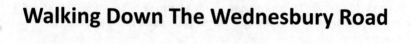

Walking Down The Wednesbury Road

Steve Jenkins

ISBN 978-1-907540-90-5

Written by Steve Jenkins

First published July 2013

Printed and Published by Anchor Print Group Ltd.

Cover design by Richard Linnett & Susan Jenkins

Cover photograph by Paul Pickard *(Steve Jenkins and Dean Keates with the League Two Championship Trophy)*.

Authors' acknowledgements
Personal thanks for work on the book go to Emily Linnett, Richard Linnett, Andrew Poole, Dan Mole and Stefan Gamble.

Also to the staff and players at Walsall Football Club I've mentioned in this book, thanks for the memories and allowing me to relay these stories.

All photographs courtesy of Walsall Football Club and Steve Jenkins personal collection.

Newspaper clippings courtesy of Express and Star, Walsall Advertiser, Walsall Chronicle, Sports Argus, Sporting Star, Birmingham Mail and Sunday Mercury.

Contents

Chapter 1
The Beginning

Back in the early sixties football was a local game; you pretty much supported the team your family supported and that was normally the one closest to home. Football was still to hit the TV screen, 'Match of the Day' was yet to be born, and it was local radio and newspapers that carried the knowledge of professional football.

As youngsters we still knew of Manchester United, Chelsea and Arsenal, they were big teams with international players, but your local team was the centre point of the town and played a huge part in the entertainment of the town, the players were well known and normally had grown up not far from where they plied their trade.

The Midlands was Football country: Aston Villa, Birmingham City, Wolverhampton Wanderers, West Bromwich Albion and Coventry City were the mighty clubs that filled the newspapers with their players, results and gossip. All of those teams could command 30 to 40,000 supporters, played in huge stadiums and were normally playing in the then First Division, now known as The Premiership. They competed against each other, drawing huge crowds and passionate support with so many local derbies, plus the visits of Manchester United, Chelsea and Arsenal constantly to the Midlands to play; the radio listenership and newspaper sales were huge.

The young Midland boys, of whom I was one, knew about football, we played it endlessly in breaks at infant and junior school, played in our Games lessons and played in the street when we got home. In the summer holidays we played everyday in the streets or on the Arboretum grass; football occupied most of our thoughts.

My family had only ever supported one club; my Grandfather Harry Jenkins was a passionate Walsall supporter and had been all his life, and maybe his Father before him had seen the birth of the club in 1888. Harry was a fixture at Fellows Park, he had two season tickets every season in the main stand and sat with the same people for season after season watching the games.

Harry must have introduced or forced my Father, William Alan Jenkins, to become a supporter of the local team. I don't recall my Dad ever saying he was forced to follow the team, he just did, and there was no question of ever visiting another football ground unless his team was playing there. The local big teams: Villa, Blues, Wolves, Albion and Coventry, held no interest in terms of passion or support, their results held a passing local interest, but no more.

I suppose, as I grew older, there was never any doubt or even question mark as to whom I would support. My Dad brought home the *Express & Star* every night and pointed at the local report, player transfer or possible team selection for Saturday. Hence, long before I ever visited Fellows Park, I was becoming aware of the local team. Saturday evenings were always spent reading about football; known locally as 'The Pinks' or 'The Pink Un', *The Sports Argus* and *The Sporting Star* gave, in great detail, reports on all the local sides, the matches, the scorers, the weeks events and rumours for the coming week, everything you could wish to know about football.

In today's world I was probably late in life attending my first football match. My Dad worked on Saturdays all his life as Manager of the Walsall and District Co-operative Shoe shops, hence he only attended midweek games; always, as is still the case today, the games were on Tuesday nights. My Grandfather, Harry, always went on Saturdays, my Uncle George, Uncle Geoff or one of his pals occupied his other season ticket.

Then, one week in September 1962, the family decided it was time that I should make my debut. Each week on Wednesday we visited my grandparents, Harry and Flo, at 25 May Street in Leamore. I always looked forward to these visits as Harry, to me, was a hero; he seemed to know everything, had every answer to my many questions, was always funny and seemed in complete control of life. I always spent most of the visit sitting next to him squeezed into his chair and was always greeted in the same way.

'Come and sit here little man.'

Harry and my Dad were talking about Saturday's game and Harry suggested that it might be time for him to take me to my first match.

I remember looking at my Dad to see his reaction.

'Do you want to go, Steve?'

'Yes, Dad.'

'Ev, can he go on Saturday?' My Dad asked my Mom.

'It's okay with me.'

And so it came to pass, all was agreed; my Dad would pick up Harry with me already in the car and take us to Fellows Park in plenty of time for the game. Dad had to be back at work just after 2:00pm and so dropped us off at 1:45pm, an hour and a quarter before kick-off, when the crowd would be light entering the ground, which ensured my safe entrance.

Parents are always concerned about their offspring and Mom and Dad wanted to make sure everything would be as safe as possible, especially as I was out on my own with Harry. It is safe to say that Harry was a bit of a lad, liked a beer and liked a bet on the horses and football. Hence, there was some concern that Harry may be distracted from his duties of taking care of me and it only takes an instant for a young one to disappear into a crowd.

I, however, felt completely safe with Harry and always had done.

I can still remember my first sight of Fellows Park, being dropped off at the main entrance, everything painted in red and white: the gates to the Directors' car park, the rails that led to the turnstiles, the six turnstiles and the directors' and players' entrance. The back of the main stand loomed in front of me and at eight years of age looked huge; the letters painted just below the roof spelt out the name that would occupy my thoughts, hopes, dreams and passion for the next fifty years: WALSALL Football Club, it would always be home to me.

Harry passed over his season tickets, the turnstile twisted round and clonked as the ratchet clicked. I followed him in to the same sound, I was there at last. We passed through a small area; an entrance directly in front led below the main stand and to the left was the mesmerizing sight of the door to the dressing rooms where every player passed. As we walked passed the players' dressing room entrance, I caught my first sight of the Hilary Street End, traditionally the Walsall supporters' end of the ground; this was where the most noise was and where the most passionate supporters stood. It was sparsely populated at 1:50pm that day but come match time it would be full and the crowd noise plentiful.

In moments I saw the Fellows Park pitch for the first time, I caught my breath as if entering Wembley: the green of the pitch surrounded by the Hilary Street End to my left, The Popular side that ran the length of the field opposite, although this was re-christened by the locals as the Cowshed due to its structure, the Laundry End, which at the time was just a wall painted white as it was indeed a working laundry and, finally, I turned to face the main stand. Back then it seemed huge, row after row of seats facing the pitch; I'd never seen that many seats before.

Harry and I walked up no more than five steps to enter the stand and walked passed a few seats at the front before reaching the first gangway going up.

Harry stopped and pointed at some seats right on the edge of the gangway four or five rows from the back.

'That's our seats, little man, go sit there and I'll be back in a minute.'

I walked up the steps heading for the seat that Harry had pointed at and sat on the outside seat next to the isle. I was in awe of the pitch and the surroundings and the people entering the ground to find their seat or particular spot they liked to stand when someone tapped me on the shoulder. I turned and heard:

'Yow corr sit there little mon … that's Harry's seat.'

I wanted to say Harry was my Granddad, but a combination of fear and unfamiliar surroundings caused the cat to get my tongue. I quickly scuttled into the next seat along without a murmur or a glance at the man behind me, just happy that he was no longer offended and that he let me be.

Harry returned within minutes, I guess from a quick beer or most likely a bet on the match. Harry never moved from his seat again until the game was over and neither did I.

I watched as the ground began to fill the closer and closer it got to 3pm, and then, with only ten minutes to game time, it seemed they had just opened all the gates as people flooded in. The Hilary Street End fans began to find their voice as the numbers increased and I was transported to my first buzz of anticipation inside a football ground. I didn't know the feeling then, but I began to fidget in my seat trying to take it all in, my stomach was tied in a knot with anticipation, I knew something was going to happen but had no idea what and then it began.

The players entered the stadium from my left, the top corner of the ground, and would run out directly in front of the Hilary Street End. The first sight of the players lining up to come out would be seen by the supporters directly opposite at the top end of the Cowshed, as the players moved forward they would then come into view of the Hilary Street End before stepping onto the pitch and into the view of the supporters throughout the Cowshed and the main stand.

The rumble of noise and arm waving started in the corner of the Cowshed, which triggered the Hilary Street End, which in turn triggered the whole ground; to an eight-year-old first-timer it was a colossal sound filled with arm movements, waving and punching the air. It was that day that I saw my first rattle: the young supporters all had one and twirled them with great determination and vigour to cause incredible noise as wood against wood clacked together, the faster you wound it the more noise it created. I wanted one and badly.

I remember little about the actual match, trying to take everything in; the game, the supporters and the stadium makes the memory all a bit of a blur, but history shows that Rotherham United were the visitors that day, September 22nd 1962.

The Walsall side was Boswell, Palin, Sharples, Hill, McPherson, Dudley, Meek, Pearson, Richards, Hodgkisson and Taylor.

Walsall won the game 1-0 with a goal from George Meek. 10,616 people were at Fellows Park that day and the game was part of the Second Division fixture list, which is now known as The Championship.

Harry and I left the ground to be picked up by my Uncle George and transported back to 25 May Street. Around 6:45pm my Dad arrived from work to take me home to 26 Regina Drive and my debut was complete. I would forever be a Walsall Football Club supporter and a Saddler.

My next visit to Fellows Park would not come until April 16th 1963 an Easter game against Cardiff City; my Dad on Easter break from the Co-op had a rare opportunity to take me to a match. Now nine years old it was a special day; I guess football supporters everywhere remember the first time their Dad takes them to a match. This time we stood in front of the main stand towards the Laundry End of the ground. At the time, as the ground was starting to change with the Laundry being demolished, there was no wall between the supporters and the pitch. I sat on a breezeblock right on the touchline and had an unhindered view of the game, I could almost touch the players as they attacked or defended that flank. My Dad stood behind me as we watched the game.

Again, Walsall recorded a win that day, a 2-1 victory, with goals from O'Neill and Newton. Records show the attendance was 10,381, the team: Boswell, Palin, Gregg, Hill, McPherson, Dudley, Meek, Hodgkisson, O'Neill, Newton and Taylor. The game would be my last for the 1962/1963 season and the team would be relegated from Division Two (The Championship) to Division Three (Division One) on the final day of the season.

Walsall, with 4 games to go of that season, fought hard to stave off relegation; a 2-1 win away at Rotherham on May 4th gave everyone hope, with goals from O'Neill and Newton. On May 8th the same scorers recorded a 2-0 victory away at Newcastle United and belief was established. Two games to go, May 14th brought Norwich City to Fellows Park and a third consecutive win, 3-1, with goals from Meek, O'Neill and Newton, setting up a tense final game.

Walsall needed a draw and 1 point to escape relegation in the final match at Fellows Park against Charlton Athletic. The town was full of hope that this could be achieved after three consecutive wins and a confidence running through the team. The supporters were to witness a false start when the first attempt to play the game was abandoned at halftime with the scores level. The rearranged date was May 24th 1963. The towns' people turned up to cheer the Saddlers on with the biggest gate of the season, 16,761. The team that lined up that day: Boswell, Palin, Sharples, Hill, McPherson, Rawlings, Meek, Hodgkisson, O'Neill, Newton and Taylor.

Walsall suffered that day with crippling injuries to both goalkeeper, Alan Boswell, and goal scorer, Graham Newton. With no substitutes as in today's game, the two players fought on gamely, but, alas, escape from relegation was not to be, we lost the game by 2 goals to 1, Colin Taylor scoring our consolation but relegation a reality.

That game brought to a close Walsall Football Club's glory years, the 1959/1960 season had seen the team rise from Division Four to Division Three as Champions, for many years our one and only Championship. The following season brought promotion from Division Three to Division Two as league runners up, in the days when only two teams were promoted. The 1961/1962 season saw the team return a respectable 14th league position in Division Two.

The relegation of 1962/1963 saw the break up of the team that had achieved such a monumental rise through the divisions. I knew all of the players from the stories my Grandfather and Father had told me of their exploits and victories, but never really saw them at the peak of their powers.

Tony Richards had been transferred to Port Vale, Tim Rawlings left after over 200 hundred games, Ken Hill moved to Norwich City, Colin Taylor joined Newcastle United and Alan Boswell joined Shrewsbury Town after a quarrel with the then Chairman, Ernie Thomas. The backbone of the team was broken.

Little did the people of Walsall know then, that it would be twenty-five years before we returned to Division Two (The Championship) and the effort and years of trying for that achievement would become the Holy Grail to generations of Walsall folk.

Tony Richards. Centre-Forward.

A local lad born in Smethwick, Tony would become a Walsall legend for his goal scoring feats. Originally released from his first club, Birmingham City, and following two years of National Service, trials were completed with both Tottenham Hotspur and Wolverhampton Wanderers to no avail.

A depressed and demoralised Tony Richards, on the brink of giving up football, made one final attempt and wrote to Major Frank Buckley, the then Walsall manager, to request a trial.

Richards instantly impressed in a reserve match and would be handed his first team debut twelve days later. Although I only ever saw Tony Richards play once and he didn't score that day, the general view was that he was not the most stylish of centre-forwards but just had that knack of being in the right place at the right time, all great goal scorers have to have that knack and Tony Richards had it in abundance.

Season 1954/1955			
League appearances	32	goals	22
F.A. Cup appearances	3	goals	4
Season 1955/1956			
League appearances	35	goals	15
F.A. Cup appearances	4	goals	2
Season 1956/1957			
League appearances	36	goals	17
Season 1957/1958			
League appearances	40	goals	21
F.A. Cup appearances	1	goals	0
Season 1958/1959			
League appearances	43	goals	28
F.A. Cup appearances	1	goals	0
Season 1959/1960			
League appearances	46	goals	24
F.A. Cup appearances	2	goals	2

Season 1960/1961			
League appearances	45	goals	36
F.A. Cup appearances	1	goals	0
League Cup appearances	1	goals	0
Season 1961/1962			
League appearances	36	goals	15
F.A. Cup appearances	4	goals	4
League Cup appearances	2	goals	1
Season 1962/1963			
League appearances	21	goals	7
F.A. Cup appearances	1	goals	0
League Cup appearances	1	goals	0

Tony Richards was transferred to Port Vale during the 1962/1963 season and would add a further 63 league appearances and a further 30 goals to his tally before joining non-league Nuneaton Borough and finally retiring from the game.

Tony Richards was my Father's hero, his legend made him a hero of mine and at least I saw him play for Walsall on one occasion.

George Meek. Right-Wing.

A fast, direct, tricky ball-playing right-winger, a crowd pleaser, sums up George Meek. Major Frank Buckley spotted him playing for Hamilton Academicals and took him to Leeds United. Meek's first spell with Walsall lasted fifteen months on loan from Leeds whilst completing his National Service, playing 44 times in Walsall colours. National Service completed, he returned to Leeds United and amassed 200 league appearances scoring 19 goals. He then transferred to Leicester City; his spell at Filbert Street was a short one and ended after only 13 appearances. In July of 1961, George signed for Walsall on a permanent basis.

Total Walsall appearances 187, goals 29.

In my two visits to Fellows Park during the 1962/1963 season, George

Meek made an impression on me, the crowd buzzed in anticipation every time he got the ball, he constantly demanded it and once in possession attacked the opposition instantly.

Many years later I was invited to play in the Mark Rees Testimonial match on Monday May 15th 1989 at Fellows Park. It was a huge night in my life; getting changed ready to play alongside some of my heroes, running up the tunnel and onto the Fellows Park pitch to the roar of the crowd will never leave my memory.

George Meek had returned to Fellows Park that night to play in the match. Just before we began to assemble to run out onto the pitch, George, then fifty-five years old, took the centre of the dressing room.

'Come on lads, just remember, enjoy it, enjoy every minute and the golden rule: get it, give it and move! Now, come on, let's go!'

Mark Rees Testimonial Programme

Mark Rees Testimonial Plaque

I consider it an honour to have seen George give that little speech and to have passed to and received the ball from him a few times during the game.

George played great that night, still amazingly fit and a bundle of energy, if I had the ball and he demanded it believe me I passed straight away.

My Dad would never have believed that there I was playing for Walsall on the Fellows Park pitch and knocking a short one to the great George Meek.

One of my treasured possessions, a commemorative half pint glass tankard from the 1959/1960 Walsall Fourth Division Championship season, remains in tact and proudly displayed on my trophy shelf.

My Grandfather Harry bought two of these mugs, one for himself and one for my Father. Dad gave me his when my enthusiasm for Walsall Football Club began to grow. I drank my orange squash from that mug as a child and no matter where I have subsequently lived or moved house the mug has travelled with me; an object to the memory of my Dad and a constant reminder of Walsall's Championship winning team. The team's autographs on the tankard are: goalkeeper, John Christie; full-backs, Harry Haddington, John Sharples and Captain Bill 'Chopper'

Commemorative Tankard 1959/60 Champions

Gutteridge; half-backs, Peter Billingham, Albert McPherson and Jim Rawlings; wingers, John Davies and Colin 'Cannonball' Taylor; inside-forwards, Ken Hodgkisson and Roy Faulkner and centre-forward, Tony Richards. Trainer, Vic Potts, is also featured, along with Manager, Bill Moore and Secretary, Earnest Wilson. I'll bet that few of these tankards remain from the thousands sold all those years ago.

Chapter 2

Where F.A. Cup 'Giant Killing' Began

One night, in January 1933, the start of F.A. Cup 'giant killing' began at Fellows Park, Walsall. The magnitude of this event filled Britain's national newspapers and radio stations, never before had a small Football Club taken on and beaten the then best football team in the country, Europe and the World.

To set the scene, Walsall Football Club had beaten Mansfield Town 4-1 in the F.A. Cup Round One, Round Two had seen Hartlepool United dispatched 2-1, bringing in the big clubs to play in Round Three. Walsall were drawn at home to play the mighty Arsenal.

Arsenal had won the F.A. Cup in 1930, been runners-up in 1932, lifted the First Division Championship in 1931 and been runners-up in 1932. In 1933, Arsenal were expected to 'do the double,' winning both the First Division and F.A. Cup, their team now at the peak of their powers.

The first decision to be made was: should the tie be played at Fellows Park with a capacity of 22,000 or should Walsall agree to move the tie to Arsenal and benefit financially from a certain 60,000 crowd.

Finally, the decision was made, Walsall would play the tie in front of their own supporters at Fellows Park.

One newspaper stated the difference between the two teams: Arsenal, the rich, the confident, the league leaders, the 30,000 pound aristocrats, against a little Midland Third Division team that cost 69 pounds all-in.

Arsenal train on ozone, brine-baths, champagne, golf and electrical massage, in an atmosphere of prima donna preciousness. They own 87 pounds worth of boots. Walsall men eat fish and chips and drink beer and the entire running costs of the club this season has been 75 pounds.

The Arsenal team that day included seven international players: David Jack, the first player to cost over 10,000 pounds and scorer of the first ever goal at Wembley in the 1923 F.A. Cup final. Scotland's inside forward, Alex James; left-winger, the legendry Cliff Bastin, known as the 'Ice Cool executioner of goals,' who had won all the games' honours by the time he was twenty-one years old. Goalkeeper, Frank Moss; England full-back, George Male and centre-half, Herbie 'The Policeman' Roberts, who was considered the finest defender of his era.

The 69 pounds worth of Walsall team: Joey Cunningham, goalkeeper. full-backs, Sid Bird and Jack Bennett, Halfbacks Johnny Reed, George Leslie and Harry Salt, wingers, Billy Coward and Freddy Lee, inside-forwards Chris Ball and Bill Sheppard and centre-forward, Gilbert Alsop

The press report of January 14th 1933.

1933 Programme

F.A. Cup Round Three.

Walsall versus Arsenal.

Walsall began the match with a rush, as was expected, but when their enthusiasm waned they refused to allow Arsenal to settle down and dictate the play. Some of the tackling was grim and on two occasions an Arsenal player ended up over the wall surrounding the pitch!

Walsall players went to meet the ball, whereas the Gunners waited for it!

Walsall full-backs Bennett and Bird and big centre-half Leslie were magnificent as Arsenal strove forward in search of the opening goal.

Walsall's confidence increased and when the halftime whistle sounded, the Londoners had managed just one shot at the Saddlers' goal.

After the break, and attacking the Hilary Street

Walsall v Arsenal 1933 Kick-Off

End, Walsall continued to run the show, and on the hour Gilbert Alsop's brave header from Lee's floated corner kick broke the deadlock, sending the Saddlers' fans wild with hundreds of hats and programmes flying into the air.

Arsenal Manager, Herbert Chapman, immediately went to the touchline to order a reshuffle, telling Jack to lead the attack.

Five minutes after the first goal, Walsall grabbed a second, and again Alsop was deeply involved. The bustling centre-forward darted into the Arsenal penalty area following a long punt downfield by George Leslie. The ball ended up in the hands of goalkeeper Marks, but unfortunately for the Arsenal, their young full-back, Tommy Black, aimed a reckless kick at Alsop, who fell to the ground. Walsall's Chris Ball charged at Black and there was a general free-for-all before calm was restored. Referee, Mr. Arthur Taylor of Wigan, pointed to the spot and awarded the Saddlers a penalty. Bill Sheppard duly stepped up and smashed the ball into the net past a groping Frank Moss, thus scoring his first goal in Walsall colours.

This certainly put the skids under Arsenal, who never really recovered from this double body blow, although Cunningham in the Walsall goal saved well from both Bastin and Black, who was eager to make amends for his misdemeanour at the other end of the field!

So, the biggest shock in football had been recorded at Fellows Park, Walsall.

Walsall 2   Arsenal 0.

In the years that followed, Walsall's monumental achievement grew in stature and more and more of the people that played and attended the game made further comments; more was written about that moment in football history and why that particular game would be remembered as the greatest F.A. Cup upset of all time.

Herbert Chapman would become known as the first truly great manager, not only for his achievements with Arsenal and his great haul of trophies, but for personally revolutionizing the game of football. Chapman introduced a new football team formation, known as the 'third back game' or 'WM' formation, when most teams stuck rigidly to the long used 2-3-5 style of play. He was also a master of the press and used them as PR to build Arsenal into the biggest club in the land. It would be partly this mastery that would help elevate this match into one of the most remembered in history. It is believed that the victory grew further in stature in the years that followed because of the incredible achievements of the Arsenal team in those years.

Cliff Bastin, who would go on to hold the Arsenal goal scoring record for more than fifty years, commented that Arsenal despised trips to Third Division sides, even though they never lost, the opposition would fling themselves into the game with reckless abandon, and the gashed bruised legs of the Arsenal players would bear grim testimony to their misguided enthusiasm. Bastin stated, 'The Third Division footballer may not be a soccer artist, but when it comes to the heavy tackle he ranks with the best.'

Bastin was the best player on the field that night; throughout the first half he whipped in cross after cross, which was either confidently punched clear by Cunningham or cleared by the Walsall backs who flung themselves at the Arsenal forwards when they had the remotest chance of a shot. These efforts were acknowledged by the home crowd who cheered them on with great enthusiasm.

At halftime it was believed that Arsenal always considered tactics and would discuss weaknesses in the opposition and then concentrate on them for the second half. That day the halftime talk was short as every word could be heard in the neighbouring Walsall dressing room. The plan, however, was to win the match through Cliff Bastin's play down Arsenal's left-flank.

No tactics were discussed in the Walsall dressing room, the players still on a high from their first half efforts. Walsall enjoyed oranges and a quick cigarette before reappearing, clearly revved up and ready to continue to bite Arsenal legs for the cause.

Bastin, his temper already at boiling point from the treatment he was getting from the Walsall backs, was becoming more annoyed in a game he was wishing was over. During halftime the crowd had encroached from the stands to the touchlines, at first it was just children, but gradually adults began to climb over the perimeter walls and settle along the side of the pitch, the tension began to increase. Bastin knew the pitch was too narrow for his play and now every time he got the ball not only were the Walsall players on him in an instant but the crowd were within touching distance and extremely vocal about the state of the match and the Arsenal team.

Walsall v Arsenal 1933

In the first fifteen minutes of the second half, Walsall were non-existent as an attacking force, Bastin and Arsenal peppered the Walsall defence, then came the corner from which Alsop scored Walsall's first. They say the roar of the crowd as the ball hit the net was the loudest ever heard at Fellows Park.

Arsenal were now stirred and Walsall looked like a side clinging on for dear life. Full-backs Bird and Bennett just launched the ball as far up field as they could to allow the defence a few moments of rest and to reform for the next Arsenal attack.

Again, Walsall had a rare attack where the unfortunate Tommy Black was beaten and launched a desperate kick at Alsop, Sheppard scoring the penalty.

The final ten minutes of the match were played exclusively in the Walsall defencive third of the pitch, so quiet was the Arsenal goal that keeper, Frank Moss, found his net surrounded by Walsall fans awaiting the final whistle and constantly told them to get back behind the lines.

The crowd of 22,000 had paid double the usual admission fee to watch the game not expecting a Cup upset or a victory, more to see the stars of the Arsenal team play. With fifteen minutes to go of the match, as usual, the gates were opened to let out the supporters; no one left, but a further 3,000 fans rushed into the ground swelling the crowd for the climax.

It was customary in those days that the home side changed their strip in the event of a colour clash. Walsall had done this. 'Saddlers' Manager, Bill Slade, a former Coventry City Director, had returned to Coventry to recruit over a period of time the entire Walsall forward line: Coward, Ball, Alsop, Sheppard and Lee were all ex-Coventry City players. Walsall played that day, not in their usual red and white strip, but in blue and white-stripped shirts which had been borrowed by Slade from Coventry.

The final whistle went and the local supporters rushed onto the pitch and mobbed the Walsall players, lofting them shoulder high. Arsenal players ran for the safety of the dressing room where Herbert Chapman awaited them.

Chapman, furious, unleashed his venom upon his players, paying special attention to the unfortunate Tommy Black, a tirade that ended with the instruction that Tommy, once back in London, was never to set foot in Highbury or the training ground ever again.

Sure enough, Black was officially banned from Arsenal and sold to Plymouth Argyle seven days later, a team he served with distinction.

The progamme of that day also became famous; it displayed the size of the task ahead with special artwork. Arsenal Captain, Alex James, was pictured and told his artillery would have to battle a Walsall teddy bear armed with a stick if they were to return to Wembley that year.

Arsenal went on a six-game unbeaten run after the match and would win the First Division League Championship that year.

Walsall still on an enormous high thrashed an unfortunate Mansfield Town in their next match five days later 8-1; they would finish the season in 5th place, their best finish for a decade.

Harry and Alan Jenkins, my Grandfather and Father, were in the crowd at Fellows Park that night, my Mom, then Evelyn Smith, was at home in Dora Street and could see the sky lit up by the floodlights from her backyard. The roars of the crowd drifted in along the breeze, both my Mother and Father told me in detail of the famous night we beat the Arsenal.

Many years later, when I was around the club at both Fellows Park and the Banks's Stadium, Gilbert Alsop would be there watching the current crop of Walsall players. Gilbert attended both first team games and reserve team games, a true football lover; I got to know him and would chat to him especially at reserve games when the ground was quieter.

Gilbert always said very little but stood watching the game with a concentrated eye; a bad pass or a missed opportunity to play in a forward would always bring a very quiet 'tut' or 'aahh' but never a shout or comment.

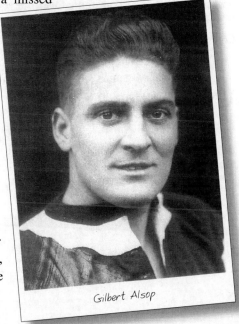

I liked Gilbert, it was an honour to stand with him and be in the presence of a centre-forward that took on the might of Arsenal and won.

Gilbert Alsop. Centre-Forward.

Gilbert was born on September 10th 1908 in Frampton Cotterill, Bristol and died in Walsall on the April 16th 1992.

Gilbert Alsop

Without doubt one of the greatest centre-forwards of his era, Gilbert Alsop, was hard, robust, a never-say-die striker who feared no one.

After leaving school Gilbert played for Latterbridge F.C., then Bath City, before joining Coventry City in 1929, before linking up with Walsall in September 1931.

A total of 448 competitive matches with a goals record of 308; Coventry City 16 games, 4 goals; Walsall 195 games, 151 goals and Ipswich Town 39 games, 30 goals. During the war, Gilbert hit 56 goals in 100 matches for Walsall, but he also guested for Leicester City, Luton Town, Mansfield Town and Northampton Town.

Gilbert scored four goals in a game for Walsall on five separate occasions, he surprisingly left Walsall in 1935 for 3,000 pounds and joined West Bromwich Albion but would return in 1938 until 1947. A further twenty years were spent at Walsall F.C. working behind the scenes and when he left he became grounds man of the playing fields adjoining the Arboretum.

Although born in Bristol, Walsall was where Gilbert was truly loved and respected.

When Walsall F.C. moved from Fellows Park to the Bescot Stadium in 1990, the stand where the most passionate Walsall supporters gathered was named the Gilbert Alsop stand. Over the years, due to sponsorship and financial income, the stand has had many names, but it will always be known as the Gilbert Alsop stand to generations of supporters.

I would personally witness several more 'giant killing' acts over the years from Walsall teams and I believe that those victories came from an inner belief that anything is possible, due mainly to the team that played on January 14th 1933.

Chapter 3

Building My Team

Walsall Football Club did not adapt easily on their return to Division Three, players came and went and over the next two seasons we would have three Managers and a change of Chairman.

My visits to Fellows Park were now only with my Dad and restricted to Tuesday evening games and Bank Holidays due to my Father's shop-keeping hours. My Grandfather had passed on; he was sorely missed by both the family and me and by his Saturday gang at Fellows Park.

Mom and Dad did not believe that I was old enough to go to the ground on my own; this caused me great frustration but was a non-negotiable issue.

The Tuesday evening games began to become huge events in my life. I loved the atmosphere, the floodlit ground, the smells of hot food, tobacco and pipes, the expectation and the roar of the crowd; to me it was magical. Whenever the team won the sweet smell of success was intoxicating.

The reserve team also played matches on a Tuesday night and my Dad and I would also attend these games. Unlike today, the reserves used to attract a crowd of anything from five hundred to over a thousand. All of the facilities were open and it was easier to get a hot cup of tea to keep away the winter chills; we could also move around the ground more easily and could stay with the attacking end of our play by moving position at halftime.

Walsall's reserve team was on a good run during those years, winning the Midland Intermediate League Cup in two out of three years. Little did I realize at the time that the young players coming through would be the backbone of our first team for years to come. All I knew was that I loved being there and I was equally as excited by the reserves and youth players as I was about the first team.

During our Tuesday night and Bank Holiday visits, my Dad, Uncle George and me would always assume position under the Cowshed just around the half way line, probably ten yards closer to the Laundry End. Supporters in those days liked the same position for viewing and although we were standing, we were always just inches from the same position of the previous match; creatures of habit.

Walsall's team was in transition during 1963/1964, it would be my third visit to Fellows Park that season before I saw them win, beating Crewe Alexandra 2-1 with two goals from Newton on October 14. I would manage a further 3 games that season but only 1 more victory; I witnessed 2 wins, 3 draws and 1 defeat. I enjoyed some performances from the flying winger Roger Smith and a couple of goals from another favourite, Trevor Forster.

Walsall escaped a second successive relegation by beating Peterborough United in the last home game of the season 2-0; we settled for 19th position but retained our Third Division status.

The reserve side gave me much more joy that season: goalkeeper, Dave Tennant; full-back, Frank Gregg; centre-half, Stan Bennett; midfielders, Nick Atthey and Colin Harrison and striker, Allan Clarke, were all regular reserve team players and beginning to make an impact on the first team with a few appearances.

The first half of the 1964/1965 season was a disaster. Walsall lost 5 of their first 6 matches and up to the turn of the year lost 18 out of 27; rooted to the bottom of the Third Division, something had to be done. Ray Shaw replaced Manager, Alf Wood, and several new signings were made.

Colin 'Cannonball' Taylor, who had been sold to Newcastle United for 20,000 pounds, returned for 10,000 pounds. Johnny Harris signed from Wolverhampton Wanderers. Graham Sissons signed from Peterborough. Jimmy McMorran signed for 6,000 pounds from Third Lanark. Ken Satchwell signed from Nuneaton Borough for 1,200 Pounds. During October, Stan Bennett and Nick Atthey became first team regulars, Frank Gregg switched to right-back from left-back for the incoming Johnny Harris. Allan Clarke had become a first team fixture from our reserve side and the team I would always love was beginning to form.

My visits to Fellows Park again fell on Tuesdays and Bank Holidays. It would be December 26 before I saw the team win that season, a 2-1 win against Mansfield Town with two goals from Colin Taylor.

My first game that season had seen us lose 1-4 to a Workington Town side; the one moment of joy was Allan Clarke's second senior career goal.

I watched as we were hammered by Watford in October 0-4 and Scunthorpe 1-2.

Following the victory on December 26th, things got a little better. Allan Clarke went on a blistering goal-scoring run and I watched as we beat a Bristol Rovers side in March 1-0, with Jimmy McMorran scoring his first Walsall goal.

Then, in April, I witnessed a thriller as we drew with Hull City 3-3, Allan Clarke scoring twice and Ken Satchwell adding the third.

The team that I would love for my entire life, the team that fuelled my unquenchable passion for Walsall Football Club, was almost complete.

Walsall escaped relegation almost with ease with a few games to go that season; they were gelling and we finished 19th in the league. Our free-fall after our Division Two years had been arrested and there was genuine hope for the coming season.

As we entered the 1965/1966 season my life was changing, I'd left Butts Junior School passing my Eleven Plus exam and graduated to Joseph Leckie School. This brought with it massive change, short school trousers were exchanged for long ones and I became familiar with travelling alone on the bus routes of Walsall. At the start of the season, I was approaching my twelfth birthday and Mom and Dad had agreed I could now attend Walsall matches on a Saturday. The routine would be that my Dad would drop me off at 1:45pm so he could return to work by 2:00pm, I would then walk over the bridge and enter the ground at the Laundry End, where I would position myself on the wall just to the left of the goal. I was not allowed at that stage to stand at the Hilary Street End, my parents thought I was still not big enough to go there and thought that if I was going to get into trouble it would be at that end of the ground. The Laundry End was less populated and visiting fans were normally housed in part of the Cowshed. I would meet a couple of school friends during those days at the ground, Michael Ward and Stephen Bird.

The town was buzzing in anticipation of the coming season. The F.A. had decided one substitute for all games and so twelve players were named for each match. No longer did an injured player have to remain on the pitch, normally pushed into a Forward Wing position to do whatever he could to occupy the opposing full-back.

The final piece of my team's jigsaw was signed during the summer, the great George Kirby arrived to play centre-forward for a fee of 10,000 pounds.

The Walsall team would now be stable for the coming seasons, but the team of 1965/1966 will always remain in my heart. That team inspired my love of both football and Walsall Football Club, so much so, that I could rattle off the eleven names at any point over the next fifty years with perfect clarity.

Terry Carling. Goalkeeper.

Terry was the first Walsall goalkeeper that I saw on numerous occasions in my first full season as a supporter. He was signed from Lincoln City in a player exchange for our previous goalkeeper, Malcolm White. Carling would be first choice for two and a half seasons, amassing 115 appearances before being transferred to Chester City.

Frank Gregg. Right-Back.

Frank came through the ranks at Walsall and his final tally of appearances would amount to 444, with 3 goals. Born in Stourbridge, all his professional appearances were for Walsall. Frank was a solid full-back, defencively strong, great anticipation and he was rarely given the runaround by opposition wingers.

Johnny Harris. Left-Back & Captain.

John had spent his early career at Wolverhampton Wanderers but had suffered two broken legs, which hindered his progress; his career would eventually be cut short by injury. While at Walsall, his performances made him a favourite and a class act as a footballer, along with being an outstanding Captain, urging the team on with his stylish play and determination. Johnny would play for Walsall 85 times, scoring 2 goals; both came in the same match against Shrewsbury Town.

Graham Sissons. Right-Half.

Signed from Peterborough United, Graham had previously played for Birmingham City. Sissons was another solid performer in that Walsall team, quiet, classy and did his job seemingly with ease. Playing exactly 111 times and scoring 1 Goal.

Stan Bennett. Centre-Half.

I have appreciated many Walsall centre-halves over the years but my all-time favourite

Stan Bennett

will always be Stan. He would only play professional football for Walsall and would be with the club for fifteen years, playing 438 times and scoring 13 goals. The 'Blonde Bombshell' was fierce in the tackle and powerful in the air, no one ever got the better of Stan. I witnessed several opposing centre-forwards flattened, eating the Fellows Park turf. Stan always gave them a glance and a smile after a heavy tackle. He feared no one and played every game at full stretch with a massive heart. I was there the day he retired, far too early in my view at twenty-nine years of age. The crowd stood to applaud him off in that final match and I must admit I shed a tear, I knew I would never see the great Stan Bennett play again. Stan was a Walsall player through and through and would name his house in later years 'Saddlers Barn.'

Nick Atthey. Left-Half.

Born in Tantibie Newcastle, the Atthey family moved to Coventry where Nick began playing football. In the following years Nick would Captain the County side and join Walsall in 1961, he would make 502 appearances for Walsall scoring 18 goals and spend his entire professional career with the Saddlers. Nick Atthey bossed our midfield for years playing with an outstanding dedication to our cause; honesty, heart and soul sum up Nick's play. Following his years at Walsall he played for local side Rushall Olympic. I went to watch them a couple of times out of respect for Nick Atthey who had given me so many glorious memories even though he never knew.

Ken Satchwell. Right-Winger.

Ken's amateur career was with Aston Villa, Nottingham Forest and Wolverhampton Wanderers before turning professional with Coventry City.

Signing for Walsall in 1965 after a spell at non-league Nuneaton Borough, he would make 63 appearances for Walsall scoring 8 goals. I must admit I was not a huge fan of Ken's although a consistent trier. I felt in my favourite Walsall team that he was the weakest link. One of my fondest memories of Ken was when he had to move from his right wing position to centre-forward to cover for an injured George Kirby in a match against Swindon Town on February 19th 1966. The crowd was dismayed that George was not fit and that Ken would be taking his position, we had never seen Satchwell play anywhere but on the right wing. Ken Satchwell was magnificent that day causing all sorts of problems to the Swindon defence. Ken did not play like a normal centre-forward and hence had the Swindon defenders all over the place, it resulted in a 5-0 victory with Howard Riley and Colin Taylor scoring two goals each and Ken Satchwell scoring in between. Ken was applauded off the field that day for his immense contribution.

Allan Clarke. Inside-Right.

See next chapter.

George Kirby. Centre-Forward.

Kirby had a much-travelled career, starting with Everton then Sheffield Wednesday, Plymouth Argyle, Southampton, Coventry City and Swansea City, before signing for Walsall for 10,000 pounds. George was well known in football when he arrived at Fellows Park, an accomplished performer, a fine header of the ball with a strong right foot, he played in the style of an English traditional centre-forward: tough, uncompromising, confident and took no prisoners in his pursuit of victory. The town folk of Walsall waited in anticipation to see George Kirby lead our line for the coming 1965/1966 season. George would play 87 times for Walsall scoring 30 goals.

Jimmy McMorran. Inside-Left.

Jimmy secured Scottish International honours at Schoolboy level, which brought him south to sign for Aston Villa. After signing professional he made 14 appearances for Villa before moving north to Third Lanark. Signing for Walsall for 6,000 pounds, Jimmy would have two spells at Walsall and also play for Swansea City, Notts County and Halifax Town. McMorran was a clever midfield player, a schemer. Our midfield was based around him and he could hold onto the ball and see opportunities and flaws in the opposition before threading balls through to our forwards and wingers. McMorran had the supporters' respect for his talent, he also had a fiery temper, didn't take kindly to being fouled or kicked and left the pitch early on a few occasions after taking a swing at his offenders.

Jimmy, however, laid on an abundance of goals for Colin Taylor, George Kirby and Allan Clarke and was a firm Walsall favourite making

120 appearances and scoring 7 goals. Jimmy was serenaded endlessly by the Hilary Street End's dulcet tones to the Martha Reeves and The Vandellas hit 'Jimmy Mack.'

Colin 'Cannonball' Taylor. Left-Winger.

Colin Taylor remains a hero to this day with the fans of Walsall Football Club, best known for his enormously powerful left foot; for season after season, none of the opposition teams wanted to give away a free kick anywhere near their penalty area. If they did the Walsall fans would go into rapture chanting 'Taylor, Taylor, Taylor.' Colin was not a David Beckham type free kick taker, he based his success on sheer brute force and timing, his thigh and calf muscles were enormous, complemented by a huge barrel chest. Taylor would place the ball and take his position for the 'run up.' The opposition would form a wall much to the amusement of Walsall fans; Taylor's power was famous and the opposing teams usually argued over who should be in the wall. Fear played a huge part in Taylor's success; the wall under that pressure would normally break or flinch in a protective move, Taylor just blasted the ball directly at goal. I don't know how many goals I saw 'Cannonball' score from free kicks but we, as supporters, knew whenever we had a free kick within range there was a great percentage chance the net would bulge. Taylor was not only a hammer, he could play with great pace and skill on our left wing and cut inside on many occasions before shifting it onto his left foot and letting fly at goal. His goal scoring record on the left wing during our promotion season to Division Two totalled 33 goals, only matched by Cliff Bastin at Arsenal for any league Left-winger in the history of the game.

The nickname 'Cannonball' came from the popular TV series of the time. Colin would appear in 502 Walsall matches and score 189 goals. He would play in three different spells at Fellows Park from August 1958 to May 1963 when he joined Newcastle United for 20,000 pounds, returning for 10,000 pounds in October 1964 until May 1968. Taylor then joined Crystal Palace before returning to Walsall for good in 1969; he would then play a further two seasons for non-league Kidderminster Harriers continuing to score from the left wing.

The rest of the squad that season was made up of young players making appearances for injuries and lack of form, but the main eleven were pretty stable. Some new players joined in the second half of the season as we transferred Allan Clarke and tried to improve the team.

The young players were Colin Harrison, who made the biggest impression, Geoff Morris, Trevor Meath, Clive Ford, Barry Holbutt and Mick Evans. The new acquisitions were Harry Middleton, Howard Riley, Trevor Smith, Gerry Harris and Gerry Summers. Ken Hodgkisson made the last of his Walsall appearances early in the campaign.

Walsall started the season in fine form and didn't lose until the ninth game bringing great hope to the Walsall Faithful. Allan Clarke and George Kirby were on fire, one or both of them scoring in practically every game.

My first ever away match was at The Hawthorns home to West Bromwich Albion in the Football League Cup. Albion were then an accomplished First Division side. Our First Round opposition were Queens Park Rangers and we drew at Loftus Road 1-1 with a George Kirby goal to earn a replay. 12,376 people turned up at Fellows Park to watch the game and suffered, as we were 0-2 down with twenty minutes to go. This Walsall side, however, did not know when they were beaten, George Kirby pulled one back, which inspired both the team and the crowd as we went in search of the equalizer. In the mayhem, Frank Gregg thrashed in one of his three career goals and the pressure on QPR increased. A penalty was awarded with a minute to go and Allan Clarke stroked home the winner. This set up a local derby in the Second Round at West Bromwich Albion. My Dad got the tickets as this was a 'must watch' occasion and we set off for West Bromwich on September 22nd 1965 to play in front of 41,188 screaming fans.

The size of the ground and the support was nothing I'd ever experienced before. I could not keep still prior to kick-off and the noise as the teams entered the arena was enormous. Walsall were inspired and took the game to The Albion. Tony Brown opened the scoring for WBA, but Walsall did not back off and scored through Colin Taylor confidence grew even further and we attacked with wave after wave. Nick Atthey scored, but it was ruled out as the Walsall fans went wild, another of our players slow at coming out. Ten minutes to go and the score line was still 1-1. There was a howling wind that night and Stan Bennett, in relieving some pressure, chipped a ball back to our goalkeeper, Terry Carling, standing on the penalty spot. At first as the ball was airborne there seemed little trouble, but the more it stayed in the air the more concern crept in. It all seemed to happen in slow motion to me; Carling started going backwards towards his own goal, but he could not get back quick enough and the wind carried the ball over his outstretched arms and into our net. Stan Bennett sunk to his knees and I began to well-up. It was a crippling blow;

Albion capitalized and scored a third a few minutes later through Chippy Clark. Walsall had put on a fine show but had come up just short. West Bromwich Albion would go on to win the League Cup that year at Wembley.

Our Cup exploits that year were not over. In the F.A. Cup First Round we defeated Swansea Town 6-3 in front of 11,651 fans; Allan Clarke scoring 2, Summers, Satchwell and Kirby 2. The Second Round saw us defeat Aldershot away 0-2 with Taylor and Clarke scoring. This brought in the big clubs from the higher divisions and we were drawn away at First Division Stoke City. We were given no chance and the bookies had Stoke in the Fourth Round before the game was played.

The score was 0-0 when Jimmy McMorran was put out of the game with a crude tackle that went unpunished except for a free kick. It took some time for the game to restart but when it did, justice was done, the rebound from the free kick went to Howard Riley who cracked home a beauty to put Walsall one up. Unable to get to the match I listened on the radio to reports from the ground and went wild in our lounge as Allan Clarke put away a penalty to make it 2-0, the halftime score. We were down to ten men for the second half and George Kirby dropped back to help our over stretched defence, defending as if his life depended on it. Somehow, the ten men held out to record another of our 'giant killing' acts. 10,047 fans turned up at our next home match to welcome back our heroes and watch as we beat Bournemouth 2-1, with goals from Clarke and Kirby on January 29th 1966.

The Fourth Round draw took us to Norwich City, another radio day for me, and although we took the lead twice through Kirby and Taylor we would eventually lose 3-2.

Walsall had a great run through the winter period and were looking possible promotion contenders with 7 games to go, but unfortunately we had a poor finish, only winning 1 of those 7 games, and eventually we finished 9th.

However, it had been a great season, my first as a full-blown supporter. It had brought many highs and lows and I was incredibly proud of the team; we were strong in defence, had a controlled midfield and free scoring forwards. Allan Clarke scored 23 goals in 32 appearances, Kirby 19 goals in 44 appearances and Taylor 19 goals in 55 appearances.

Walsall had also played in what was my favourite all-time Walsall strip: white socks, red shorts and white shirts, with WFC across the chest. My Dad bought me a souvenir shirt and I wore it until it just disintegrated. My Mom stitched the number 8 on the back as homage to the great Allan Clarke.

Stoke City v Walsall, 3rd Round F.A. Cup. Howard Riley hammers in Walsall's first goal.
" By Courtesy of the Sunday Mercury."

Newspaper Clipping

Chapter 4

All-Time Football Hero

I guess in all aspects of life a 'first' is always remembered with great love, in some ways life changing and somehow deeply set in the memory, where it remains forever.

Of footballers, strikers are normally singled out for worship; they are the 'death or glory' boys, game-turning moments fall mainly to them.

As an impressionable 11 and 12-year-old, my first Walsall hero will forever live in that space in my mind.

Allan Clarke

Allan 'Sniffer' Clarke. Inside-Right.

He came to Walsall F.C. straight from school in 1962 and turned professional on August 12th 1963. I watched him develop in our reserve team and he made his first team debut on October 1st 1963 in a 1-1 draw against Reading as a sixteen-year-old. Allan played four more games towards the end of that season without scoring, however, Walsall supporters could see that he was something special.

Allan played in the second game of the 1964/1965 season and never again lost his place – he was eighteen years old. He scored his first goal away at Shrewsbury Town in a 3-1 defeat. I saw him score his second in the following home match, a 1-4 defeat at the hands of Workington Town.

The team that season was struggling and only just staved off relegation, however, Clarke just got better and better and scored more and more goals as the season went on. His final tally being 23 goals in 46 appearances. He scored his first hat-trick in his 11th first team game and would score two goals in each of a further five matches.

By the start of the 1965/1966 season Allan Clarke was well known in the third tier of professional football and would be a marked man. There was some concern around the club that Clarke would come in for some rough treatment during the campaign. Clarke, at only just nineteen years old, was tall but still slight of build, not yet fully developed. Walsall signed George Kirby to, not only lead the attack, but to act as 'minder' to the young Clarke. Kirby took his job seriously and when opposing defenders singled out Clarke for a little treatment, George responded using his full physical force and knowledge from many professional games. The Walsall supporters knew George's job and would scream 'Sort him out George' whenever Clarke was fouled. George was clever too, in that retribution wasn't always taken immediately, but would nevertheless come a few minutes later. Clarke blossomed in this protective environment and went on a scoring spree, scoring 23 goals in 31 appearances.

Coupled with the goals from the previous season there was a great confidence within the ranks of Walsall supporters, we felt that we could win many games and Allan Clarke would score us to victory. He became an instant legend and a hero to the young and old that followed the Saddlers.

Personally, I tried to make myself 'run' in a similar style to Clarke, to celebrate my goals in street games with his scoring reaction and practiced endlessly to take penalties in his style. The penalty practice worked for me in that I took penalties during our inter-house matches at Joseph Leckie and for the school side.

Allan Clarke winning penalty strikes home. 1st and replay—League Cup.
" By Courtesy of the Express and Star."

Newspaper Clipping

The technique was to run to the ball on the spot, looking as if you were going to hit it hard to the goalkeeper's right (or your left) as you approached the goal, just at the last moment opening the right foot to side foot it into the goalkeeper's left hand post (or your right) as you approached. The key was to play the ball so close to the post that it rolled inside the post and down the side netting. Having wrong-footed the keeper, he had no chance of getting anywhere near it, and even if the keeper didn't take the dummy, he still had little chance of getting a hand on a ball played that tightly to the post. I watched Allan Clarke do it time after time and practiced for hours to be able to repeat the feat. Wherever and whenever I scored a goal in street games or at school I reeled away shouting 'Clarkey' every time.

Allan Clarke's last game for Walsall came on March 12th 1966, versus Grimsby Town, a 1-0 victory with a goal by Colin Taylor and I was at the Laundry End that day oblivious to the fact that it would be my last sighting of Clarke in a Walsall shirt.

Clarke had scored 46 goals in 82 appearances and he was 'hot property.' I was completely unaware that a player could be so in demand by the big clubs and could disappear overnight. Fulham signed Allan Clarke at nineteen years of age for a then record fee for a Walsall player of 37,500 pounds.

My Dad came home with the *Express & Star* that night and informed me 'Clarkey's gone.' I just couldn't understand it. Why would he want to go? How could they sell him? It was all too much for my twelve-year-old brain. I retired to my room and cried at the loss of my hero.

Allan Clarke's career blossomed; he played 86 games for Fulham, scoring 45 goals, before being transferred to Leicester City in 1968 for 150,000 pounds. He spent one season at Leicester and was not so prolific in their colours, scoring 12 times in 36 games. However, Leicester City got to the F.A. Cup final in 1969 to face Manchester City, Clarke scoring the goal that got them there by defeating West Bromwich Albion.

My Dad, knowing that I was still a huge Allan Clarke fan, had been offered two tickets for the final and asked if I'd like to go to watch Clarkey. My Dad would be at work as usual that day and so my friend Steve Baldwin and I boarded a coach to Wembley for my first look at the stadium.

I became a Leicester City fan for the day and stood with their supporters. I was surprised when the teams lined up that Clarkey was not playing his usual upfront role but was playing more in midfield, somewhere I'd never seen him play before. Manchester City took an early lead through Neil Young and although the game was exciting that was the only goal of the game. I constantly shouted throughout the second half 'Get Clarkey up front.' I felt he was bound to score, but the Leicester Manager never took that option. Allan Clarke played magnificently that day and although being on the losing side he was voted 'Man of the Match.' I returned to Walsall disappointed, but happy I'd watched Clarkey in my first F.A. Cup final at Wembley.

FOOTBALL ASSOCIATION CHALLENGE CUP COMPETITION

FINAL

Leicester City
v
Manchester City

SATURDAY 26th APRIL 1969 · Kick-Off 3 p.m.

EMPIRE STADIUM WEMBLEY Official Programme 2/-

Soon after, Don Revie signed Clarke for Leeds United for 165,000 pounds. He would play for the great Leeds side of the seventies 273 times and score 110 goals. I watched their matches on TV just to see Clarkey.

His honours at Leeds:

Charity Shield 1969, Runner-up 1974

Fairs Cup 1971

F.A. Cup 1972, Runner-up 1969, 1970 and 1973

League Champion 1974

European Cup Runner-up 1975

Allan Clarke played 19 times for England, scoring 10 goals. He also collected 6 Under-23 Caps, scoring 4 goals on his debut. He was a member of the England squad under Alf Ramsey that competed in Mexico in the 1970 World Cup.

After nine seasons with Leeds United, Clarke sustained a knee injury that stopped him playing top-flight football, he went to be Player Manager at Barnsley and I watched his progress there through the newspapers.

In his first season, Barnsley won promotion to Division Three. Clarke played in 34 Games and scored 12 goals almost on one leg. In his second season as Player Manager, Barnsley finished in a comfortable mid-table position; he played in 13 games and scored 3 goals.

Allan Clarke's career total 514 appearances and 223 goals.

He would return to Elland Road as Manager for two years and then manage Scunthorpe United, Barnsley again and Lincoln City, before retiring completely from the game.

The name 'Sniffer' came from his predatory instinct to 'sniff' out goal scoring opportunities in crowded penalty areas; he was always in the right place at the right time.

Allan Clarke gave me twenty-five years of football as I followed his career and he still remains probably the Walsall player that achieved the most and my hero.

Harry Middleton

In my world, the story of Allan Clarke would not be complete without a mention for Harry Middleton. When Clarke was sold to Fulham, I was distraught and thought I would never see such a goal scorer again at Walsall Football Club. I didn't then know that in life when one door closes another one opens and in through the door came Harry Middleton.

Harry Middleton. Inside-Right.

Harry's career started at Wolverhampton Wanderers, but he only managed 1 game before being transferred to Scunthorpe United, then Portsmouth, before returning to the Midlands with Shrewsbury Town, playing 85 times and scoring 37 goals. He arrived at Walsall as a replacement for Allan Clarke, a masterstroke by Manager Ray Shaw. He made his debut for the Saddlers at Brentford on March 19 in a 2-2 draw, returning to Shrewsbury in a Walsall shirt six days later in our 1-2 victory. Harry's home debut was on March 26th against Bristol Rovers, a 1-1 draw. I was there to see Harry's first Walsall goal. Harry Middleton could then not stop scoring. Two weeks later, we demolished Gillingham at home 6-1, Middleton scoring 4 goals and Colin Taylor scoring 2, 1 of which was a high whacked lob from just inside the Gillingham half, which flew over their keeper into the net. I watched the strike and ball hit the back of the net just in front of me as I stood at the Laundry End wall. In total, Harry Middleton hit 14 goals in 18 appearances. Middleton became a hero in the weeks after Allan Clarke's departure.

Harry Middleton never quite hit those heights again, but he finished his career at Walsall having scored 30 goals in 66 appearances. His league career totalled 236 appearances and 103 goals.

Alan Ball in Dubai reminisces about Fellows Park

Chapter 5

1966 And All That

After Walsall's exciting season, football was in my blood and would remain so forever. Although I was also a big cricket fan, the summer of 1966 will be forever imprinted on a football brain.

The excitement of the coming World Cup gripped the nation; the souvenirs, including 'World Cup Willie,' the flags and the debate over the make-up of the England squad all led up to the opening match.

England and 'Swinging London' were at their peak; The Beatles and The Rolling Stones were worldwide successes, our music dominated the airwaves everywhere. Mary Quant led the fashion industry and the 'mini skirt' spread throughout the world like a plague; male blood pressure and testosterone rose in abundance. Vidal Sassoon remodelled our hairstyles and it seemed the world was at our feet; all we needed was a World Cup victory to complete the set.

History now shows that it would be achieved with a 4-2 victory in extra time over Germany; it just couldn't have played out in a better way.

After watching the early rounds of the competition, my family: Mom, Dad, Sister Helen, and I, went on a touring holiday of Cornwall for just over two weeks. I was deeply concerned that we would find a television to watch the final. My Dad knew, no matter what, that he would find a way and so it came to pass.

We were staying at a small farm on a bed, breakfast and evening meal arrangement and we watched the game from the dining room table through the serving hatch into the kitchen where the TV had been positioned. The owners of the farm sat in the kitchen and we, as guests, sat at the dining table.

Germany's equalizing goal just before the end of fulltime to make it 2-2 was devastating; it lifted me off my seat to a prostrate position on the floor.

Alf Ramsey was more controlled than I, his famous instruction: 'You've won it once, now you'll have to go and win it again. Don't sit on the floor, stand up, don't let the Germans see you are tired.' England's two goals in extra time brought the Cup home.

As soon as the programme was over my Sister Helen and I went outside onto the farm and we spent an hour chasing cows and sheep all over the fields to release some of the pent up energy.

Over the years since, I've only ever met one of that World Cup winning side, our right midfielder and youngest in the team that day, Alan Ball. I was fortunate enough many years later to play golf in some of The Footballers' Golf Classics, held in Spain and Dubai. I first met Alan in Dubai; after all those years, all the professional players held him in high regard, after all, there are very few World Cup winners. As I got to know Alan I told him my team was Walsall and Alan told me he would never forget Fellows Park.

At the very end of Bally's career, at 37 years of age, he was playing for Bristol Rovers; Bristol came to Fellows Park in a league game on October 29th 1983. Walsall would win the match 2-1, with goals from Richard O'Kelly and Mark Rees; Alan Ball was playing central-midfield for Bristol and David 'Mini' Preece playing central-midfield for Walsall.

Alan told me, 'I retired from professional football at Fellows Park in the dressing room after the game. A guy named David Preece had given me the run around all match, every time I got the ball he was on me and whenever he had it, I couldn't get near him. I knew that day my time was up and retired straight after the match. So, you see, I'll never forget Fellows Park, Walsall.'

I met up with Alan a few more times on golf trips and we became golf buddies; always fun to be with and a pretty good golfer. I was devastated to hear of his death, which came so suddenly, and only a few weeks after we had played golf together.

God bless Alan Ball, World Cup Winner.

The summer of 1966 rolled on and when we returned to Walsall I spent days at Fellows Park collecting autographs from around 9:30am as the players returned for pre-season training.

One day, the coach turned up as the players were going to Aldridge airport to train. I decided I had to see the training session and caught the bus from Fellows Park into Walsall Town centre and then the bus to Aldridge and I appeared at the training session watching them go through their paces.

Our family home was in Regina Drive, just off the Mellish Road, and so I had planned to return home after the session, which was not too far away. The players finished training and started to board the coach, still signing autographs for me as they boarded.

Stan Bennett stopped and said 'Were you at the ground this morning?'

'Yes, Stan.'

Stan then got on the bus, spoke to a couple of people and came back off the bus to me.

'OK, you get to ride on the team bus back to Fellows Park, come on, what's your name?'

'Steve Jenkins.'

I knew by getting on the bus it would take me an hour to get back home rather than ten minutes down the road, but I could not miss a chance to ride on the team bus.

Stan led me onto the bus and said 'Sit there with me,' then he stood in the gangway: 'Hey, lads, this here is Steve Jenkins, who was at the ground today. He followed us all the way here, so we're giving a ride back!'

There were many shouts of 'Hello, Steve,' 'Alright, Steve,' 'Good lad.'

I sat next to Stan all the way back to Fellows Park while he chatted and I asked him questions. I was proud as punch.

I couldn't wait to tell my Mom and Dad that I'd been on the coach with the players and when I returned to Joseph Leckie I told all my mates the same and that Stan Bennett and me were mates.

All these years later, thanks Stan, I still remember.

The Walsall squad reassembled for the 1966/1967 season, our major off-season signing being Alan Baker from Aston Villa for 10,000 pounds. Alan was a good ball player and had won both schoolboy and youth international caps for England. He had appeared in the League Cup final, playing over 100 games and scoring 17 goals for Villa. When he signed for Walsall everyone thought we had bought a class performer and so he proved to be, playing for five seasons before a serious injury ended his career.

The season opener was at home versus Mansfield Town, a World Cup enthused crowd turned up; 10,287 souls hoping for a winning start to the season. Unfortunately, we went down 2-1 and worse was to come when Johnny Harris was badly injured; we lost our inspirational Captain for almost two seasons. He eventually got back into the team and made a further 10 appearances, but he was never really fit enough for professional football again.

This left an opening in the team at left-back and a young Mick Evans, from our youth and reserve side, jumped in and would become a regular fixture in that position for the next seven seasons, amassing 263 appearances and 8 goals before moving on to Swansea and Crewe Alexandra. Mick was a fine athlete, whenever I saw the team in training Mick was way out in front with the exercises and running. He was fair but tough in the tackle and nicknamed 'Chopper' after another Walsall full-back, Bill Gutteridge. Not many wingers got the better of Mick Evans and if they did, it was usually a painful experience.

Years later, I got to know Mick whilst playing in a few ex-Walsall players' games. The first time was during Mark Rees' Testimonial match at Fellows Park. I started on the bench not expecting to appear until after halftime, when after only three or four minutes Mick pulled up with a hamstring problem and signalled to the bench immediately that he was off. Brian Caswell, in charge of our side that night, looked at me and said 'Warm up, you're on.' I was excited and nervous all at the same time, but running up and down the line, warming up at Fellows Park, was a fantastic feeling. The crowd being so close gave me plenty of stick even before I got on. I had long hair during those days and could hear the fans: 'Oh no, we're putting a girl on!' 'Get your hair cut!' 'Part your hair you might see the ball!' 'Shirley bloody Temple's coming on!' I enjoyed all of the banter and because I couldn't help but laugh the fans all joined in, a great moment for me.

Mick was still a fearsome tackler in his late forties and early fifties, I was forever grateful I played with him and not against him.

The team started poorly in 1966 and Terry Carling, our goalkeeper, paid the price. In came Bob Wesson, from Coventry

Steve Jenkins pass to Mick Evans at Fellows Park

City, who would stay with the club for seven seasons making 220 appearances. Although not always first choice, Bob was a good keeper and turned around our fortunes that season, we won 10 of our next 15 games; Baker, Kirby and Taylor forming a great strike force and scoring regularly. Just when we were looking good, we stalled in January and February, but the signings of Alec Jackson and Terry Simpson and our Walsall born reserve keeper, Keith Ball, being promoted to the first team steadied the ship and we finished a respectable 12th in the league.

Our main scorers were Colin Taylor 19 goals, Alan Baker 16 goals and George Kirby 11 goals. Some of our homegrown players made an impact; along with Mick Evans, Trevor Meath had 22 appearances with 5 goals, Colin

Harrison 11 appearances and the highly thought of Geoff Morris 1 appearance, to add to the 1 appearance from the previous season as a sixteen-year-old.

Trevor Meath was a giant and although he had good skill, when he was in full flow the best course of action was to get out of the way. Meath normally broke from the right-wing half position, but he did play a few games at centre-forward. The supporters loved it when he did; he absolutely battered opposing defenders with an all-action style. Meath was never a regular in the team but would play in periods over the next five seasons, making 76 appearances and scoring 13 goals.

Walsall would have a good run in the League Cup that year beating Port Vale 3-1 at Vale Park, with goals from Middleton 2 and Taylor. Our only home leg was in the Second Round, which I watched with 13,599 others as we came up with another 'giant killing' act against Stoke City, winning 2-1, Taylor and Middleton scoring again. Round Three saw us away at Exeter City, again 2-1 winners; Baker scored our first and big Trevor Meath came on as our substitute centre-forward and battered in the winner. Finally, we were knocked out at Sheffield United going down 2-1, with Colin Taylor scoring our goal. It had been another exciting run in a Cup competition and Walsall fans always believe we can turn over the big boys.

I was thirteen coming on fourteen at the end of the 1966/1967 season, the summer was here and a period that would forever be known as the Summer of Love. 100,000 hippies descended on San Francisco and forced themselves and their beliefs into the world consciousness. Scott McKenzie had a number one record in the U.K. with 'San Francisco (Be sure to wear some flowers in your hair)' and The Beatles topped our album charts with *Sgt Pepper's Lonely Hearts Club Band*.

I was already in love with music, but that summer made a big impression on me. Music could change the world and the youth movement was at the peak of its powers. The government was so nervous of music, and how it grouped the youth together, that they outlawed Radio Caroline and Radio London. Later, on September 30th 1967, the government, through the BBC, launched Radio 1. If youth was so in love with music then the government had to have some control over the speech that went with it. The youth of Great Britain had embarrassed the government into launching Radio 1.

Obviously, I didn't know that my future life would be spent in the record industry, but I'm sure that summer had a huge influence on what was to come. The hits that year came from The Beatles, The Who, The Beach Boys, The Turtles, The Bee Gees, The Tremeloes, Petula Clark, The Small Faces,

Donovan, The Rolling Stones, The Four Tops, Cliff Richard, The Hollies, The Monkees, Tom Jones, The Kinks and Lulu.

Walsall returned to pre-season training and the real shock was that George Kirby had been released. George went to try his luck in America with The New York Cosmos before later ending his career with Brentford. Our one addition to the team was Jimmy Murray, a former Wolves player, he signed after four seasons at Manchester City. Murray had been a fantastic goal scorer, 166 goals for Wolves, winning two League Championship medals and an F.A. Cup winners medal, then a further 43 goals for Manchester City.

Jimmy played for two seasons at Fellows Park, scoring 15 goals in 64 appearances and although it was considered a good spell, the fans never really took to him. George Kirby had been such a favourite; I believe Jimmy had to take some of the backlash for the club releasing Kirby. He was soon christened 'Ruby' by the supporters, after the singer Ruby Murray and long before 'Ruby' became a national name for curry.

The 1967/1968 season started with a bang, we won 13 times with 5 draws and 5 defeats and we went into Christmas looking as though promotion was on the cards. I was at Fellows Park to witness the opening match, a 3-0 win against Gillingham, and the next home match saw us thrash Leyton Orient 5-0. A few games later we signed a flying winger who would become a real favourite, with Colin Taylor on our left wing and Tommy Watson on the right, we were a handful for any team. Tommy burst into the team as we walloped Tranmere Rovers on his debut 5-1, Watson getting his first for the club. I was standing with my Dad that night on the halfway line under the Cowshed. Dad watched Watson score and make a couple of other goals and constantly run through Tranmere's left side of defence.

He said 'Hey, Steve, we've got a good one here.'

Watson scored 4 times in his first 4 games and we notched 5 consecutive wins.

As good as we were in the first half of the season; we were equally as poor in the second half. From Boxing Day until March 2nd 1968, we wouldn't win a match. That period blew our chances of promotion; we rallied again towards the end of the season but all too late, finishing 7th from a start that promised so much.

There were some moments that season which stay in the memory: Watson scored 15 goals from the right wing, Taylor 14 from the left and 'Ruby' got 12 through the middle.

Finally, I had graduated to the Hilary Street End. At fourteen years of age I felt I could hold my own with the big lads behind the goal. I was joined by school pal John Oebel and we would stand behind the goal for years watching games.

We were there on a cold November 11th 1968, Bury were the visitors in front of 12,169 supporters. Bury had taken the lead and were hanging on as we pushed and pushed to equalize, slowly the minutes were ticking away and the end of the game was drawing in fast. In a last throw of the dice, Stan Bennett went up front and we hammered the ball continually into Bury's box.

John and I thought it was over, a minute left and Bury are punting the ball up field with every chance they have, suddenly the ball is back in the Bury box, Stan turns and lashes it into the corner of the net, 1-1. The Hilary Street End erupts, screaming, shouting, punching the air and finds an enormous voice: 'Come on Walsall, Come on Walsall,' rings out around the ground. John and I are in pretty good voice too. Bury kick-off, we steal the ball, Harry Middleton is put through and Harry slides it home, 2-1. The Street End is now jumping, the fans start to move forward and one of those old-fashioned crushes occurs as everyone moves a few steps down, still singing, dancing and chanting. Bury kick-off and the referee blows for fulltime. The team pass the Street End on their way back to the dressing room and the atmosphere was as if we had won the F.A. Cup.

The crushes were scary, the arm pumping equally, an unintended punch could land easily. The pushing, the jumping and the noise of the singing, scary, but equally exhilarating, and those two goals in the final minute that caused so much chaos, I will always remember.

We won a few games at the end of the season as we rejigged the side. Stan Jones came back to Walsall after 267 games for West Bromwich Albion. On March 16th 1968, I was behind the Laundry End goal as Stan made his return against Bristol Rovers, we won the match 2-1, with goals from Watson and McMorran, but Stan tried to stop a Rovers shot, half caught it and deflected it into our net for an own goal on his debut, right in front of me. This may have caused a lesser player some problems, but I remember Stan just looked at the ball in the net, turned and played a fantastic game as if nothing had happened. Stan Jones would remain in our backline for another five seasons and then return again as trainer years later. In 1980, Stan was looking after our reserve side and on a couple of occasions I sat on the bench with him. Although he was working, we chatted at times through the games and I got to know Stan Jones a little. Great player, great guy. Strangely, after Stan Jones' debut in that match, we signed a Bristol Rovers centre-forward. I left the ground and headed home and by the time Dad got home from work the signing had made 'The Pinks' sports paper. Alfie Biggs was now a Walsall player. Although Alfie was at the end of his career, he was a true goal scorer, ending his career with 213 league goals. The fans took to Alf; he started scoring straight away and managed 5 in our last 11 games. The crowd responded with the song 'What's it all about Alfie,' whenever he got the ball and especially when he scored.

Allan Clarke's brother, Derek, played in those last few matches as an eighteen-year-old, 10 games and 2 goals. Wolverhampton Wanderers came straight in and bought him, believing they just might have another Allan. They didn't, but Derek had a good career with Oxford United and Leyton Orient.

Our F.A. Cup exploits were again in the news. We beat Leytonstone in Round One, Exeter City in Round Two, finally beating Crystal Palace in a replay 2-1 after drawing the home leg 1-1 in Round Three and out of the hat came Walsall versus Liverpool in Round Four. We all thought, here we go again, there might just be a chance. I was in the 21,066 fans that packed into Fellows Park and we put in a spirited performance and ended with a credible 0-0 draw. The replay at Anfield two days later was played in front of 39,113. Liverpool were just too good for us that night winning 5-2, Tony Hateley getting 4 of their goals and Tommy Watson scoring our two goals. My Dad and I listened to the radio for bulletins every fifteen minutes. The fog that night was so bad that you could not see the other end of the pitch. The Kop were singing 'Who scored?, Who scored?' to the other end of the pitch and it kept coming back 'Tony, Tony Hateley.'

Our Cup exploits were over for another year.

Colin Taylor fires away against our famous visitors, Moscow Dynamo.
" By Courtesy of the Express and Star."

Newspaper Clipping

Chapter 6
Saturday Jobs, Girls And 'The Pinks'

During the summer of 1968, my parents decided that I would become what was known in those days as a 'Saturday boy' in my Dad's main shop at the Walsall Co-op, Bridge Street. I had been to work there before, in the basement moving shoeboxes, stacking shelves and taking in deliveries, in fact, everything behind the scenes. Sure enough, that would be the case again, but eventually, when they thought I was ready, I would move into the Men's department to sell shoes. All of this was to get me used to work, earning my own money and beginning to manage it and taking more responsibility for my own life.

I was up for the task and started to feel a little more grown up. I would be fifteen in the coming October and I remember starting to notice a difference in girls. At first, I couldn't quite understand why they looked different and seemingly more interesting. I had not been that interested before, but suddenly my interest seemed to come from nowhere and 'out of the blue.' It would take a little while for me to get a hold of all that emotional surge, as it did for us all, for the time being, however, I wouldn't miss a match for one.

I was excited about working at the Co-op, but disappointed that this would put an end to Saturdays at Fellows Park. My Dad assured me it would be okay and that on occasions I wouldn't be needed and I could have the day off. I'm sure that happened although I don't remember it that often.

Walsall Football Club was in the middle of change; the Chairman Bill Harrison, who was much loved for his enthusiasm and effort, suddenly died in the close season. Bill's son Ron took over and that brought about more managerial change.

The previous season had seen Dick Graham brought in to manage the team, although Ray Shaw was not sacked. Ron Harrison then brought in Ron Lewin to start the coming season, with Ray Shaw as General Manager. All this change affected the team and finally, in February 1969, back to the club came Bill Moore.

The 1968/1969 season began with Colin 'Cannonball' Taylor off on his travels, this time sold to Crystal Palace. We received a good offer from Palace; Colin wanted to try his luck again and we had Geoff Morris in our reserves who everyone thought would be a fine left-winger. Geoff had been knocking the first team door for some time and had managed to have a run of games at the end of the previous season scoring 3 times in 11 matches; he looked ready. Dislodging Colin Taylor had been difficult, but Walsall felt they had a ready replacement.

Keith Ball our goalkeeper had lost his place to Bob Wesson again and moved to Port Vale, but we had found a fine young goalkeeper who would go on to achieve plenty in the game. Bob Wesson's understudy that season was Phil Parkes. Terry Simpson moved to Gillingham and Graham Sissons retired from league football. We made only one signing and looked a little thin on the ground; Mike Tindall joined from Villa, but would only play a few games into the season and was then injured.

Our defence would remain stable for several seasons and that would always keep the side in a mid-table position; whenever we developed a good forward line we had a chance to get promoted.

The defence was built around goalkeeper, Bob Wesson; right-back, Frank Gregg; left-back, Mick Evans; right-half, Nick Atthey; centre-half, Stan Jones and left-half, Stan Bennett. Well, that's the way they numbered them in the programme; football was changing and the system was changing to the now common back four. It would read today: Gregg, Jones, Bennett and Evans, with Atthey in midfield. Those players had been together for two seasons already and would manage another five.

The season started poorly, we won on the opening day 1-0 against Shrewsbury but wouldn't win again for 10 matches. During that time, we bought in a couple of players to bolster the team. Davie Wilson arrived from Grimsby Town, a blonde haired bundle of energy and commitment to play centre-forward. Derek Trevis joined at the same time to bolster the midfield from Colchester United. I remember the night my Dad came home with the *Express & Star* and said 'Look at that.' Somehow, I missed the report of the signing of Davie Wilson and had to have it pointed out to me later by my frustrated Dad.

Due to my Saturday job, it would be October before I got to Fellows Park that year. I watched a 0-0 game on October 8th against Watford, but on October 19th got a rare Saturday off and saw a 2-1 victory over Wigan Athletic. It was my first sight of Davie Wilson, who gave what was to become a normal fully committed performance in a Walsall shirt and scored both goals in front of me standing at the Laundry End. Derek Trevis also played in midfield that day and I remember being impressed by his skill and workrate. I reported my opinion back to my Dad later that night.

It was around this time I became aware that all was not right with my Dad. Little by little he became more and more tired and started sleeping for twenty minutes at lunchtime before returning to work. Mom was always cooking baked fish almost every day for him to eat at lunch. The smell of all that baked fish has put me off fish for my entire life. Nothing was ever said to Helen, my Sister, or I, but being a little older I knew everything was not quite right. Only a few weeks later my Dad was admitted to the Walsall General Hospital having suffered his first heart attack. In those days, the heart attack method of recovery was one week complete bed rest, one week being allowed to walk to the toilet only and then in the third week, sitting up and a walk a day around the ward in preparation for returning home. Visiting times were limited in the evenings to one hour, but I used to sneak up to the hospital in the afternoons after school and see my Dad through the window to the ward. We couldn't talk as he was too far away but the message would be passed down the ward that I was there and he would wave.

All seemed to be going well with my Dad, he was only two days from coming home when a second massive heart attack came, bringing with it a stroke. Our family world was shattered that day and would never be the same again. Dad eventually made it back home and fought against his paralyzed left side for another 18 months before being readmitted to hospital and finally succumbing.

My Dad and I were under the Cowshed for a 2-0 victory over Luton Town on November 5 and in the same place for the December 30 game against Brighton, our biggest win of the season, a 4-0 victory.

The last match I remember going to with my Dad was January 4th 1969. We had progressed to the Third Round of the F.A. Cup again and drawn Tottenham Hotspur at home. Within the Tottenham side was the legend Jimmy Greaves, both Dad and I could not wait to see Jimmy play at Fellows Park, but also hoped he may leave a little disappointed.

My Dad decided that he wanted to get seats in the stand that night and got some as close to his own Father's seats as he could. We watched as Walsall charged at Tottenham with Davie Wilson giving everything he had got, how they kept out one of his attempts was beyond belief. Our defence was tight, Jimmy McMorran prompted all night and Watson on our right wing and Morris on the left gave it a real go. Dad and I urged the boys on, but as we began to tire, up popped Jimmy Greaves to break our hearts and score in front of the Hilary Street Faithful. We lost the match 1-0. Jimmy Greaves was a cut above anyone on the park and it seemed to me that all of the Tottenham side were just that little bit quicker than us in all aspects of the match. Our commitment, enthusiasm and passion, however, were there for all to see.

I have never known Walsall play Tottenham in all the years that have passed since that night and so still to this day the last time we played them William Alan Jenkins was watching, a Walsall Football Club supporter all his life and I'm proud as his son that I've been able to support the same team all these years.

One of my duties during the time I worked at Walsall Co-op was to go and get 'The Pinks' on a Saturday evening. *The Sporting Star* and *Sports Argus* were huge selling papers and covered all the local football teams with reports on the day's games. Regular as clockwork at five forty-five pm I would leave the shop, cross Bridge Street, past 'The Dirty Duck' and wait on the corner next to the Nationwide, where the papers were delivered and sold. Around five fifty a van would pull up and sell both 'The Pinks' sporting papers, I would take them back to the Co-op and then Dad and I would take them home and during dinner would read a paper and then swap at some point later in the evening. It always amazed me how only an hour after fulltime, whole newspapers could be produced and distributed.

During the second half of the season, from January onwards, I was lucky that a lot of postponed home matches were rearranged for Tuesday nights. All of the games I stood with my Uncle George under the Cowshed just on the halfway line. George, like my Father, preferred that position.

In those 5 games, I only saw wins or draws. Alan Baker found his scoring boots again, Trevor Meath returned to the side to play centre-forward and batter in four goals. In March, we won 4 games on the bounce as Ray Train, another Walsall find, made a big impression on the first team. In addition, on April 1, I was there to witness a 3-1 victory over Mansfield and the debut of another find, and possibly the greatest goalkeeping discovery in Walsall history, Phil Parkes.

Ray Train would have a twenty-year career in football, making 621 appearances for nine clubs, including 104 for Walsall in two spells, starting and finishing his career with the Saddlers. After coming through the ranks at Walsall, we eventually sold Ray to Carlisle United for 15,000 pounds, playing in Division One and making 154 appearances, then going to Sunderland for

80,000 pounds. After winning the Second Division Championship, Bolton paid 80,000 pounds to sign him. Again, he won the Second Division Championship and made 57 appearances before signing for Watford for 50,000 pounds, there he won promotion twice from the Third Division to the First. Oxford United for 10,000 pounds was his next move, before playing for Bournemouth, Northampton, Tranmere and, finally, coming home to Fellows Park as Player Coach to our reserve side. Ray Train also had a spell as our Caretaker Manager, but he is best remembered as a great little player.

Phil Parkes, a goalkeeping giant in more ways than one; 6 feet 3 inches tall and 14 stone 9 pounds in his prime, he made 60 appearances for Walsall before being transferred to QPR for 15,000 pounds. Phil stayed at QPR for nine seasons, making 408 appearances before joining West Ham for 500,000 pounds. He was West Ham's keeper for ten seasons before ending his career with one season at Ipswich, keeping goal for his four clubs in more than 900 senior games. Phil won England caps at all levels, an F.A. Cup medal and Second Division Championship with West Ham; another great Walsall find and a truly great goalkeeper.

During the 1968/1969 season, Walsall were no longer the free scoring side of previous seasons, Morris got 10, Wilson 10 and Baker 8; other players scored 3, 4 and 5 goals, but the days of 23 and 19 had gone.

We would finish a reasonable 13th in the table, but it had been an unsettled season apart from our defence. Bill Moore was now back in charge and all Walsall folk hoped that he would repeat the magic he had brought before when we rose from Division Four to Division Two in consecutive seasons.

The summer of 1969 was different in that I worked for a few weeks in my Dad's shop and we left as a family for Bournemouth for our holidays as we had the year before, but little did we know at the time that it would be the last of our family holidays. We had travelled around the U.K. for many years in the summers previously and Mom and Dad had decided that Bournemouth was the place they loved most; had our holidays continued I'm sure we would have found ourselves in Bournemouth each year. My parents loved The Chines, which are the walks through the woods that lead to the coast and the beach; there are four Chines of various lengths. They also loved Poole, its town and harbour, along with the New Forest. My Dad was not in a position to expend energy and so we had a beach hut that my parents were around all day and I was allowed to explore the town, pier and Winter Gardens alone. Helen, being younger, was normally around the beach hut and beach. I'd always return at meal times as Mom had a stove and cooked bacon, eggs, tomatoes and sausages for us, while Dad had much less tasty fare not rich in fat.

Dad and I did visit Dean Court to watch Bournemouth play a few times over a couple of years. We were part-time Bournemouth supporters; it did not have the adrenaline rush of watching Walsall, but our genuine love of football made it a good day out.

In the years that followed, I went to Bournemouth many times, I don't know if that was because it was my parents' favourite or because I knew the town so well. In times I needed to think things through I used Bournemouth as a 'bolt hole' or 'safe house.' The sea air and the beautiful scenery always seemed to calm my mind and help me think through my next life plan or objective.

When I was older I went there again with some mates and found Chelsea Village, a nightclub, which remains in my memory a favourite. It was there that I would see Hot Chocolate and The Emperor Rosko perform. I also got up early one morning to see Tony Blackburn do the Radio 1 breakfast show live from the Winter Gardens; music, records and radio were becoming all important to my life.

On my return to Walsall, I managed to sneak into a pre-season training session at Fellows Park. I think the players and staff just let me hang around; I made sure I made no comments or a nuisance of myself, just watching as they trained.

I remember one day that the boys were warming up in front of the main stand; each player had to step forward and do an exercise that the others copied. Geoff Morris stepped forward and started doing an exercise, throwing each leg out sideways alternately, the others started to follow. I must admit it did look a little odd. For some reason that I was not privy to why they called Geoff 'Bubbles.'

Mick Evans then chimed in 'Hey, Bubbles, what's this,' meaning the exercise. Colin Harrison responded 'It's what he's been doing with that new girlfriend of his.' Stan Bennett replied 'God help her,' followed by laughter.

Bill Moore was now in charge for his first full season back at the club. Throughout the season he would change players' positions change our plan of attack in an attempt to get things moving. Our defence remained solid; Phil Parkes had his one full season at Walsall before being transferred to QPR and was magnificent. The full-backs were still Frank Gregg and Mick Evans, although it became Colin Harrison's breakthrough season where he displaced both Frank and Mick as their form dipped and he made more appearances that term than either of them. The Halfback line of Atthey, Jones and Bennett remained as solid as ever. It was in front of this defence that Bill Moore tried everything to fashion an attacking force.

Bill bought back Colin 'Cannonball' Taylor from Crystal Palace; he was in great form and would be top scorer with 13 goals. It became a struggle to fit both Geoff Morris and Taylor in the same side; both had spells on the right wing to try and accommodate both talents. The other main signing was John 'Woody' Woodward from Aston Villa. 'Woody' would play for the Saddlers for three seasons making 145 appearances and scoring 29 goals. Stan Bennett and Derek Trevis would move forward to have spells at centre-forward to try to spark some life into our attack with occasional success as Bill Moore rang in the changes to make it work. We tried several midfield players to get the middle of the park right with signings Chris Crowe and Alan Deakin, but they found it hard to fill the boots of the departed Jimmy McMorran.

Gone during the summer were Jimmy Murray, Alfie Biggs, Mike Tindall and Johnny Harris, who became Reserve Coach, and Davie Wilson was sold after only 4 matches in January.

Towards the end of the season, Jimmy Seal came on loan from Wolverhampton Wanderers and managed 8 goals in 17 appearances and we would only lose 2 of our last 13 games and finish again a comfortable mid-table 12th. Bill Moore had found an answer after so much effort and trying, but it was too late for the 1968/1969 season.

I would attend 9 games that season due again to working Saturdays; on September 16th, a 1-0 win against Barrow secured with a Ray Train penalty. September 30th, a 1-3 defeat against Luton Town, 'Cannonball' getting the consolation. The Boxing Day win against Mansfield Town, 1-0, Train again scoring. January 27th, a 1-3 defeat, Train again getting the consolation; it would be Train's last game before joining Carlisle. In March 1970, I visited Fellows Park twice to see a 1-1 draw against Bury and a 0-1 loss to Gillingham. During April, I watched a 2-0 win against Leyton Orient, a 2-2 draw against Plymouth Argyle and the best result of the season against Reading, a 4-1 win, with goals from Colin Harrison, Colin Taylor and 2 goals from the very lively Jimmy Seal.

Colin Harrison. All Positions.

In Walsall terms, whatever you write about Colin Harrison will not be enough. Colin spent his entire professional career at Walsall Football Club and played in every position for the club, full-back, central-defence, midfield, both wings and striker. He played in our first team for eighteen seasons and retired as the Walsall appearance record holder with 529 appearances and 34 goals. He is also a gentleman and a player much loved to this day, his name is part of Walsall Football Club and will forever be so.

Colin Harrison

Many years later, on May 21st 2005, I played my final football match. I was fifty-two years old. Although I ran most days and could be considered fit I was no longer fit enough to play football, the twisting and turning and pushing off in short bursts was to prove my undoing.

Chris Marsh had phoned me to say that he was organising a game in charity for the Walsall Hospice and would I join in and play at the Bescot Stadium. A lot of my Walsall professional football mates would be turning up and many of them had asked for me to be included as we got together less and less over the years.

I wanted to support the day as the Walsall Hospice had been so kind to my Mom in her final days, but I said to 'Marshy,' 'I'm only good for fifteen minutes at the end of the game.' I knew my legs were gone, over the past few years I had only played in five-a-side games where I found it easy to position myself properly and play at a canter. Playing on the Bescot pitch would demand much more and I knew I didn't have it, especially playing with all ex-professionals. 'Marshy' agreed fifteen minutes would do it and up I went on the day to the Bescot.

I was having a great time; Ron Green, Mark Rees, Martin O'Connor, Dean Keates and Andy Rammall, just to mention a few, had all turned up to support 'Marshy' and the Hospice. I spent time in both dressing rooms before the match chatting to the lads before Reesy kicked me out saying I wasn't playing for his team, all in jest of course.

The match was between Walsall Old Dogs versus Walsall Mad Dogs.

I cannot remember which team I played for and looking back I certainly qualified for both, we managed to pull a 1500 crowd and donate good money to the hospice.

We went out to warm up and 'kick in' and I put a few crosses in for Ron Green to warm up in front of the big stand. I was having a great time and looking forward to warming the bench for most of the game. As the ref blew to line-up and kick-off, I started jogging to the bench when 'Marshy' said, 'Sorry mate, Don Goodman cannot make it until halftime, you'll have to play the first half.' Now, that was not in the plan,

Short ball to Chris Marsh at Bescot Stadium

but what can you do, if you're on, you're on. 'Marshy' said 'Play right-midfield in front of me and I'll take care of it.'

So, I lined up on the right-flank just hoping I could make it to halftime, the other team's left-back was Colin Harrison, then in his sixties, but still fit and able to move around comfortably. Well, I never got passed him once and my play consisted of getting close to him and then laying it back for either 'Marshy' or Keatesie to cross it in. I once ventured into the box and 'Marshy' just yelled 'Get out of there, too much trouble for you up there.' Probably right.

I spoke to Colin Harrison a few times during the match and managed to play twenty-seven minutes before having to come off, I'd ripped both Achilles and I knew I was in serious trouble. Colin came up to me as we went down the tunnel at halftime and inquired what I'd done, when I said Achilles, he gave me a knowledgeable nod. Colin managed the whole second half; I was long gone and changed, back in the stands.

We all had a meal afterwards, which was great fun. Sitting and eating took quite some time and by the time it came to leave, I got up and could hardly walk, the steps down to the car park were a nightmare, made even worse by Rammall, Reesy, Ron Green, Keatesie and alike giving me almighty stick all the way to the car.

The achilles took twelve weeks to heal and quite a bit of massage and therapy.

On that day I'd had the idea before the match that it might be my last, by the end of the game I knew it was. I've never pulled on a pair of boots since, not even for a five-a-side game, but I'm delighted in the knowledge that my football career ended at Bescot Stadium, home of the Saddlers.

Walsall Mad Dogs v Walsall Old Dogs

Steve Jenkins No. 14 late defending Bescot Stadium

Chapter 7
Trouble Brewing At Fellows Park

During the spring and start of the summer in 1969, my thoughts should have been focused on getting my O'levels or GCSE's as they are known today. Looking back, and in all honesty, I had little focus in that area. I'd really had enough of Joseph Leckie School and they had really had enough of me; I was considered a disruptive influence and only got any respite when playing football and cricket for the school teams.

Hindsight is a wonderful thing and we are all geniuses with it. Although I think I've always had a happy demeanour and been satisfied with my lot no matter what was going on in my life, I did have an anger in those years that was just below the surface. What had happened to my Father I was particularly unhappy about; my Dad was talented, a hard worker and had a great sense of humour, he got through life without injuring others and looked after his family. To see every day what he had to go through hurt me badly. My Dad was also a man that never hit me, choosing always to discuss, educate and enlighten, hence, when I was hit at school by teachers who I had little respect for, pent up anger was released and usually in abundance. Consequently, I was instructed not to attend school in the final couple of months and just return for the GCSE's, where I was met at the gate and escorted to and from a desk for the exam and had no interaction with the other pupils.

This led to no preparation for the exams. Joseph Leckie didn't care and quite frankly neither did I. The only thing I did care about was trying not to upset my Mom who had enough to cope with.

I spent all my days at Walsall Football Club, playing with the boys, junior teams and apprentices and doing any unpaid job I could do; sweeping the terraces, making tea, carrying the water buckets, you name it I'd do it.

On Tuesdays, my fascination with records saw me selling records on Walsall market. I hung around the stall that much that in the end they said why don't you stand this side of the stall and help us sell the records. I was in my element. I just loved being around those records; they were imported from America and you couldn't buy them in W.H. Smiths or Boots, it was a more specialised market. Whatever money I earned during those days I gave it straight back and bought the records I just had to have. I loved the R n B sound of Stax Records from Memphis and bought Otis Redding, Carla Thomas, Sam & Dave, Rufus Thomas, and Booker T & The MG's, all American import singles that I still have to this day.

My record collection was growing and most of the money I received from Walsall Co-op on Saturdays went into W.H. Smiths as I bought the more popular chart records there.

The inevitable happened I suppose, I managed an English GCSE from Joseph Leckie and no more, I couldn't force my way into Walsall Football Club and Mom insisted I re-sit my GCSE's at Walsall Technical College where I attended throughout the 1969/1970 season. I enrolled at the Tech, still working Saturdays at Walsall Co-op and I was disappointed I had not made my escape from the education ranks. Walsall Technical College worked better for me in that you really didn't have to be there by law, you were there more or less off your own bat, even if my bat was really my Mother's. I agreed with Mom that I must get a Maths GCSE to go with my English and she believed that would give me some sort of qualification and a possibility of a decent job. I managed my Maths GCSE and would soon be working as Walsall approached a new season.

Walsall F.C. had a small squad in 1970/1971. Bob Wesson would reclaim the number one goalkeeping jersey after Phil Parkes transfer to QPR and would become Player of the Season. Normally, when your keeper is Player of the Season, it means he has seen a lot of action and usually reflects a poor season. 70/71 was that.

Our defence was still based around Gregg, Harrison, Evans, Bennett, Jones and Atthey. Morris, Taylor and Train dominated the wings, Woodward, centre-forward, and Baker and the newly signed Willie Penman as inside-forwards.

Willie Penman was signed from Swindon for 6,000 pounds and was a highly skillful midfielder, having played for Dundee, Glasgow Rangers and Newcastle United. He knew how to play and was a welcome addition to the team. The combination of both Penman and Baker would make us a real ball-playing team, but alas, the best laid plans.

I was at Fellows Park on September 12th 1970, we were playing Tranmere Rovers and were 1-0 up with an Alan Baker goal, when Baker, as ever, was twisting and turning, ball at his feet, attacking the Laundry End, then, he seemed to twist, turn and take a heavy tackle all at the same time. After watching so many football matches and seeing so many tackles, I think you instinctively know when something bad has happened. Without going into too much detail, the moment had dislodged Alan's kneecap and that moment would be the end of his career. He tried hard to regain fitness but eventually had to concede that his knee would never hold up to the vigours of professional football. It was a great loss to the club, the town and the fans. Many loan players came in over the following months to fill the gap Alan had left behind, it was difficult to replace a player of Baker's quality and we never really did that season.

The only highlights of a poor season came with a good trouncing of local rivals, Aston Villa, at Fellows Park. I joined 19,202 fans on January 2nd to see Geoff Morris torment the Villa and score twice and Colin Taylor blast a penalty, which the keeper did well to get out of the way of. I also attended the return at Villa Park hoping for another scalp in front of 37,642, but Villa held on for a 0-0 draw.

We were in trouble on the last day of the season, it looked like Walsall or Reading for the drop to Division Four. We drew 1-1 at Port Vale and Reading lost 2-1 at Villa Park, we just and only just retained our Division Three status, thanks in part to all those lovely people at Aston Villa.

The summer once again came around and we breathed a sigh of relief that Walsall had escaped relegation; it almost felt like promotion, we were seemingly doomed with 3 games to go.

That season, fortunately, I had managed my Maths GCSE from Walsall Tech, with not much else but enough to please my troubled Mother. Dad had finally left this mortal coil after much suffering; our family was now three and my responsibilities much larger.

I needed money first and foremost, mainly to pay rent to my Mom for my keep and to help with the household bills, then to get a car to enable me to move around and seek opportunities. I attacked relentlessly, working all the previous summer at Walsall Co-op. I knew it would be my last; after my Dad's passing I didn't really want to be there anymore but felt it was a summer job and it would swell the coffers. I also got a job on the petrol pumps at a garage on the one-way system, by the Arboretum, six pm to midnight, so I could work in the day, then go straight to the garage and work on. I had two regular nights but would fill in where necessary and on occasions worked four nights.

In September 1970 I soon got a job in Darlaston at Charles Richards Fasteners in the office. I must admit, I didn't like it. Playing football for the works' team I did like, and I also liked the typing pool of girls, who were far more attractive than my football teammates. Soon, my car arrived, a maroon M.G Magnet. I made further money by picking up Steve Lawton and giving him a ride to work and back each day. I still see Steve at the Banks's Stadium watching matches to this day.

After completing my summer job at Walsall Co-op and getting a fulltime job at Charles Richards Fasteners, I quit the shoe department at the Co-op. The people there had been good to me and a lot of them had great respect and affection for my Dad, but I just felt that it was time I left. I stayed on at the petrol pumps as that added a good amount of income to my weekly wage and provided the money I spent on records. Leaving the Co-op meant that Saturdays were now my own again and guess where I was going to spend them.

The 1971/72 season still had our stalwart defencive unit of Wesson, Gregg, Harrison, Bennett, Jones and Atthey. Forwards of Morris, Train, Taylor, Woodward and Penman played in the majority of matches for the first half of the season and the new signings were John Manning at centre-forward from Bolton Wanderers, a much-travelled striker with a good eye for goal, he would play in 14 matches and score 6 goals before departing for Tranmere Rovers. John Smith, who you could tell had been a fine player with West Ham, Tottenham, Coventry, Leyton Orient, Torquay and Swindon Town, was coming to the end of his career; he would play in 13 matches before retiring to become our first team coach. Some new signings work and others don't, the one that did was Brian Taylor. Signed from Coventry City, Taylor would play for Walsall for six seasons and was excellent in all of them, making 247 appearances and scoring 29 goals, he played on both wings, at full-back and in midfield during that time.

It would be the eleventh game of the season before I saw the Saddlers win a match; we had a poor start to the campaign. I turned up at Fellows Park to watch a 2-0 victory over Port Vale and an impressive debut from Bernie 'The Bolt' Wright, promoted from our reserve side. The goal scorers that day were Brian Taylor and Bernie Wright.

Bernie 'The Bolt' Wright. Centre-Forward.

Born in Birmingham, Bernie was signed to Birmingham City as an amateur but not offered a professional contract; in

Bernie 'the bolt' Wright

September of 1971 he signed professional forms with Walsall and within three weeks made his debut in that Port Vale match. We all knew that day, Bernie Wright was special; speed, skill, fine left foot and good header of the ball and built like a centre-forward, you would not want to mess with Bernie. Wright played only 19 games and scored 5 goals before Everton bought him and took him to Division One. In those 19 games Bernie had caused chaos in Division Three defences, playing in a direct and powerful fashion, he was frightening to face.

Bernie's stay at Everton would be for just under a year, 11 games and 2 goals later returning to the Saddlers, where he would play for the next four seasons scoring 38 goals in 152 league appearances. Bernie was more than a fan's favourite; he was a hero, feared no one and nothing. No defence was too big or solid enough to stop the rampaging Bernie 'The Bolt' Wright; he went on to play for Bradford, Port Vale and Kidderminster Harriers and would have a great non-league career, finally hanging up his boots playing for Gloucester City at the age of 40.

All was not going well as we started our F.A. Cup campaign that season, but, as ever, the chance of 'giant killing' spurred on the team. Round One saw us defeat Dagenham 4-1, Woodward, Wright, Taylor and Morris scoring. Round Two, Brighton and Hove Albion were defeated 2-1 at Fellows Park following a 1-1 draw in Brighton, Train and Wright scoring. Round Three, Bournemouth 1-0 at Fellows Park, the scorer Bernie Wright had a taste for the F.A. Cup. In the Fourth Round we were drawn away at Everton and would lose 2-1, Evans with our consolation, but we had given the 'Toffees' a rough day, especially the rampaging Bernie Wright. Everton were so impressed by his performance that they signed him within days.

Bernie had gone from playing amateur football with Paget Rangers, to the First Division in six months.

We were disappointed to lose 'The Bolt' but I think all the supporters were aware that our club were in a little financial trouble and needed the money.

At more or less the same time we had discovered another fantastic goalkeeper, he would only play 12 games for Walsall before being sold at almost the same time as Bernie to balance the books, he played only one Cup game for us and that was in front of 45,462 in that Everton game at Goodison Park.

Mark Wallington. Goalkeeper.

Mark joined Walsall as a junior in 1969 and made his first team debut just after signing professional forms, there was always no doubt he would become a fine goalkeeper. Walsall sold him to Leicester City for 30,000 pounds where he would spend thirteen seasons before another five at Derby County amassing 490 league appearances. He also played for England at schoolboy, amateur, youth and Under-23 levels.

We had sold three of our homegrown players in a matter of eight weeks: Ray Train for 15,000 pounds, Mark Wallington 30,000 pounds and Bernie Wright for 40,000 pounds. I cannot remember any demonstrating fans; I believe we all knew that there was trouble brewing at Fellows Park.

In February 1972, when we were languishing at 19th in Division Three and it looked like a relegation battle was on the cards again, we signed two forwards and everything changed.

Chris Jones. Centre-Forward.

Jones would play for nine different clubs in a long career of 500 games and 150 goals. We plundered Swindon Town for his services and he clicked in our team during February 1972, finally making 63 appearances and scoring 15 goals.

Jones was a team player with good pace and control and led the line well. Walsall fans liked his wholehearted displays and he turned the season around along with Bobby Shinton.

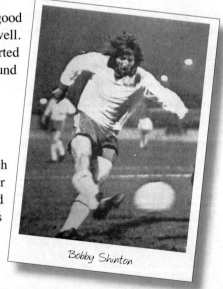

Bobby Shinton

Bobby Shinton. Striker.

Bobby was born in West Bromwich and he was spotted while scoring for Lye Town; he was immediately offered a professional contract and two weeks later made his debut for Walsall. He would play 86 times and score

23 goals before being transferred to Cambridge United for 22,000 pounds; Wrexham then signed him where he scored 37 goals, a 300,000 pounds move to Manchester City came next, but he soon switched to Newcastle United; his final league club was Millwall before retiring from the game.

Bobby Shinton's debut came on March 4th 1972 against Swansea City. We hammered them 4-0 that day. I had gone to see this new striker and came away seriously impressed; Shinton was everywhere, he had skill in abundance and seemed to have no nerves at all. Harrison and Penman scored before Bobby got the loudest cheer with a goal on debut, Geoff Morris finishing the scoring.

A week later, we were at home again to Bradford City, we won again 3-0 and Chris Jones and Bobby Shinton hit it off as a pair of strikers, Shinton scoring twice and Jones adding the third.

We would go on a sixteen game unbeaten run that lifted us from 19th and possible relegation to a solid and comfortable finish of 9th in the table.

Suddenly, there were goals all over the team: Shinton 6, Morris 4, Harrison 4, Jones 3 and Brian Taylor 3 in those last 16 games.

The season finished with a triumphant whacking of Shrewsbury Town, always great rivals for Walsall. They arrived at Fellows Park on April 25th, Shinton started the rout, before Jones, Harrison and Evans finished the season's scoring in a 4-1 win. The fans were delighted and left with high hopes for the coming season.

Some years you just didn't want the season to end and this was one of them. The team was in great shape, we all wondered if the 1972/1973 season was to be, finally, a promotion year. Bill Moore was in charge and had somehow manufactured another winning side. Bill was a proper football man and could see and knew more than others about building a football team. John Smith, having been a great player, was turning into a good coach, backed up by Jimmy MacEwan as trainer who had seen it all in a long career. Jimmy had been seriously injured at Villa before joining Walsall and he struggled thereafter, but during 1966, when we had both George Kirby and Harry Middleton up front, both good headers of a ball, Jimmy played Outside Right almost on one leg. He was such a fine crosser of a ball he did not need to take on and beat the full-back, something he clearly couldn't do in his final few matches. However, in those 10 games the opportunities he made by perfect crosses to George

Kirby was a wonder to behold. I wish I'd seen him in his prime. Jimmy was so well thought of that he was offered the trainer's position as soon as he retired from playing.

We didn't sign anyone during the close season; it seemed we had a good side and just wanted the new season to start, but the real reason was that we were in serious financial trouble.

We started the campaign in the same form as we had finished the previous season, winning 10 of our first 13 games and shooting us to 3rd in the table. All in the garden of Fellows Park looked rosy, the undercurrent though was just about to burst to the surface.

In our fourteenth game, we lost away to Brentford 2-0 and following the match Bill Moore resigned. It seemed an outrageous decision at the time, the team were playing well and so high in the table and yet history would soon show that Bill Moore knew more about football teams than most.

In hindsight, Bill knew our stalwart defence was ageing and that major surgery was in desperate need. Bill had obviously told Ron Harrison, the Chairman, and Ron had said 'We're broke.' Bill did not want to stay around for what was about to happen.

John Smith took over the team from his coaching position, with Jimmy MacEwan assisting. We won the next match 1-0 at home against Rotherham United with a Brian Taylor goal and then inexplicably we took 1 point from the next 7 games and 'fell off a cliff' in terms of league position.

Chairman, Ron Harrison, resigned and our Club Secretary of forty years, Ernest Wilson, died after a four-month illness and Walsall Football Club faced oblivion. Somehow, the club survived. Ken Wheldon became Chairman and John Westmancoat was promoted to Club Secretary. Wheldon's famous quote on taking over the club was 'I found it wrapped in waste paper and tied up with string.' Wheldon set about satisfying the creditors, bringing in new ideas and trying to inspire results.

We won 2 games during the Christmas period and thought we may have 'bottomed out' only to get 2 points in the next 7 games including a five game losing streak.

John Smith began to wheel and deal, we sold Mick Evans to Swansea and Geoff Morris to Shrewsbury, with that money we bought Dave 'Sugar' Robinson from Birmingham City and John Saunders from Leeds United to bolster the defence.

Bernie 'The Bolt' Wright returned from Everton and George Andrews signed from Shrewsbury in the deal that took Morris to 'The Shrews.'

Although John Smith would be proven to have bought some good players, the disastrous run of results cost him his position. Jimmy MacEwan, our third Manager of the season, took over, fashioned the new signings into the team and we avoided relegation by 2 points. We were sweating right to the end, but Bobby Shinton, Chris Jones and Bernie 'The Bolt,' scored goals just when we needed them.

Dave 'Sugar' Robinson. Centre-Forward.

'Sugar' was definitely not sweet in the tackle and would spend nearly 6 seasons in our defence making 181 appearances and scoring 3 goals; signed from Birmingham City where he had made 127 appearances scoring 4 goals.

John Saunders. Right-Back

A welsh schoolboy international; John signed for Newport County before a big move to Leeds United, things did not work out as hoped for with Leeds, leading to a transfer to the Saddlers.

John played at full-back or central-defence making 108 appearances and scoring 2 goals before injury ended his playing days at the age of 25.

George Andrews. Inside-Forward

'Georgie Boy' was to become a firm Walsall favourite and was well known in the lower Divisions as a fine goal scorer. For Cardiff City he scored 21 goals in 43 games, for Southport 41 goals in 117 games, for Shrewsbury 50 in 124 games and finally at Walsall 38 in 159 matches, before playing non-league football until he was 40 years of age.

George Andrews

Having survived relegation at the end of the 1972/1973 season the end of an era had arrived and what Bill Moore could see months earlier happened, some of our most trusted players had reached the end of their Walsall days, our solid defence of so many years finally conceded.

Leaving the club that season were:

Bob Wesson 220 appearances
Mick Evans 263 appearances and 8 goals
Frank Gregg 444 appearances and 3 goals
Stan Jones 265 appearances and 7 goals
Geoff Morris 241 appearances and 41 goals
John Woodward 149 appearances and 29 goals
Willie Penman 135 appearances and 6 goals

And, finally:

Colin 'Cannonball' Taylor 502 appearances and 189 goals

Colin Taylor

Chapter 8
New Boots And Panties

My life seems to have been linked so many times to the fortunes of Walsall Football Club it seems uncanny. As we concluded the 1971/1972 season, I was eighteen coming nineteen in October 1972.

As 1972 began, I was working at Ductile Sections in Willenhall, although the people there were friendly and I liked them, I hated the job. After a year of working at Charles Richards Fasteners and four months of Ductile Sections, I'd seen enough of offices attached to factories. My record collection had now grown in size and I wanted with all my heart to be a disc jockey doing gigs that might lead me into the Birmingham clubs and with that experience onto my passion, radio.

Walsall Football Club were about to have a massive change with Ken Wheldon, John Westmancoat, a new Manager and a host of new players. It was new boots and panties for all.

My girlfriend Carol Darnley's Father had been in the car trade all his life and had managed many showrooms. One night, at their house on Barr Beacon over dinner, he asked what I wanted to do with my life. I told him of my desire to be on the radio and how I planned to get there, however, I needed money to buy equipment, speakers, turntables and microphones to enable me to get on the ladder by doing what was termed 'mobile gigs' at the time.

Les Darnley suggested I should try his occupation of car sales. There the basic wage was not determined by age or experience, it was just a basic wage, then, if you were good enough and sold plenty of cars, the bonus for selling made your wages much higher than any job I could get at the time. Good salesmen bought houses and fed their families by selling a lot of cars all from the same basic wage. The job also had more freedom, you could at least walk around the showroom and visit prospective buyers and you were not chained to a desk. The clincher was you were given a company car or, at the very least, drove 'trade in' cars privately.

Les Darnley would inadvertently change my life; within a couple of weeks I applied for a car sales job at J. W. Stocks on Broad Street, Birmingham, and got it, selling a car on my sixth day.

During the off-season and summer, I retired from the petrol pumps near

The Arboretum, sold my Mini, obtained a company car and collected some sales bonuses and went directly opposite the showroom to The Music Exchange on Broad Street and bought turntables, speakers and microphones. The boys in the shop knew that I worked opposite and didn't quite have enough money, but let me have the equipment and pay them as I sold cars.

A couple of weeks later, I took a Vauxhall Victor Estate Car in part exchange for a new car, the boys in the garage, now friends, checked out the car and said it was 'a good 'un.' I made a deal with Stocks to get the car at a very reduced price and I also paid that off with future car sales. I was in business.

Not knowing any better I put an advert in the Walsall Observer as a DJ for hire and within a week got my first gig at Pelsall Community Centre. That first gig at Pelsall got me a Monday night residency at a youth club in Pelsall and I was off and running. More and more gigs came in around Walsall, Bloxwich and Aldridge and on New Year's Eve I played a gig just south of Stoke-on-Trent for fifty pounds, almost a month's basic wage. I felt I was on my way, doing something I was good at and loved, my massive record collection fitted all venues from youth clubs to weddings.

The changes by Ken Wheldon were ringing in at Fellows Park, Ronnie Allen, then a household name, became our Manager, after scoring 354 goals in 804 appearances for Port Vale, West Bromwich Albion, Crystal Palace and Wolverhampton Wanderers, collecting an F.A. Cup winning medal and five England caps. Ronnie managed Wolverhampton Wanderers and Athletic Bilbao before joining Walsall. A major coup by Ken Wheldon. Ronnie instantly started to rebuild our squad for the 1973/1974 season. In came:

Mick Kearns. Goalkeeper.

'The Cat' would play 322 times for Walsall and be forever linked with the club, playing 18 times as the Republic of Ireland's goalkeeper, 15 times while at Walsall, Mick is our most capped international. Kearns signed from Oxford United and would play in 293 of our next 298 games, before joining Wolverhampton Wanderers, then returning to Fellows Park.

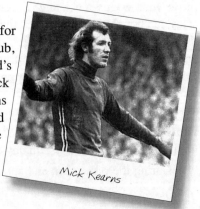

Mick Kearns

Mick became Community Relations Officer at Walsall F.C. in 1990, a position he retired from in the summer of 2013.

Doug Fraser. Full-Back & Midfield.

Fraser played for Aberdeen, West Bromwich Albion and Nottingham Forest, winning an F.A. Cup Winners medal, a League Cup Winners medal and two Scotland caps before signing for Walsall for 8,000 pounds. Winding down his playing career, he would replace Ronnie Allen as Manager in January 1974 and remain in place until March 1977. Doug was highly thought of during his time as Walsall Manager and he would preside over possibly our greatest ever F.A. Cup run.

Roger Fry. Full-Back.

Fry would make 136 appearances and score 2 goals for the Saddlers, playing equally comfortably at right or left-back, signing on from Southampton.

Alan Buckley.

Alan Buckley. Striker.

'Buck' would prove to be one of Walsall's finest ever signings; arriving from Nottingham Forest he would go on to hold our all-time scoring record and be our best-known striker. His final total would be 483 appearances and 205 goals, many of which I witnessed personally. Buckley would also become our Manager on four different occasions and he is still held in high regard by the Walsall Faithful. We would sell Buckley to Birmingham City for 175,000 pounds in October 1978 and buy him back for the same figure in June 1979, making him, after all these years, still our most expensive signing.

There is no doubt that Ronnie Allen brought some great players to Walsall during the summer of 1973, our squad took a different shape and again we were hopeful.

The squad consisted of goalkeeper, Kearns; defenders, Fraser, Fry, Harrison, Saunders, Robinson and Bennett; midfield, Atthey, Brian Taylor, with homegrown youngsters Caswell and Birch and strikers, Wright, Shinton, Buckley and Andrews.

Our only other main signing that year was David Sloan, a winger from Oxford United, who would play 52 times and scored 3 goals.

Our league form was to be a disappointment, but in our second game of the season, a League Cup match at Fellows Park against Shrewsbury, Alan Buckley announced himself and what was to come by scoring his first hat trick. We would run out 6-1 winners with Buckley 3, Shinton 2 and Harrison scoring.

The Second Round brought another 'giant killing' opportunity drawing Manchester City at Fellows Park. We gave a great account of ourselves but could not get the goal our play deserved, resulting in a 0-0 draw. We went to Maine Road for the return twenty days later. Again, we gave everything we had and even after extra time the scores were still 0-0. A third replay was scheduled at Maine Road after a toss of a coin for ground advantage. Eight days later, we succumbed and City ran out 4-0 winners, our League Cup campaign was over and there would be no joy in the F.A. Cup that season either.

Our league form was terrible and by December we were rooted at the bottom with only 3 wins but with a team that was beginning to take shape.

Ronnie Allen departed and Doug Fraser was the surprise choice to take over, instantly, everything changed. Buckley, Andrews and Shinton found their scoring boots and we won 7 out of our next 8 matches, catapulting us up the Division.

Bobby Shinton was sold to Cambridge United for 22,500 pounds and he would go on to have a great career. I was disappointed that 'Shinner' was sold, however, the offer was a good one and Alan Buckley and George Andrews were forming a great partnership.

Buckley would finish the season with 52 appearances and 24 goals, our best striking return in years. Buckley was a hero and his goals had brought us a reasonable 15th place finish after a disastrous start.

The new season hopes would be high again; we had a goal scorer for sure.

1973 had seen my DJ career move at a pace. I'd done plenty of gigs and had got a good name locally, my next move was more by luck than judgement.

John Oebel, my best mate from school, was working at Leon Berner, the steel company in Aldridge, and on two occasions had a crossed line with a woman who was involved in opening a new club in Lichfield. After getting into conversation, John told her I was the best DJ locally and she should sign me on. I auditioned, got the job as DJ and Compere in the main cabaret room and by September had become a fulltime professional DJ working six nights a week. I quit the car trade, sold my mobile equipment and Vauxhall Victor Estate, bought an Austin 1100, that would be reliable for late night driving and headed for Barnaby's in Lichfield six nights a week.

1974 blew in and we had a good Christmas and New Year period at Barnaby's, however, as the New Year began, the club started to falter. I remained as DJ/Compere in the main room Thursday, Friday and Saturday and operated in the Disco room on Monday, Tuesday and Wednesday, but by May, I was an unemployed professional DJ.

Mother was none too pleased and said 'enough is enough, get a proper job.' I told Mom I would not give up on my dream and proceeded to get two jobs, one driving a van delivering office furniture and assembling desks from eight thirty in the morning until five at night. Then, almost immediately, Eddie and Chris Fewtrell gave me a DJ/Compere job at Barbarella's in Birmingham, six nights a week from eight pm until two in the morning. The summer of 1974 was tough, I existed on four or five hours sleep but had the power of youth to keep me going.

John Oebel's parents had both died and John used to eat a lot at our house, getting some home comfort from my Mom. I'm sure Mom talked John into trying to get me settled down and John came up with the plan of me being a representative for Leon Berner where he worked. I told John that I was going to be a DJ and it would not be good for him if I joined Leon Berner's as I would definitely leave at some point. John as a true friend said, not to worry, he would cover for me in the job and when I had to go that would be fine. I quit delivering desks and joined Leon Berner. Quickly, and after only three months at Barbarella's, I was offered a DJ job at a new club, Chaplin's in Broad Street and so I continued working six nights a week, but had the cover of working at Berners with John during the day. I knew, however, I couldn't keep up the day and night working, something was going to have to give.

The Saddlers were preparing again for another campaign, season 1974/1975 and one that would be memorable and make an unforgettable mark in our history. My life would also change and I would embark upon a career during the first half of the season that I would never have thought possible.

Chapter 9
Lightning Can Strike Twice

The 1974/1975 season commenced with no new additions to the squad, the team were a more settled unit and lined up in a 4-4-2 formation. There was goalkeeper, Kearns; Defenders, Harrison, Robinson, Bennett and Fry; midfield, Sloan, Andrews, Atthey and Taylor B. and strikers Wright and Buckley. Brian Caswell and John Simpson also featured heavily in terms of appearances. David Sloan would leave the club in December and be replaced in the team with the ever improving, Alan Birch, whilst Dave Serella would join from Nottingham Forest completing the season's changes.

August was not a good month, we drew 2 and lost 1 in the League and went out of the League Cup at the first attempt. September was as good as August was indifferent, Buckley hit form scoring 7 goals in 7 games, we won 5, drew 1 and lost 1. Form then started to slip away again; October brought 2 wins, 1 draw and 3 losses and during November and December we had a poor period where we lost 4 games on the bounce.

In the middle of all of this indifferent form, the F.A. Cup came around. Round One saw us drawn away at Ashford Town, given our form, a potential banana skin. 2,700 people from the town of Ashford attended looking to turn over the Saddlers. Fortunately, it was not to be and we ran out 3-1 winners, with goals from Alan Buckley twice and Roger Fry adding a third.

On December 14, again, we were drawn away, this time at Newport County, another difficult match. Again, the people of Newport fancied their chances and 4,764 watched on as Walsall again came away victorious, another 3-1 win with goals from Brian Taylor, Bernie Wright and Alan Buckley.

Walsall were now in the hat for the Third Round. Third and Fourth Division teams at this time of year are all dreaming of a big draw, financially it can be a huge lifesaver for small clubs, a good draw also ignites regional towns and there is always the chance that history might be made with a victory by the underdog.

The town of Walsall was hoping when out of the hat came Manchester United versus Walsall. There is no bigger draw, every small club wants to have their day in the sun and a match in the F.A. Cup against Manchester United brings that warmth.

The tie was to be played at Old Trafford on January 4th 1975 and the town's people began to make their arrangements for the migration north. On this occasion, I was to travel with my Mom's Brother Frank, wife Iris and Cousin Robert, along with some of their friends, in a hired minivan.

The ride up to Manchester I can still remember as being an uncomfortable one. The van was cold, damp and the seats hard, what was worse was that my Cousin Robert from Tipton had declared himself a Manchester United fan and proceeded to tell us all the way up the M6 what United were going to do to Walsall that day.

To say I was incredibly 'pissed off' by the time we reached Old Trafford is an understatement. I couldn't wait to get out of the van and away from Robert, who was big and loud and still going on about how awful Walsall were. We all had seats together in the Walsall end of the ground, I made sure that Iris, Frank and others were in between Robert and me. For some reason Robert was a lot quieter sitting in the Walsall end, I wonder why.

Doug Fraser, our Manager, had changed a couple of positions in the side: Kearns as ever in goal; a back four of Saunders, Robinson, Bennett and Harrison; midfield, B. Taylor, Andrews, Atthey and Birch, with Bernie 'The Bolt' Wright and Alan Buckley up front.

Walsall did not play a defencive game at Old Trafford, we went after Manchester United with full belief and commitment, this shocked the home side as they expected us to defend and they never got into their stride during the whole match. As the game wore on, there was only going to be one winner, such was our dominance. The Walsall Faithful, seeing the 'boys' were on top, roared them forward and enjoyed 'winding up' the United Manager, Tommy Docherty, who was becoming more and more frustrated. No matter how close we came United held on and we cheered loudly our 0-0 draw in front of 43,353 fans.

The minivan ride back was seemingly more comfortable, warm and quiet. As we approached Walsall, Robert began to predict the score line and what would happen in the return leg in three days time at Fellows Park. I didn't have to respond, the warm smug smile stuck steadfastly to my face.

The newspapers were full of the battling Walsall performance against the giants of Manchester. In no uncertain terms they commented that Walsall should have won the game but the return and surprise element of the Saddlers was now gone. There was some belief that something might happen, such was the magnitude of our performance, and the TV cameras arrived at Fellows Park just in case a 'giant killing' might occur. On January 7th 1975, 18,105 souls packed into Fellows Park and Walsall announced an unchanged team.

I attended the match with my Uncle George and we took his favoured position in front of the Cowshed just on the half way line. They say that lightning never strikes twice, we were all hoping it just might.

Bernie 'The Bolt' was on fire that night in front of the home fans, challenging for everything, charging at the United defenders, heading, shooting and unsettling their whole defence.

Brian Taylor ran fifty yards down our right wing and wrong footed the whole United defence with a cross that landed at Bernie's feet. Bernie shifted it to his better left foot and whacked it home. The Saddlers fans went ballistic, the whole ground erupted and United were on the back foot again, wave after wave of Walsall attacks followed as United tried to stay in the game.

As halftime approached, disaster struck, a penalty was awarded to United after the ball seemed to strike Stan Bennett on the arm, Gerry Daly duly scored. In the after match interviews Tommy Docherty would comment that the penalty should never have been given. As the players left the pitch at halftime, the scores level, 1-1, the crowd roared off the Saddlers trying to wash away the disappointment of the unjust equalising goal.

Walsall returned to the pitch for the second half and they were not put off by the injustice, they carried on as before and went after United again, wave after wave of attacking play. Again, United held on and the tie went into extra time.

During the first period of extra time, Walsall twice and United once were denied penalty claims as the game went end-to-end and became fraught, still no one could break the deadlock. The second period of extra time started with Walsall charging towards the Hilary Street End, John Saunders got down our right wing and crossed, Alex Stepney fumbled and in whipped Alan Buckley to score from close range. Manchester United's will was broken, in disarray Walsall rushed forward to kill them off and George Andrews was upended in the United box. Buckley stepped up and although Stepney got a hand to it, the ball flew high into the net. The terraces were now singing and dancing, me included, as we took a commanding 3-1 lead. Two minutes later, in the mist of all the chaos, Sammy McIlroy pulled one back for United, but they were already beaten. We never looked like we were losing our lead and Stan Bennett was completely solid at the back, nothing was going passed him.

The final whistle came and the Walsall players were slow to leave the pitch taking in the celebrations, which went long into the night.

Tommy Docherty's comment on TV after the match: 'Walsall played well and good luck to them.'

We had disposed of the mighty Manchester United and now looked forward to the draw for the next round; there was great anticipation in the town and a feeling of 'we fear no one.'

The draw was made and the match would be played at Fellows Park on January 24th 1975, this time the visitors would be Newcastle United. It couldn't happen again, could it?

John Oebel and I got there early that day, we wanted to be right behind the goal at the Hilary Street End to bask in the atmosphere, the noise and have a good sing and shout to urge the boys on.

It was with disappointment that the hero in beating Manchester United, Stan Bennett, was not fit to play, out with a bout of flu. John Saunders switched from full-back to centre-half, Harrison from left-back to right-back and in came Roger Fry at left-back.

We lined up: goalkeeper, Kearns; back four, Harrison, Robinson, Saunders and Fry; midfield, B. Taylor, Andrews, Atthey and Birch and forwards, Wright and Buckley.

Long before kick-off the noise was enormous; Fellows Park had a limit of 20,000 and the recorded total was 19,998, although it seemed there were more people than that.

The pitch was in poor shape that day and didn't look playable, however, with so many packed into the ground the referee, David Wallace, decided the match would be played.

The introduction of Roger Fry at left-back was to prove a stroke of luck as Bernie Wright in full flow was up-ended out on our left-flank. Fry stroked the perfect cross into the Newcastle box, George Andrews rose above the pack and headed past Ian McFaul into the Newcastle net. Our early arrival was rewarded, the Hilary Street End rose as one, arms aloft, with a deafening roar of 'Goal.' The singing began in unison 'Georgie, Georgie Andrews.'

Newcastle were now on the back foot as Walsall went in for the 'kill.' Alan Buckley was just robbed in his final stride when looking likely to score and another Andrews header whistled over the bar. Newcastle had little to offer in return and the Saddlers went in at halftime 1-0 to the good.

After the break, Newcastle regained their composure and started to put some passes together. Malcolm MacDonald, Tudor and Nulty all had opportunities that led to nothing. Back came Walsall; Buckley, Wright, Atthey and Birch all troubling Newcastle's goalkeeper McFaul as the minutes ticked by.

The one big chance of the match fell to Malcolm MacDonald, played through by Nulty and eight yards out, somehow he pulled his shot wide, that seemed to knock the stuffing out of Newcastle and Walsall played their way into fulltime.

The scenes again around the ground were memorable, no one wanted to leave and the players waved and strolled around as the fans serenaded them off.

It was an unbelievable feeling, not only had we beaten both Manchester United and Newcastle United, we had out played them, we were the better team in all three matches and fully deserved our Fifth Round placing.

The town's people were positioned around radio's and TV screens as the Fifth Round draw took place, we wanted a home draw as we now fancied we had a chance against anyone at home, unfortunately, that was not to be, out of the hat came:

Birmingham City versus Walsall.

The match was to be played on February 15th 1975 at St Andrews.

Our team showed just one change, Stan Bennett was fit again to resume his position at centre-half, Saunders moved to right-back and Harrison switched to left-back.

The team lined up: goalkeeper, Kearns; back four, Saunders, Robinson, Bennett and Harrison; midfield, B. Taylor, Andrews, Atthey and Birch and forwards, Wright and Buckley.

John and I made our way to St Andrews where the Walsall fans had taken over half of one side of the ground and behind one of the goals. We made our way to the half-way line so we could see both ends of the ground clearly. This was to prove a mistake; we were far too close to the 'amped up' Blues supporters who could not live with a defeat by local 'Cinderella' side Walsall, nevertheless, we had come to 'The Ball.'

The match, full of local issues and passion, was an end-to-end affair. The longer Walsall held on the more aggravated the Birmingham City fans became. At halftime the police were separating the Birmingham City and Walsall fans with a line down the middle. The only problem being that they had not controlled the toilets in the middle. All of a sudden, hoards of City fans came flying through the toilets and into the Walsall fans. All hell broke loose with John and I in the middle; the ground being packed with a crowd of 43,841, there was no backing away. Arms, fists, elbows and kicking became the order of the day. John and I were separated in the melee and, in the end, we were just hitting anything that came near. Slowly, the police regained control and they ushered the City fans back.

The match had already resumed as I found John and we dusted ourselves down. Walsall just kept on going at the Blues; it was a tremendous contest that we eventually lost 2-1, with Brian Taylor scoring for us.

Our next problem was to get out and away from the ground; the Blues fans not content with their victory wanted Walsall blood. There were people running here, there and everywhere as chaos reigned in the streets around St Andrews. To be honest, it spoilt what could have been a great day. Walsall had given everything on the pitch and we had no complaints, we had lost, but once again 'held a candle to the devil.' We were all proud of our team and the players are still heroes to this day. The Cup run of 1975 is written into Walsall history.

Blues lost in the semifinal that year, shame.

Since that day I have only returned to St Andrews a couple of times, once was to see an ageing George Best and Rodney Marsh play for Fulham against Birmingham City; it was a pleasure to see their skill and fun with the game.

Inspired by our famous Cup run, during January, February and March we won 7 games, drew 1 and lost 2, putting us in a great position for promotion, however, we began to run out of steam and would only win 3 of our last 11 games finishing 8th in the league. Disappointing, but no complaints, the team had done us proud in a season to remember.

Alan Buckley top scored with 27 goals, George Andrews managed 14 and Bernie Wright 10.

Personally, it had been a great season for me off the field; I'd left Leon Berner but continued as a DJ six nights a week at Chaplin's. Commercial radio was beginning to happen in the UK and the government was awarding licenses, this meant a new job in the regions rather than London had occurred. Record Companies now needed Promotion people to get their records played on these stations. I applied to Nems and Immediate Records and on my 21st birthday was awarded the job. I was in the music business. I believed that if I was calling on Radio stations weekly I would get to know when jobs might occur 'on air' and still might fulfill my dream. After the Christmas and New Year period, I cut my DJ nights from six to three; Thursday, Friday and Saturday, whilst working five days for Nems.

I had registered with all the Record Companies and they had begun sending me free records to play at my gigs but told me I needed a bigger audience to qualify for all of their releases.

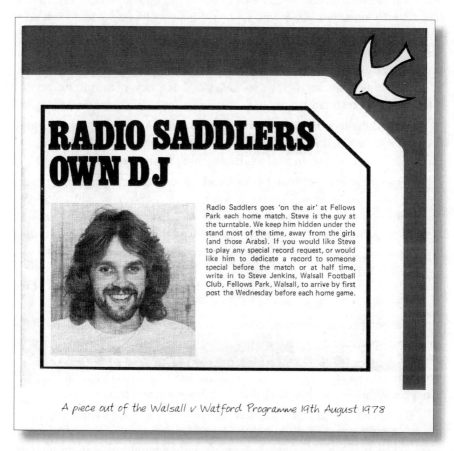

RADIO SADDLERS OWN DJ

Radio Saddlers goes 'on the air' at Fellows Park each home match. Steve is the guy at the turntable. We keep him hidden under the stand most of the time, away from the girls (and those Arabs). If you would like Steve to play any special record request, or would like him to dedicate a record to someone special before the match or at half time, write in to Steve Jenkins, Walsall Football Club, Fellows Park, Walsall, to arrive by first post the Wednesday before each home game.

A piece out of the Walsall v Watford Programme 19th August 1978

I thought if I could do the broadcasting at Fellows Park that would solve my problem, giving me a 6 or 7,000 audience and, if we had two games in a week, a 12 to 14,000 audience. I wrote to John Westmancoat at the club telling him of my experience as a DJ and my job with Nems. I was invited to meet with him and he said that Cyril did the broadcasting and I could sit with him and see how it went.

I turned up on February 28ᵗʰ for the match against Preston North End, a 2-0 victory, with two goals from George Andrews for the record.

John Westmancoat, who I got to know well, along with his wife Betty, took me under the main stand, through a doorway into a small room with three or four steps leading from the back of the room. Up the steps, I went into a small box with bench seats either side of the steps and a shelf table that ran the length of the small box. Once you sat on the bench, all you could do was slide your way into position with your legs under the shelf, like sitting behind a tight desk. The windows were no more than nine inches deep all around the box and it was directly on the halfway line. It was high enough that we were above the heads of the standing fans below the main stand; the view of the ground and the pitch took my breath away.

I played the records while Cyril did the announcing during the remaining six games of the season and I was always on time and did the job professionally. I liked Cyril and we got on well whilst watching the matches together.

Cyril was in his sixties and I think had had enough of broadcasting at the ground. My records energized the ground as they were new and up-to-date and I believed they provided a more up-to-date entertainment. At the end of the season, John Westmancoat asked me if I would like to do the broadcasting for the coming season, Cyril had told him he thought I was reliable and a true Walsall fan. I said 'yes' and John said, 'we cannot afford to pay you though.' I laughed, 'No problem John, you got me.' John would send me the dates of the pre-season friendlies and I would not miss a match for the next six seasons.

That box became my home. I loved everything about it; I got into all of the games without paying, would know all of the players as friends, was invited into the players' bar after every match, could park my car in the directors' car park and, almost most importantly, on those freezing winter days and nights I had a heater under the shelf desk that kept me warm and toasty.

The record companies addressed my new large audience and for the next five years free records arrived at 26 Regina Drive almost every day of the week. So much so, that Mom thought the weight would put my bedroom through the ceiling and into the dining room.

One last thought from the 1974/1975 season: I was in the box as we finished the season with a home match against Watford, it was an exciting closer and we would run out winners, 3-2, with goals from George Andrews and two from Terry Spinner, who played only a few games for us. That was the night that the great Stan Bennett retired. I had tears in my eyes as Stan walked off waving to each part of the crowd before the Hilary Street End descended into the corner of the ground by the tunnel and chanted Stan back inside.

Stan Bennett will forever be my favourite centre-half; he retired completing 438 appearances and scoring 13 goals over fourteen seasons. Thanks Stan.

Editor's Notes

Firstly, I should like to bring to your attention a Programme Fair that is being held at the Hawthorns on Sunday, May 15th from 10.0 a.m. to 1.30 p.m. This will be similar to the one held here not so long ago and they really are a must for any programme collector. There are thousands of programmes on sale and included will be many Walsall home and aways from this season and way into the past. So if you've got nothing to do pop along for a couple of hours. Incidentally if you have any programmes that you would like to sell take them along, there will be many dealers willing to buy them from you.

Talking about programmes, I was pleased to hear that this programme came fourth in the Third Division poll.

Crystal Palace won the award followed by Gillingham and Port Vale. Next season we shall have to try and do that little better and beat the lot. don't forget if you've any ideas for improving it write to me and I'll see what I can do about introducing them for next season.

I should like to give special thanks to Steve Jenkins who does such a wonderful job on matchdays with his Radio Saddlers spot before the match and at half time. Steve that's him in the photograph, is a top D.J. but gives his services free of charge to Walsall. Many thanks, Steve. Keep up the good work. If only he was as good at football as he is at spinning records playing alongside him on Sundays would be much easier.

Before I end, don't forget to buy your season ticket. It really does save you a great deal of money in the long term. Have a nice break and I look forward to joining you all here again next season.

Walsall v Bury Programme 14th May 1977

Chapter 10
Radio Saddlers

As the 1975/1976 season began everyone reassembled at Fellows Park, including me. Radio Saddlers was now completely my domain and I would soon become part of Walsall Football Club.

The broadcasting was not a complicated issue, pre-match music and a few notices building up to the game. Five minutes before the match, the team sheet would arrive and I would inform the crowd of the side that was due to play, the changes to the programme and the visitors.

Halftime was again music and notices and then, at fulltime, the size of the gate at the match and the next fixture. Pretty simple stuff, but I was broadcasting to the Walsall Faithful, which I grew to have an affinity with over the years through the broadcasting and content. They all knew me and they sent in requests and name checks they wished me to read out.

The team had only one change at the start of the season; we had signed Miah Dennehy from Nottingham Forest.

Miah Dennehy. Right-Wing

He played 41 times and scored 4 goals for Nottingham Forest before joining Walsall. Miah would spend the next three seasons at Fellows Park making 151 appearances and scoring 22 goals. Always a favourite for his skillful, direct and speedy right wing play, he supplied many crosses for our forwards and worried many Third Division defences. He was capped for the Republic of Ireland on 10 occasions.

Dave Serrella. Centre-Half

Dave had a slow start to his Walsall career, after playing 76 games for Nottingham Forest. Following the retirement of Stan Bennett during the 1975/1976 season, Serella began to make an impact on our first team. It would still be another year before he made the centre-half position his own, but when he did he would be a mainstay of our defence and complete eight seasons in our colours, making 304 appearances and scoring 13 goals. Dave was strong and reliable as a player and similar off the pitch. I became friendly with him over the years and was disappointed when he signed for Blackpool in 1982.

The two most impressive players to come through from our youth and reserve teams at that time were Alan Birch and Brian Caswell, both would go on to have long league careers, both were now considered fixtures in our 1975/1976 squad.

Alan 'Acker' Birch. Left-Wing.

Acker played his initial games for Walsall on our left wing, later, occasionally moving to the right-wing and central-midfield. He had good skill and an eye for goal, which would become keener as his career went on. Birch would play 191 times for Walsall and score 24 goals before being transferred to Chesterfield for 40,000 pounds in July 1979. He had two fantastic seasons at Chesterfield, which led to a 180,000 pounds transfer to Wolverhampton Wanderers. Later he would play for Barnsley, Chesterfield again, Rotherham United, Scunthorpe United and Stockport County.

Brian 'Casa' Caswell. Right-Wing

'Casa' would become one of my great friends in football, along with his wife Tina. I first met Brian when he was playing midfield for our youth and reserve teams and watched as he became a first team regular and Walsall favourite. Caswell played in many of our Cup runs and always acquitted himself well against higher league opposition. He would make 458 appearances for Walsall scoring 19 goals before signing for Doncaster Rovers, then shortly afterwards, Leeds United. While at Leeds United, Brian went on loan to Wolverhampton Wanderers and sustained a knee injury whist playing in midfield. Brian told me he knew, at the moment of the tackle, his knee would not regain fitness to play league football again. I believe Brian would have played league football for many more seasons without that injury, he was a natural athlete and his fitness levels were way above the norm.

I played a few matches in later years with 'Casa' and a few against him. I played for Walsall Old Boys in one game and for some reason Brian was playing for West Bromwich Albion. I had put in a couple of good tackles on their left-winger from our right-back position. All I could hear was 'Casa' encouraging West Brom's winger to get at me because I was crap! Well, what are friends for?

Brian Caswell will always be known around Walsall as a legend and he still lives in the town to this day.

Our season did not start as well as we had hoped even though we had a settled side. Miah Dennehy added to our striking options from the right wing, Brian Taylor switched to the left-wing, Wright and Buckley up front. The midfield of Andrews and Atthey remained; our Defencive unit had Kearns in goal, Fry and Harrison at full-backs, Robinson at centre-back with either Saunders or Serella alongside. We lost 6 of our first 12 games, then held our own through October and November. At the start of December, two important reinforcements joined the club.

Roger Hynd. Centre-Half

Hynd signed from Birmingham City and soon became a favourite at Walsall, no nonsense, hard tackling, fully committed player; he slotted into our backline and stayed there. Previously, Roger had played for Glasgow Rangers for eight years and had featured in their European Cup Winners Cup final. I was with some of our team when Roger was relaying the story of how he was so disgusted with the result and his own performance, after collecting his loser's medal and walking around the stadium, he threw it as hard as he could into the crowd. He told us, disappointingly, he never got it back, this caused a few of our lads to comment sarcastically, 'No Rog,' 'Didn't give it you back Rog?' Roger answered until he realised there was a little 'micky taking' going on, then stood up and said 'Right,' we all scattered and quickly. Hynd left Rangers in a 12,000 pounds deal to join Crystal Palace and then 25,000 pounds took him to Birmingham City where he made over 200 appearances and became a favourite. At Walsall he played 106 games and scored 1 goal, before becoming Manager of Motherwell.

Alun Evans. Midfield

Alun was a famous player mainly due to his transfer from Wolves to Liverpool in September 1968, he became Britain's first 100,000 pounds teenager. The football world thought Alun was a star of the future, having already played for England at schoolboy, youth and Under 23 levels. He spent four seasons with Liverpool but never really lived up to expectation and he joined Aston Villa for 72,000 pounds in June 1972. Alun played in an F.A. Cup final for Liverpool and a League Cup final for Villa before joining Walsall in December 1975. Three years later, he left for Australia, playing for South Melbourne and Hellas.

I got to know Alun well in his years with Walsall, you could tell he had plenty of ability on the pitch. I discussed with him regularly why Walsall played him in midfield and why we did not play him as a striker. I was trusted to take his girlfriend to away matches on several occasions so she could watch him play such was our friendship.

Alun also gave me one of my most difficult moments in the broadcasting box, we were playing Leicester City at Fellows Park in the F.A. Cup Fourth Round during the 1977/1978 season, another of our famous Cup runs. That day we had slugged it out with the First Division side and were still attacking with less than a minute to go with the scores at 0-0. The ball came back out the box and fell to Alun who rifled it into the top corner, which made the crowd and me inside the broadcasting box erupt. I was yelling and screaming inside my own enclosed environment, the teams lined up to kick-off and the referee instantly blew for fulltime. I had no time to compose myself and had to do the end of game announcements. To be fair, I struggled, I have no idea what I sounded like that day, but I'm sure it could not be described as 'completed with composure.'

Alun Evans moments after his goal v Leicester

I refrained from announcing 'How do you like them apples?'or 'Hold that!' professionalism somehow kicked in.

The addition of Roger Hynd and Alun Evans sent us on a nine game unbeaten run and boosted us up the table. At the end of March, we were in with the promotion chasers only to win 1 of our last 6 games and slide to a finishing 7th position.

Alan Buckley would have his best ever goal scoring season and it was fantastic to watch, in 47 games he would score 35 times; in the last 19 games, he would score 20 of his goals. On February 13th Walsall smashed Rotherham United 5-1, with Buckley scoring 4 times. In our next home match on February 27th, we beat Gillingham 4-0, with Buckley scoring 3 times and on March 20th Aldershot were the visitors to Fellows Park losing 4-1, with Buckley scoring another 3. That period was the most devastating example of goal scoring I'd ever seen, it seemed that whenever 'Buck' got the ball it ended up in the back of the net.

Alan Buckley became well known in the football world for his goal scoring exploits. The fans, press, radio and TV were all about Alan Buckley. This upset Bernie 'The Bolt' Wright. He rightly concluded that Buckley's goals were due to his (Wright's) outstanding performances, which were creating both space and passes to Buckley. 'The Bolt' became so aggrieved that he suggested he would not pass to Buckley and so Bernie was paid a bonus whenever Buckley scored to maintain the avalanche of goals.

Bernie, himself, scored 12 times that season with George Andrews getting 9 and Miah Dennehy 8. Some say that was the best Walsall strike force for many years.

We missed promotion that year by only 6 points.

I had completed my first season at Fellows Park Radio Saddlers and had enjoyed every minute. I was now a full member in the players' bar and would always meet up with the boys after the match. Occasionally, we would go out afterwards to the local clubs and discos, as the players would always get the following day off. This was long before it became the custom to 'stretch off' the morning after a match.

I rarely took a holiday in those days, it seemed what with record company work, gigs at the weekend and the football season broadcasting, there was just not enough time. If I did take a few days away it had to be Sunday to Wednesday, when I didn't have gigs, and so I always just went to Bournemouth.

The 1976/1977 season was soon upon us and our only signing of the summer was Mick Bates. Everyone knew Mick Bates and looked forward to his addition to our midfield and team. We felt it was a great capture.

Mick Bates

Mick Bates. Midfield.

Mick was part of the Leeds United side that won just about everything; he was always the first name on the sheet if either Johnny Giles or Billy Bremner were injured in their midfield. Hence, Mick was always on 'Match of the Day' and a well-known face and player in those days. It came as a surprise that we should be able to sign a player of his quality.

Mick had played in over 150 games for Leeds United and would stay at Walsall for two seasons, making 105 appearances and scoring 6 goals; later playing for Bradford City and Doncaster Rovers.

I didn't know Mick well in his time at Walsall, he still lived in Leeds and travelled back after games. Years later, I would meet him on a 'Footballers' Golf Classic' played at La Manga in Spain. We were all assembling for the opening dinner outside on the terrace of the hotel. At these dinners, one or two of the ex-professional players would be included in your team group table. Susan and I sat down at our table and a few moments later Mick came and sat next to me. He said 'Hello, I'm Mick Bates.' I said 'I know, I'm Steve Jenkins ex-broadcaster at Fellow Park, I watched you for two seasons at Walsall.' We got on famously after that for the whole trip and enjoyed our time in Spain.

Mick also got me a Footballers' Classic head cover for my driver and signed it Mick Bates, Walsall F.C.

Our team changed a little for the season. Roger Fry left the club and Brian Taylor moved from Left wing to right-back, Colin Harrison would break a leg and Brian Caswell would establish himself at left-back. Serella, Hynd and Robinson would share centre-half duties. Miah Dennehy would occupy the right-flank and the left by either Alun Evans or Alan Birch. In midfield, the evergreen Nick Atthey and Mick Bates, with Bernie Wright and Alan Buckley, up front.

We started poorly which came as a surprise, not winning a match until the seventh game. Then, after winning 2 games, we got hammered away at Brighton 7-0. We would only win 2 of our next 14 games and were at the wrong end of the table.

As February approached, it seemed we had finally found our form, winning comfortably 4 out of 5 games, beating Sheffield Wednesday 5-1, Grimsby 1-0, Reading 6-1 and Shrewsbury 2-1.

As quickly as we were looking good, we lost 3 games on the bounce and that spelt the end for Doug Fraser as our Manager. Doug had been a good Manager and brought some exciting times to Walsall, had built a good side, but, unfortunately, the small changes from the previous season's team had not worked. Doug had also sold Bernie Wright to Bradford City at the beginning of February and that did not go down well with Walsall fans, Doug's popularity had gone.

Chairman, Ken Wheldon, seeing our side slide towards the bottom of the table, took action and we wondered who would be our next Manager.

Dave Mackay. Manager.

Mackay needs no introduction to football fans; he won everything in the game in terms of medals with Hearts, Tottenham Hotspur and Derby County. He managed Nottingham Forest and Derby County, taking them to their second First Division League Championship. Mackay had been out of the game for four months after leaving Derby County and arrived at Walsall with his assistant Des Anderson. It was a major coup by Ken Wheldon.

I got to know both Dave and Des during their time at Walsall, at first by just picking up the team sheet from their office before the game, but over a period of time they both chatted to me around the ground, especially when I was there on non-match days. After we beat Brighton at home on April 16th 1977, 1-0, Brighton were top of the League and flying at the time, I had to drop something off to their office, their celebration was in full swing and the scotch was flowing as I knocked and walked in. Des said 'Have a small one young Steve,' I responded shyly 'No you're okay Des.' Dave butted in 'We won, you'll be havin' a small one Steve,' 'Yes, thanks, Mr Mackay.'

The players also told me that they hated Mackay playing in the five-a-side games in the gym; he was evidently as fearsome in those games as he was all those years earlier for Tottenham and Derby. In Dave Mackay's days, tackling from behind was fair play, Dave had mastered the art of 'taking everything,' the ball and player dispatched up the pitch.

Personally, I loved Mackay's attitude, it was win at all costs and he was a professional winner.

Dave Mackay

Following Dave Mackay's appointment, we would only lose 2 of our final 15 games and relegation was avoided.

The F.A. Cup that year had brought more excitement to Walsall. It all started against Bradford City, drawing 0-0 at Valley Parade and securing a 2-0 victory at home with goals from Taylor and Wright. Round Two drew us away to Chesterfield, a 1-1 draw, followed by a 0-0 draw at Walsall, and then finally at the third attempt we won 1-0 with a Bernie Wright goal.

The Third Round draw, as always, can bring a dream tie, we were lucky again, Manchester United versus Walsall.

The game was played at Old Trafford on January 8th 1977. 48,870 watched the match and Walsall moved north to see if we could tweak the lions' nose again.

It was a hard fought match but we went down 1-0 just before halftime and could not get the equaliser, finally ending in a 1-0 defeat. It was a great day and I believe Manchester United were never going to allow a repeat of the events of two years previous.

In the League Cup, Walsall beat Shrewsbury home and away 1-0 to progress to the Second Round, where we were beaten at home 4-2 by Nottingham Forest.

In terms of goal scoring for the season Alan Buckley again came out on top with 23 goals in 51 appearances, George Andrews 8, Miah Dennehy and Alan Birch 6 goals each.

On a personal front, in September 1976 I had joined Chrysalis Records from Nems and Immediate. Chrysalis were a Rock based label at the time and built their artists on constant touring. Hence, as Regional Promotions Manager, my job entailed radio, press and TV promotion during the day and constant gigs during the evening, with a multitude of bands on tour.

Radio Saddlers would change my job status; on Tuesday 30th of October, I was in Manchester with a band, Split Endz, we had completed interviews during the day and they were playing a gig that night in Manchester. I went along to the sound check and made sure everything was okay. I was due to stay and be at the concert, however, Walsall were at home that night and so I left and drove down the M6 and straight to the ground to broadcast.

My boss at the time lived in the Midlands but originally came from London, we had not discussed football and I had no idea he was interested. The match was a 0-0 draw against Crystal Palace, I did as usual, the before the game, halftime and end of match broadcasting.

The following day I got a call:

'How was the Split Endz gig last night Steve?'

'Yeah, all good, went well.'

'You know I'm a Crystal Palace supporter?'

'Oh, no, I didn't actually.'

'I was listening to you all last night when you should have been in Manchester.'

Well, sometimes you are completely nicked aren't you, with no way out? I apologized, but from then on, although I did well for Chrysalis and won Promo Man of the Month a couple of times, I knew that my future there was stained and to be honest I would do it again if I had too. Fortunately, only three months later I was head hunted by M.C.A. Records, offered more money and I felt a better opportunity and so left Chrysalis after only six months.

Walsall at the time had a fine youth and reserve side, I used to go and watch them on the Saturdays that the first team were away from home, many of them would go on to have long league careers. As a group, they were outstanding and the future looked very bright in terms of players coming through, they smashed their opponents consistently.

That team also became some of my best mates in football and, over thirty years later, we are still friends. They also came on occasions and sat with me in the broadcasting box where we all got to know each other well.

That team had Ron Green in goal, Ian Paul and Kenny Mower at full-back. The centre-backs were John Horne and Kelvin Clarke; midfield, Wayne Secker and David 'Mini' Preece; wingers, Mark 'Rico' Rees and Paul Waddington and centre-forward, Don Penn.

It was a truly great team and I enjoyed then, as I do today, the youth players coming through, getting professional contracts and watching their career develop. Over the next couple of seasons, they would all make their first team debuts and some would go on to be Walsall legends.

Dave Mackay began to change the squad during the summer of 1977 in preparation for the coming season and his first full season in charge, there would be comings and goings all season as Dave set about a promotion campaign. Somehow, with Dave Mackay in charge, we all believed we had a chance.

During the summer, two of our midfield heroes departed the club. Nick Atthey after 14 seasons, 502 appearances and 18 goals slipped into non-league football; it was strange not to have Nick in our midfield. Atthey would be the last departure of the famous Walsall defence of Wesson, Gregg, Evans, Bennett, Jones and Atthey, which had been such a steady backline for so many years. A part of Saddlers history disappeared as Nick Atthey departed. George Andrews also left the club after five seasons, 177 appearances and 40 goals; George was a fans' favourite and would always be remembered for his header that knocked Newcastle United out of the F.A. Cup. Brian Taylor would also depart 13 games into the season and join Plymouth Argyle after seven seasons, 247 appearances and 29 goals. Roger Hynd would leave in December to join Motherwell as Manager.

Gary Shelton. Midfield.

Gary Shelton would only make 29 appearances for Walsall and 15 of those as a substitute. Signing in June 1974 and turning professional in March 1975, Gary made his debut aged eighteen as a substitute at Southend United in April 1976.

Aston Villa would sign Gary for 80,000 pounds in January 1978, he was sold to Sheffield Wednesday for 50,000 pounds in April 1982, five seasons later he signed for Oxford United for 150,000 pounds then onto Bristol City and, finally, Chester City. Gary's final league appearance for Chester City was one month before his fortieth birthday, tribute to his fanatical approach to fitness. Gary, even as a youngster, would train all week, play on Saturday and then turn out for my Sunday afternoon five-a-side team. We would play for one hour nonstop, which kept up our fitness levels, Gary must have played for eighteen months on a Sunday with me. When he left for Villa I went along with him to watch his debut and was well looked after by the Villa players of the day. Since then we have met up over the years at games or played in old professional matches, we have known each other for most of our lives and I was very proud of him when he captained the England Under-21 side. Great player, great career, great mate.

Mackay signed a new crop of players to help our push for promotion, in came centre-forward, Alf Wood, from Middlesborough. We all knew Alf for his goal scoring at Shrewsbury and Millwall and were hoping that would continue in a Walsall shirt. Sadly, it didn't, but Alf put in some fully committed performances that season.

Tony Macken would prove to be the best of the new signings, coming in to play right-back from Derby County for a fee of 9,500 pounds. Macken was a tough tackler and would stay at Walsall for five seasons, amassing 214 appearances and scoring 2 goals.

Terry Austin would join the club in March 1978 to bolster our attack, previously playing for Crystal Palace, Ipswich Town and Plymouth Argyle. After leaving the Saddlers he would play for Mansfield, Huddersfield Town, Doncaster Rovers and Northampton Town. For Walsall, he led the line well and made 51 appearances, scoring 19 goals.

Mackay also bought in a couple of players almost at the end of their careers, having played with or for Mackay before they made their way to Fellows Park.

Both great players it would be a pleasure to see their undoubted skill and time on the ball. Henry Newton, ex-Nottingham Forest, Everton and Derby County, would make 16 appearances for us that season before retiring. Jimmy Robertson, formally of Tottenham Hotspur, Arsenal, Ipswich Town and Stoke City joined the Saddlers and was a favourite for his right-wing play. Jimmy made 16 appearances before joining Crewe Alexandra and then playing in the U.S.A. for a couple of seasons.

Jeff King would also join in December and play on our left-flank; staying for a couple of seasons, he made 59 appearances and scored 6 goals. Jeff was a tough and tricky player and in his 59 appearances we would be awarded 10 penalties. King was the best at obtaining penalties; always attacking the opposition box from the left he would first look to go across the goal and then flick it left and change direction heading for the goal line. The full-back's first reaction is to stretch out his right leg, and whether it touched Jeff or not, he would seemingly trip himself up. His fall, however, was not the 'dying swan' leaps you see in today's Premiership; it was an understated fall, one of surprise. Jeff would only pull this stroke occasionally; he was too smart to keep trying continually. We as supporters, however, knew it might come at any time. There was much more to Jeff's game than penalties, but he definitely had a rare talent in getting them.

So, the season started full of hope, we were not losing many but not winning many either. The first half of the season we would draw 12 games, this with a win here and there kept us in touch with the leaders. In February and March, we won 6 and drew 2, pushing us into position for a run at the top of the table. We stuttered over a five game period and then finished strongly but it was all too late. The 5 match stutter of 3 losses and 2 draws had ended our real chances, we would finish 6th in the league. Buckley hit another 29 goals, Dennehy 8 and Austin 6 in the final flourish.

We had another year to remember in Cup runs:
The League Cup saw us defeat Bristol Rovers and Preston North End, both over two matches, before losing 2-1 to Sheffield Wednesday.

The F.A. Cup would throw up all those memories of 1933 as we progressed to the Fifth Round. Round One saw us at home to Dagenham, who we dispatched after a tough match 1-0, with Alf Wood scoring. Round Two was at home to Port Vale, where they managed a 1-1 draw, our goal again from Alf Wood. On December 19th we headed for the replay at Vale Park.

I had been doing a lot of broadcasting work at Fellows Park for Goldliner, the Walsall lottery that was bringing in good returns for the Football Club. As I was now a staff regular, I was asked if I would like to go in the Directors' box at Vale. I was not too sure because I liked being in the crowd at away matches; I spent so much time in the broadcasting box at Fellows Park. However, having been kindly asked, I accepted, and had a good time in the Directors' area. The Directors' box at Vale Park was pretty big, thankfully. We assembled on the front row in the area reserved for visiting Directors, which had a low wall in front and a perfect view. All was going well and the score was 1-1 when, out of the blue, my great friend Gary Shelton hit one and it flew into the net. Not remembering where I was, and the combination of 'Shelts' getting his first senior goal, lifted me off my seat and onto the wall in front joining in the Walsall celebrations. Slowly, it dawned on me that I was standing on the Directors' box wall and as in most Directors' boxes goals are gently applauded not given the full celebration. I sort of slid back into my seat and wanted the ground to open up; it would be a long time before I would again venture into a Directors' box. Jeff King added a third that night and we were in Round Three. On January 6th 1978, Swansea City were dispatched 4-1, with Alan Buckley getting another hat trick and King adding a fourth.

Round Four was the Leicester City game at home where Alun Evans scored with seconds to go to put us through 1-0 and my emotional broadcasting skills were stretched.

Then, Round Five, and out of the hat for February 18th 1978 came Arsenal versus Walsall.

Everyone in the town was excited about the match, the papers were buzzing about our 1933 victory and although this match was to be played at Highbury, everyone hoped we might just have a chance.

I travelled down to London on a staff coach from Walsall Football Club and enjoyed the day. The team was goalkeeper, Kearns; back four, Macken, Harrison, Serella and Caswell; midfield, Dennehy, Bates, Evans and King and strikers, Wood and Buckley.

We would lose the match 4-1 but put up a good fight. Things could well have been different as Colin Harrison ripped through the Arsenal defence only to miss very early on. Had that gone in, all may have changed, however, Stapleford 2, MacDonald and Sunderland saw us off, with Alan Buckley replying.

We all left Highbury believing our team had a real go at Arsenal, but on the day they were just too good for us. We arrived back at Fellows Park and we were soon joined by the team in the bar. We stayed to watch 'Match of the Day' re-run the game and I was standing next to Mick Kearns when David Coleman in commentary suggested what big hands Mick had got. The whole bar gave Mick a lot of stick and it was a most enjoyable evening. Our Cup run was over but we had enjoyed our 'run' and visit to the big time.

The summer of 1978 was disruptive. Dave Mackay left to manage Arabic Sporting club in Kuwait, he would later return to manage in England, but our driving force had gone and it would take some time to recover.

Chapter 11

Sixteen Seasons In Division Three

The stability and hope of the 1977/1978 season had disappeared with Dave Mackay, his departure being sudden and swift. Some players left during the summer. Miah Dennehy went to Bristol Rovers, Mick Bates to Bradford City, Alf Wood to Stafford Rangers and Alun Evans to Australia, all of which had been first team regulars. Signings were thin on the ground during the summer as we had no Manager in charge. Jimmy Kelly, a tricky left-winger, signed from Wolves and would make 27 appearances and score 3 goals during the campaign.

Alan Buckley, our most experienced player, took charge of the team for a month; we started with 3 straight losses and in came former West Bromwich Albion Manager, Alan Ashman.

Ashman was a totally different character to Dave Mackay. Alan was easy going and his style was to encourage players gently rather than Mackay's iron fist. Such a drastic change of style did not work well and we would win only 6 matches before the end of January and find ourselves rooted at the bottom of the Division.

Ashman had tried to change our downward spiral with signings, three of which would have good Walsall careers.

Steve Waddington. Midfield.

He signed from Stoke City for 40,000 pounds; a busy and feisty midfield player who would play in our side for four seasons, making 142 appearances and scoring 14 goals before being transferred to Port Vale.

Roy McDonough. Striker.

He signed from Birmingham City for 15,000 pounds. Roy played every match with 100% effort, but he was never really loved by the Walsall Faithful. I thought McDonough did a great job in leading our line and taking the 'hits' for our other strikers. The Walsall fans expected Roy to score more goals, but did not realize it was his play that enabled others to score our goals. Roy was a good mate of mine and we saw each other at matches and get togethers over the years. Roy got his reward for good play at Walsall with a 15,000 pounds move to Chelsea in October 1980, before playing at Colchester, Southend, Exeter and Cambridge United. For Walsall, he appeared 93 times and scored 17 goals.

Ricky Sbragia. Centre-Back.

He signed for Walsall from Birmingham City for 15,000 pounds in February 1979 in an attempt to sure up our leaky defence. Rick would stay at Walsall for a season and a half before transferring for 35,000 pounds to Blackpool. After a long professional career, he became a youth coach at Sunderland and Manchester United, before returning to Sunderland and managing them in the Premiership.

Ricky made 77 appearances for Walsall, scoring 4 goals and he was a very popular player during that time with our team.

Ian Turner. Goalkeeper.

Turner returned for his second spell at Fellows Park and displaced Mick Kearns as we tried to stop the flow of goals against us. Turner had been at Southampton and had won the F.A. Cup with them in 1976. In two spells, Turner played 46 times for the Saddlers.

Unfortunately, nothing worked and Alan Ashman was fired in February 1979, with the Saddlers still rooted to the bottom of the table. In came Frank Sibley, from Queens Park Rangers, to manage the team in the last throw of the dice. The now disillusioned Walsall supporters did not appreciate Frank. In came striker Dave Syrett from Swindon, scoring 3 goals in 11 games and Steve Jones from QPR, making 15 appearances, before moving to Wimbledon during the summer. Sibley also sold Terry Austin our centre-forward to Mansfield.

Sibley lasted only two months in charge, our fate was sealed, relegation to Division Four was now guaranteed.

In amongst the mayhem of that season, Birmingham City had signed Alan Buckley for 175,000 pounds in October 1978, scoring 8 goals in 24 appearances for them. 'Buck' would return to Walsall in July 1979 for 175,000 pounds and be named our Player-Manager.

The 1978/1979 season could only be described as chaos; three Managers, endless changing and chopping of the team and only 10 wins all season from 46 games. Terry Austin scored 13 goals to top score and only Alan Birch 45 appearances, Dave Serella 43, Tony Macken 42 and Brian Caswell 41 stood firm in a team that was unrecognizable.

In all my time as a Walsall supporter, we had always competed in Division Three. Our 'Holy Grail' was to compete again in the Second Division; no thought had been given that we would find ourselves in Division Four. That was now the case, and Alan Buckley set about putting a team back together in less than a month for the coming season.

Season 1979/1980, life in Division Four started with Alan Birch being transferred to Chesterfield for 40,000 pounds, 9 goals and 45 appearances in a losing team had proved his worth and he moved on. Jimmy Kelly soon moved to Portland Timbers in the U.S.A. and Jeff King also left the club. The biggest shock and disappointment was Mick Kearns was sold to Wolverhampton Wanderers.

The coming campaign would feature mainly homegrown players, most of which were good friends of mine, and so although we had to compete in Division Four I was looking forward to the coming campaign.

The players that would begin the rebuilding of Walsall Football Club:

Ron Green. Goalkeeper.

Ron signed from non-league Alvechurch in July 1977 and performed brilliantly in our youth and reserve winning team. Five games into the season Ron displaced Ian Turner. His first game that season was a 3-0 home win against Lincoln City. I was in the players bar that night with both Ron and Dave Serella. Ron had been promised that if we won he would stay in the team. Dave suggested that we were expected to win and that Ron's position might not be totally secure to which Ron

Ron Green

became a little upset. He need not of worried he was not displaced all season.

Ron would make 265 appearances for the Saddlers and have a great career playing for, Shrewsbury, West Bromwich Albion, Bristol Rovers, Scunthorpe United, Wimbledon, Manchester City, Kiddiminster Harriers, Colchester United, Happy Valley F.C. in Hong Kong and a host of non-league clubs.

It is fair to say in Ron's professional career he always struggled with his weight. He once told me he only had to walk past a curry house and he put on five pounds. Strangely, when his career was over, he had no weight problems at all, could eat what he liked and never put on weight. Explain that!

Ron is a good mate of mine and along with Mick Kearns, up to that point, they were my favourite Walsall goalkeepers. I've been fortunate to play games at both Fellows Park and Banks's Stadium with both of them.

Ian Paul. Full-Back & Midfield.

All the lads knew Ian as 'Chef.' He graduated through our youth and reserve teams in the right-back position, but as he became a regular in the first team he moved forward into our midfield. I believe that Ian Paul was the most talented of the group of players that came through the youth system during that time. I also believe that Ian would have gone on to play in the First Division without any doubt, had injury not finished his career. 'Chef' was awesome. Ian had vision on a football field above the norm, great control, pace, determination and a fighter's heart, all done with maximum efficiency.

We always took the mickey about Ian being booked by the referee. It went like this:

Referee, 'That's enough lad, what's your name?'

'Paul.'

Referee, 'Paul who?'

'Paul.'

Referee, 'Are you telling me your name's Paul Paul?'

And, so it went on.

'Chef' always got his own back mind you, he was also brilliant at pool, snooker, in fact, anything you wanted to challenge him to he'd beat you.

Ian would play 83 times for Walsall scoring 11 times and the season 1979/1980 would be his best.

Kenny Mower. Left-Back.

Ken also came through that same youth and reserve side, making his debut in the last game of the previous season 1978/1979. At that time, I was talking with Ken and he asked me if I thought he was ready for the first team, I answered honestly, not quite yet but soon. Ken told me I was wrong, he was right.

Kenny played the first game of the 1979/1980 season and out of 52 games that year he missed 3. What do I know?

Playing for twelve consecutive seasons, making 494 appearances and scoring 10 goals, Kenny Mower became a Walsall legend.

Ken Mower

Don Penn. Striker.

Don again came through the ranks, and after scoring a bundle of goals in the youth and reserve sides, had made a few first team appearances over the previous two seasons. The 1979/1980 season would be his breakthrough year. Walsall fans knew that Donald was that rare breed of striker, he could look disinterested and not involved much in the game and then bang, out of nowhere, he would strike and turn the match. Personally, I loved to see the fear on defenders' faces when Don came short into midfield, received the ball, turned and went straight at the centre of their defence. Panic, sheer panic.

The more you are around football and

Don Penn

footballers, the more you realize it is a game of chance, in some ways like the Music Industry. Don would score 26 league and cup goals in his first full season, we were all proud of him as in front of players from Villa, Wolves, Blues, Albion and Coventry, that season Don stepped forward to receive the 'Midland Golden Boot Award' for goal scoring.

Don would make 159 appearances and score 58 goals in Walsall colours before a knee injury ended his career. A month earlier, Don had been the subject of a big offer from Manchester City to take him to the First Division. I think Walsall were holding out for more money as was their right and during that month Don got injured. I sat with Don many times watching reserve games as he worked a weight on the bottom of his foot to strengthen the knee, which eventually was to no avail. We spoke many times that if, just if, the Manchester City transfer had gone through, the better doctors and the ability to protect a huge investment might just have saved his career if the injury happened at City. A game of chance.

Mark 'Rico' Rees. Right-Winger.

'Rico' and I have been mates for thirty years. Towards the end of the 1979/1980 season Mark would become a first team regular, another member of the youth and reserve side. His play was always direct, with exceptional pace and power, loved by the Walsall Faithful. 'Rico' would spend twelve seasons in our first team making 274 appearances and scoring 42 goals. Best remembered for ripping apart the

Mark Rees

Liverpool defence in our Cup run in 1983/1984 where England's left-back, Alan Kennedy, couldn't get anywhere near the flying 'Rico.' There are many tales of Mark Rees, my favourite is after a game at Sheffield United, which had been a relegation battle that would decide if Walsall or Sheffield United were relegated, played at Brammall Lane. As the final whistle went, chaos ensued, the pitch was invaded and disgruntled Sheffield United supporters were out for blood. The players were trying to exit the pitch as quickly as possible. 'Rico' was ten yards from the tunnel when a United supporter hit him round the head and started to run. At this point, there must have been three thousand people on the playing surface. The wise move at this point is to ignore it and get into the dressing room as fast as possible. Not in 'Rico's World.' Mark turned and I watched in dismay as he chased the offender forty yards across the pitch and battered him. The guy was never going to beat Reesy in a sprint race. After which Mark suddenly realized he was fifty yards from the safety of the dressing room, but I think many of the United supporters had watched the sequence and decided it was best to leave Mark alone as he weaved his way into the tunnel. What a huge heart!

Mark Rees snowy Feb 1986 v Wolves

Paul Waddington. Left-Winger.

'Sid' or 'Wadda' as he was known to us all was a gifted player. His left wing play for the youth and reserve sides was outstanding. 'Wadda' had such skill and balance that he was not content to beat a player once, he used to double back and beat him again, preferably 'nutmegging' in the process. 'Sid' also took the penalties for those sides and we had many conversations about it. My belief was to make sure and bury it, but 'Sid' liked to only put it in the top corner, chip the diving keeper, faint one way and roll it in the other, in other words any way he could think of rather than just hitting it. 'Rico' joked for years that he made all those league and cup appearances and yet 'Sid' had all the talent. 'Sid's left foot was as good as Merson's right. 'Sid' used his right foot for balance and it didn't interfere with the ball; the left was magnificent and could do anything. Sadly, Buckley did not fancy 'Wadda' for his team, although 'Wadda' did force his way in and score a tremendous goal in a win against Colchester United he never really had a good run in the team. I believe had Chris Nichol been in charge and seen 'Sid's talent he would have worked him into being a great player for Walsall. It's a game of chance, possibly wrong place, wrong time and 'Sid' was definitely 'one that got away.'

Paul Waddington would go on to have a great non-league career and score goals for fun for Halesowen, for Walsall he only played 19 games and scored 1 goal.

If the 1978/1979 season was one of our worst, then season 1979/1980 was one of our best. Alan Buckley had created a team from within, moulded it together and believed in our rich vein of homegrown players.

The game stats were amazing. We would not lose until the fourteenth game of the season. We would lose only 2 games in the first 38. We would go 21 games unbeaten in the middle of the season and, finally, lose only 5, including losing the last 2, which cost us the Championship and we ended Runner-up in League Division Four and promoted back to Division Three at the first attempt.

The team was solid throughout. Ron Green, our goalkeeper, made 39 out of a possible 46 appearances. Full-backs, Tony Macken 42 and Kenny Mower 44; centre-backs, Ricky Sbragia 45 and Dave Serella 37; midfielders, Brian Caswell 45, Steve Waddington 37 and Ian Paul 37; forwards, Don Penn 45, Alan Buckley 44 and Roy McDonough 40. Jimmy Williams, signed from Worcester City, also contributed with 22 appearances.

Goals came from everywhere, Don Penn 26, Alan Buckley 18, Roy McDonough 7, Brian Caswell 6, Ian Paul 6, Steve Waddington 5, Dave Serella 4 and Mark Rees 3.

Our biggest win of the season came on January 26th 1980 at home to Northampton Town. The Cobblers brought a large support as the travelling distance is not too far and they had been given a large segment of the Cowshed.

The game was memorable for me as my good pals scored the goals. Don

Penn opened the scoring before Northampton equalized, we went ahead again through Ian Paul before halftime. During the first half, Brian Caswell had landed an enthusiastic tackle on Northampton's right-winger right in front of the Cobblers fans. After that moment, they had proceeded to give 'Casa' unmerciful stick every time he touched the ball throughout the remainder of the first half. During the second half, 'Casa' was on the other flank, but the boos and calls could be heard across the pitch whenever he touched the ball. The next goal in the match was crucial, we attacked and suddenly the ball fell to 'Casa' who thumped it in. Brian then went on a curving run that went all the way down the side of the pitch in front of the Cobblers fans. 'Casa' was waving, laughing and thoroughly enjoying himself as the Northampton fans went ballistic, surging towards the wall. Fortunately, they stopped and did not invade the pitch as that would have triggered the Hilary Street End into a response and probably an almighty brawl. I'll never forget that run, it signalled the end for Northampton in the game as Alan Buckley made it four. Then onto the pitch came Mark 'Rico' Rees who proceeded to make it five and score his debut league goal. Four of the goal scorers that day were all graduates from our youth team, plus one from the Manager; it doesn't get much better than that.

Brian Caswell

After the sixteen seasons in Division Three, the relegation in 1978/1979 was not a pleasant experience, but on reflection, it was worth the trauma to see an almost homegrown team provide the first promotion I'd experienced as a supporter. 1979/1980 is a lasting memory. Working at Radio Saddlers made me feel that I was part of the whole thing. I truly loved it.

With Ron Green

With Kenny Mower

Chapter 12
The Great Escapes

The 1980/1981 season found Walsall Football Club in a buoyant mood. At the start of the season, we felt our team was young and building for the future, if we could stabilize in Division Three that season we could then press on the following season when our young players would have more experience.

The summer signings looked solid and two of them over the coming years would become Walsall legends.

Peter Hart. Defender.

Peter started his career at Huddersfield, making his league debut at 16 years of age. Captaining their youth team to the F.A. Youth Cup Final, he soon was a regular in their first team, making a total 229 league and cup appearances. After winning the Fourth Division Championship with the Terriers by just beating Walsall into second place, he signed in August 1980 for a fee of 70,000 pounds. It was obvious that Alan Buckley rated him highly and we were all looking forward to his inclusion in the team. Peter began his Walsall career in midfield but would soon drop back to centre-defence and be the corner stone of our backline for seasons to come. 'Harty' would Captain our side and make 474 appearances and score 13 goals during the next eight seasons, qualifying for legend status.

Peter Hart

The Peter Hart Testimonial game at the end of his career was the last match ever to be played at Fellows Park in May 1990. I was lucky enough to play in that game for the 'All Stars Team' and wave my personal farewell to Fellows Park, Peter Hart and the Hilary Street Faithful.

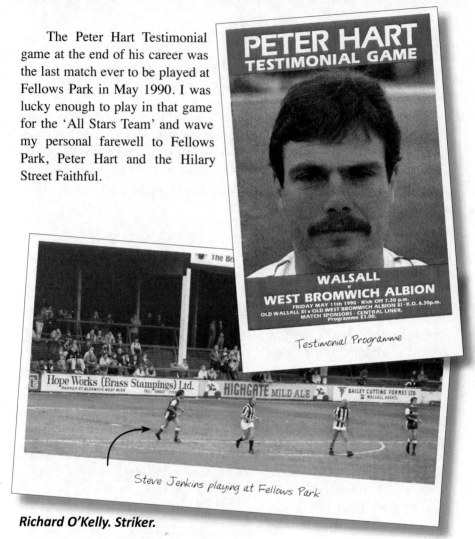

PETER HART
TESTIMONIAL GAME

WALSALL
v
WEST BROMWICH ALBION
FRIDAY MAY 11th 1990 - Kick Off 7.30 p.m.
OLD WALSALL XI v OLD WEST BROMWICH ALBION XI - K.O. 6.30p.m.
MATCH SPONSORS - CENTRAL LINER.
Programme £1.00.

Testimonial Programme

Steve Jenkins playing at Fellows Park

Richard O'Kelly. Striker.

Richard signed from Alvechurch in October 1979 and made our first team at the start of the 1980/1981 season. Rich would have a long career in football, both as a player and coach. For Walsall he would have two spells making a total of 254 appearances and scoring 65 goals, in between he had a season at Port Vale before returning to Walsall and then onto Grimsby Town. After injury ended his playing career, he joined Alan Buckley at Grimsby as Assistant Manager, then he went with 'Buck' to West Bromwich Albion, then onto Aston Villa, Hereford United, Bournemouth and Doncaster Rovers. Richard was a supporter's favourite for his 100% effort in every game, so much so, rumours abound that one day he would return to manage our team; eventually he would return as Assistant Manager to Dean Smith.

Steve Baines. Centre-Back.

Steve arrived at Fellows Park to replace Ricky Sbragia who had been sold to Blackpool after his commanding season in our promotion side. Baines played for Nottingham Forest, Huddersfield Town, Bradford City, Walsall, Scunthorpe United and Chesterfield. I would say his time at Walsall was not his best. After injury ended his career, he qualified as a referee and he would return to Walsall to referee one of our games. Baines may remember the jolly banter and 'stick' he got that day.

In September, Roy McDonough would move to Chelsea and Ian Paul would play his last game in December. In a short period of time Sbragia, McDonough and Paul, three huge players for us from the promotion team, were gone. Consequently, the team that had been so solid was chopped and changed and positions moved as 'Buck' tried to find the winning formula. We would win only 7 of our first 27 games and find ourselves close to the bottom of the table. In came more of our homegrown players to try to turn our fortunes around. Paul Waddington had a run of 14 games, David 'Mini' Preece made 6 appearances in our midfield and Mark Rees 21 appearances. We simply could not get the wins to move us away from the bottom of the table; we won only once in 12 games from February to almost the end of April. In all honesty, we were doomed to Division Four again. We had 2 games left and we were 3 points behind Sheffield United and safety, the first of which was a home game against Swindon Town. We didn't go into the match with any kind of confidence but with nothing to lose the boys went for it and pulled off a 2-1 victory, with goals from Don Penn and Mark Rees.

Sheffield United drew their game at Hull and so we were now just 1 point from safety and our final match was at Brammall Lane against Sheffield United. We needed to win, but a draw would be enough for them, we still had a chance, although only a small one.

The Walsall Faithful made their way up the M1 to support the lads and swelled what would be a huge crowd for the game with so much at stake for both sides.

Our team that day was goalkeeper, Green; back four, Macken, Baines,

Serella and Mower; midfield; Rees, S. Waddington, Hart and Caswell and strikers, Penn and Buckley.

The atmosphere was electric and the crowd wound up tight as both sets of supporters drove their teams forward and prayed for clearances out of defence. The score line at halftime was 0-0 and would remain so until five minutes from time. I was in the stand at the end of the ground where our team were attacking towards our own supporters during the second half. The stand had not been segregated, and so Sheffield United supporters surrounded us, although by some distance. In the eight sixth minute with Walsall teetering on the edge of the cliff and Division Four, Buckley cut into the box and was upended. Penalty; the cry was huge and deafening from the Saddlers supporters as the referee pointed to the spot. Buckley was injured and he was our usual penalty taker. Minutes passed by to see if 'Buck' would be able to take it, the eventual decision being, no. The kick was to be taken by Don Penn who had not taken one before for the first team, tension mounted. I could hear the movement and rumble of seats behind me and said to Sue, 'If Don scores, don't jump up' as Don placed the ball all that was going through my mind was 'Come on Don, Come on Don.'

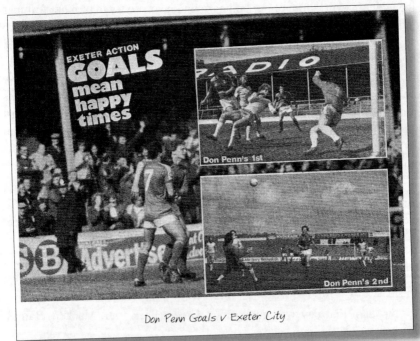

Don Penn Goals v Exeter City

Don went back to his run up and smashed it home. I just about remained in my seat but Sue jumped up and started waving, within seconds we were surrounded by thirty Sheffield United supporters. They wanted to tell me exactly what I was and what they were going to do to me. There really was no way out of this one, hemmed in by all sides. Fortunately, three Police Officers who had watched the penalty from the front of the stand saw the movement and started to walk up the gangway to our rescue. I decided this was the only route out and started to push my way along the seats dragging Sue behind me. I took a good few punches to the ribs and a few kicks to the calves and made it to the gangway. Sue, fortunately, was untouched in the movement, but now totally scared. The Police said 'Time for you two to go, get out now.' We began walking to the exit and the corner of the stand, when, with one minute to go, Sheffield United were awarded a penalty. I just had to see it. We stood ready to run; the Sheffield fans' mood had now changed as their escape from relegation rested on the penalty and positivity came rushing back. Don Givens, a Republic of Ireland international, stepped up to take the penalty and all the money was on him scoring. Ron Green in our goal threw himself to his right and pushed the shot away, Walsall had escaped. The referee decided to blow for the end of the game and all hell broke loose. I stayed for a couple of minutes as the Sheffield fans stood in shock before they gathered themselves and went looking for retribution from the people of Walsall. My last view of Brammall Lane was the run of Mark Rees as he battered one of their supporters. I grabbed Sue and said 'Run.' We made it back to the car, which I'd positioned for an escape two hours earlier just in case, but hardly breathed until we hit the M1. Many Walsall supporters over the years have told of their after match experiences that day; it was war on the streets, United fans chased the Walsall fans who would stop, stand and fight for a few minutes before running again, totally overpowered by numbers. Eventually, the Walsall boys made it to the railway station but with nowhere to go the whole thing erupted there. Fortunately, I had made my escape, but I bet there are still a few body scares from that day, 'the great escape' of May 2nd 1981.

During the off-season, I had finally retired from DJing in nightclubs. I'd been working Friday and Saturday nights for years and my last gig would be at Snoopy's in Weston Super Mare. I had a residency there for my final few months on Fridays and Saturdays and had enjoyed my drives up and down the M5 from Walsall. It was sad to finish but I knew it was time. I'd loved every moment, all those gigs, all those nights and the crowds, but I'd hardly had a

Friday or Saturday night off in eight years. I'd not been on holiday except for a few days in Bournemouth since the family holidays in my teens, I was ready and I knew it.

I was also starting a company in London with the backing of Tom Edmunds, my friend and Walsall F.C. Director. Although originally I had not intended spending five days a week in London, I could see it was coming. That brought into question Radio Saddlers, although I could still do Saturdays, the Tuesday nights were going to be a problem and Cup replays too would cause concern. Although I loved being part of Walsall F.C., I knew it was probably also time for me to give it up. Tom Edmunds offices were at the Hilary Street End and we decided that we would sit and watch the games together although not in the Directors' box. We enjoyed being more passionate and vocal, something that is frowned upon with the Directors. It's much easier to sit relatively quietly away from home in Directors' boxes, but at home I still needed to let go with a 'Come on Reesy' every now and again.

I started the season with Radio Saddlers and did make a couple of Tuesday night 'runs' from London, but I had told the club I would soon be finishing. A chance meeting with my friend and Northern Soul DJ, Neil Rushden, got us into a conversation about Radio Saddlers and soon Neil took over from me. Again, I was sad to leave but I was so well known by the staff and club that I continued to wander around at will and was always welcome in the Players' bar after games.

I finally laid down the microphone against Portsmouth in front of 4,408 fans and a 3-1 victory for the lads, Kenny Beech, Dave Serella and Alan Buckley concluding that part of my career. I'm proud that I was involved in Walsall Football Club for so long as a member of staff. It had been over six seasons, I'd made a lot of lifelong friends and it wasn't as if I was going anywhere, I'm still going 30 years later. Thanks Walsall F.C. and Radio Saddlers.

The new season came as it always does, 1981/1982.

Neil Martin had returned to the club to be joint Manager with Alan Buckley. The thinking being that 'Buck' needed assistance on match day with the team and to concentrate more on his playing career, being our main goal scorer along with Don Penn. 'Buck' had still top scored in the previous season but his total had been 13 goals, a poor return for him.

The Saddlers added Kenny Beech to our midfield, a box-to-box player with a great engine and great effort in every game. He signed from Port Vale and he would play in 89 games, scoring 5 goals over the next two seasons. David Preece and the blossoming Lee Sinnott started to make more impression on the first team, proving our youth system was again working well.

1981/1982 would be a definite season of two halves. We started well with a great run up to Christmas; in 18 matches, we achieved 9 wins, 5 draws and 4 losses, it seemed we would be making a promotion push come the new year.

A brutal English winter arrived in early December and the team would not play for six weeks, whatever happened in those six weeks changed the course of our whole season.

At the beginning of January, in a strangely timed move, Neil Martin became our sole Manager with 'Buck' returning to the playing ranks. This would prove to be a difficult arrangement and Buckley would end the season scoring only 7 goals in 33 games, not the Alan Buckley we knew.

The second half of the season was the exact opposite to the first. During the next 28 matches, we would achieve 5 wins, 9 draws and 14 losses; no matter how we chopped and changed the team, we could not find a winning formula. So much so that we went from a side pushing for promotion in December to a side doomed for relegation by the end of April.

Neil Martin departed in one final throw of the dice, Alan Buckley was re-instated and we had 4 games left.

We finally won on May 1 against Exeter City at Fellows Park, 2-1, with Don Penn scoring both goals and providing valuable points, hope seeped back into the Saddlers. Then came two quick defeats: Wimbledon away 2-0 and Burnley away 2-1, with Mark Rees getting the consolation.

Bad news also came when it slipped out there was a possible ground sharing arrangement with Wolverhampton Wanderers. Barry Blower, a fierce Walsall supporter, galvanized the supporters in a march to the ground on the final day of the season. The thought of playing at Wolverhampton Wanderers was just too much for the people of Walsall. Had it have happened, hardly any Walsall supporter would have made the trip, it would signal the end of the Saddlers.

Under this cloud of uncertainty, poor form, small crowds and facing relegation, we hosted Doncaster Rovers at Fellows Park. We needed a win and Newport County to beat Swindon Town; if Swindon got anything from the game and we lost, the Saddlers would be relegated. Walsall fielded a defensive team, low on confidence, with the aim of getting something out of the game and trying to sneak a win in the second half. At halftime, we were still in the match and the hunt for safety, with the game locked at 0-0; Newport and Swindon were positioned similarly. During the second half, we tentatively pushed forward in search of a winning goal, encouraged by a crowd of 3,799. The winning goal would not come and the game finished 0-0, news soon filtered through that Newport had beaten Swindon and we had survived by a solitary point. 'the great escape two' had been achieved.

Our strikers that season had not fired on all cylinders although Don Penn top scored with 15 goals, Buckley 7, O'Kelly 6 and Rees 6. Our most consistent appearance makers were goalkeeper Ron Green with 50 and centre-back Dave Serella 50; both had stood firm in a season of turmoil.

The season also signalled the end of a record-breaking career; Colin Harrison played his last league match on September 12th 1981, rightly, in front our fans at Fellows Park. The visitors were Chesterfield and we drew the match 1-1. Colin had played in our first team for eighteen seasons and would hold our all-time appearance record of 529 appearances, scoring 34 goals. Walsall would be the only professional club he played for; they don't make them like that anymore!

Only three players had beaten the 500 appearance mark for Walsall, the other two, Colin 'Cannonball' Taylor with 502 and 189 goals and Nick Atthey, 502 with 18 goals. These appearance records would stand for thirty years and would only be overtaken later by the goalkeeping appearances of James Walker.

Chapter 13

Milk Cup Glory

The past six seasons had been a rollercoaster ride for the people of Walsall, we had two famous Cup runs in two seasons ending at Old Trafford and Highbury. Relegation from Division Three, an immediate promotion from Division Four and then two 'great escapes'. I have always said you have to be mentally tough to be a Walsall Football Club supporter; anything can happen and normally does.

Personally, having returned to the ranks of Walsall supporter rather than employee, I had attended all the Saturday home matches of the previous season, spending Monday to Friday in London and weekends at home in Walsall.

The company that Tom Edmunds and I had set up was doing well but we had decided to relinquish our shares in the Company and return to Walsall. Soon after, I left for Los Angeles and an elongated stay meant that I missed the comings and goings in the summer along with the first matches of the campaign. I returned to Fellows Park for the 2-1 victory over Reading on November 13, goals that day from Ollie Kearns and Kenny Beach. Within five weeks we would be anchored to the bottom of Division Three again for Christmas.

In my absence, Dave Serella had moved on to Blackpool, Tony Macken back home to Waterford and we had signed Ollie Kearns, Mick's brother, to play centre-forward. Ollie joining from Oxford and previously with Reading, he would only play for us that one season, making 42 appearances and scoring 12 goals, before moving on to Hereford and Wrexham.

In our first 20 matches, we won 3, drew 7 and lost 10. During that period, we lost Don Penn to a serious knee injury that would end his career by the close of the season. The team, although bottom of the league, was beginning to take shape.

Ron Green in goal, Brian Caswell after seasons at left-back and left-midfield switched to right-back and looked a new, improved and solid performer. Kenny Mower, more experienced, was looking the part as well at left-back. The centre-backs were the dependable Peter Hart and from our youth and reserve side Lee Sinnott. The midfield featured Mark Rees, Richard O'Kelly, Kenny Beech, a now established David Preece and an emerging Craig Shakespeare. The striking duties fell to Ollie Kearns and Alan Buckley.

For the second half of the season we signed Kevin Summerfield, initially on loan and then permanently the following summer from Birmingham City, playing at centre-forward. Mick Kearns returned from Wolves and Phil Hawker came in from Blues. These additions to the squad began to settle the team and turned around our season.

David 'Mini' Preece. Midfield.

'Mini' was always a class player at whatever level his career took him. Playing in our first team for only two seasons, he was transferred to Luton Town for 150,000 pounds. At Luton he won the League Cup, defeating Arsenal, a game 'Mini' invited me to and arranged the tickets. It was a great day and to see him lift the League Cup, from watching him in our youth team, was a pleasure. 'Mini' won 3 England 'B' caps and even though he was controlling their midfield he could not keep Luton in the First Division. After 260 appearances and 12 goals 'Mini' moved to Derby County. The move did not really work and after loan spells at

David Preece

Birmingham City and Sunderland, he joined Cambridge United, where he concluded his playing career. 'Mini' became assistant coach at Cambridge and I was invited along to a couple of games to see the team play. 'Mini' was a great player and a good mate, I, along with many others, was devastated about his death in 2007 following throat cancer. Luton have since named their family stand, The David Preece Stand.

'Mini' played 135 times for Walsall scoring 11 goals.

Lee Sinnott. Centre-Back.

The rate of development of a young Lee Sinnott was astonishing. Playing for our Youth team at left-back, he seemed a slightly built lad, with only signs of being a good player. In a matter of twelve months, he was big enough to handle Third Division centre-forwards, played with enormous skill and was a real threat from corners in the opposing penalty area. I think we all knew as Walsall supporters he was meant for bigger and better things and would not stay in our team for long. Lee played in 46 games for Walsall scoring twice, strangely, in consecutive games. In September 1983 Lee joined Watford for 100,000 pounds, won England Youth and Under-21 Caps, played in an F.A. Cup final against Everton before joining Bradford City for 130,000 pounds, later Crystal Palace for 300,000 pounds and then Huddersfield Town, Oldham Athletic, Bradford City (again) and finally Scunthorpe United.

Craig Shakespeare

Craig Shakespeare. Midfield.

I first watched and got to know 'Shaky' in our youth and reserve teams, he was then playing left-wing, but he would soon convert to left-midfield and become an awesome player with a powerful left foot, which dispatched free kicks with venom. 'Shaky' would play in our first team for seven seasons before moving to Sheffield Wednesday, then a 265,000 pounds deal took him to West Bromwich Albion where he captained their side, before a 100,000 pounds took him to Grimsby Town and later Scunthorpe United.

'Shaky' made 355 appearances for Walsall scoring 60 goals from midfield.

As the team began to settle we played with a confidence that had not been in the side for over a couple of seasons, our next 26 league games would feature 14 wins, 6 draws and 6 defeats. This run would catapult us from the bottom of the Division to a respectable 10th place finish.

Alan Buckley rediscovered some of his form, scoring 15 goals, Ollie Kearns 12, Kevin Summerfield 9 and Richard O'Kelly 8.

Don Penn, fighting all season with a knee injury, came back with 4 games to play, he managed 2 games and scored in both but would not play another league game, the knee just could not take it. However, that was Don Penn, all heart, and he proved he could score league goals on one leg, a tragic loss.

We once again had some excitement in the F.A. Cup, beating Kettering at home 3-0, Kearns, Preece and Buckley scoring. Round Two, North Shields on their home territory lost 3-0, goals from Round, Buckley and Caswell. The Round Three draw brought Birmingham City to Fellows Park on January 8th 1983; Blues immediately called Kevin Summerfield back to St Andrews. Summerfield, on loan at Walsall from Blues, was in good form scoring twice in 4 games for us.

Birmingham turned up at Fellows Park with Summerfield in their team, their right I suppose and showing their worry about the match. 12,967 turned up to watch the match and we hoped we just might turn them over for our loss four years previously. Sadly, it was not to be, although it just might have been, if Alan Buckley's penalty had hit the back of the net instead of crashing against the bar. The game ended 0-0, the replay at St Andrews also ended 0-0 in front of 14,774. We would finally lose in the second period of extra time when Kevin Summerfield settled the match. Two weeks later Summerfield returned to Walsall.

After a poor start, the season had got better and better, there was a quiet confidence around the supporters that our team was beginning to gel.

At the end of the season I'd started my own company in London, it meant staying there for five days a week and during the coming season I would sell my apartment in Walsall and make the move to London permanent. I still maintain that I never wanted to live in London but 'needs must' and I would be on my way.

As the buildup to the coming 1983/1984 season began I was very vocal in London about this Walsall side. I had seen enough to know, that with just an ounce of luck, we could be in the race for promotion. This was to backfire on me spectacularly when, September 10, away at Bolton Wanderers, we were smashed 8-1. I had so many phone calls that week about my prediction it was unbelievable. On the teleprompter on BBC, when a team gets a high score they print the number and then spell it out, 8 (eight), it seemed like everyone I knew saw that and wanted to tell me. Better times were ahead but it was an awful start to the campaign.

The arrivals at Fellows Park for the coming season:

Kevin Summerfield, a Walsall boy who went to my school, Joseph Leckie, signed from Birmingham City on a permanent basis to lead our attack, previously having played for Birmingham City. He would make 62 appearances for the Saddlers scoring 19 goals. Later he would play for Cardiff City, Plymouth Argyle, Exeter City and Shrewsbury Town.

Colin Brazier signed from Lincoln City after playing for Wolverhampton Wanderers and Birmingham City; he would play for the Saddlers for three seasons, 145 appearances and scoring 4 goals, making a fine partnership in central-defence with Peter Hart.

Phil Hawker. Defender/Midfield.

Phil signed from Birmingham City after coming to Walsall initially on loan; he would be an important member of our squad and team over the coming years. Proficient at left-back, centre-back and left-midfield, Phil could switch position during a game or start in different positions in consecutive matches, he would go on to make 221 appearances and score 16 goals. I was lucky enough to know him and play in a few games with him, great lad.

Ally Brown. Striker.

There was genuine excitement when Ally Brown signed for Walsall, he was a well-known Midland striker and heralded for his 72 goals for West Bromwich Albion in 279 appearances, which helped him achieve 'Midland Player of the Year' in 1979. Ally spent only one season at Walsall, but it would remain historically one of our best. His 13 goals in 37 games, tireless and enthusiastic workrate all helped to make him a Walsall favourite. Ally never knew when he was beaten he just kept going until the game finished. Brown had also played for Leicester City and Crystal Palace and on leaving Walsall played for Port Vale.

Gary Childs. Midfield.

Gary would sign from West Bromwich Albion for 17,000 pounds after a short loan spell. He would make 164 appearances and score 23 goals before being sold nearly four years later to Birmingham City for 22,000 pounds, later playing for Grimsby Town, linking up again with Alan Buckley. More importantly, Gary Childs became the final piece in a Walsall team that would charge through the Division and tweak the nose of the best team in the land.

Later in the season, January would see us sign Ian Handysides from Birmingham City for 17,000 pounds. He would make 81 appearances and score 12 goals, a very talented player; he would re-sign for Blues two years later. Ian's life was tragically cut short by tumours on the brain and spine, shockingly, at the age of 27.

In March, we signed Dave Bamber from Coventry City to boost our goals. He looked the part and scored twice against Hull City on his home debut, alas, he would only score one more goal that season and his style was not appreciated by the Walsall Faithful. Bamber had a long and travelled career and scored almost 150 league goals for Blackpool, Coventry, Portsmouth, Swindon, Watford and Stoke City. Tony Godden also came on loan from West Bromwich Albion twice during the season to keep goal. Our youth and reserve side, again, was producing talented footballers; Paul Jones and David Kelly would both feature in the 1983/1984 season. During the summer, Ollie Kearns left the club and, after only 5 games, the expected transfer of Lee Sinnott to Watford occurred.

Our team that season for the most part took this shape: goalkeeper, Ron Green; back four, Brian Caswell, Colin Brazier, Peter Hart and Kenny Mower; midfield, Gary Childs, David Preece and Craig Shakespeare and strikers, Mark Rees, Ally Brown and Richard O'Kelly.

Seven of that team had graduated through our youth and reserve side: Green, Caswell, Mower, Preece, Shakespeare, Rees and O'Kelly. This side had an 'us against the world mentality,' never knew when they were beaten and refused, no matter what the pressure, to ever give in. Together, it was a magical moment when that team suddenly gelled. Our midfield three were all young, twenty and twenty-one years of age, yet they could control and would overcome First Division midfield units. The defence had the athleticism of Caswell, calmness of Brazier and Hart and pace and left side play of Mower. Both strikers, Brown and O'Kelly, were intelligent players who also had a will to win; no defenders had an easy day against those two. Ronnie Green in goal was, as ever, solid. Then there was Mark Rees, that season was his best, fully fit in the most part and at the top of his form with pace and confidence, simply unstoppable.

The season started and after losing 3 of the first 4 games Walsall suddenly started to hit form during the period from October 1st to December 17th. We would play 12 matches, winning 8 and drawing 4, this would catapult us to 4th place in Division Three.

By January 14th, we were top of the Division after beating Exeter City at Fellows Park 4-1. I took this moment to phone all that had phoned me after the 8-1 Bolton Wanderers debacle.

By March 10th, we lay 3rd and right in the mix for promotion. Again, it was not to be, our final 12 games yielded 5 wins, 2 draws and 5 defeats. The most crucial period was after Dave Bamber's debut brace, we lost 4 games on the bounce: away at Sheffield United, 2-0, home to Oxford United, 1-0, away at Millwall, 2-0, and, finally, at home to Lincoln City, 1-0. That sequence of losing and not scoring put paid to our hopes. Any kind of result in those 4 games would have kept us in it, but, hey, that's football.

Our final league position was 6th. We probably deserved more and the team assembled definitely did, they were one of our best ever sides and would be remembered for the 'big' matches they played that year.

Our Milk Cup Heroes and Memories.

It all started with a two-leg affair with Blackpool. The first match was away at Blackpool, August 30th 1983.

The team was goalkeeper, Mick Kearns; back four, Phil Hawker, Lee Sinnott, Peter Hart and Kenny Mower; midfield, 'Mini' Preece, Colin Brazier and Craig Shakespeare and forwards, Mark Rees, Ally Brown and Kevin Summerfield.

We lost the game 2-1, with Alan Buckley coming off the bench to score one of his three goals that season.

The return match at Fellows Park saw us line-up: goalkeeper, Ron Green; back four, Peter Hart, Colin Brazier, Phil Hawker and Kenny Mower; midfield, Richard O'Kelly, 'Mini' Preece and Craig Shakespeare and forwards, Ally Brown, Kevin Summerfield and Alan Buckley.

The changes and positional moves worked and we ran out 3-1 winners, going through 4-3 on aggregate, our scorers Kevin Summerfield, David Preece and Richard O'Kelly.

Round Two was another two-leg affair against Barnsley. At home in the first leg on October 4th, the team was goalkeeper, Mick Kearns; back four, Brian Caswell, Colin Brazier, Peter Hart and Kenny Mower; midfield, Mark Rees, Richard O'Kelly and Craig Shakespeare and forwards, Ally Brown, Kevin Summerfield and Alan Buckley.

The team had hit form and although we only won the game 1-0, we dominated proceedings and Mark Rees got the only goal.

The second leg was away at Oakwell and we were unsure if we had enough to deposit Barnsley out of the Cup. We need not have worried; playing superbly, we won 2-0, with goals from David 'Mini' Preece and Mark Rees again.

The team was goalkeeper, Kearns; back four, Caswell, Brazier, Hart and Mower; midfield, Gary Childs, Preece and Paul Jones and forwards, Rees, Summerfield and Buckley.

Round Three saw us drawn at home to local rivals Shrewsbury on November 8th 1983.

The team was goalkeeper, Kearns; back four, Caswell, Brazier, Hart and Mower; midfield, Childs, Preece and Shakespeare and forwards, Rees, Brown and O'Kelly.

Slowly, our first team had taken shape and we fielded the side that night that would take us so far. The match being a local derby was not an easy one; the score remained 1-1 with two minutes to go, 'Mini' Preece having scored our goal, when up popped Gary Childs to lash in the winner. 7,952 cheered on a Walsall side and belief was beginning to build around the town, Round Four awaited.

When the draw was made it was hugely exciting, our historical encounter from 1933 hit all of the newspapers again. We were to play Arsenal at Highbury on November 30th 1983 in the Fourth Round of the now called Milk Cup, formally the League Cup. Now permanently in London I was going to be there and made sure that the Arsenal supporters in the Record Industry knew who was coming to town.

Looking back, I think Walsall supporters knew we had a good team and not only that, but they were in good form and in a winning streak, just what you need when embarking on a 'giant killing' act.

I got my tickets and two of my mates Shaun King and Keith Knowles accompanied me to the game. I was most definitely revved up for the event. I didn't believe that we would win the match as Arsenal at home are formidable, however, I had hoped that we may take the lead and give them a shock, probably and hopefully, then dragging them back to Fellows Park where I believed we may have more of a chance.

On the night, I took my position with the massive travelling support from Walsall. 22,406 had turned up to watch the game, we were in good voice and letting the Saddlers know they had a firm loyal support.

The team was goalkeeper, Kearns; back four, Caswell, Brazier, Hart and Mower; midfield, Childs, Preece and Shakespeare and forwards, Rees, Brown and O'Kelly.

'Mini' Preece was now an outstanding player and flanked by clever ball players in Gary Childs and Craig Shakespeare; our midfield was formidable. We played well during the first half and were unlucky to concede and go in 1-0 down.

The second half commenced and we started wave after wave of attacks on the Arsenal defence towards our own fans, who roared on the boys as Arsenal seemed to falter. Charlie Nicholas, a good player and Arsenal favourite, was just out classed by Childs, Preece and Shakespeare. Their play and youth never let Arsenal players settle and we ran them into the ground. This led to Charlie being substituted and the Walsall Faithful chanting 'Charlie Who? Charlie Who? Charlie Who?' at the top of their lungs. The party had now well and truly started and Walsall pushed on, backed by the volume of our supporters.

A through ball found Ally Brown, his shot was blocked and the Arsenal defence tried frantically to clear, out it went to 'Mini,' who crossed again to Brown, who rolled it across the six yard line for Mark 'Rico' Rees to turn and hammer home with his right foot. The Walsall part of the crowd erupted and I went with them, 1-1, and Arsenal were on the ropes.

Straight from the kick-off we gained possession of the ball and began attacking again, wave after wave rained down on the Arsenal goal, surely, we would score. Richard O'Kelly attacked down the left, the TV commentary at this time tells of Arsenal's fatigue, O'Kelly crosses and the ball again comes out to Preece who put it back in to Brown to flick into the Arsenal net. 2-1 to the Saddlers with minutes to go, Arsenal did not have anything left. It seemed that night that Walsall were the First Division side, such was the performance of our team. Arsenal would fire their Manager, Terry Neill, one week later.

Shaun and Keith struggled to get me out of the ground, walking away with so many distressed Arsenal fans; all Walsall people were very vocal about what they had just watched. We escaped Highbury unscathed and headed for the Holiday Inn at Swiss Cottage where we indulged in a few drinks and generally danced the night away.

Walsall Football Club were now in Round Five of the Milk Cup, the town were awaiting the draw and looking for either a big team at home or a lesser side at home, so we could progress to the semifinal.

The draw came out, we had drawn a lesser team away from home, not quite what we wanted, but by now the supporters were 'game on' for anybody.

Rotherham United away, January 18th 1984, quarterfinal, Round Five.

The team was goalkeeper, Green; back four, Caswell, Brazier, Hart and Mower; midfield, Childs, Preece and Shakespeare and forwards, Rees, Brown and O'Kelly.

I made the journey from London to Rotherham with Shaun King, M1 all the way. I believed that it would be a tough and tight match, if we could nick a 1-0 win that would be fantastic. Just the thought of making the semifinal was intoxicating. Would the dream come true or would it be a massive disappointment?

Walsall seemed supercharged that night. Straight from the kick-off, we ripped into Rotherham with control and pace, with Reesy electric on our right wing. The pitch was slippy and muddy in different areas and so there was no consistency. This made no difference to Reesy; latching onto a through ball in the inside-right position he calmly threaded the ball home, 1-0. Walsall continued to attack and midway through the first half, Richard O'Kelly flicked home a David Preece chip into the box to put us 2-0 up. I was in the tunnel just as the halftime whistle went and got to encourage a Walsall team as they made their way to the dressing room. I must admit that the look on their faces as they went by was one of total concentration and focus. So far, so good, 2-0 to the good at halftime was more than we could have hoped for.

The second half resumed and again we pushed forward not content with 2-0 and preferring to attack than sit back on our lead. Again, we were rewarded as Ally Brown headed in Brian Caswell's right wing cross, 3-0. Rotherham, in front of their own fans, kept going and pulled one back, 3-1. That just pushed Walsall forward again and Mark Rees burst through to score again making it 4-1. Back came Rotherham and they finally managed another consolation goal, the final score being 4-2.

Winning 4-2 away from home is an exceptional performance in any game of any season. The crowd that night was 14,487. The noise was from a huge travelling support that made it seem that Walsall were the home side. The celebrations from the supporters and the team are lodged in my memory, as is the rejoicing as we travelled back to London in my car that night.

The draw, again, was the subject on all Walsall minds. The semifinalists were Liverpool, Everton, Aston Villa and Walsall. I guess we would have preferred Aston Villa. The tie was to be played over two legs, home and away, hence, whichever team we were drawn against it would be an almighty task to reach the final. Having come this far the town of Walsall believed in its team.

The draw was made and the toughest one possible came our way, Liverpool.

The first tie was to be played at Anfield on February 7th 1984 and nothing was going to stop me or the town of Walsall from visiting Anfield.

The team was goalkeeper, Green; back four, Caswell, Brazier, Hart and Mower; midfield, Childs, Preece and Shakespeare and forwards, Rees, Brown and O'Kelly.

Shaun King and I left London just after lunchtime on that day to make our way up to Anfield, stopping off in Walsall to see my Mom and obtain some home cooking as sustenance for the evening. The second part of the journey up the M6 we were part of the migration north, with cars, vans and coaches carrying the Walsall Faithful. We turned off to head down the East Lancashire road and head for Anfield. Along that road, we saw the team bus heading for the ground. I got passed a couple of cars and got next to the coach at a set of traffic lights. I jumped out waving frantically at Casa (Brian Caswell). Quickly realizing it was me, Reesy, Ronnie Green, Kenny Mower and 'Mini' Preece started waving and giving the 'Come on' fist pump. We were ready for the Mighty Reds.

Liverpool v Walsall

Liverpool at the time were the best team in Europe, on their way to the European Cup final and having recently won a host of League Championships, F.A. Cup's, League Cups and European Cups. Their players were internationals and household names: Bruce Grobbelaar, Steve Nicol, Mark Lawrenson, Phil Neal, Alan Hanson, Graeme Souness, Ian Rush, Alan Kennedy, Sammy Lee, Ronnie Whelan and Kenny Dalglish.

Walking into Anfield, finding our position and seeing 'the Kop' is a fantastic memory. There to see Walsall, Shaun described it as 'sticking your head in a lion's mouth' and saying 'go on then.'

The Walsall Faithful were trying their best to out sing 'the Kop', not easy, but going for it just the same.

Liverpool came out and slowly began to build momentum. Walsall were holding their own and beginning to launch some attacks when Ronnie Whelan got free on our right and met a well-delivered ball to put Liverpool 1-0 up. Whether Liverpool now believed Walsall would begin to falter I don't know, but that was not the make-up of our side. We began to launch attacks down our right wing, where Mark Rees had no respect for Alan Kennedy, then an accomplished First Division left-back and in the England squad. Encouraged by the Walsall fans, 'Rico' just knocked the ball past Kennedy time after time and raced passed him. Kennedy had only one option, foul 'Rico' or let him go. This constant pressure down Liverpool's left began to cause them concern and just before halftime their defence got in a terrible mess under pressure from 'Rico' and Richard O'Kelly. Mark Rees pressured Sammy Lee into a poor pass that found Richard O'Kelly in a position on the goal line, O'Kelly rolled the ball along the line and another mix up with Phil Neal meant the Liverpool defenders pushed the ball into their own net. Had they not Ally Brown would have tapped it in. An own goal equalizer, but caused by Mark Rees' pressure and a growing confidence from our midfield. The Saddlers fans went wild in a now quiet stadium; a growing Walsall side had quietened 'the Kop.' The halftime whistle blew and we were still in the match.

Liverpool v Walsall Report

The second half started with a more confident Walsall now accustomed to the surroundings and buoyed by the equalizing goal. Anything was now possible. The two sides traded punches with end-to-end football, Walsall giving as good as they got. With fifteen minutes to go, Liverpool, having a good spell, lashed a cross-shot at the Walsall goal, which Ron Green got his hands to and pushed out only for it to fall perfectly for Ronnie Whelan to head home.

Walsall were now 2-1 down. Immediately, Buckley substituted and brought on Kevin Summerfield, not a defencive move, he was obviously planning to push for the equalizer. Straight from the kick-off we surged forward with David Preece who chipped the ball into the Liverpool box with their defenders pushing up field. Summerfield with his first touch lobbed Bruce Grobbelaar and it sailed into the net, 2-2, the Walsall fans went wild with excitement. Shaun and I joined in the singing and dancing and huge celebrations. The match would end 2-2 but one of my great memories was Ian Rush set free down our right-flank, cutting in with Brian Caswell a couple of yards adrift, the situation looked like serious trouble as Rush was scoring all the time that season. In one of the finest tackles I've ever seen 'Casa' caught him up, slid in, took the ball and in one movement came back onto his feet, turned and headed up field. Rush left in a heap listening to the Saddlers supporters singing, 'There's only one Brian Caswell.'

After the match, Shaun and I made the long trek back to London to be ready for work the following morning.

That evening the BBC, whose cameras had been at the game, put together a thirty-minute highlights package, they had to re-arrange their schedule to make the time available. They introduced the show as a programme change, saying it was a 'must watch' show for all football fans. Walsall Football Club were nationally famous and the talk of football, they had indeed put their head in the lions mouth and come out unscathed.

Liverpool fans, being true sportsmen, stood and applauded off that Walsall side. The boys first acknowledged their fans and then showed their appreciation to an applauding Kop End. The crowd that night numbered 31,073.

The return match was scheduled for Fellows Park on February 14th 1984.

The team was goalkeeper, Green; back four, Caswell, Brazier, Hart and Mower; midfield, O'Kelly, Preece and Shakespeare and forwards, Rees, Brown and Summerfield.

Gary Childs was injured for the return match and so was Mark Rees. He was struggling with an almost gone hamstring, but nothing was going to stop 'Rico'and Walsall knew that Liverpool were in fear of our right-winger, 'Rico' made the team sheet.

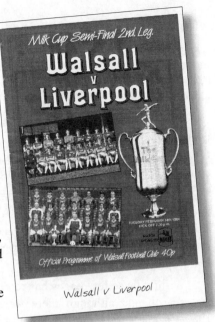
Walsall v Liverpool

I was just outside the dressing rooms that night when Alan Kennedy made his way in, this coincided with an official bringing the team sheet, which Kennedy took. Someone behind me shouted, 'Don't worry Alan; Reesy is in, get ready to run.' Kennedy smiled and said 'Thanks.'

The big change to the Liverpool side was the return of Graeme Souness.

19,951 packed into the ground. Walsall, full of confidence, attacked from the start and Richard O'Kelly had a snapshot well saved by Grobbelaar. A few minutes later, Preece put Ally Brown through and somehow when it looked easier to score the ball flashed past the post. Back came Liverpool and against the run of play Ian Rush, ever dangerous, shot Liverpool into the lead.

Halftime was 1-0 to Liverpool. Walsall opened the second half, again going at Liverpool, but after fifty-two minutes Ronnie Whelan made it 2-0.

Walsall, now going for broke, put in the most fantastic final thirty minutes. Mark Rees broke free and was clean through but dragged his shot wide. An Ally Brown shot was kicked off the line and Kevin Summerfield failed to score from ten yards. Sadly, after controlling most of the game and having five great opportunities, Walsall went down 2-0. However, we were not disgraced; most of the papers believed that over the two matches Walsall were the better side and they were most certainly heroes in our country. Liverpool marched on to the final and won. They would also win the F.A. Cup and the European Cup that season, making a historical treble. The team that gave them the most hardship was a little club in the West Midlands.

That night the wall collapsed at the Laundry End injuring 24 people, the weight of the people behind the goal was just too much when Liverpool scored their second goal. Play was held up for 13 minutes as the injured were attended to, helped by Graeme Souness.

Alan Buckley said after the game 'I am not going to decry other teams, but had we faced any other side than the most ruthlessly professional outfit in Great Britain, with wonderful skills to boot, I believe Walsall would have been at Wembley.'

For me, the great difference that night was Graeme Souness. Missing from the first match, he returned and set about our midfield, trying to snuff out David Preece, Craig Shakespeare and Richard O'Kelly. He didn't manage it completely, but he made a significant difference.

That Walsall team, I have to admit, in all of the years I've followed the Saddlers, was one of my favourites. All the players were comfortable with the ball at their feet, they were young and in their prime, as a unit, they hunted in packs, never knew when they were beaten and outplayed the best team in Europe.

Writing these few pages has reminded me of the excitement I felt during that season and although there were some magic moments to come, the 1983/1984 season is imprinted on my memory and so is that team. Maybe one of Walsall's finest.

Our Milk Cup Heroes.

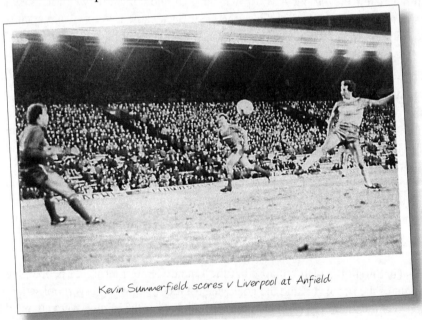

Kevin Summerfield scores v Liverpool at Anfield

Chapter 14

Wheldon, Birmingham City And 'Our Tel'

The excitement and performances of the 1983/1984 season had the town buzzing for the coming season. It seemed that all of the squad that had performed so well would be retained and we could almost start where we had finished off.

The surprises were that Ally Brown, who had played so well, joined Port Vale. Ron Green signed for Shrewsbury and Kevin Summerfield signed for Cardiff City. The Board of Directors were promising signings and players of a higher quality to augment the team. In came Steve Cherry as goalkeeper from Derby County, he would stay for two seasons and become a good Walsall keeper, making 94 appearances before signing for Plymouth Argyle and then Notts County. In the striking positions we still had Dave Bamber, our management believed he would become a good performer for the club. Unfortunately, it just never worked for Dave at Walsall, he would become a success elsewhere and after 10 games and 3 goals he joined Portsmouth. We also signed Peter Eastoe from West Bromwich Albion on loan; Peter played 6 games and scored 1 goal before returning to WBA.

The striking department was about to be revolutionized by one of our youth and reserve team players, he would go on to become an international player and score at the highest level.

David 'Ned' Kelly. Striker.

I was and always have been a 'Ned' Kelly fan. From the moment he got into our first team, he was always exciting, alert, quick, dragging centre-halves to the byline just where they don't like to go and then heading for the box, and most of all brave; 'Ned' would always go in where you knew you might get hurt. Kelly truly was a magnificent find;

David Kelly

he would play 180 times for Walsall scoring 80 goals and would become a Saddlers legend.

Kelly was sold to West Ham United in August 1988 for 600,000 pounds. At that point, it was the most money Walsall had ever received for a player. West Ham did not take to 'Ned' and so, after 61 appearances and 12 goals, he transferred to Leicester City for 300,000 pounds. Living in London, I knew a lot of West Ham fans that always used to moan to me about 'Ned.' I always told them, they didn't know what they were talking about and to send him back to Walsall any day.

At Leicester the goals started to come again, 22 in 66 appearances, before 250,000 pounds took him to Newcastle United, 35 goals in 70 games made 'Ned' a Tyneside hero. Newcastle won the First Division title and surprisingly they sold Kelly to Wolverhampton Wanderers for 750,000 pounds. 26 goals and 83 appearances later, 900,000 pounds took Dave to Sunderland, a barren spell followed of 2 goals in 34 games, although for some reason they played him on the wing. Tranmere Rovers then stepped in and paid 350,000 pounds and

David 'Ned' Kelly

the goals started coming again, 21 in 88 games. 'Ned' also played for Sheffield United, Motherwell, Mansfield Town and, finally, Derry City. Walsall fans would have all loved him to return to our team at the end of his career.

'Ned' also gained 26 caps for the Republic of Ireland, scoring 9 goals, played in a World Cup and coached Tranmere Rovers, Preston North End, Derby County and Nottingham Forest.

Paul Jones. Midfield.

Jonah was another to come through our youth team and he started making an impression on the first team in 1984/1985. He could play in midfield, on the wing and occasionally filled in at full-back. He was always a solid and committed performer with good skill. He would make 182 appearances, scoring 19 goals, before joining Wolverhampton Wanderers for 15,000 pounds in 1989.

On December 4th David Preece, following his impressive performances, was transferred to Luton Town, with Steve Elliott coming to Walsall from Luton as part of the deal. Elliott came with a good reputation, having played for Nottingham Forest and Preston North End for whom he scored over 70 goals. Steve would have a good spell at Walsall, making 82 appearances and scoring 24 goals, before moving to Bolton Wanderers, then Bury and Rochdale.

The start of the 1984/1985 season got underway. Our defence and midfield remained more or less the same apart from Steve Cherry taking over in goal. The forward line chopped and changed as we looked for the formula. We started with Handysides, Eastoe and O'Kelly, then, Rees, Eastoe and O'Kelly, next, Handysides, Bamber and Kelly, followed by Rees, Bamber, Kelly and Handysides, Kelly and Elliott. The team played well but with no consistency, then, suddenly, between December and almost the end of March we found the formula and form:

Goalkeeper, Cherry; back four, Caswell, Brazier, Hart and Mower; midfield, Handysides, Childs and Shakespeare or Jones and forwards, Rees, O'Kelly and Elliott.

During a sequence of 14 games, we won 10 times, drawing 2 and losing 2, catapulting us up the Division and into contention for promotion.

As quickly as we got there we seemed to lose our goal scoring ability.

We whacked Cambridge 5-0 with Kelly, O'Kelly 2, Rees and Shakespeare scoring and then found it hard to score at all.

The final 14 games of the season saw us win 2, draw 4, and lose 8, ending in 11th position.

The goal scorers that year in the main were Richard O'Kelly 18, Shakespeare 13, Rees 12, Kelly 11 and Elliott 7. Not a bad return, but the scoring came in clusters and not consistently throughout the campaign.

Some of our best performances were again in the Milk Cup, the First Round a two-leg affair against Swansea City; starting away from home we won 2-0 at The Vetch, goals from Childs and O'Kelly. At home we won 3-1, goals from Shakespeare, Eastoe and Hawker.

Round Two, again over two legs, brought a local derby against Coventry

City at Fellows Park on September 25th in front of 8,399 'giant killing' fans, we lost 2-1, Shakespeare getting our goal. The second leg at Highfield Road on October 9th drew a crowd of 9,214, swelled by a travelling Walsall support on a night out for an upset. I drove up from London believing we stood a chance to turn it around. David Kelly had burst into the team the previous week scoring a couple of goals and was full of confidence. Our defence stood firm, while Rees, Kelly and O'Kelly just ripped into Coventry. In the end we were easy winners, 3-0, David Kelly scoring twice and Richard O'Kelly with a third.

Again, we were dreaming of League Cup glory and when the draw came out, it was game on again. October 30th 1984, due at Fellows Park, Chelsea F.C., we were ready.

11,102 supporters filed into Fellows Park that night and our team did not disappoint, taking the lead with a 'Mini' Preece goal. Things were going to plan, then Chelsea equalized. Craig Shakespeare then restored our lead and as the clock began to tick away, it seemed as though we were on another 'giant killing' run. Pressing forward, we scored again, only for it to be disallowed, and then six minutes from time Chelsea equalized, forcing the replay at Stamford Bridge.

Stamford Bridge was like a home game for me in terms of distance and I looked forward to seeing a Walsall side play there. The November 6th replay in front of 19,502 saw the Saddlers again put up a tremendous fight. Chelsea took an early lead, only for the Saddlers to pour forward and, after intense pressure, we scored, but again the goal was disallowed. This was a blow, however, we stuck at our task and kept attacking, only to be caught on the break and finally lose the match 3-0. Our run was over, but it had been another great experience and a brilliant night out.

The season had its moments and we had hit great form at different times. Again, our 'run in' to the end of the season is what caused us to lose touch with the promotion candidates, but we still had a talented group of players and the coming season would bring with it fresh hope and a promise of money to invest in more players for a promotion push.

The 1985/1986 season brought two summer new signings.

Nicky Cross. Striker.

Nicky was to become a Walsall favourite. After 19 goals in 119 appearances for West Bromwich Albion, the Saddlers paid 48,000 pounds to secure his services and he made an immediate impact on our team. He would make 139 appearances and score 52 goals in his time with the club before transferring to Leicester City for 80,000 pounds. After eighteen months, Port Vale signed him for 125,000 pounds where he helped them secure promotion to Division Two, finally, playing for Hereford United.

Steve Daley. Midfield.

Steve had been a great midfielder for Wolverhampton Wanderers, making 212 appearances and scoring 38 goals. Manchester City paid a British record fee of 1,437,500 pounds to sign him, but he never settled at Maine Road, making only 48 appearances and scoring 4 times. Branded a waste of money and a misfit, he signed for Seattle Sounders for 300,000 pounds, returning to England to play for Burnley. He soon returned to the U.S.A., playing for San Diego Sockers before signing for Walsall, playing just one season, he made 37 appearances and scored 1 goal.

Brian Caswell, after 458 appearances, scoring 19 goals and playing for thirteen seasons in our first team, was transferred to Doncaster Rovers. Personally, I was disappointed; a Walsall team without 'Casa' took a bit of getting used too. Our youth team developed another professional first team footballer in Mark Taylor. Playing midfield or full-back he would make 138 appearances and score 4 goals in five seasons before being sold to Sheffield Wednesday.

Willie Naughton. Winger.

Willie had been signed in March 1985 from Preston North End for 35,000 pounds. Brought in to try and create chances for our 'run in' and reignite our goal scoring, it had not worked, and the Walsall Faithful had not taken to Willie's left-wing style. That was soon to change as Willie hit form and became an integral part of our team, going on to make 202 appearances and scoring 24 goals during the next three seasons, until his transfer to Shrewsbury Town.

The team had taken a slightly different shape but looked solid and started to perform well: goalkeeper, Cherry; back four, Hart, Brazier, Hawker and

Mower; midfield, Childs, Daley and Shakespeare and forwards, Cross, Elliott and Naughton.

Phil Hawker was establishing himself in the team, but some of our trusted members of the previous two or three seasons were not having as much impact, Mark Rees, Richard O'Kelly, Ian Handysides and, strangely, David Kelly, did not play as we had hoped.

In the first 9 games we won 7 times and lodged ourselves in the top 3. Nicky Cross scored on debut and was off to a flyer. Steve Elliot was also scoring and Richard O'Kelly seemed to score a penalty every time he played. David Kelly came off the bench and scored. After 9 games Elliott had 5 goals, Cross 3, O'Kelly 3 and Kelly 2, it seemed there were goals all over the team. During the next 5 games, we lost 3 and drew 2, which stopped the momentum, but we roared back with 8 wins, 2 draws and 4 losses in the next 14 games. During that time, we smashed Cardiff City at home 6-3, what a match, with Steve Elliott getting a hat trick, Shakespeare 2 and Cross. We proceeded to lose the very next match away at Gillingham 5-2, but then hit Bournemouth for 4 and as we approached the end of January we were 4th in the table. The league leaders came to Fellows Park on the February 1 and received a thrashing 6-0, Naughton, Taylor, O'Kelly, Cross 2, and Elliott scoring. Three days later, Brentford came to Fellows Park and lost 3-1, Cross, Hart and Shakespeare doing the damage; six points gained and we were right behind the leaders and looking good. Again, we immediately lost 2 games, before hitting Bristol Rovers for 6, Elliott 2, Cross, Hawker 2 and Kelly. The 'run in' to the end of the season came again and although we did not do badly, it was just not good enough, 11 games, 4 wins, 4 draws and 3 defeats, we would finish in 6th position.

It had, however, been an exciting season, the team was free scoring and there were times when we looked as though we might just end our exile from Division Two. The main goal scorers that campaign were Nicky Cross 24, Steve Elliott 17, Richard O'Kelly 10, David Kelly 10 and Willie Naughton 8.

Walsall did not progress far in the Cup competitions that season, but they did offer up a few moments, The F.A. Cup First Round saw us beat Preston North End 7-1 at Fellows Park and their ex-winger Willie Naughton gave them a torrid time scoring 3 goals; Elliott, Childs 2 and O'Kelly completing the rout. In Round Two Walsall beat Port Vale in a replay at Fellows Park 2-1, with Cross and Hawker scoring, which set up another 'giant killing' opportunity, Manchester City at Fellows Park in Round Three. On January 4th, 10,836 were ready to cheer on the Saddlers. We played well, but not well enough, losing 3-1,

O'Kelly's penalty the only home goal.

The Milk Cup would see us go out in Round Two to Leeds United, but the First Round brought some local bragging rights and the kind all Walsall folk enjoy. August 20th saw the visitors at Fellows Park get a 1-1 draw in an exciting match watched by 11,330. Nicky Cross scoring our goal against Wolverhampton Wanderers. The Wolves thought they had done the hard part, they were wrong. In the return match we defended well and then caught them, running out 1-0 winners, again, with a Nicky Cross goal. Wonderful stuff, unlucky Wolves.

During the campaign, we sold Steve Cherry to Plymouth Argyle, he had been playing very well. Mark Prudhoe signed from Birmingham City as Steve's replacement and he did well in our goal.

The summer of 1986 arrived and brought with it rumour that Walsall could be moving from Fellows Park. Saddlers fans began to demand an explanation from the Board of Directors. Chairman, Ken Wheldon, and wealthy businessman, Jack Harris, were contemplating selling Fellows Park to developers and moving the town's Football Club to St Andrews in a ground sharing arrangement with Birmingham City.

Saddlers fans were having none of it, believing that any move from the town would mean the death of the club as many suggested they would not travel to Birmingham to see the team play. Also, a big stadium like St Andrews would have little atmosphere for a smaller club with a smaller fan base, it would feel like a Birmingham City reserve game. Wheldon and Harris countered that it made financial commonsense, especially as football in general was going through a tough period.

This move had to be prevented as far as The Supporters Club were concerned. Barrie Blower, then Director of Caldmore Housing Association, a true and vocal Walsall fan who had led a protest movement before to stop the ground sharing idea with Wolverhampton Wanderers, took on Wheldon and Harris against all odds.

The Town Hall was packed as Blower, Tom Hargreaves and a number of key Walsall fans from The Supporters Club drew up battle plans, with a fight to the finish mentality. They met at the Town Hall again and again as the action plan kept going, emotionally charged.

The Football League were bombarded with phone calls and letters in an organised fashion. Day after day letters arrived from Walsall fans and the phone just would not stop ringing. Finally, the Football League caved in, announcing that the application to ground share had been kicked out.

Phase one was completed, but phase two was even more difficult, a buyer had to be found and everything depended on that someone who would invest a great deal of

Barrie Blower at the Town Hall meeting

money into a Third Division Football Club.

I've known Barrie Blower for many years and here is a story he told me of that time. Barrie and Jeff Bonser used to have their haircut at the same barbershop in Bloxwich on Saturdays. Barrie was searching for an investor to buy up the club, having come so far and shouldering the full weight of the supporters and town. Whilst the two of them chatted in the hairdressers, Barrie saw a piece in a national newspaper about racehorse owner Terry Ramsden and he said to Jeff 'This is the kind of person we need.'

Barrie then rained in phone calls to Terry Ramsden's office and eventually got himself and Jeff a meeting with the self-confessed London multi-millionaire.

Barrie and Jeff made the trip to London with great hope and not much else, selling the idea of Walsall to a London millionaire was a long shot to say the least. That day, Barrie, as always, full of enthusiasm for his projects and especially Walsall Football Club, sold the idea to Terry Ramsden. By the end of a Blower battering, Ramsden asked him to wait outside for a few minutes and when Barrie walked back into the office Terry Ramsden said 'I'll do it.'

There were many last minute snags, final deal breaking moments, before Terry Ramsden bought Walsall Football Club from Ken Wheldon for 400,000 pounds.

Barrie Blower, somehow, from absolutely nowhere and against all odds, had managed to do what no one believed he could, stopped a ground share, sold the club and retained a football team for the town of Walsall. Just magnificent.

The town was buzzing; a multi-millionaire owned our football team, was investing and going for promotion, music to the ears of the Faithful.

Barrie Blower and Terry Ramsden

Chapter 15
The Holy Grail

Terry Ramsden bought Walsall Football Club on August 1st 1986. He arrived in a blaze of publicity never seen before or since. His helicopter arrived on the playing fields next to Fellows Park and he walked into the ground in style, followed by a huge press, radio and TV gathering.

Ramsden, loved by the people of Walsall for embracing our football team, set to work immediately. Alan Buckley, Manager, and Garry Pendry, Assistant, were fired that afternoon. He wanted his own management team and was determined to remove all links with the old regime. Ramsden also announced free admission to matches for senior citizens and agreed to give them free turkeys at Christmas.

Terry Ramsden became affectionately known by the Walsall Faithful as 'Our Tel.'

Days later, when the fans were expecting a big name Manager to lead us to the Second Division, Tommy Coakley arrived with his Assistant, Gerry Sweeney. The whole town chorused 'Tommy Who?'

Tommy Coakley was a right-winger for Motherwell before transferring to Arsenal in May 1966, playing 9 times and scoring 1 goal. After playing for Detroit Cougars he returned to Scotland and signed for Morton. He then played non-league football for Chelmsford City and Maldon Town before retiring from the game and becoming Manager of Bishops Stortford. It was from Bishops Stortford that he joined Walsall.

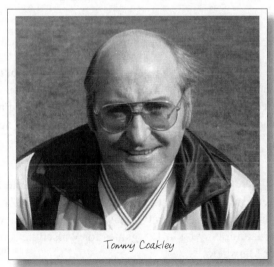

Tommy Coakley

Coakley set about putting a squad together for a promotion push immediately.

In came:

Andy Dornan. Right-Back.

Andy was a fierce competitor and started his career at Aberdeen. Motherwell then signed him for 20,000 pounds where he made over 100 appearances. Signing for Walsall for 17,000 pounds, Andy was by then an accomplished and confident full-back, he settled in straight away and would hold the number two shirt for 3 seasons, making 149 appearances and scoring 1 goal. Andy was one of the lads and fitted in, he was always up for a night out and I got to know him well during his time in the Midlands. After Walsall, Dornan moved back to Scotland and played for Montrose, Ayr United and Forfar Athletic.

Graeme Forbes. Centre-Back.

Forbsie also signed from Motherwell for 80,000 pounds and had made 185 appearances for them before arriving at Fellows Park. Graeme would become the lynchpin of our defence and a Walsall favourite for his fully committed displays, making 214 appearances and scoring 14 goals before returning to Scotland to play for Dundee and Montrose.

In late September, Ray Train would return to the Saddlers and during October we would make further signings.

Fred Barber. Goalkeeper.

Signed from Everton for a fee of 95,000 pounds, Freddie was to become a huge Fellows Park favourite and a fine goalkeeper. Always up for a laugh, he used to run out onto the pitch wearing a full head mask, looking ancient, as he made his way to the goal. Fred would make 189 appearances for the Saddlers.

Trevor Christie. Striker.

Trevor was an experienced striker when he arrived at Walsall and was seen by all as a great signing, having played for Notts County, Nottingham Forest and Derby County. Walsall paid Manchester City 30,000 pounds for his signature. Playing in 128 games for Walsall he scored 32 goals before leaving for Mansfield.

Colin Brazier would be one of the only players to leave, joining Kiddiminster Harriers after a couple of early season games and Richard O'Kelly left for Port Vale. Richard would return 20 months later and then leave again for Alan Buckley's revolution at Grimsby Town.

So much had happened during the off-season that hopes were high as the campaign started, only for the most disastrous sequence of results to dump us firmly at the bottom of the table.

In our opening 10 games we would only win 1 match away at Carlisle, 3-0, drawing 3 and losing 6. The new signings arrived and we began to find our shape and our form. The team in the main looked as follows: goalkeeper, Barber; back four, Dornan, Forbes, Hart and Mower; midfield, Jones, Childs and Shakespeare and forwards, Cross, Kelly and Christie.

The new signings worked and we started to make steady progress up the division, during the next 11 matches we won 8, drew 1 and lost 2. We hit a poor patch over Christmas and January not winning in 5 games, but we were soon back on track; our final 20 games produced 13 wins, 2 draws and 4 defeats. The side had clicked and in a great run through April we produced 7 wins out of 9 games, it took us to the verge of the playoffs, but we had suffered too poor a start to the season and that cost us the opportunity, having to finally settle for 8th position.

Our goal scorers looked in good shape. David Kelly, with confidence and belief from Tommy Coakley, blossomed, scoring 26 goals. Trevor Christie scored 19, Nicky Cross 19, Craig Shakespeare 16 and Gary Childs 8.

We also had another great F.A. Cup run. Round One saw us beat Chesterfield at home 2-0, with Shakespeare and Mower scoring. Round Two, Port Vale at home 5-0, Naughton, Cross, Shakespeare 2 (pens) and Christie. Round Three, away at Charlton Athletic, 2-1, Kelly and Shakespeare scoring.

Then, the unbelievable; after a summer of being threatened with playing our football at St Andrews, Birmingham, the Fourth Round Draw for January 31th 1987 and out of the hat came Walsall versus Birmingham City.

Walsall fans were not only up for this one they demanded victory over the old foe. 14,824 packed into fellows Park, including yours truly; the opportunity was too good to miss.

The tension and the drama were at a higher level than those games against

Manchester United and Newcastle United all those years ago. The pitch was icy and would play in our favour. The home fans were incredibly noisy and revenge and venom was in the air. Birmingham City could not be blamed had they have not fancied the match or the surroundings, however, they put up a brave fight as we penned them in, driven on by a frantic crowd. Then, up popped Nick Cross to fire the Saddlers in front. We held on to our 1-0 advantage not being able to kill the game with a second goal. Birmingham City came on strong towards the end of the match, desperate for an equalizer, piling on the pressure, but our defence held firm. Walsall 1 Birmingham City 0 and the Saddlers marched on to the Fifth Round of the F.A. Cup. On February 21st 1987, First Division Watford arrived at Fellows Park. We had been given another home tie and we thought it just might be our opportunity to get to the quarterfinal stages for the first time ever. 15,621 believed it was possible as we set about Watford with complete confidence. It was Watford who opened the scoring, but such pressure was built on the Watford defence that they conceded a penalty, Trevor Christie converted, 1-1. Walsall went in search of a second and gave the First Division side a good mauling and were unlucky not to win. Watford hung on to scrape a draw to take us back to Vicarage Road on the evening of February 24th.

The TV cameras turned up to show highlights of the game, Walsall were now an attraction in F.A. and League Cups, they had achieved the impossible before and might just do it again, you simply didn't know. The crowd swelled to 20,350 and the game started at a frightening pace.

I had misjudged the parking arrangements that night as we went the relatively short distance to Vicarage Road from our Willesden offices, in a mad scramble we parked and ran to the ground tight to kick-off. After slowly getting into the ground the match had already started as we were making our way to our seats. Walsall were attacking as we were watching the match and half looking for the seats, almost treading on the already seated. The ball went into the penalty area and Nicky Cross shot Walsall in front. It was breathtaking. Still half looking for our seats we were jumping up and down celebrating the goal. Walsall were still piling on the pressure and played a great first half; Trevor Christie scoring to put us 2-0 in front, only for Watford to pull one back just before halftime with a penalty from Kenny Jackett. Watford, with Blissett, Barnes and Falco up front, came out fighting and levelled at 2-2. The game then went into extra time with breathless cheering supporters from both teams, a real end-to-end affair. Watford went in front for the first time through John Barnes, 3-2, but back came Walsall again, this time through Phil Hawker, 3-3. The final period of extra time came. Watford attacked again and scored 4-3. I think the TV and radio people thought that might be it, with minutes to go, Walsall surely had nothing left. Not true, David Kelly, a thorn in the side of Watford all night, just kept on going and finally, from one of his runs, an opportunity for Trevor Christie arose and he didn't miss, 4-4. A real cracker of a game, one you always remember. A coin was tossed and the next replay was scheduled at Fellows Park for March 2nd.

15,897 were at Fellows Park and we still thought a quarterfinal place might be ours. Watford took the lead from an unfortunate own goal by Andy Dornan, a slice at a clearance and Watford were in front. Walsall continued to fight and attack all night, but we just couldn't find that equalizing goal. First Division Watford would go through 1-0 to the quarterfinal. Watford would lose in the semifinal that year to Tottenham Hotspur.

'Our Tel' and Tommy Coakley had provided a great season, but were unhappy that in their first season in charge they had not achieved promotion to Division Two.

The town were united behind Ramsden and the team, hoping again that this just might be our year. The added incentive was that 1988 would arrive and on January 1 it would be our centenary year. Roy Whalley had joined the club as secretary and he was busy preparing for the celebrations. hopefully, a double celebration.

The team was more settled and didn't need major surgery. Tommy Coakley always had great confidence in the group of players we had at the time. Coakley added Mark Goodwin from Notts County to our midfield. Mark would be a Saddler for three seasons, making 114 appearances and scoring 3 goals. Walsall's homegrown youngsters Paul Jones and Mark Taylor would both feature heavily during the coming campaign and establish themselves, making 48 and 50 appearances respectively. Mark Rees would spend his third season fighting hamstring injuries, getting fit, playing a few games and then tearing a hamstring again. No matter how hard he fought for fitness, the injury kept breaking down. We joked he was now Dr. Mark Rees, Hamstring Specialist or the Hamstring King.

Next, from the Walsall Academy and making his debut that season was a young Chris Marsh. More about 'Lucky' later.

Players moving out of Walsall that season: Gary Childs moved to Grimsby to link up with Alan Buckley and, surprisingly, during January, Nick Cross, after scoring his first league hat trick against Rotherham, was sold to Leicester

City. Richard O'Kelly returned for a short spell to cover Nicky's position. It was a surprise that Coakley sold Cross. No one could quite believe it. With everything going for us at that stage of the season why should we sell one of our main assets?

The season started with great upset as the admission prices to Fellows Park were increased, the best seats going up a hundred percent. The supporters didn't like it one bit, however, we had some very experienced and talented players on unusually big contracts for a Walsall team. Hence, the opening day of the season saw a small gate of 4,691 attend as some sort of protest. For those that did attend, including me, it was a bad day at the office as we lost to Fulham 1-0.

The clouds parted and the sun came out after that day, we would only lose two of our next 22 games, chalking up 12 victories and charging up the Division.

We did not do well in the Cup competitions, but during this run one match does deserve a mention, Round One of the now called Littlewoods Cup saw us drawn away at The Hawthorne's, home to West Bromwich Albion, only just up the road. Well, well, the 'giant killers' just happened to beat WBA 3-2 on their own patch, with goals from Shakespeare, Jones and Forbes. The return at Fellows Park was a 0-0 draw. Charlton knocked out Walsall in the next round, all worth it though for a glorious night at The Albion.

At the start of February, we had a small blip in that we drew 3 games and lost 1, before roaring back. 6,631 saw us defeat Doncaster Rovers 2-1 at Fellows Park on April 9th, goals from Christie and Kelly. Then, 11,913, with the smell of promotion in their nostrils, watched us beat Notts County 2-1, goals from Kelly and Naughton. We were second in the league and needed two wins from our last two matches for promotion. Surely, after twenty-five years since we last played in Division Two, in our centenary year of 1988, promotion had to be ours.

Unfortunately, it was not. We lost 3-0 to Bristol Rovers and drew at Fellows Pak 0-0 in front of 8,850. We were in the play-offs. The dream was still alive.

The play-offs in any division are scary, if you win, the memory lives with you for the rest of your life, if you lose, the closeness of the Holy Grail being lost is excruciatingly painful. You live those two weeks on a knife-edge of emotion, wishing away the days to Match Day. If you get through the first legs to the final, the hope is increased and the pain of losing increases twofold.

Notts County, who we had recently beaten, were our opponents. The first leg was to be played at Notts County on May 15th 1988. Our team was goalkeeper, Barber; back four, Taylor, Forbes, Hart and Hawker; midfield, O'Kelly, Goodwin, Shakespeare and Naughton and strikers, Kelly and Christie.

I travelled up to Meadow Lane and sat with an injured Kenny Mower and Mark Rees. We were all on edge and hoping for a result. After a tough game, we had been the better side and dominated for large spells, we ran out 3-1 winners.

We had been professional in our celebrations of our goals, but when the third one went in the dancing and celebrating of Kenny, Rico and me, probably left a lot to be desired. 'Rico' will always claim to be a great dancer though.

The second leg at Fellows Park on May 18th was a tough and tight affair; we named the same team and fought to a 1-1 draw, with Trevor Christie getting our goal. We were through and would play Bristol City over two legs, home and away; this was before the finals were held at Wembley.

May 25th saw us go to Ashton Gate. Again we named the same team. We were hoping for at least a draw. That would do. We could then bring them back to Fellows Park and go for it there. Bristol City were tense and David Kelly was on fire, pulling their defence all over the place. Unbelievably, we won 3-1, with Kelly scoring twice and Christie claiming the other.

The second leg almost seemed a formality, promotion would most certainly be ours and 13,941 came to be at the party. Richard O'Kelly was injured and we brought back Andy Dornan at right-back and switched Mark Taylor to left-back.

Walsall v Bristol City - Play-Off Final 1988

The team was goalkeeper, Barber; back four, Dornan, Forbes, Hart and Taylor; midfield, Goodwin, Shakespeare, Hawker and Naughton and strikers, Kelly and Christie.

The balance of the side had changed, maybe that was a problem, maybe some nerves, who knows, but City's right-winger, Milne, destroyed us that day. Bristol City claimed a 2-0 victory and then we had to face a penalty shootout to decide where the match was to be played.

I was sitting in the main stand with Kenny and Dr Hamstring. I was trying to be tough and not cry, we had lost the match, promotion had disappeared out the window, there was to be no, as expected, party, and the last thing we needed was to have to play at Ashton Gate in front of their fans and try to win again. The emotional seesaw was swinging again; we had to win the penalty shootout. Fred Barber saved twice, if David Kelly scored, we would play again at Fellows Park. 'Ned' took his run up and smashed it in. The relief was shattering. May 30th would see us go through all that emotion again.

A smaller crowd of 13,007 was in the ground that day, 940 less than the previous match two days earlier. I believe they just could not go through it again and chose home and the radio in preference.

We played the same team. I was in the stand again with Kenny, Rico and Paul 'Sid' Waddington discussing the game before the match. 'Rico' told me that Taylor would move into midfield and Phil Hawker had been given the left-back position and was 'on a mission.' Phil's job was to stop Milne on Bristol's right-flank bombing crosses into our box. 'Sid' had driven David Kelly to the ground that day and told us Dave had said there was no doubt we were going to win and that he was going to do it for the fans.

Hence, we sat awaiting the match with a degree of confidence. The first half that day was one of the best halves of football a Walsall team under pressure has ever played. We were attacking the Laundry End, our preference in the first half of matches; allowing us to attack the Hilary Street End during the second period of games, urged on by the loud support from that end of the ground.

Straight from the kick-off we surged forward in waves of attacks, putting ball after ball into their box. On the rare occasions they got the ball out to Milne on their right-flank, he met a brick wall in the shape of Phil Hawker.

Bristol's defence was battered for eleven minutes in an unbelievable display of passionate attacking football, then, 'Ned' Kelly drifted in and we were 1-0 to the good. Straight from the kick-off we got possession and went after them again, six more minutes of pumping balls into their penalty area and 'Ned' Kelly scored again, 2-0. Again, we got possession from the kick-off and attacked again, this time resulting in a corner. As the ball was swung in, Hawker got in front of his man and scored, 3-0. Well, we were flabbergasted, reeling in the stand, the four of us were up on our feet, yelling and screaming. Bristol were all at sea, there was no way they could come back from that.

Halftime came and went with the ground shaking in expectation. Bristol tried but were done for and, on sixty-four minutes, David Kelly thrashed one in at the Hilary Street end to make it 4-0 and complete his hat trick. The promotion party started after twenty-five long years of waiting. I was with the players on the pitch, unable to control myself, the singing and dancing was immense, we would finally play again in Division Two.

Terry Ramsden had 'come good' with his promise. His unknown manager, Tommy Coakley, would be only the second manager in the history of Walsall Football Club to achieve promotion from the Third to the Second tier of British football. There would never be anymore 'Tommy Who?' in Walsall.

David 'Ned' Kelly had done what he said he would do in the back of 'Sid's car earlier in the day, he had scored a hat trick and done it for Walsall and the fans.

And that's the true story of the Holy Grail.

Chapter 16

Boom And Bust

We were back in Division Two and the first match of the season on August 27th was at Fellows Park versus Plymouth Argyle.

David Kelly had been transferred to West Ham United for 600,000 pounds, then the largest sum ever received by the club for a Walsall player. Everyone was sad to see 'Ned' go, however, he had got us promotion and deserved to go and seek a career at a higher level. Great player. Walsall legend.

Kelly top-scored in our promotion season with 30 goals, Paul Jones 14, Christie 11, Shakespeare 10 and Cross 9, being the other main scorers.

Tommy Coakley had to try and replace 'Ned,' but that was nearly impossible to do. Alex Taylor looked a great player and a fitting replacement in his few games before injury ruined his career, he signed from Hamilton for 100,000 pounds. Howard Pritchard arrived to play on our right wing for just over one season before moving to Maidstone United. Howard had played for Bristol City, Swindon Town and signed from Gillingham.

Keith Bertschin. Centre-Forward.

The signing of Bertch brought a great pal for me, someone I would know all these years and watch many games with. I loved Keith's style of centre-forward play. Totally committed, he pulled centre-halves all over the pitch, ran at them full pelt and was beyond brave when sticking his head anywhere in the penalty box. When a cross came in Bertch knew no other way than to fling himself at it. The strain as he tried to jump an extra inch or two to head it was beyond normal determination.

By the time Keith arrived at Fellows Park, he had scored 8 goals for Ipswich, 29 for Birmingham City, 29 for Norwich, 3 in 14 games for the Jacksonville Tea Men in the U.S.A., 29 for Stoke City and 7 for Sunderland. He had gained 3 Under-21 England caps and was a well-known First Division striker.

Keith was a little 'miffed' as he had scored a hat trick for Sunderland in his last game before they sold him. He told me he couldn't believe they had done it.

Bertschin would play 69 times for Walsall, scoring 15 goals, before departing for Chester City and then playing until he was forty years old in non-league football. I was with him at Peterborough United on January 13 1998 at the match where Walsall were trying to get to play Manchester United in the next round of the F.A. Cup. Keith said sadly, 'I've retired from playing today, just can't take the injuries anymore.' It was obviously a sad moment; Keith had played football all his life and loved every minute. In his non-league career he had played for Aldershot, Solihull Borough, Evesham United, Barry Town, Worcester City, Hednesford Town, Tamworth and, finally, Stafford Rangers. You don't do that without loving the game.

There are many stories about Bertch, the one I truly love is when he went on loan from Norwich City to Jacksonville Tea Men. In the days when he had hair and being a stylish trendsetting centre-forward, he sported the Afro perm, lovely, and was shipped off on a long flight to Jacksonville. Now, Keith is not a fan of flying and so, to assist with his discomfort, he lubricated himself with alcohol. Having had more than sufficient, he slipped off into a deep sleep or passed out and laid his full weight on the left side of the perm.

The plane duly arrived in Jackson and Keith came around a little worse for wear, quickly making for the exit. He was expecting to get through customs to a waiting car and be whisked off to the hotel to complete a jetlagged, alcohol sleep.

Little did he realize that the 'Big Time' English centre-forward would bring out Jackson's media to greet him. Immediately, they surrounded a confused Bertschin, who at the time had no idea who he was playing for, however, he somehow got himself through the interview and on to the hotel. Reaching the room, our Keith turned on the TV and there carefully coming down the plane steps was the centre-forward from England. As the interview started and Keith came into close up, he realized that the heavy sleep had committed one side of the perm into a flat wall, the other side being the usual Afro shape.

It seemed that an alien was now about to play for the Jacksonville Tea Men. The interviewer's face was a picture; his face said 'What on earth have we got here?'

If you ever get to watch a game with Keith, it's an all-action affair. Whenever the ball goes in the box, he's moving, pushing, squirming in his seat, still the same as always, a great player.

The season started well, our first game against Plymouth Argyle ended 2-2 in an entertaining game; Alex Taylor had the perfect debut, scoring twice. We drew the first 4 games and then on September 20th Birmingham City came to Fellows Park. In a period of twenty-nine minutes during the match we scored five times and smashed them 5-0. Forbes, Shakespeare, Alex Taylor, Naughton and Mark Rees came off the bench to score. Mark had the hamstring scraped and it seemed to be working, he would feature in 27 games that season, which was a relief from constant injury.

In our first 12 games, we achieved 2 wins, 8 draws and 2 losses. We were rewarded with a comfortable mid-table position and what was considered a good start to playing football at a higher level.

All seemed well, however, behind the scenes Terry Ramsden was in trouble, his company was over extended and the collapse of the stock market and the repercussions almost destroyed him. As the banks reclaimed the loans, the plane went, the helicopters went, 151 racehorses went and still it was not enough. The fans and I might have felt all was not well, but we did not know the size of the problems. 'Our Tel' was trying to stand good on his promises and was paying wages from his personal money into the club, which could not and would not last.

On the pitch we hit one of our worst ever runs, which would haunt us for the next few seasons. We lost 15 consecutive games, 10 of which we didn't score in and the team were devoid of confidence. Coakley could not regain it and his employer had huge problems. The final straw came with the visit of Chelsea to Fellows Park; we were smashed 7-0 in our own backyard.

The euphoria of only a few months before was over, we were rooted to the bottom of the table. Barrie Blower, our Chairman, made the only move he could to try and balance the club. Out went Tommy Coakley and his Assistant Gerry Sweeney, Ray Train our ex-player and reserve team coach took the reigns while we searched for a new Manager. Shortly afterwards, John Barnwell was appointed.

Barnwell was a good football man, a fine player and an experienced Manager. His appointment was considered a good one. He immediately signed:

Stuart Rimmer. Striker.

Rimmer signed for 150,000 pounds from Notts County, Barnwell's previous club, in an attempt to bring goals to our team. Rimmer had previously played for Everton, Chester City and Watford. He would become a Walsall favourite and eventually a prize asset, playing 106 times and scoring 44 goals. He would stay with the club for two seasons before being sold to Barnsley for 150,000 pounds to ease our money problems. Later playing for Chester City again, Rochdale and Preston North End.

Soon after, Andy Saville arrived from Hull City for 100,000 pounds as we tried to pull out of the relegation zone. Saville did not achieve a goal scoring run at Walsall but scored a good amount of goals for Barnsley, Hartlepool United, Birmingham City, Preston North End, Wigan and Scarborough in a much travelled career.

Barnwell also picked an eighteen-year-old from our youth and reserve team, Dean Smith, and thrust him into the relegation battle, where he kept his place in the side, making 15 appearances at the end of the campaign.

Dean Smith. Centre-Back.

Deano's league career began with a baptism of fire. The team were losing and had no confidence and yet this eighteen-year-old came into the team and played like a seasoned professional. It would be a glimpse of what was to come in Dean's career. After 165 appearances and 2 goals, Walsall, again balancing the books, sold him to Hereford United for 80,000 pounds, then a Hereford transfer record. 117 appearances and 19 goals later, 42,500 pounds took him to Leyton Orient. Smith played 239 games and scored 32 goals before signing for Sheffield Wednesday. 55 games and 1 goal later, he joined his final club Port Vale for 13 games. Dean Smith was a born leader, was appointed Walsall captain at twenty years of age and captained all the sides he played for.

Dean Smith

After finishing at Port Vale, he went straight back to Leyton Orient as Youth team coach and then spent four seasons as assistant manager, before returning to Walsall as Head of Youth, becoming Manager of the club in January 2011. His first managerial position was with Walsall again in dire straights, bottom of Division One and adrift on points.

Deano was a great and intelligent footballer and was one of the group of players I knew well during his Walsall days. We also met up on occasions throughout his playing days at Hereford, Orient and Sheffield Wednesday. On his return to the club, he had a difficult task following the celebrated Mick Halsall, but he took to the task and impressed everyone before being named first team Manager.

No matter how John Barnwell juggled the team and the effort he put in, Walsall were devoid of confidence and could not muster a winning streak, only winning 3 games in the second half of the season. The Holy Grail of a return to the Second Division was obtained and lost in twelve months, we returned to the Third Division with a shattered town, support and players.

During the summer of 1989, I was made Managing Director of Jive Records, a position I would hold for fifteen years and would bring enormous record success over those years. I also became Chairman of my own company, Impulse Promotions, with part-time Walsall supporter, Shaun King, becoming Managing Director. My time in London took on further demands, but I managed to visit Fellows Park regularly. I would drive up on a Saturday morning, visit my Mom for lunch and then go to the game, usually watching with the injured or out of the side players, before spending the night at Mom's and returning to London at some stage on Sunday. Once a Saddler, always a Saddler.

The chaos of relegation and a low confidence team did not stop the people behind Walsall Football Club, mainly Barrie Blower and Jeff Bonser, pushing through the building of a new stadium, situated about half a mile from Fellows Park near the Bescot railway sidings. The new stadium would cost 3 million pounds and have a capacity of 12,000 and was due to be completed for the beginning of the 1990/1991 season. The original plans and timing of the new Stadium was to coincide with our future in the Second Division, that would now not be the case unless we bounced straight back by achieving promotion.

The 1989/1990 season would bring changes, re-shuffles, signings and transfers all season long as we tried to find a formula.

During the summer, we signed Steve Gritt on a free transfer from Charlton Athletic. He had spent most of his career at Charlton and would return there after only 20 games for the Saddlers. John Kelly signed from Swindon Town for 35,000. He would make 39 appearances and score 1 goal before being transferred to Huddersfield. Graham Thorpe signed for 75,000 pounds from Notts County, playing 33 times and scoring 1 goal before moving on to Northampton Town. Peter Skipper signed from Oldham Athletic. Spending two seasons with the Saddlers, he made 99 appearances and scored 3 goals before moving to Wrexham. 'Skip' was probably the most successful in a Walsall shirt of the summer signings. Our own Ron Green would rejoin the club and return to our goalkeeping position.

Craig Shakespeare joined Sheffield Wednesday after 355 appearances and 60 goals, another of our homegrown legends to leave the club. Howard Pritchard would leave for Maidstone, Andy Saville for Barnsley and Paul Jones for Wolverhampton Wanderers.

Towards the end of the season we would try Gary Ford on loan from Port Vale and Gary Shaw, ex-Aston Villa. In his 9 games he would score 3 times before joining Shrewsbury.

We did not start too badly, winning 4 of our first 10 games, drawing 3 and losing 3, but after that we were on a downward slide. In our next 22 games we would only win 1 and that signalled the end of John Barnwell. For the second year in a row we were rooted to the bottom of the table, this time bottom of Division Three. Mark Rees got himself fit again, made the first team, scored in a rare 1-0 win at home to Mansfield and went off injured, not to feature again that season.

Rimmer and Bertschin scored most of the goals during the campaign. Rimmer top scored with 18 goals and Bertschin with 14.

Our youth academy had success with Steve O'Hara making 19 appearances, Adrian Littlejohn 14, Chris Marsh 13, Martin Goldsmith 9 and 3 goals, Dean Smith 8. Of those players, Steve O'Hara would go on to make 122 appearances in our defence, scoring 4 goals, before moving to Hong Kong. Adrian Littlejohn, 53 appearances and 1 goal, before being sold to Sheffield United, then in the Premiership, where he had a great season and a long career that took in Plymouth, Oldham, Bury, Port Vale, Lincoln, Rushden & Diamonds and Mansfield Town.

Paul Taylor took control of the side for the last two months of the season and, although we began scoring again, it was all too late; we were doomed to the second relegation in two years.

The only respite during the campaign had been in the Leyland Daf Trophy. We had played for seven seasons in the competition, originally called the

Associate Members Cup, The Freight Rover Trophy, The Sherpa Van Trophy, The Simod Cup and then The Leyland Daf Trophy. We beat Cardiff City 5-3 at Ninian Park, with goals from Skipper, Bertschin 2, Rimmer and Kelly in the preliminary round and although we lost 1-0 to Shrewsbury next time out that initial win was enough to see us through. We beat Aldershot 4-1 away, with goals from Rimmer 2, Forbes and Kelly in Round One proper. Southend at Fellows Park 4-1 in Round Two, with goals from Rimmer 3 and Bertschin. Before losing 3-2 on penalties after a 0-0 draw at Bristol Rovers in the area semi-final.

The last game at Fellows Park had a carnival feeling; bands and dancers served up the entertainment before the visit of Rotherham United on May 1st 1990. I was there for the game, saddened that we should be leaving Fellows Park. It had been the ground of my boyhood dreams, the pitch on which my heroes had played and the scene of so many 'giant killing' victories. Only two years before we had romped into Division Two with that victory over Bristol City, we were now doomed to Division Four.

The match would finish 1-1 with Andy Dornan scoring his one and only goal for Walsall and the last ever league goal at Fellows Park. A whole host of former players attended to leave the ground they had graced, at the end of the match they stood in the centre circle as everyone sang 'Auld Lang Syne.' I stayed in Walsall for the next few days and did not return to London. I would be playing in the very last match at Fellows Park, the Peter Hart Testimonial game. It was an emotional night, but it didn't really hit me until days after. I was concentrating that much on not making a fool of myself playing with my professional mates. Fortunately, I held my end up playing left-back with a few over-lapping runs as my confidence grew. I was looked after defencively by Roy McDonough, who came to my rescue whenever I was in trouble down our left-flank, fortunately, that was not too often. It was sad to see Peter Hart leave after so many Walsall games, but great to meet up again with some old pals. I left that night not quite realizing that I would never return to Fellows Park, it was gone and soon would become Morrison's Supermarket.

All things in life must move on, for Walsall it was Division Four, the new Bescot Stadium and a huge rebuilding job for our club and team.

Chapter 17

Skint, Hibbitt And The Rebuild

Walsall Football Club was in trouble, we had a brand new stadium to look at, but, as they say in the U.S.A., we were 'All Hat and No Cattle;' in Walsall the saying is more like 'Fur Coat, No Draws.'

The Bescot Stadium was just about finished for the new campaign. The formal official opening ceremony was in a friendly match against Aston Villa, Sir Stanley Matthews cutting the ribbon to open the Stadium. The first home league match was the opening day of the 1990/1991 season. Torquay United were the visitors, Stuart Rimmer would claim the first ever goal at the Bescot and the final score 2-2, included our second goal from youngster Martin Goldsmith.

During the summer, Barrie Blower and the Board had invited Kenny Hibbitt to become our Manager.

The new Bescot Stadium

Kenny Hibbitt. Manager.

Kenny was a well-respected First Division footballer, playing for Bradford Park Avenue, Wolverhampton Wanderers, Coventry City and Bristol Rovers, making 694 appearances. He gained an England Under-23 Cap, won two

League Cups in 1974 and 1980, promotion to the First Division twice with Wolves in 1977 and 1983, played in the UEFA Cup final against Tottenham Hotspur and scored 114 goals from midfield.

Kenny Hibbitt played a massive part in rebuilding Walsall Football Club. We were broke, had a shattered team, a new Stadium and it was probably the toughest managerial position to take at the time. Ken went at it with all the enthusiasm that he had as a player, did not moan, just endlessly wheeled and dealed to build a side. He moulded players from our youth academy with senior professionals at the end of their career and the best of non-league players. Without Kenny's enthusiasm, courage and dedication, I believe Walsall could have lost their League status and plummeted into the Conference.

To save the club's financial state most of the Coakley signings on long and highly paid contracts had to go; the team that had delivered the Holy Grail all left, were sold or were sent out on loan to cover their wages. Peter Hart retired; Graham Forbes, Mark Goodwin, Adrian Thorpe, Mark Taylor, Andy Dornan, Keith Bertschin, Phil Hawker, Fred Barber and Mark Rees were all no more. It was incredibly sad to watch, but it just had to be done. Walsall F.C. was going down like the Titanic.

In came, Chris Hutchings ex-Chelsea, Brighton and Huddersfield and Tony Grealish ex-Orient, Luton, Brighton, West Bromich Albion, Manchester City and Rotherham; both towards the end of their careers but arriving to steady the ship.

Colin Methven arrived from Blackpool and became one of the oldest players ever to make his debut for Walsall. He would not only play 117 times for our club scoring 3 goals, but he had a great teaching effect on our young defenders Dean Smith and Steve O'Hara, holding our defence together for the next three seasons. He would pass the career total of over 700 appearances while at Walsall.

Non-League players joining the club for the season were:

Charlie Ntamark. Midfield.

Charlie was to become a Walsall favourite. After playing for Canon Waounde in Cameroon, he made his way to England playing for Boreham Wood in non-league football, where Kenny Hibbitt found him and signed him for Walsall. Charlie would go on to make 336 appearances for Walsall and score 14 goals, gaining 31 Full International caps with Cameroon along the way. Much loved and a great lad at Walsall F.C..

Rod McDonald. Striker.

Rod had been playing for Colne Dynamoes before signing for Walsall. He was

With Charlie Ntamark

fast, determined, tough and played with immense drive and passion. Rod became a favourite with the fans for his 100% effort in every game, making 178 appearances and scoring 46 goals before joining Partick Thistle.

Kenny Hibbitt also managed to get 25,000 pounds from a strapped for cash board, which he spent on:

Mike Cecere. Striker.

'Cec' would make 131 appearances scoring 35 goals. He had played for Oldham Athletic before a 100,000 pounds move to Huddersfield that had not really worked for him and he subsequently joined Walsall. We would later sell him to Exeter City in another balancing of the books move.

It would be the eighth game of the season before we recorded our first win at home to Scunthorpe United, 3-0. We would then win 6 out of the next 11 games, Stuart Rimmer really hitting form with 13 goals in 27 games. This made him a valuable asset and he would soon move to Barnsley for a much needed 150,000 pounds. The fans were obviously upset, seeing our goal scorer and crowd favourite leave; the club was in more trouble than we knew and needs must. Kenny Hibbitt again got on with the job without his main striker. Willie Naughton came back for a short spell to bolster our left-flank and go someway to appeasing the fans. We had a poor run to the end of the season winning 5 games in 21 attempts. Fortunately, there were worse sides than us in the Division and we finished 16th, we had escaped another relegation almost comfortably and gone someway to steadying the ship.

The players that did the most to steady the ship were goalkeeper, Ron Green; centre-backs, Peter Skipper, Colin Methven and Dean Smith; full-back, Chris Hutchings; midfielder, Charlie Ntamark and striker, Rod McDonald. Our leading goal scorer was the departed Stuart Rimmer with 17 goals.

The attendances at the Stadium were poor, only three times did we achieve over a 5,000 crowd. The team were struggling and the Bescot Stadium was like a house not yet lived in. Smaller crowds meant a poor atmosphere and I remember feeling we were all spread out and sitting in silence as the team performed.

I did like the new stadium. I thought if we could get a winning side then the atmosphere would build and the good times might just roll again, although it seemed as though it might be a long way off.

Your Football team is your Football team and come what may the new season will come again and with it fresh hope.

The summer of 1991 saw another exodus of players from the team. Departing were goalkeeper, Ron Green; centre-back Peter Skipper, Chris Hutchings, Willie Naughton, Adrian Littlejohn, and we witnessed the end of left-back, Kenny Mower, 484 appearances and 20 goals, Kenny had established himself as a Walsall legend, it was sad to see him go.

Kenny Hibbitt worked tirelessly again and brought in former England left-back Derek Statham, defenders Wayne Williams from Northampton, Russell Musker from Torquay United and even spent 15,000 pounds on goalkeeper, Mark Gayle, from non-league Worcester City. Former Liverpool and Coventry midfielder Kevin MacDonald joined to calm our midfield. Our young players were now given more appearances in the side as they developed. Dean Smith, Steve O'Hara and Chris Marsh became regulars and the latest academy player to emerge was striker, Neil Tolson.

The 1991/1992 season got under way. We won 7 of our first 13 games and were positioned inside the top ten in the Division. There was more and more going on off the pitch as the weeks rolled by. The fans were being made aware openly for the first time what a poor state the club was in. The Supporters

Club rallied around donating 100,000 pounds to the Football Club early in the season.

Barrie Blower resigned as Chairman and handed over the reigns to Jeff Bonser. During November, Board member, Mike Lloyd, came out into the press and claimed Walsall Football Club was losing 7 to 8,000 pounds a week and the club must look to other avenues of income to support the team rather than the traditional turnstile income.

Plans were set in motion to turn Besot Stadium into an entertainment complex in the years to come; Sporting Events, Pop Concerts and a Sunday Market were all on the agenda. In a short statement Jeff Bonser said 'At the moment it's a case of balancing the books and we must generate commercial income other than from football, otherwise we shall be in deep trouble.'

The Board went after generating the income to provide the town with a Football Club in the future. In March a planning application for a floodlit all-weather pitch on the car park behind the Gilbert Alsop Stand was submitted. If granted, it was estimated revenue of 50,000 pounds a year would come into the club. It was the shape of things to come. The club was being rebuilt.

On March 26th 1992, Neil Tolson, after only a few first team games, was transferred to First Division Oldham Athletic for 150,000 pounds. 'Tolly' had played 12 games and scored 2 goals but had scored a bundle for the youth and reserve sides. The club also received a grant from the local council of 250,000 pounds. Jeff Bonser said, 'We were in a critical financial position needing a large injection of cash, we got it.'

It's easy to see the problems that were occurring at the Bescot Stadium in those days. The Board must take credit for sticking to the task and preserving League Football in Walsall, it would have been much easier to call it a day and pull the plug.

On the football side, Mark Gayle had trouble stepping into the League from Non-League Worcester City. He soon lost the form that had brought him to Walsall; he would regain it in the second half of the season, but Kenny Hibbitt moved swiftly.

Ronnie Sinclair joined on loan from Bristol City to provide a steady goalkeeper and when he returned to Bristol, in came Alan McKnight, a former West Ham keeper; he would only make 11 appearances before Mark Gayle resumed. In four long months, November, December, January and February, we gained 1 win, a Boxing Day victory over Blackpool, 4-2; Rod McDonald scored 3 and Kevin MacDonald the other.

At the end of February we won 3 out of 5 games and then had another indifferent spell before winning 2 out of the last 4 games. Finally, we finished 15th. Never in trouble of relegation, but never troubling the top of the table. Rod McDonald scored 17 goals, Mike Cecere getting 9.

We had survived another season. We still just had our heads above water and we were still in business. That was the real result of the 1991/1992 season.

During the 1992 summer our big signing was Wayne Clarke from Manchester City, brother of former Walsall players, Allan, Derek and Kelvin. The signing was seen as an end to our scoring woes. The previous two seasons had been hard work in front of goal and it was hoped that Wayne would solve the problem by converting half chances into goals. The team was also more settled and a much younger side. The team was goalkeeper, Gayle; back four, Williams, Smith, O'Hara and Statham; midfield, Ntamark, MacDonald and Marsh and strikers, Clarke, Cecere and McDonald.

Stuart Ryder would make an impact on the side later in the season moving up from our youth and reserve sides. Martin O'Connor would come on loan from Crystal Palace and Colin Methven would come back into the team to calm the defence.

The support started to increase as Walsall began to perform more consistently. The Stadium began to feel a little more like home, a Clarke brother was in our team and we started to feel like the Saddlers again.

After two seasons of not being able to score freely, suddenly we were scoring goals from all over the park; in 46 league matches we would fail to score in only three. In the first 19 games we would win 11 and start to bring back a good feeling around the ground and move us up the table to 4th position at the beginning of 1993. We then had our poor spell and lost 4 and drew 2 of our January games dropping us down to 9th position.

A good sequence of results then occurred until the end of the season, only 3 defeats in 17 matches, with an outstanding run of 5 straight wins at the end of the season. This catapulted us to 7th in the league and the final qualifying position for the playoffs.

It had been our best season for five years, since the promotion campaign in 1988. The side looked like a team, were playing for each other and were in tremendous form going into the playoffs. Our opponents would be Crewe Alexandre, the first match on May 16th would be in Crewe.

Kenny Hibbitt dropped Wayne Clarke to the bench and played a more defencive team for the first leg of the playoff. In this instance it didn't work. Walsall were soon under pressure and would eventually lose the tie 5-1. This was a great shock. We had been in great form and Kenny took a lot of stick for the makeup of the team that day. Had the game gone our way and we had secured a 0-0 or a 1-1, Hibbitt would have been hailed a genius. The second game at Bescot Stadium on May 19th was really a formality, however, 7,398 turned up to see if we could get out of this one. Unfortunately, we couldn't and in being forced to relentlessly attack we ended up losing 4-2, Clarke and O'Connor getting our goals.

The season ended in disappointment but we had started to create a team and had a good go at the Division. Wayne Clarke top scored with 24 goals, Cecere 18, and McDonald 14.

This had also been the first season of the newly shaped English League. The Premiership at the top had been there for a few seasons, this season they made the Second Division now The Championship, The Second Division was now the old Third Division and the Third Division was now the old Fourth Division. Simple but complicated. The upshot meant we were in the Third Division instead of the Fourth, but stayed in the same Division. Well, that's the F.A.

Belief was beginning to come back into the Walsall consciousness. After a playoff season, we all felt, a couple of good signings and we may just have a chance of promotion. The mass comings and goings of the last few seasons seemed to be slowing down, the summer brought bad news in that Wayne Clarke was sold to Shrewsbury and Mike Cecere to Exeter, that sent Kenny Hibbitt, still with no money, trawling the non-league clubs for talented footballers.

Instead of a couple of new faces and off we go, we were now back rebuilding the side, our 42-goal strike force from the previous season gone.

Players coming in:

Wayne Evans. Right-Back.

'Evo' was to prove a great signing from Welshpool and be a consistent performer for six years in our team. Always dependable and solid he would make 228 appearances and score 1 goal. He would move to Rochdale and stay with them for another six years operating in just the same fashion, 259 appearances and 3 goals. 'Evo' later played for Kiddiminster Harriers and finished his career back at Welshpool. Everyone always took the 'micky' out of 'Evo' for his goal scoring prowess, finding the most extraordinary ways to miss when in position. Both the team and the fans wildly celebrated his one goal on March 1st 1998, against Gillingham in a 1-0 win.

Stuart Watkiss. Centre-Back.

Big Stu was signed from Rushall Olympic after being on Wolves' books as a youth. He was fully committed centre-half and a good man to have in the team; solid, dependable and one of the boys. After three seasons Stuart left for Hereford and then Mansfield. I had a good friendship with Stuart and when he got his first managers job at Mansfield Town, who he coached to promotion from the Third Division, I remember

With Stuart Watkiss

getting Britney Spears to sign a photo for him, which they put up in the dressing room for luck. For Walsall he had 78 appearances and 3 goals.

Jimmy Walker. Goalkeeper.

'Super Jim' was on his way to becoming a Walsall legend, much loved by all the Walsall fans. 'Wacka' would play for eleven seasons in our side, winning promotion three times, two 'Player of the Season' Awards and the goalkeeper with the most appearances in our history. In 2004 he left for West Ham United and won promotion to the Premiership, injuring a cruciate ligament in the playoff final with minutes to go. 'Wacka' went on loan to Colchester and on leaving West Ham, joined Tottenham before returning to Walsall on October 29th 2010.

I once took some of the lads on a night out in London. 'Marshy,' 'Wacka' and a few others piled into my car. After the first club, the boys told 'Wacka' to get in the boot of my jeep. I went to close the tailgate and 'Wacka' looked at me and said 'This is the first time you've had a 2 million pound goalkeeper in your boot!'

Kyle Lightbourne. Striker.

Kyle Lightbourne

'Killer' joined Walsall from Scarborough and what a fantastic signing he turned out to be. Spending 4 years at Bescot Stadium, he would be our leading scorer for three consecutive seasons. Tall, a good header of the ball, good control and great pace, Kyle was a huge favourite with the fans. Although a quiet, relaxed man, on the pitch 'Killer' had a real will to win and led our line immaculately. In 1997, Kyle joined Coventry City for 500,000 pounds, also playing at Fulham on loan. His next move, again for 500,000 pounds, was to Stoke City, finally, playing for Macclesfield Town before returning to Bermuda. A Bermudan International he was awarded 26 caps for his country. 'Killer' played 198 games for Walsall, scoring 83 goals.

Dean Peer. Midfield.

Signed from Birmingham City, Dean had one good season with Walsall, but he faded during the second season and was transferred to Northampton Town and he then played for Shrewsbury. He made 56 appearances for Walsall with 8 goals.

John Keister. Midfield.

The one thing about 'Keist' is you never want to mess with him in midfield. If John Keister is marking you, it's not going to be a fun afternoon. Commitment was John's game and we all loved him for it. Arriving at Walsall from Sierra Leone, John would play international football for his country. In nearly seven seasons at Walsall he would make 125 committed appearances, scoring 2 goals, later playing for Chester City, Shrewsbury Town, Stevenage

Borough and Margate, enjoying a long career.

Evran Wright. Striker.

Evran had a long non-league career playing for Halesown, Barry Town and Stafford Rangers. In the 1993/1994 season, Kenny Hibbitt gave him a chance at league level and Evran enjoyed every minute of it, making him a favourite with the Walsall fans. Every time he played or came off the bench he tried everything he knew to score. Playing 35 times, although coming off the bench on numerous occasions, Evran netted 5 goals and we enjoyed every one as much as him.

Jason Lillis. Striker.

Jason was another player Hibbitt gave a chance to and he put in some committed appearances for Walsall that season. Having played a few games at Gillingham and more at Maidstone United, Walsall signed him from Sittingbourne. He would later play for Dover and Cambridge United. For Walsall that season he made 27 appearances and scored 6 goals.

The big signing of the season would arrive in February 1994.

Martyn O'Connor. Midfield.

'Skip' started his career with Bromsgrove Rovers and showed such promise in non-league football that Crystal Palace signed him for 25,000 pounds. He would only make 4 first team appearances for Palace and came on loan to Walsall, his hometown club, during March and April 1993. Finally, he signed permanently in February 1994 for 40,000 pounds, another great signing by Kenny Hibbitt. 'Skip' would become our Captain and midfield General with his fully committed displays, a true Walsall boy. After two seasons he would be transferred to Peterborough United for 350,000 pounds having made such an impression in our side. Walsall fans, including me, were dismayed at the transfer. Had it been to a Premier League or Championship side it would have been a little easier to take, but not Peterborough United. Martyn did not settle at Peterborough. We were good friends and Martyn told me he hated the daily commute to Peterborough for training, having chosen to stay living in Pelsall. It would not be long before another transfer came along, this time 500,000 pounds took him to Birmingham City where he excelled in their midfield, playing in their League Cup final team of 2001, losing on penalties to Liverpool. 'Skip' would play in Blues midfield for six seasons, making 186 league appearances and scoring 6 goals, before rejoining Walsall, at first on loan in 2002 and then resigning for the 2002/2003 season.

When 'Skip' returned to the Bescot I was in the crowd to see his debut. The teams lined up and just as the referee blew for kick-off Martyn rushed through the centre circle at the ball and put in a brutal tackle on the opponent in possession, the ref blew and booked him, all in about 5 seconds. Yes, 'Skip' was back.

In the summer of 2003 he joined Shrewsbury Town and played for them for two seasons, before winding up his playing career at Kiddiminster Harriers. Martyn then managed Hednesford Town and played a great part in the development of our striker, Troy Deeney.

In January 2009, 'Skip' returned to Walsall as Assistant Manager to Chris Hutchings, he was a popular addition to the management team. Although Chris Hutchings was to prove extremely unpopular, the Walsall fans were always respectful of our Skipper and midfield general. When Hutchings was fired, 'Skip' also had to go, which was unfortunate. Some of us hoped he may get a couple of games to have a go as Boss, but that was not to be.

The season also saw another of our youth players making an impression on the first team.

Martin Butler. Striker.

Another great mate of mine over all of these years, 'Butt' had a seriously tough time establishing himself with the Walsall Faithful, for some reason they just didn't take to him and gave the young player some serious 'stick.' Around the club, however, we all knew that Martin would become a great player, his pace and control could only develop and he had the heart to lead the line. 'Butt' would spend three seasons in and out of our team trying to turn the supporters around. In the end, Walsall reluctantly sold him to Cambridge United for 22,500 pounds. Walsall supporters thought we had made a great deal, how wrong they were. Freed from abuse, Martin hit 41 goals in 104 appearances. I was with him and 'Marshy' at The Professional Footballers' Awards at the Grosvenor Hotel in London, that night he was named in the Third Division Team of the Year. Soon afterwards Reading paid 750,000 pounds and he scored 32 goals in 103 games for them, including one at the Millennium Stadium in the playoff final against Walsall. I remember going to that match and knowing before kick-off, we would have to score two, because 'Butt' would definitely get one.

Rotherham for 150,000 pounds was his next move, scoring 28 in 97 games, before returning to Walsall as a proven goal scorer and now fans' favourite. I was at the club when Martin came back; he walked through the door, looked at me and said 'You can't still be here.' After two seasons he would leave to play for Grimsby Town and then Burton Albion. Now living in Worcester, he joined them to wind down his playing career. Good player, good mate.

After the previous season's 7th position and Kenny Hibbitt's wheeling and dealing we hoped for a continuous rise up the table and possible promotion. The club was finally stabilizing and the support would grow again for a third season running, if only slightly. We were becoming used to Bescot being our home, the memories of Fellows Park were hazing in the isles of Morrison's.

The team that developed in the first half of the season was goalkeeper, Gayle; back five, Evans, Watkiss, Ryder, Smith and Marsh; midfield, Ntamack, Keister and Peer and strikers, Lightbourne and McDonald.

'Evo' and 'Marshy' pushed on from the full-back positions and our centre-backs were solid; Stewart Watkiss, Stuart Ryder and Dean Smith were all magnificent. Our overall problem would again be scoring goals; from the free scoring side of the previous season we were a shadow of that attacking force. 13 out of 46 games we failed to score and a further 17 saw us only register 1 goal. The defence had to be good if you are only going to score that many goals. We did hit a couple of teams, Lincoln City at home 5-2 on November 20th, goals from Dean Peer 3 and Lightbourne 2, also a 4-2 beating of Wycombe Wanderers at home on New Years Day, goals from McDonald, Marsh, Lightbourne and Lillis. That win lifted us to 3rd in the table. It followed our best run that season between October 9th 1993 and January 1st 1994, where we played 12 games, won 8, drew 1 and lost 3.

The following 12 games we only won 2, drew 3 and lost 7, dropping us back down the division. After Martyn O'Connor's arrival, the team began to rally again and we finally finished 10th in the Division. Not the season we had hoped for, but we now had some players we had faith in; defencively sound, the midfield, with Charlie Ntamack and Martyn O'Connor, had skill and 'Killer' Lightbourne was getting better and better.

The scorers that season were Lightbourne 9, McDonald 8 and Peer 8.

It had taken Kenny Hibbitt a long time, a succession of incoming players and youth members to establish themselves, but it finally seemed we had a great basis for a team that just might do something. They definitely enjoyed being in the team and playing as a unit. The opportunity given to a whole host of players, who might just have thought a professional career could be passing them by, galvanized themselves into a group that played for each other. They were becoming heroes to the population of Walsall again, after what had been six long years.

The Faithful behind the goal at Bescot were beginning to find their voice. 'Sing you're heart out for the boys' and 'Walking down the Wednesbury Road, to see the Walsall Aces' were beginning to reappear.

There was even more hope for the 1994/1995 season. Could they? Would they just manage to have a real go for promotion?

Chapter 18

1-0 The Best Result In Football

Kenny Hibbitt was once again in the transfer market. Dean Smith was sold to Hereford United for 80,000 pounds and again we could not believe that a club the size of Hereford would be able to buy one of our best defenders. It was a record fee for Hereford to pay and one that we could probably not turn down; it was, however, disappointing. Hibbitt made two great signings with the money that would go towards making our team into something special.

Kevin Wilson. Striker.

Wilson would become a key player in our line-up. Having started with Banbury United he was transferred to Derby County for 20,000 pounds, scoring 41 goals for the Rams. He then moved to Ipswich Town for 100,000 pounds and hit 49 goals. Chelsea took him to Stamford Bridge for 335,000 pounds and he played 191 games with 55 goals before heading for Notts County and then signing for Walsall. He was capped 42 times for Northern Ireland and was without doubt a clever and purposeful footballer. He would spend three seasons at Walsall making 152 appearances and scoring 50 goals, his partnership with Kyle Lightbourne was exceptional.

Trevor Wood. Goalkeeper.

'Woody' had a superb first season with Walsall, displacing a young Jimmy Walker; he would remain first choice during the 1994/1995 season. 'Wacka' would then reclaim the jersey the next season, lose it to Trevor again and then finally reclaim it for good. This caused 'Woody' to move to Hereford United, but the Walsall fans will always remember him as a good and solid keeper during the campaign.

Jimmy Walker

Charlie Palmer. Centre-Back.

Charlie was a solid centre-back brought in to replace Dean Smith. Charlie had played for Watford, Derby County, Hull City and Notts County. In a season and a half Charlie made 64 appearances for Walsall.

The season did not start too well, winning only 1 of our first 4 games. After the Carlise match at Bescot on August 30th, which was our first defeat in those 4 games, Kenny Hibbitt was sacked. It came as a surprise, 1 win, 2 draws and then the first loss, it seemed a little harsh, especially as Kenny had worked so long and so hard with no money to spend and his best players were always sold to keep the club afloat. Maybe it was just time after four seasons in charge, maybe the Board had decided they wanted a promotion season. Who knows? And we never will. Hibbitt would go on to manage Cardiff City and I would get to know him well as the years passed by at the Footballers' Golf Tournaments. A good guy, Kenny Hibbitt, he did well during a tough time for Walsall Football Club.

Soon afterwards, two more new signings came to Walsall which coincided with the arrival of our new Manager.

Scott Houghton. Left-Winger.

Scotty would have 2 great seasons at Walsall. He started his career at Tottenham Hotspur and burst into their team as a teenager, but he failed to establish himself. He joined Luton Town and from there signed for Walsall for 20,000 pounds. He would leave for 60,000 pounds shortly after Martyn O'Connor to join Peterborough United as well. Later playing for Southend United, Leyton Orient and Halifax Town. For Walsall he had 93 appearances and scored 18 goals.

Colin Gibson. Left-Back.

Colin signed from Leicester City, but was most famous for his time at Aston Villa, winning the Football League First Division title and European Cup before playing for Manchester United for five seasons. 'Gibbo' played just one season for Walsall before retiring, making 40 appearances and scoring 1 goal.

Chris Nichol. Manager.

I guess its no secret that Chris Nichol is my favourite Walsall Manager, he represents everything I believe a Manager should be. He was an outstanding defender for Halifax Town, Luton Town, Aston Villa, Southampton and Grimsby Town. Playing at the very top, winning two League Cups with Villa and losing one with Southampton. Winning promotion with both Villa and the Saints and constantly playing in the First Division. Then, after a spell in charge at Grimsby, bouncing straight back into the Premier League as Manager of Southampton, leading them to their highest ever position of 2nd and steering them into the UEFA Cup.

Chris Nichol

Chris's mantra: '1-0 is the best result in Football,' you don't concede, important for a defender, it would mean you always get a point and you are always in the game. One goal and you are off home with the 3 points. Simple, but difficult. Nichol's management of players is fantastic; treated as men and asked to do their job, he was always prepared to stay behind and coach the youth players he saw potential in. He also has a temper; essential, I believe. I've never witnessed the dressing room in one of these moments, however, I'm told it rivals Alex Ferguson's 'hairdryer' and can blister the paint on the dressing room walls. Obviously, one or two of the lads didn't get the point on those days it occurred.

I got to know Chris better as the years went on, mainly through golf, of which he is a great player and he is also exceptional at tennis; a sporting all-rounder.

Chris Nichol came in and brought with him a passion and organization that had been lacking. Everyone had specific jobs to do and the lads did them. The team mainly featured throughout the season was goalkeeper, Wood; back four, Evans, Ryder, Palmer and Gibson; midfield, Marsh, Ntamark, O'Connor and Houghton and strikers, Lightbourne and Wilson.

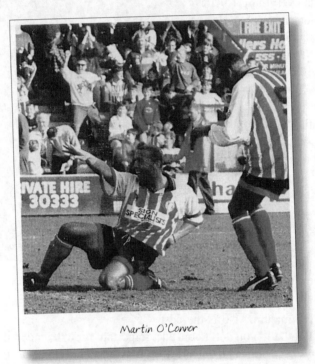

Martin O'Connor

In a great run up to January 1st under Chris Nichol we played 14 games, winning 10, drawing 3 and losing 1. We were 2nd in the table and the team had clicked. The arrival of Wilson had freed Lightbourne and the service from O'Conner, Ntamark, Marsh and Houghton brought goals from all over the park. We smashed Fulham 5-1 on September 17th, Marsh 2 and Lightbourne 3 goals. We hit Scarborough 4-1 on October 8th, O'Connor 2 penalties, Ryder and Houghton. We won 4 matches in December, Hereford beaten 4-3, scorers Houghton, Lightbourne 2 and Ryder. In the next game, Barnet, 4-0, Palmer, Wilson and Lightbourne 2. A day later, Rochdale, 2-0, with Wilson and Lightbourne and four days later, Doncaster Rovers, 1-0, with Marsh scoring.

'Going UP, Going UP, Going UP,' came the cry from behind the goal at the Gilbert Alsop End.

We hardly played in January due to the weather, but resumed in February with 11 wins, 4 draws and 3 defeats in 18 games. Carlisle were the leaders and we were in 2nd place going into the last game, an away match at Bury. We needed 1 point for promotion and a return to Division Two. Jimmy Walker came back in goal for the game, one of only three appearances that season. Nevertheless, you can rely on 'Wacka.' 3,000 Walsall supporters made their way to Bury that day to see the boys home. We got what we went for, a 0-0 draw, and Walsall were promoted back to Division Two and at Chris Nichol's first attempt.

The town and the players started to party, it was a real relief to leave that division behind. The club was on its way again after years of struggle. I don't think we believed we could run through Division Two, but if we could stabilise the club in that Division who knows what might occur in the next couple of years.

Martin Butler

We had a couple of small Cup runs that year. In the Coca-Cola League Cup we beat Plymouth Argyle over two legs and drew West Ham United. On September 20th, the Bescot Stadium would see the first of its 'giant killing' acts; we beat them 2-1, with Watkiss and an own goal from Potts, scoring for us. Unfortunately, we lost the second leg 2-0 at Upton Park and couldn't quite claim their scalp, although we were close.

In the F.A. Cup we beat Rochdale 3-0 at Bescot in Round One, Lightbourne and Butler 2, drew away 1-1 with Preston North End, a goal from Wilson, before beating them 4-0 in the replay at Bescot, Houghton, Wilson and Lightbourne 2. The Third Round came and we thought that might just bring a huge 'giant killing' to Bescot, the visit of Leeds United on December 4th. 8,619 turned up, as did the 'Match of the Day' cameras. Maybe, just maybe.

Our usual team lined up and went after Leeds United. With our backs to the Gilbert Alsop Stand we attacked the end where the Leeds supporters were, always loud and passionate in their support. It was an end-to-end game and Leeds gave as good as they got, but after half an hour, the cameras and our supporters got what they came for. A ball across the six-yard box and there was 'Marshy,' one touch and smashed it in the near post. The Walsall supporters went ballistic; it would be one of the major moments in 'Marshy's' career and at first he seemed a little stunned, before the boys jumped on him in celebration. Leeds built momentum during the second half, but Trevor Wood was in great form,

Chris Marsh
scores against Leeds

we kept them out for most of the second period and just when we thought we had them, they equalized and forced a replay.

'Marshy' came out with his classic during an interview at the end of the match, 'Cometh the hour, cometh the man.'

December 14th 1994 saw us at Elland Road. I was listening to the radio in London, where I was getting fifteen-minute reports from the match and whenever there was a goal. We did well that night and were on top before a floodlight failure came and allowed Leeds to regroup, they got ahead and we chased the match, finally losing 5-2, Wilson and O'Connor getting our goals.

It had been a great season in the league and we had done well in the Cups, enjoying our games against both West Ham United and Leeds United. Our goal scorers had hit form, Lightbourne with 27 goals, Wilson 22 goals, O'Connor 12 goals, Marsh 11 goals and Houghton 9 goals.

Chris celebrates after scoring against Leeds

Chris Marsh scoring against Leeds

About to Tee off with Chris Nicol in The Footballers Classic Spain

Chapter 19

Stability

As the 1995/1996 season approached our long exile in the Third Division was over. The Kenny Hibbitt years of making teams from the lower leagues and a host of youth players and senior professionals had, in a way, come to an end. The Second Division allowed us to obtain better players, as they were probably only dropping down one division rather than two. Our youth system would still be a key factor but now we did not trawl the Conference and below for players, they would rarely be able to make the leap instantly to Division Two.

Chris Nichol did not lose players in the summer, even promotion had not caused bigger teams to come in for our best players and so the basis of the team stayed together. Chris brought in players to strengthen the defence, expecting a rougher ride in the higher division. Two of his signings proved to be magnificent and would become the mainstay of our defence for the next three seasons.

Adrian Viveash. Centre-Back.

Adie was a success from the moment he joined the club. Having started at Swindon Town and coming through the ranks, he made 64 appearances for them and had experience from loan spells at Reading and Barnsley, joining Walsall on a free transfer. Nichol knew a good centre-half when he saw one; he worked and developed Adie into an excellent player. He would play for five seasons in our defence and become a crowd favourite making 202 appearances and scoring 13 goals. I spent a lot of time

Adrian Viveash

with Adie after matches in the players' bar and he always made great comments and analysis of the game. I was not surprised when retiring from playing he later became youth team coach at Chelsea.

Derek Mountfield. Centre-Back.

Derek had played at the highest level and won the First Division Championship twice with Everton in 1985 and 1987, the F.A. Cup in 1984 and the EUFA Cup in 1985. He had also played for Tranmere Rovers, Aston Villa, Wolverhampton Wanderers, Carlisle United and Northampton Town. Nichol signed him to play alongside Adrian Viveash and together they became the heart of our defence. Derek would play in 119 games and score 2 goals for Walsall. He was another of the Walsall players and managers who would later feature in the Footballer's Classic Golf in Spain and Dubai.

Darren Bradley. Midfield.

Darren had played for Aston Villa before having an amazing career with West Bromwich Albion, Captaining their team and making 254 appearances before signing for Walsall. Darren would play for us for two seasons, making 85 appearances and scoring 3 goals. He was a quality midfield player with great control and delivery. Darren had several injury problems but still managed to play in our midfield when his knees had seen better days.

Ray Daniel. Left-Back.

Ray had a good career with Luton, Hull City, Cardiff and Portsmouth. Chris Nichol signed him on a free transfer from Portsmouth and he fitted straight into the team at left-back. Ray stayed with us for one season making 43 appearances; a solid, comfortable and experienced full-back.

My opinion was that if we could stabilize in Division Two that would be a reasonable season. I was not expecting us to run through the Division and get promoted again. Chris Nichol would have had other ideas and would have wanted a minimum push for the playoffs.

The season did not start well, goal scoring was more difficult at this level and it took almost half the season for the team to settle and for Lightbourne to find his scoring touch. By the middle of November we were hovering above the relegation zone. Nichol produced the 'hairdryer' and vocal paint blistering of the dressing room and we started on a run of 5 wins and 3 draws in 8 games and suddenly the playoffs were in view. We stumbled again and only won 1 of our next 7 games with 5 defeats, leaving us again just above the relegation places. The team gathered themselves again and in the last 14 games we won 9, drew 2 and lost only 3. Kyle Lightbourne suddenly found the form in front of goal that was missing and was scoring regularly, during one spell hitting 6 goals in 6 games. We would finally finish in 11th position and only four points off the playoffs; it had been a seesaw season but it had its moments to remember.

When you live in London and support the Saddlers a home game is a 250-mile round trip. Now, I've been making that journey all my life, either living in Walsall and driving to London or the other way round. Saturday games were usually not a problem unless I was travelling from out of the country or had a concert with any of our artists. Tuesday games were a little more difficult and that always depended on whether I could get away early enough to make the match and then would get back to London late into the night. Sometimes you just have to make a 'call.' One that I will always regret happened during this season. I'd been to the December 9th game at Bescot when we beat York City 2-0, with goals from Mountfield and 'Marshy,' which pleased me greatly. Our next home match was on Tuesday 12th against Torquay United in the replay of the Second Round F.A. Cup tie. I couldn't get away in time to make the journey and so I had to settle for missing the match; also, having just made the trip three days earlier, it would have been a tough call. So, I finished work and met up with a few mates to pass the evening, ending up at a pal of mine's flat. I asked him to turn on the radio in the background so I could get an occasional bulletin from the game and find out how the boys were doing. We heard the halftime score was 1-1, 'Marshy' having scored our goal. The next report said Torquay had taken the lead and the boys I was with started 'taking the piss.' We equalized through Kevin Wilson and then Torquay scored again and the banter rose some more; there was twenty-five minutes to go at the time. Six minutes later, Darren Bradley scored to make it 3-3 and we heard nothing more. We were searching around the radio dial, as there was now a few quid being put on the table regarding who was going to win. The bulletin came in saying the match had gone to extra time. A few more quid went down and this could have turned out to be an expensive night for yours truly.

Three minutes into extra time and 'cometh the hour, cometh the man' 'Marshy' scored, 4-3. Well, I'm now dancing in a front room in Highgate much to the disgust of my three mates. Two minutes later the radio sparks up and you know what my mates are hoping for. Unlucky, 'Killer' Lightbourne makes it 5-3. The radio states 'and we are back to the Bescot Stadium again,' my mates gather round hoping for a Torquay revival. Unlucky again, Martyn O'Connor scores for Walsall, 6-3. The boys are now a little dismayed, but the money has not been pushed towards me, back the radio goes to Bescot and Torquay make it 6-4. A glint of hope is now in their eyes. Four minutes later they go back to Bescot again and all of us are up round the radio, Scott Houghton makes it 7-4 to Walsall. Amazingly, five goals went in during that fifteen-minute period, the game was won, but Kyle Lightbourne did finish it off just before fulltime by adding another, 8-4 being the final score. Now, I came out of the evening a few quid richer, but I would have traded that money and more to have been there to see it. One that got away from me, not that many have, but the night we hit 8 did.

Our Youth Academy was still working well and producing the next batch of players that would go on to have long careers. Three made the first team that year, one during the season and two right at the end. I've always enjoyed watching the development of our own players, it brings great joy. In November 1995, up from the reserve team and making his debut was Ian Roper.

Ian Roper. Centre-Back.

The development of Ian Roper and his subsequent career had a lot to do with Chris Nichol. Chris used to stay behind after training with 'Ropes' and give him extra coaching in the art of defending. Ian Roper was deceptively quick; he looked like he was not moving that fast but his legs just ate up the ground. When he became established in the side, the fans used to sing, 'You'll never beat Ian Roper' and very few ever did. 'Ropes' saw danger before anyone else and just cleared it, his tackling was fierce and his heading ability was first class. 'Wacka' once told me he couldn't leave Walsall unless 'Ropes' went too, he always wanted 'Ropes' in front of

Ian Roper

him. You never really wanted 'Ropes' starting the attack from the back, that would always be someone else's job; passing along the back four was not his skill, but in clearing his lines and defending he was the best. I once sat at Luton with the former England player, Ricky Hill, watching Luton versus Walsall. Ricky said 'Got any good defenders?' I said 'Yeah, the best defender, not the greatest footballer, but the greatest defender!' I then told him about 'Ropes.' Ricky watched for the first half and said 'You're right, he just sniffs out trouble and clears it. I'd sign him any day.' 'Ropes' would become a Walsall legend, making 325 appearances and scoring 7 goals before leaving for Luton Town, maybe Ricky remembered. Later, joining Kettering Town, I watched the match on TV between Kettering Town and Leeds United in the F.A. Cup and was delighted when 'Ropes' came up for the corner and powered in Kettering's goal in their 1-0 win. 'Ropes' was the hero and as always looked uncomfortable in the interview afterwards, a man of few words. During Ray Graydon's reign in charge, Ray couldn't come to terms with 'Ropes.' In the off-season Ian always took a full rest and didn't really train that much, hence, it was normally September before he was fit enough to start the campaign. When he did start, however, he was magnificent. Ray called in 'Ropes'' wife and said that she must start steaming the vegetables and boiling the potatoes, eating salad and keeping the weight at the right level. He is a professional footballer you know. 'Ropesy's' wife said 'Our Ian likes fish and chips, burger and chips and a good roast on Sunday with all the trimmings and if that's what he wants, that's what he's getting.'

Sir Ray's heart must have sunk at that one.

Clive Platt. Striker.

I am and always have been a Clive Platt fan. He is a classic centre-forward, good in the air, strong, fearless, good with his back to the opposition's goal, holds the ball up and scores. When I first saw him play for our reserve side I thought he just had that something that would develop into an accomplished professional.

Personally, I think we sold him too soon and we should have kept him at Walsall. I believe he would have become a great player for us rather than everyone else.

Bill Jones our Youth Development Officer at Walsall, and someone I've watched a couple of hundred Walsall matches with, told me he found Clive

Platt as a fourteen-year-old playing centre-forward against grown men. Now that is a tough young man; you are always going to get some treatment with your back to the opposition's goal, yet there was Platty giving as good as he got. Bill said, 'I love Platty, great player.'

Platty made his debut this season coming off the bench four times and scoring twice. He would stay with Walsall in and around the first team for four seasons before going out on loan to Rochdale. Platty was loved at Rochdale and a hero to the fans in a short period of time. Rochdale offered Walsall 100,000 pounds for him and considering he was not a first team regular, we sold him. That fee was four times Rochdale's biggest outlay on a player. He made 169 appearances and scored 30 league goals for Rochdale before joining Notts County, only staying a short while, 19 games and 3 goals. Peterborough United was next, 37 appearances and 6 goals before joining MK Dons. Platty wanted to go to MK Dons, 'Marshy' phoned and asked me to tell Pete Winkleman, their Chairman and an old friend of mine, that he wanted to join them. I did, and shortly afterwards Clive Platt was an MK Dons player. I wouldn't suggest my involvement had anything to do with the deal. A year later, I was in Spain at the Footballers' Classic Golf Tournament and sitting with Danny Wilson, MK's Manager and the man that signed Platty. I told him I knew Clive and he said to me that the signing of Clive Platt was the sole reason for MK Dons not being relegated that season. He led the line and inspired the team to escape relegation. Unfortunately, he couldn't do the same the following season and they went down. Danny did tell me about MK Dons playing in a match where the opposing centre-half had it in for Platty and kept elbowing him and trying to wind him up. Platty told him, not now, but I'll see you in the tunnel after the match. Sure enough, the centre-half was waiting just inside the tunnel, Platty walked into the tunnel and smashed him, breaking the guy's jaw and his own fingers at the same time. Both went to hospital and were in the room next to each other getting fixed up. We did have a laugh about that one. The moral of the story: don't wind Platty up!

The following season Clive scored 18 goals and that earned him a 300,000 pounds move to Colchester. One of my friends in the music business comes from Colchester and is a dedicated supporter and he told me they loved Platty down there. He made 124 appearances and scored 25 goals before being transferred to Coventry City, where again he was a crowd favourite. If I was Walsall Manager, anytime he wanted to come back I'd take him, what he does for a football team is exceptional, committed, passionate; a proper centre-forward.

As uncomplicated as Clive Platt is, his strike partner in our reserve side was the opposite.

Michael Ricketts. Striker.

On May 4th 1996, at Bescot versus Brighton & Hove Albion, Michael Ricketts burst into Saddlers consciousness. He came off the bench in the second half, picked up the ball after two minutes and smashed it in. Michael had everything: great physique, good control, pace, good in the air and could always do the unexpected; that made him into a class act. It seemed as though the higher the level of football Michael played the better he became. I like Michael as a person, a lot, but he is frustrating on the pitch. Everyone can see the enormous ability he possesses, however, with his complications, you just never know when he will be brilliant or if the match will just pass him by. After 76 games and 14 goals for Walsall he signed for Bolton for 500,000 pounds. His 37 goals for Bolton brought promotion to the Premiership and he made the leap in class look easy. In 2002 he made his one and only appearance for the full England team. Things started to go wrong after that. 3 million pounds took him to Middlesborough, then Leeds United, before he began to become a nomad. Playing for Stoke, Cardiff, Burnley, Southend, Preston, Oldham and, finally, returning to Walsall. In his second spell for the Saddlers, where he was once again loved, he scored 12 times in 40 games and we were all hoping that he would return to the great striker he had promised to be. Sadly, he moved on again and joined Tranmere Rovers. Some of the lads told me that with Michael you could always tell when he got on the coach what was going to happen in the coming match. If he got on with the headphones on and didn't really talk to anyone, he was not going to have a good game, if he got on all chatty and laughing, the boys knew he'd be great that day and we were in with a good chance of him scoring. I believe Michael can play well whenever he wants to, but sometimes it just gets complicated. I always enjoyed watching him play and was always happy when he was at Walsall. You just never knew when he was going to be brilliant - tough for a Manager.

The more you know about Football the more you know of tragic stories. Yes, there is the glory and the memories, but alongside that, some terrible unfortunate tales. This season saw one of those moments occur, which you wished had not, the case of Stuart Ryder.

Stuart Ryder. Centre-Back.

Stuart took the same route as many before him, joining Walsall as a youth and progressing through the youth and reserve teams before making his debut for the senior side. He would make 124 appearances for Walsall and score 5 goals. He was a member of our promotion side in 1994/1995, a great reader of the game, his positional sense was immaculate and as a centre-back he could bring the ball out of defence with aplomb. He would have been the most brilliant centre-back in our promotion year such was his class. He earned an Under-21 England cap whilst playing in the Third Division to add to his England Youth caps. After recovering from injury, Stuart played a reserve match to regain match fitness against Carlisle United's reserves. Steve Hayward, born in Walsall, hit Stuart with a horrific tackle and broke his leg, which brought more injury complications. Even though Stuart, after over a year, regained a level of fitness he was never the same player and eventually left the club. Stuart was well liked by the lads and whenever Hayward was in an opposing team, the boys dished out some serious stick and deservedly so. Years later, when Hayward came to the Bescot to play for Fulham, he still got stick from the crowd and the players.

At the end of the 1995/1996 season with our grand finish, hopes were high for 1996/1997. Our season of stability had occurred and we all, including Chris Nichol, were positive about the coming campaign.

It was, therefore, unfortunate that two of the most influential players would leave the club; both Martin O'Connor and Scott Houghton left for Peterborough. The offers were too good to resist I suppose, 350,000 pounds for Martyn and 60,000 pounds for Scott, and it did disrupt our start to the season.

Walsall as a Football Club relies on the money it makes from finding youth players or professionals from other clubs and bringing them on, without those sales the wage bills for the season would be hard to find. The philosophy, although correct in business terms, is sometimes hard to take; the supporters don't like it as the player is normally a crowd favourite. The manager doesn't like it as he has worked hard to blend a team together, seems to be getting somewhere and then has to start all over again. Walsall players, however, are not usually so concerned about it all, they know players will leave and are pleased that one of their mates and fellow professionals have got the chance of more money and most times a better club and higher division. In fact, they hope one day it just might be them. That's all part and parcel of supporting a lower league club; it makes the highs, higher and the lows, lower. You have got to be mentally tough to support Walsall Football Club.

After 4 games of the season we were bottom of the league with only 1 win. Chris Nichol began rebuilding the team.

Mark Blake. Midfield.

Blakey was a neat midfield footballer signed to replace Martyn O'Connor. He did not have the drive and passion of O'Connor but he was a good player. He started at Aston Villa before a 400,000 pounds move to Portsmouth, he never settled on the South Coast and soon signed for Leicester City for 360,000 pounds before joining Walsall. He played in 70 games for Walsall, scoring 5 times, before moving on to Mansfield Town and Kiddiminster Harriers.

John Hodge. Winger.

'Hodgey' was a great lad; always fun to be with and he became a favourite at Walsall. After playing for Exeter City, he signed for Walsall from Swansea City, making 96 appearances and scoring 14 goals before he moved to Gillingham and then Northampton.

Andy Watson. Striker.

Andy was a quiet lad, a great athlete, and he would score some important goals for Walsall. He developed a great curving run that enabled him to escape the offside trap, which, when he timed it well, set him free on goal. Clubs always paid transfer fees for Andy. After starting at Halifax Town, Swansea City paid 40,000 pounds for his services, after a short stay, he joined Carlisle United for 30,000 pounds, before transferring to Blackpool for 55,000 pounds. Walsall paid 60,000 pounds and he made 96 appearances, scoring 24 goals, before joining Doncaster Rovers.

After these new signings the team began to play better and we edged our way out of the relegation zone, but by the start of November we were back in the bottom four. Out came the Nichol 'hairdryer' and we won 2, drew 2 and lost 1 in the next 5 games.

On Boxing Day that year we played away at Wycombe Wanderers. My girlfriend at the time did not understand my infatuation with the Saddlers. I had been saying since the beginning of December, I'm willing to be wherever you want to be over the Christmas period, but I am going to Wycombe on Boxing Day to watch Walsall play. I thought I had made an agreement and all would be fine, but Boxing Day arrived and an almighty bust-up occurred because I was leaving her family to watch a football team. Well, come what may I was going, 'Marshy' got me a ticket and I made it to Wycombe. It was freezing cold, grey, damp and just plain horrible. I had arrived in a state and stood on the terraces just praying that we would win; to return home and have lost would have made the whole Christmas a disaster. I have to thank Mark Blake for cracking one in that put us 1-0 to the good and raised my spirits. Maybe, just maybe, it might turn out all right. 'Killer' Lightbourne added a second and we ran out 2-0 winners. That victory remains in my memory. The victory would also signal a rise up the Second Division table. We won 8 out of the next 10 matches and all of a sudden the playoffs were in view. Then again, maybe they weren't. From the last 13 games we only managed 15 points and had to settle for 12th position; safe, but no real forward movement during the season.

November and December provided some memories of that season. First the home match against Peterborough United on November 9th 1996, probably our best performance of the season. Walsall were two places off the bottom of the table and on a losing streak, Peterborough came to town, with Martin O'Connor and Scott Houghton in their team the Saddlers fans were still disgruntled about their transfers and were very much up for loud vocal support in an attempt to turn them over. We all knew what dangerous players Martyn and Scott could be so only the best would do from our lads.

After twenty-three minutes, 'Killer' Lightbourne opened the scoring from a pass from Wilson. Just before halftime, Mark Blake was fouled in the box and Kevin Wilson converted the penalty, his 200th professional goal. Halftime was a pleasure, the Saddlers were on top and we were ready to sing them home. After seventy minutes an on loan Louie Donowa, with incredible pace, raced onto Lightbourne's pass and made it 3-0. This caused the fans to start chanting for Donowa to be signed on a permanent basis, it never occurred. A minute later, a now frustrated Martyn O'Connor launched into a clumsy tackle and got sent off. The crowd, now enjoying the moment, chanted 'You should have stayed a Saddler.' Peterborough, now down to ten men, O'Connor off and Houghton substituted, were done, and Lightbourne netted with three minutes to go to make the final score 4-0.

The F.A. Cup came around and we had a 2-2 draw at Northwich Victoria in the First Round. The replay was scheduled for November 26th 1996 at Bescot.

About four months earlier, Jive Records was now becoming a major force in the record business. I also made a label deal with my old mate, Pete Waterman. We had been mates but hadn't worked together for five years since all of those hits in the eighties. As the deal had developed and we were working on records, Pete had asked 'where do you keep going to on Tuesdays and Saturdays?'

'The home of the Saddlers, Bescot Stadium' came the reply. I told Pete he should come, that most of the players were mates of mine and it really took my mind off records and getting hits. When I was watching Walsall I was mentally free from it all. I was only thinking about my mates winning and Walsall F.C. doing well.

Pete got in touch and said some of his friends were Directors of Northwich Victoria, so he would like to come and watch the match. I said 'No problem, but they are going to lose.'

Pete came to that first match against Northwich Victoria and they did lose, 3-1, Lightbourne 2 and a Wilson penalty accounting for them. Pete had a good night and I introduced him to the players after the game. After that he became a Walsall supporter and would go to games with me for the next nine seasons.

Pete was born in Coventry and grew up a Coventry City supporter. In fact, I went with him to Wembley in 1987 for the Coventry City versus Tottenham F.A. Cup Final, which was a great match, Coventry winning a thriller, 3-2. For Pete, that was one of his finest days, seeing his boyhood team win the F.A. Cup.

Since he converted to being a Saddler in 1996, I've been to watch Walsall play at Coventry with him and trust me he is a Saddler. I think he still watches for Coventry results, but he is not embraced in his hometown the way he is in Walsall.

The next round we drew Burnley at home and drew 1-1. We went to Burnley on December 17th in the replay and the team were really on that night. We went 1-0 up, Lightbourne scoring again and Burnley could not cope with us. At halftime, with their team never getting a kick, somehow, the floodlights failed and the match was abandoned. Some of the team told me something wasn't right; they thought Burnley, needing a big tie in the Third Round, just pulled the plug to get the match abandoned. Might be true, might not, but the team were really upset about the whole affair. When the match was rescheduled, we drew 1-1 and then lost 4-2 on penalties.

You see it's always interesting supporting a team in the lower leagues. There is as much passion in those divisions as in the ones above and when you do hit the big time you are most definitely part of the whole thing and it will remain in your memory forever.

Our youth system again featured during 1996/1997. Making their debuts were two midfield players:

Wayne Thomas. Midfield.

Wayne spent four years at Walsall, coming through the youth and reserve teams before making his debut in this season. He was a quality midfield player that always looked as though he had time on the ball. I was always impressed with him and the way he moved from the reserves to the first team and didn't look out of place. He would make 40 appearances for Walsall, scoring 5 goals, before moving on to Shrewsbury and Kiddiminster Harriers.

Dean Keates. Midfield.

'Deano,' a Walsall fan who had stood on the terraces at the Bescot Stadium, made his debut on October 12th 1996 coming on as a second half substitute and playing on our left wing. Soon after he came on, he took off chasing a long ball down the left, which he had no right to get and he got it. That was many fans' first introduction to Dean Keates. They would go on to be huge fans and 'Keatsie' would become a Walsall legend. Jeff Bonser once told me 'If you break Keatsie in half, Walsall F.C. runs through him like a stick of rock. We need 10 more like him.' I believe everyone thought that about Keatsie.

Bill Jones, Youth Development Officer, told me he once took Keatsie with him to talk to the parents of another young player we were after. They went in and chatted, then came out after the meeting and Keatsie said 'Eh, Bill, they're posh ain't they, they've even got grapes on the sideboard and nobody's ill.'

Later a great friendship developed between Dean Keates and Darren Wrack and Jimmy Walker, 'Wacka,' dubbed the pair 'Dumb and Dumber.'

Deano would play for Walsall, Hull, Kiddiminster, Lincoln, Walsall (again), Peterborough, Wycombe Wanderers and Wrexham. He so nearly came back to Walsall after Peterborough, before signing for Wycombe, we all wished he had.

Dean Keates

212 league appearances for Walsall and 24 goals in two spells, 'Deano' would become a favourite wherever he played and normally the main cog in midfield.

Our leading scorers during the 1996/1997 season were Lightbourne 25, Viveash 10 and Wilson 9.

Kyle Lightbourne would score 12 in our last 18 games and Adie Viveash, although being our centre-back, scored 10 times, due to the magnificent delivery of Darren Bradley's free kicks.

We had finished 11th and 12th in the last two seasons since our promotion, we had consolidated in the division and had a few periods where we looked like we might challenge for the playoffs, but each time had fallen short. The team had five or six players that had now played together for a while and some good new youth players were coming through, the supporters were not down, we were still looking up and believed we were not far off a good side. The new season was coming and everything would change again.

With Adrian Viveash

Chapter 20
Big Fat Jan's Barmy Army

The summer of 1997 saw the end of Chris Nichol's reign. We all sort of knew before the final match that Chris was thinking about calling it a day. The reception he got at the last match was terrific, we all knew he was a proper manager and had given everything to building a team for Walsall. The reason he left, well only Chris knows for sure, but we all thought the sales of O'Connor and Houghton and the imminent sale of Lightbourne had not helped. I'm sure there was more to it than that but losing Chris Nichol was a blow.

Soon afterwards, Kyle Lightbourne was sold to Coventry City for 500,000 pounds. 'Killer' would never reach the goal scoring levels with any of his future clubs that he achieved with Walsall. In that there are maybe three factors: Walsall played under Chris Nichol in a way that was tailormade for 'Killer,' we played to his strengths. Kevin Wilson's experience brought out the best in Kyle and the boys reckon 'Killer' was scared to upset Nichol and so played with more determination, passion and fear than at any other club.

There was a big rebuilding job to do at Walsall. Along with Lightbourne, out went Ray Danial, Charlie Ntamak, Darren Bradley, Martin Butler, Trevor Wood and Kevin Wilson. Rumour had it that Wilson was offered the manager's job; he declined and joined Northampton Town, where he did eventually become manager.

The interviews for our new manager took place and we waited to see who would follow Chris. When he was announced we all had to research where he had come from and who he was.

Jan Sorenson. Manager.

Jan had been a naturally gifted footballer, he had played for Ajax, F.C. Twenty, Enschede, Feyenoord and F.C. Bruges, had won the Belgium Championship in 1977 and played against Liverpool in the European Cup final of 1978, losing 1-0. He was capped 15 times by Denmark and he had previously been Player Manager of Portonese in Portugal before taking over at Walsall.

It is safe to say that Chris Nichol was all about discipline, organization, preparation and routine. Jan Sorenson was a complete opposite.

Coaching under Chris was about practice, corners, free kicks, defending properly, creating space for Lightbourne. Jan was off-the-cuff, get it down and pass it, try something, if you think you can, you can. Training went from extreme fitness to five-a-side games with small goals. Tactics became: go out and enjoy it, smile and pass. The style of management was a complete opposite. Jan usually watched training sitting on a stool and smoking cigarettes. Jan Sorenson made the town of Walsall and it's football team international. First, in came two French players:

Roger Boli. Striker.

Roger came in to replace Kyle Lightbourne. He was a different style of striker but he could play, super quick. He signed from French club Lens on a free transfer; he had been a former French Under-21 International. Roger had an explosive start to his Walsall career and would remain with the Saddlers for only one season before being sold to Dundee United for 150,000 pounds, later joining Bournemouth for 100,000 pounds. He was another that would never find his Walsall form with another club. The boys told me that when Roger signed he thought Division Two meant the one lower than the Premiership, not the third tier of English football. He had no idea where Walsall was and thought we were going for promotion to the Premiership. Roger also claimed that he didn't speak English. Only when Sorenson blasted him in the papers, did he come in the next day and hit Sorenson with a stream of perfectly linked English abuse; it stunned the rest of the dressing room, the cat was out of the bag.

Jean-Francois Peron. Left-Midfield.

Jean-Francois was too much for the Walsall boys to cope with, so within a day he was re-christened 'Jeff' and would remain so throughout the campaign and known as such by the supporters. Peron had played for Caen, Racing Club Strasbourg and signed on a free transfer with Boli from Lens. 'Jeff' would have the most magnificent season on our left-flank before being sold to Portsmouth at the end of the campaign,

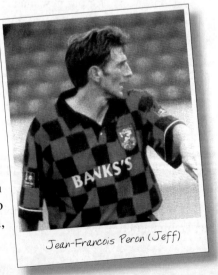

Jean-Francois Peron (Jeff)

again for 150,000 pounds. He later played for Wigan Athletic.

Gary Porter. Midfield.

Gary, I got to know well during his eighteen month stay at Walsall. He signed from Watford where he was their third highest ever appearance maker, with 472 games and 51 goals. Gary was the mainstay of their midfield for years. He had gained 12 England Under-21 caps and had been a quality footballer. That quality would show through in his first season at Walsall. After eighteen months Gary joined Scarborough United and later became a football agent.

At the start of the season came 'The Curious Case Of Christopher Marsh.' With the changeover of managers and the transfer of Martin Butler, 'Lucky' had found himself training at Cambridge United with a possible transfer in the offering. Whilst not allowed to play for Cambridge, I presume the transfer fee being under discussion, he was away from first team duty for the Saddlers. Walsall tried Darren Rogers, Dean Keates, Stuart Ryder and Jeff Peron in the left-back berth. Then, our new left-back appeared for training in the middle of September, Chris Marsh was back; he slotted in to the left-back position behind Jeff Peron and stayed in the team all season.

Later in the season we would also sign two more French players on loan. striker Didier Thorlot from Sion was a good striker; he made 16 appearances and scored 5 goals. Midfield player J.J. Eydelie, also from Sion, J.J. had won the European Cup with Marseille but had been involved in their famous match fixing scandal, he played 12 games in our midfield and proved to be another good player for us.

The season started badly, we won only 1 in our first 7 games and ended up two places from the bottom of the league, the one win, however, was spectacular. Jan Sorenson had promised attacking football and that certainly was true. We were 'gung-ho' for the first few matches, John Hodge playing down our right wing and Jeff Peron down the left, with Boli and Watson up front. On August 30th Southend United visited the Bescot. The poor start to the season meant that only 3,304 fans turned up to watch the match, I was one of them, and I was rewarded for the familiar 250-mile round trip. Boli and Peron were on fire that day. During the first half, Peron went down the left wing and was well marked by Southend's right-back. Peron, under pressure, swung over a cross that was not the best directed, slightly behind the incoming Roger Boli.

Boli stopped, turned, twisted in the air and hit the most unbelievable overhead kick into the top corner. To watch that movement, an overhead shot, 'live' is something those 3,000 fans will never forget. The ground seemed stunned for a split second before going wild with the excitement at what they had just seen.

Boli, then buoyed by the crowd and the achievement of that goal, 'jinked' his way into Southend's box and passed in another, 2-0. Southend did pull one back in the second half, but with minutes to go Boli got free again, rounded the keeper and rolled in his hat trick goal. It had been fantastic to watch. Waterman, me and a host of Walsall supporters were now Boli fans. He had arrived in the cultural backwater of Walsall, but he was now a real Saddler.

Roger Boli scores v Southend United

We slowly began to get better over the next few games and the team started to settle. The team was goalkeeper, Walker; back four, Evans, Viveash and Mountfield/Roper Marsh; midfield, Hodge, Porter, Keates and Peron and strikers, Watson and Boli

A young Dean Keates got into the team and stayed there. 'Marshy' returned and shored up the defence and the midfield worked as a unit and all of them were comfortable on the ball. Whether it was luck or judgment, the team started to click and find confidence within themselves. The defencive unit were experienced, Walker was on fire and with 'Ropes' beginning to find his game at league level he backed up Viveash and Mountfield without any problem.

Our league campaign was to prove a poor one, slowly we moved up the division to 16th around Christmas, but we rarely achieved better. Boli kept scoring and would get 17 goals before Christmas, whether it was the bad weather or just a loss of form, he became less consistent during the second half of the campaign and scored 7 after Christmas. We fortunately got ourselves into a mid-table position with 10 games to go, but we would only win 2 of those games and finish in 19th position, just a couple of places above the relegation zone.

During the league campaign, Waterman and I had always joked that Jeff

Bonser had a removal van 'on hold' each week for Jan, yet every time we had a series of bad league results the team would come up with a victory at a crucial time and Jan survived the chop, which must have been seriously close all season.

That is not the story of the 1997/1998 season. During the previous ten or twelve seasons we had not had those glorious Cup runs of the past. Yes, we had the odd game and frightened a few big teams before running out of steam, but we had not made our way through the rounds to the latter stages. Somehow, this team that could not make a real fist of the league campaign, became 'one-off' Cup fighters, which brought with it a season of 'Walsall days out.' Now, we all love a 'Walsall day out,' usually vocally supported by the chant 'Walsall Boys, We are here! Way Oh, Way Oh.'

The Coca-Cola Cup.

Started at Bescot Stadium on August 12th 1977 with a two-leg affair against Exeter City, winning the first leg 2-0, with goals from Clive Platt and Roger Boli. We went to Exeter on August 26th and won 1-0, Boli scoring again.

Round Two saw us drawn against Nottingham Forest then going well in Division One and on their way to the Premiership. The away leg on September 17th, when we were due for a good hiding, produced a 1-0 win for the Saddlers, with Justin Skinner, on loan from Bristol Rovers, scoring our goal. Chatter came from Forest on how the return match was going to go. Evidently, we were lucky and lightning does not strike twice, preceded the return at Bescot on September 24th. Now, in Walsall, we know that it can and so a crowd of 6,037 above our poor average at the start of that season, decided that it just might and they should be there to see it, should it happen.

Waterman and I assumed our position, pumped up for the match. During the first half we played well, 'Deano' Keates and Jeff Peron out playing the Forest midfield, the halftime score being 0-0. We were still in front on average. Forest came out in the second half and laid siege on our defence, Pierre Van Hooijdonk looped a header over 'Wacka' and the scores were level on aggregate. There was now the chance that we may crumble, but we didn't. We had chances to win and so did Forest, the best of which was a fantastic long shot by Hooijdonk, who looked a great player, which smashed against our crossbar, with 'Wacka' back peddling. Extra time was called and Pete and

I knew it was going to be a long night before we got back to London. The first half saw Forest gain the lead from a corner; the ball bounced around and squirmed through Walkers grasp. Jan Sorenson then brought on Clive Platt and signalled the team to go all-out attack. This team needed no second asking, they flew at Forest and pinned them in. With 7 minutes to go, Platty slipped Andy Watson through and he beat Dave Beasant, 2-1, aggregate 2-2, but Forest would still go through on the away goals rule. Four minutes later, with Walsall still attacking a bewildered Forest side, John Hodge twisted and turned and confused himself, Forest and our own team, before laying off the most perfect cross. Andy Watson smashed it into the roof of the net and the party started. There was no coming back for Forest with only two minutes to go. The chatty ones from Nottingham faced a ride home a little quieter than the ride in.

The Third Round saw us at home versus Sheffield United, they were fifth in Division One and another good side, we, however, were in a winning streak of four matches when they arrived and fancied our chances. Sheffield were indeed a good side and took the lead at Bescot during the first half, only for Andy Watson, our Cup scoring hero, to score again, levelling the tie early in the second half. Slowly, encouraged by a crowd of 8,239, we began to build momentum before Sorenson signalled to go for it with five minutes to go. Again, with our last reserves of strength, we powered at Sheffield United, forcing Carl Tiler to dump the ball into his own net and bring a breathless close to the match, a 2-1 victory. We all cheered the boys off.

The Fourth Round draw was not as kind but gave us a chance of another big night out, West Ham United away at Upton Park on November 19. We had given West Ham a rough ride only two years earlier, beating them 2-1 at Bescot before going down 2-0 at Upton Park. They were still aware of our fighting spirit and left nothing to chance. Pete and I went along to Upton Park in hope of maybe a replay. It was also like a home match in terms of travelling, however, it was not to be. West Ham played well and ran out 4-1 winners, no complaints. We gave them a run for it for a while but they had been bitten before and it was not going to happen that night. Andy Watson, again, scored our goal.

So, our League Cup run was over for another year. Four days earlier we had commenced our F.A. Cup campaign at home against Lincoln City on November 15th, winning the match 2-0, with goals from 'Cup King' Andy Watson and Roger Boli. Round Two saw us drawn away to Macclesfield Town on December 6th. I could not make the match as I was on tour with the now famous Backstreet Boys and playing the NEC in Birmingham. As the match progressed I was driving up the M1 listening to the radio, screaming to no one as the boys went on the rampage. We were in our run of form. Macclesfield were unbeaten at home and fancied their chances of turning us over. 3,566 turned up to see if they could progress and knock Walsall out of the Cup, which would have been a feather in their cap. According to reports of that match, Macclesfield did not play badly, just everything we did came off and Jeff Peron's performance that day, some say, ranks with the very best ever seen by a Walsall left-winger; he totally destroyed Macclesfield's defence.

Boli opened the scoring after twenty-one minutes after being set up by Peron. Fourteen minutes later, Keatsie was upended in the box and Hodge scored from the penalty, 2-0 at halftime. Three minutes into the second half and a Walsall free kick from Gary Porter found Adie Viveash and it was 3-0 and game over. Fifteen minutes into the second half and Boli was poorly tackled in the box and the defender sent off before Boli stoked home the penalty, 4-0. The noise level in my car was now at a good level as on my own I roared on the Saddlers. During the last thirty minutes, Walsall powered on against a demoralised Macclesfield, Porter slammed one in, 5-0, Peron put through Porter again, 6-0 and in the last minute Hodge completed the scoring, 7-0. That day Walsall chalked up their biggest ever away from home F.A. Cup win in their long Cup history.

Round Three brought an away tie at Peterborough United on January 13th 1998. The tie had been delayed from the Saturday to the Tuesday due to the poor condition of their pitch and during that time the draw for the Fourth Round had been made, the winners would face Manchester United at Old Trafford. The game leaped in magnitude with this draw and so the gate rose to 12,809 and the whole place was rocking before kick-off. I sat with Pete Waterman and Keith Bertschin, the day he told me he had retired from playing. We all wanted the chance to visit Old Trafford again. Peterborough, being at home, were favourites and wanting the Old Trafford trip for themselves. Walsall fielded the following side: goalkeeper, Walker; back four, Evans, Viveash, Mountfield and Marsh; midfield, Hodge, Porter, Keates and Peron and strikers, Boli and Watson.

Peterborough could not find a way through our defence that night, no matter how much effort they put in, and that scorer of Cup goals, Andy Watson, delivered again, scoring twice in a 2-0 victory. It was a fantastic Walsall night out. Cars, vans and coaches had made the trip from Walsall to Peterborough;

the noise coming from the away end was enormous and the fans just kept on singing and urging the team on. The singing and terrace dancing at the end was a sight to behold, we were on our way to Manchester. The Fourth Round tie at Old Trafford was scheduled for January 24th 1998.

We now had a settled side and set off on our way that Saturday to Old Trafford. I drove from London to Walsall early, went to my Sister Helen's for a bite and took her with us to Manchester. Waterman was on a fishing holiday in India but had arranged to fly into Heathrow, change flights to Manchester, cab from the airport and he came bursting into the ground just as the players walked out. Keith Bertschin joined our crew, along with Mark Rees, Kenny Mower and Paul Waddington. It was going to be a fun day. The gate that day was 54,669, the second largest crowd ever to see a Walsall side play.

Never let it be said that Walsall fans don't know how to enjoy themselves when they get the chance. Way before kick-off the away end was full, singing and chanting, their favourite being 'Big Fat Jan's Barmy Army.' When our players nervously came out to kick in, the crescendo of noise was enormous, a noise that would continue throughout the game and would be applauded by a Manchester crowd on the fulltime whistle, along with our players.

The boys were in a hotel the night before and Hodgey was too wound up to sleep, playing pranks and keeping our goalkeeper up all night. 'Wacka' would later say that Hodgey's antics stopped him worrying about facing United. Our team was treated to a trip around the Old Trafford stadium; Jan had insisted no matter what may happen they should enjoy the day. A film was made by the team of their arrival that day: greeting the Walsall fans, visiting the trophy room and a tour of the stadium. They asked me to make about twenty copies and clip in the BBC footage of the game, which I did in our studios in London and distributed them to the team a couple of weeks later, keeping one for myself.

The boys lined up in the tunnel next to Giggs, Scholes, Beckham, Neville, Schmeichel and Solskjaer, reality hit them; this was the big time. Walsall did not freeze that day, we played well, attacked United at Old Trafford and being a side capable of retaining possession, we did ourselves proud. 'Marshy' playing left-back had to face Beckham. Chris hit 'Becks' with a couple of crunchers early on, but David didn't react or say a word he just got up and kept playing, a true professional. Becks also went into the Walsall bar afterwards and sought out 'Marshy' and bought him a drink whilst talking with the other Walsall players. David Beckham - class act!

The match also had its moments. I'd seen Walsall sides play at Old Trafford before, drawing 0-0 and losing 1-0, this, however, was a different United side. Premiership winners and European Cup Winners we were no match for them. We lost the game 5-1. I think the score flattered United, we played better than the score line suggests, however, we did score through Roger Boli who loved the big stage. That moment filled the papers the day after due to Walsall's celebration of the goal. Hodgey had instigated a plan that if we scored the team would all fall to the ground as if fainting in disbelief. When we did score, Boli, obviously having scored at Old Trafford, was having none of the falling down bit and raced along the Walsall fans who were shouting and cheering the moment. The instigator of the fainting scam, forgot all about it and raced after Boli in celebration, the two of them turned, looking for the rest of the team who were all laid flat out on the ground. I've never seen that before or since, as they say, only at Walsall.

At the end of the match, the Walsall players stayed on the pitch enjoying the occasion with our still singing fans. The boys threw their shirts into the crowd and only one shirt made it back to the dressing room - that was Clive Platt's. The team saved it for me, signed it and it has hung in the dressing room in my home since then. It is still there today. Happy memories.

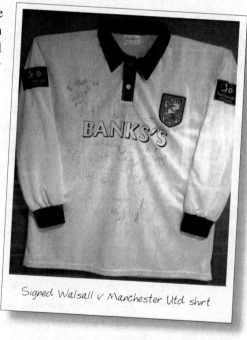

Signed Walsall v Manchester Utd shirt

'Big Fat Jan' was still in a job, the removal van still not summoned. Even though our league form was poor, the income made from our Cup runs was, as ever, much needed by the club. Jan and the team were still not finished yet.

Back in December we had been drawn away at Barnet on December 9th in the Auto Windshield Trophy. As a contrast to the Old Trafford crowd, Walsall played in front of 754 on a cold night in Round One. Pete Waterman and I were in that 754, taking advantage of a short ride to Barnet. We won the game 2-1, with goals from Blake and Boli. Round Two saw us at home to Brighton and Hove Albion on December 6th, we had just had three wins on the bounce in the league and probably our best run that year and we were firing on all cylinders. Brighton were washed away on a joyous night in front of 2,562. Watson, Boli 2, Keates and an own goal completed the 5-0 rout and the Third Round drew Bristol Rovers away. The game was on January 28th. Pete and I missed a 1-0 victory with another Roger Boli goal. A seriously good win as Bristol Rovers are normally a good side on their own ground and do not lose too many there.

The next round, named the regional semi-final, meant we had to go back to Peterborough, after ruining their hopeful day out at Manchester United. We were given no chance, as missing out and looking for revenge were a hurt Peterborough. Lightning struck twice again and we were victorious by two goals to one, with Boli and Michael Ricketts coming off the bench to score the second. Unbelievably, 'Big Fat Jan's barmy army', were in the regional final to be played over two legs against Bournemouth. The winners would appear at Wembley in the final. Walsall have never played at Wembley and the chance of doing so brought the whole town to life. The first leg was to be played at the Bescot on March 10th. 6,017 thought we stood a chance. Pete and I were on edge. Could Walsall, a team made up of our mates, yet claim the ultimate 'day out'?

The home crowd were buzzing, but this was a decent Bournemouth team. I remember they had a training ground corner play that they executed perfectly. Everybody moved to the near post and one player came round the back, the ball got delivered right over all of the players and to an unmarked Bournemouth player on the back post, he scored, 1-0. Bournemouth would dampen our hopes with a second goal and we were 2-0 down from the first leg. Walsall fans, a sturdy bunch, still believed. Off we went to Bournemouth on March 17th. Pete and I drove down eating dinner at a Little Chef. As pop stars, we know how to live it up.

When we arrived at Dean Court we had been put in a small part of the stand, there were probably only about 200 Walsall fans but, squashed in, they made an enormous noise. They were the real hardcore Walsall fans. It seemed they would be rewarded, we raced into the lead with goals from Wayne Thomas, Roger Boli and Dedier Tholot. Bournemouth nipped one in between, but with the score at 3-1 and the away goals rule we were set for Wembley.

Unfortunately, Bournemouth would get another goal. A wicked deflection off Wayne Evans flew into our net and our dreams of Wembley were over.

Pete and I still talk about that night. Our team were magnificent, they once again gave everything they had to make an appearance at Wembley, it was, unfortunately, not to be.

Pete and I had promised the lads that if they got to Wembley we would make a record with the team for what would have been a big 'Walsall day out.' We would make it at our studios and put the record out on our label. The boys were really up for it, especially 'Wacka' and Hodgey, both of whom were always singing to both Pete and I. We heard so many songs from those two. 'It's Now or Never' and 'In the Ghetto,' were two I remember. I don't know who Hodgey thought he was but 'Wacka' definitely thought he was Elvis. We all know what 'thought' did. The two of them thought they were the lead singers of the team. We were all disappointed not to make it to Wembley, but, in hindsight, we saved the country from the dulcet tones of James Walker and John Hodge.

The team returned to the league programme after a short break in Marbella to re-focus. It didn't work. Jan was trying to make a real push for the playoffs, but I believe the team were more mentally fatigued than physically after their exploits in all three Cup competitions. We just could not get going again. We had 11 games left and we would only win 3 of them, which caused us to slide down the table. With 2 games left we were in trouble, just above the relegation zone. We went to Bristol City, nervously needing something from the match and we lost 2-1, with Tholot getting our consolation. Fortunately, all of the clubs around us lost as well and mathematically we were, unbelievably, safe. Fortunately so, as we would lose our last match to Wycombe 1-0 at Bescot.

We finished 19th in the league and days later the removal van, on hold all season, was called. Big Fat Jan was on his way out.

The Walsall fans were upset by our poor finish and were particularly vocal about the Board of Directors, Jan Sorenson and Jeff Bonser. Jeff responded by sacking Jan, resigning as Chairman and putting the club up for sale. I guess it's been up for sale ever since.

My opinion, for what it's worth, is that it was a season of magnificence and one I will never forget. The Cup runs were David and Goliath stuff, all that supporting a small Football Club is about. Pete and I loved the whole season, we could have done without the nervousness at the end of the season, but the team had given all they had got for nine months, you cannot have it all.

Jan Sorenson was much ridiculed for his loose, lack of discipline ways, but he believed in his team and believed they were professional players and should go out, get it down and pass it. Without him we would not have enjoyed the freedom the boys played with and the Cup runs that came.

After the Manchester United game Alex Ferguson, having seen our side play, said to Jan 'Your wages should be doubled for the job you've done!'

The arrival of the French players changed the thinking of our team. After a match, the following day would be off, be it a Saturday game, Tuesday or Wednesday match. Our lads were surprised that the French players went in to Bescot on these days off to religiously 'stretch off.' The French lads could not believe that our lads did not do this. Peron and Boli explained it elongated your career and kept overworked muscles loose. From that season on, our boys stretched off the day after a game.

Walsall had become international during this campaign. Peron and Boli had been huge successes and that would bring further players from abroad to England and a little town Football Club in the West Midlands.

Our leading scorers that season were Roger Boli 24, Andy Watson 15 and John Hodge 10.

Another season had ended and we were again manager-less, Bonser had resigned, the club was up for sale, all after a most exciting season. Who would come in and what would happen next?

Derek Mountfield at Footballers Classic Golf in Spain

With John Hodge

Chapter 21

The Walsall Team With The Most Heart And Passion

During the summer of 1998, I was away from England working in New York. I returned to our shores and phoned the 'Walsall Club Call.' Back then it was the only way to get information about the club and what was happening. The Manager of the team always introduced the news bulletin the same way, 'Hello, I'm so and so, welcome to Walsall Club Call.' I phoned on my return and heard, 'Hello, I'm Ray Graydon, welcome to Walsall Club Call.' That was the first I knew of Ray's appointment at Walsall Football Club.

Ray Graydon. Manager.

Ray Graydon

Ray had been a professional footballer for eighteen seasons, playing for Bristol Rovers, Aston Villa, Coventry City, Washington Diplomats and Oxford United. An orthodox right-winger with an outstanding shot, he scored plenty of goals from the right-flank, playing in those two League Cup finals for Villa alongside Chris Nichol. After finishing his playing career at Oxford United, he coached there and at Watford and Southampton. Walsall was Ray's first chance at League management and he came with his own ideas that were non-negotiable. Within days the players had to be properly dressed to come to training with suits and ties. Gone were the earrings, the mobiles, the baseball caps and the stereos in the dressing room, a return to discipline after the looseness of Jan Sorenson was ordered.

Balancing the books at Walsall has always been at the top of the agenda and so players were sold, although I do believe they were great deals. Roger Boli signed for Dundee for 150,000 pounds. Jeff Peron fell out with Ray and didn't like the strict regime, so he went on the transfer list and was promptly sold to Portsmouth for 150,000 pounds. This disappointed the fans, but when you look at those deals both players arrived on free transfers and both were thirty-two years of age, under those circumstances, they were great deals, coupled with, Roger never returned to his Walsall goal scoring form and Jeff had an in-and-out career at Portsmouth before moving to Wigan.

John Hodge was sold to Gillingham. Mark Blake's contract ran out and was not renewed and Derek Mountfield moved to Northampton to join Kevin Wilson.

Ray started a re-building programme with no money to spend, moving swiftly into the free transfer market.

Neil Pointon. Left-Back.

'Points' was a class player and a great lad; he fitted straight away into the Walsall team at left-back. Having played for Scunthorpe, Everton, winning the Premiership, Manchester City after a 300,000 pound transfer, three seasons with, then Premier League, Oldham Athletic and a move to Scotland with Heart of Midlothian, he signed for Walsall from Hearts, playing in 61 games for us before joining Chesterfield.

Andy Rammall. Centre-Forward.

'Rambo' would become a Walsall legend for his performances over the next two seasons. Andy was playing for Atherstone United when Alex Ferguson spotted him and took him to Manchester United for 40,000 pounds. A year later, without playing in United's first team, 'Rams' joined Barnsley for 100,000 pounds where he blossomed as a centre-forward, playing there for six seasons, making 220 appearances and scoring over 50 goals. He then signed for Southend, playing 79 times and scoring 14 goals before moving on a free transfer to Walsall. After 69 appearances and 23 goals he would join Wycombe Wanderers to become a hero there over the next three seasons, before ending his playing days at Bristol Rovers. Pete and I were great mates with Rambo; he led the Walsall team, especially

Andy Rammall

during that first season. A couple of seasons later, when he was playing for Wycombe, Walsall played there in the league and lost 3-1, Rambo scoring twice for Wycombe. A strong Walsall support that day after seeing their team lose, chanted 'There's only one Andy Rammall' out of respect as Rambo left the field. He was and always will be a Walsall hero.

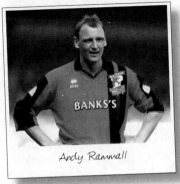

Andy Rammall

Jason Brissett. Striker.

Jason started at Arsenal before playing for Peterborough United and Bournemouth, signing for Walsall on a free transfer. He would make 40 appearances and score 3 goals before moving to Cheltenham Town and Leyton Orient.

Bjarni Larusson. Midfield.

Bjarni is Icelandic and another that just fitted straight into our team in central-midfield. Signed on a free transfer from Hibernian, he would play 59 times and score 3 goals for Walsall before moving to Scunthorpe and then back to Iceland with IBV and KR.

Darren Wrack. Right-Midfield.

'Wracky' became a Walsall legend staying with the club for ten seasons before moving on to Kettering Town. Starting at Derby County and making 26 appearances, Wracky moved to his hometown club Grimsby for 100,000 pounds, things just did not work out for him there and he signed on a free transfer to Walsall. He would make 380 appearances and score 52 times during his stay at Bescot Stadium and be a mainstay of our side during those years.

Darren Wrack

Richard Green. Centre-Half.

Greeny was another that fitted straight into our squad. An experienced centre-half, when he arrived at Walsall he had already played in over 330 league games for Shrewsbury, Swindon and Gillingham. Ray spent 35,000 pounds on Richard and he would be the only player we bought that season. Playing 30 times for Walsall and scoring 1 goal he later moved to Rochdale and Northampton Town.

As the season was about to commence the bookies and pundits were vocal in their predictions of what the campaign would bring for Walsall F.C.. Unanimously, they said we had no chance, an inexperienced manager, no money to spend, a rash of free transfers, we would be going down, definitely.

Inside the camp, the players were in good spirits; they felt that as they had played so many teams above them in the Cup competitions last season and come out on top, that they might just do something during this campaign. Ray's discipline, at first, they liked, it was much more of a return to what they knew under Chris Nichol. Ray also had a system that they believed in the more matches we became successful in.

Unusually, the Football League computer had made it possible for me to attend our first seven league and cup games. August 8th 1998, our first fixture, was away at Gillingham, not far from London. I joined the Walsall Faithful and watched a tight game, which we won 1-0, with a deflected Chris Marsh shot. 'Marshy' tried to claim it, but the League wrote it in as an own goal by Carr of Gillingham. (Lucky strikes again).

August 11, Pete and I watched the 0-0 draw with QPR at Bescot in the Worthington Cup and four days later the 0-0 draw with Northampton in the league, also at Bescot. It was clear even then Ray had built a team that would be difficult to beat. August 22nd, the computer took us to Wycombe Wanderers, again not far from London, we won 2-1, another forced own goal by McCarthy of Wycombe and Rammall scored his first. The away leg in the Worthington Cup was at QPR and we were invited by Barclays Bank to watch the game from their box. Pete had made the arrangement, as they wanted his business. They said they would take us to a football match to bond. Pete chose QPR versus Walsall, much to Barclay's surprise. We lost 3-1, but had a good night, Rambo scored the consolation and we didn't do business with Barclays, for the record. August 29th brought Burnley to the Bescot. We were there again to see a 3-1 victory, Brissett and Wrack 2. September 2nd and Pete had an involvement in a country hotel close to Manchester, they were City supporters and they arranged a day out at Maine Road for us with lunch, Mike Summerbee hosting and with seats in the large Directors' box. They rejoiced as we went down 3-1, Rambo scoring our goal and Michael Ricketts missing an easy chance at a crucial moment. September 8th at home to York City saw us lose 3-2, with Rambo and Wracky scoring. The first match I missed was away at Chesterfield where we pulled off a 1-0 victory, Rambo scoring again.

The team would win 5 of the next 7, lose 1 and win 6 of the next 8, drawing 2. Walsall favorites for relegation were now heading for the top of the league, in 2nd place behind Kevin Keegan's Fulham.

In January 1999, we were still up there when the rejoicing Manchester City fans came to Bescot and swelled the crowd to 9,517. We invited Pete's partners to Bescot for lunch and again they were very vocal about the upcoming game and what might happen. They were a subdued bunch when they left, still behind us in the table and lucky to scrape a draw after Andy Watson had put us ahead. In 19 games from January 1st 1999 we would only lose 4. We were chasing Fulham at the top hard. Preston and Manchester City were chasing us hard from behind.

Five games to go and a pressure match away at Preston North End ended in disaster, Brissett got sent off in a tense affair and we lost 1-0. Our next game was away at Lincoln City. 'Marshy' was injured and in the stand with reserve loan keeper, Stuart Naylor. Our team were under constant pressure from Lincoln and hanging on. Ray Graydon switched Wracky from the right-flank to the left, Wracky hated the left-flank and reluctantly drifted over, with ten minutes to go Wracky got free and cut inside onto his favoured right foot from the left-flank and scored. 'Marshy,' having visited the bar, went ballistic in the stand cheering on his mates. A couple of disappointed Lincoln supporters thought the celebration was out of order and were persistent in telling 'Marshy'. Chris decided enough was enough and headed for the offenders. Naylor, fortunately, older and wiser, got hold of 'Marshy' and pointed him towards the dressing room. At fulltime 'Marshy' welcomed the boys in with the news that the results had gone our way, both Preston North End and Manchester City had lost, surprisingly, and little old Walsall were back in the driving seat, destiny in our own hands.

As May 1st arrived there were 3 games to go but Walsall only needed 3 points for promotion, a return to Division One, soon to be called The Championship. The Holy Grail was beckoning.

On that day, 9,184 turned up at the Bescot, we all wanted the 3 points that day and our lungs were ready to burst to drive the boys over the line. It had been eleven years since we had been in that division. The club had been rebuilt, after spending five years in the Third Division and building up the playing staff along with the business side, we had a new home and it would be Bescot Stadium's first visit to Division One. Everything, life itself, seemed to hang on getting 3 points that day in the town of Walsall.

The starting line-up of the side that day had not cost one penny. The relegation favourites and no-hopers of the Division were on the cusp of promotion. Could they? Would they?

Walsall came out that day to a crescendo of noise. The team was goalkeeper, Walker; back four, Marsh, Viveash, Roper and Pointon; midfield, Wrack, Henry, Keates and Brissett and strikers, Steiner and Rammall.

The noise was infectious. Oldham tried to upset us by winning the toss and forcing us to play towards our own fans; traditionally we preferred to do that in the second half. Oldham, in trying to be clever, upset our team and we just flew at their defence from the whistle. Wave after wave of attacks, enormous noise in the stadium, Oldham just had to crack under the pressure. twenty-two minutes into the game Pointon floated in a cross from the left that originally did not look too dangerous, but Oldham's keeper came out and misjudged the flight, the ball falling at the feet of Darren Wrack who rammed it in from a tight angle. The crowd noise was enormous and the traditional 'Come on Walsall' rang out around the ground. On thirty-four minutes, Nick Henry laid the ball up to Rob Steiner. Steiner, back to goal, controlled it and held off the defender before pushing it to his left and straight into the path of Chris Marsh bursting into the box. 'Lucky' took one touch and then dispatched it into the roof of the net; the roof came off the stadium. We were not only 2-0 up, but one of Walsall's favourite sons had scored. 'Marshy' continued his run across the front of the goal and towards the corner flag in front of a wildly celebrating Gilbert Alsop End. Rambo, Wracky, Keatsie, Steiner and Brissett all chased 'Marshy' down, jumping all over him as he celebrated. As Chris ran across the goal after scoring, his mouth wide open as he screamed with delight, it was ten years of graft exuding from his lungs. 'Lucky' deserved to be the one to score the crucial goal that day. It was his moment.

With 'Marshy' being my mate I was uncontrollable in the stand. Pete and I were jumping up and down like teenagers and, to be fair, we were way passed that. The halftime whistle came and the stadium was breathless but still knowing we had not won it yet. 2-0 at halftime never secures the points; the crowd gathered themselves for the second half.

Oldham, with 1,000 travelling fans who had come to spoil the party, set about us from the kick-off and after eleven minutes put a cross into our box that Duxbury planted into the top corner, 2-1. Momentarily the Saddlers support was silenced, before gathering themselves again and driving the team forward. Graydon substituted Steiner and brought on, crowd favourite, Siggi Eyjolfsson. Within seconds, Siggi hit a powerful shot that was well saved. The crowd started with their 'Siggi, Siggi, Siggi' chant. After some end-to-end play, with twelve minutes remaining, Brissett got free on the left, sliding a perfect ball to Siggi, who turned and lashed it into the bottom corner, 3-1. We were up and we knew it. The crowd went wild and the celebrations started. 'Wacka', still not sure, was shouting and shouting at our defence to concentrate. Adie Viveash, forever cool, responded with 'For God's sake enjoy it, we've done it.'

Chris Marsh Goal v Oldham

The whistle blew. The players did their lap of honour and then returned to the stand to pour champagne over a delighted Ray Graydon in front of thousands now assembled on the pitch. Pete and I stayed in the bar with all the lads for hours as we celebrated our return to Division One, a wonderful 'against all odds' success and a season to remember. We assembled again for our last home match, a 2-2 draw, with champions Fulham, before losing our last game of the season 2-0 away at Stoke, not that anyone remembers that.

Ray Graydon had pulled off the impossible and was an in demand manager, but stated instantly, he would stay and lead us into the Division One campaign next season.

Ray keeps on winning

Ray Graydon Celebrates

Andy Rammall had led the team during the whole campaign. He had been told by Ray Graydon at the start of the season that he would not be able to score 20 goals in a season. The bet was taken. 'Rambo' top scored with 20 goals and Wracky got 14 from the right wing. One of our greatest ploys of the season was 'Wacka's' goal kicks, aimed at the centre circle, with a little draw, they came off like a perfectly struck seven iron. Rambo, moving in from a left-wing position, met the ball time after time heading it across the field onto the incoming Wrack, Larusson, Keates or 'Marshy' pushing forward. Pointon fed ball after ball into the penalty area from the left, and the right-wing partnership of Marsh and Wrack was probably the best ever from a Walsall team. Both could play right midfield well and both could play right-back well, hence, they covered for each other, could overload the opposition full-backs and defend as a unit. We were structured, professional and had the most heart and team spirit I've ever seen from a Walsall side; unfancied and written off, they smashed the whole division.

Ray Graydon also worked the loan market better than any other Walsall Manager. During that season, he chose loan players with character and commitment and they came for short periods and played their part in our success. Paul Simpson did well on our left wing during two spells. Colin Cramb, a determined striker, played 4 games scoring 4 goals. Nick Henry played well in our midfield, Rob Steiner scored 3 times in 10 games, Darko Mavrak played well on the left wing during his 12 matches scoring twice and Siggy Eyjoffson scored twice coming off the bench, including the all-important third goal against Oldham.

Walter Otta joined from Argentina not speaking a word of English, but he definitely had the striking instinct, playing 9 games and scoring 4 goals. Walter would play all over the world, Spain, Germany and back to Argentina and he scored goals wherever he went. His only club in England was Walsall. Ray, being a very pleasant man, had invited Walter for Christmas lunch at his home as Walter was alone in the U.K. with a language barrier. The boys, hearing this, had taught Walter the delicacies of the English language in preparation for his lunch with Ray. They told him, when lunch is served the proper response is 'Fuck you very much' etc. etc. Walter, however, was not stupid and he tried out the phrases and words in a pub visit a few days before his lunch with the Graydon family. On seeing the response, Walter sidestepped what our boys had in mind, fortunately.

The promotion-winning season might seem like enough, but that is not the full story. We were out of the Worthington League Cup at Queens Park Rangers in the First Round. The F.A. Cup was also short-lived that season; we were beaten at Preston North End in Round Two, 2-0.

December 8th 1998 we began again in the Auto Windscreen Trophy, the trophy we had so nearly made an appearance in at Wembley the previous season. The team, having been successful the season before, believed they could do it this time and concentrated their efforts again on reaching Wembley. With the departure of Hodgey, 'Wacka' now felt that he was the sole lead singer of the team and was quick to strike the deal with Pete and I about making a record with the team if they got to Wembley. We agreed.

Bristol Rovers at home in Round One proved a tough match at Bescot, a 2-2 draw led to penalties. Larusson and Otta had scored our goals during the game and we progressed after winning 5-4 on penalties. January 5th 1999 took us to Luton Town where we progressed relatively easily 3-0, with goals from Watson, Wrack and Keates.

Round Three drew us away at Brentford on January 20th. The computer had been kind to Pete and I again, giving us away matches at both Luton and Brentford. We were both outside the ground when our team coach pulled up. As the players embarked we noticed two new faces, we joked that Ray had signed two Bosnians, was paying them twenty-five pounds a week and they would be in the team soon. They were, in fact, Siggi Eyjoffsson and Darko Mavrak; neither played that night.

The game ended 0-0 and after extra time went to penalties. That night I saw 'Wacka' pull off the best save I've ever seen during a penalty shootout. The Brentford player hit it great and straight at the top corner, but somehow 'Wacka' lept at it and just got a couple of fingers to a shot he should not have got anywhere near and tipped it over. It was truly unbelievable. 'Wacka' would and could do anything to sing on a record. The save was soul destroying for Brentford and we went on to win 4-3 on penalties.

On February 16th we were drawn at home to Cambridge United. I couldn't make the game as I was at The Brits with The Backstreet Boys and the record company staff. I kept nipping out all night to get the reports from the game. At fulltime it was 1-1, Rambo getting our goal. Extra time produced no goals and by this time everyone on my table was annoyed that I kept leaving and coming back. When it went to penalties I gave up on The Brits and went and listened to the 'live' report on my phone. I returned to the table delighted with our 4-3 penalty win and everyone on the table was delighted I wouldn't keep leaving. 'Wacka' was still going for the recording contract.

We were now in the area final against Millwall over two legs, if we beat them, Walsall were at Wembley and 'Wacka' was lead singer on the Walsall record.

Pete and I went to The Den with a crowd of 11,626, mainly Millwall supporters and we lost the match 1-0. We were still in it and the return at Bescot was scheduled for March 16th. Pete and I travelled north full of hope again. 9,128, mainly Walsall fans, turned up to cheer the boys on to Wembley.

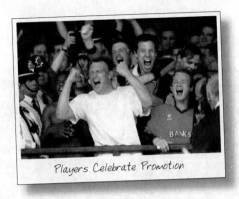

Players Celebrate Promotion

We went 1-0 down, but Siggi came off the bench to put us back in the match at 2-1 on aggregate. We pounded the Millwall defence in an all-out attack to get the equalizer, but sadly, we couldn't. For the second year in succession we fell at the final hurdle. The team were down and 'Wacka' was distraught.

We had played Millwall three times in the space of seven days; the middle game was a league match, which we won at The Den 2-1, with two goals from an on-loan Colin Cramb. At the end of the sequence of three matches, having lost in the Auto Windscreen Trophy, but won in the league, Ray Graydon calmly remarked 'Well, maybe we won the right one.' Never was a truer word spoken. Those 3 points that day were part of the reason we were in the position against Oldham to get promoted.

Walsall would start the coming season as a Division One team. We were back.

Team photo 1998-99 Season

With Neil Pointon

Chapter 22

The Pride Of The Midlands

There was great pride and expectation as Walsall began to prepare for the coming 1999/2000 season, back in the now called Championship. Quickly, both the Board and Ray Graydon realized how difficult it was going to be. The recruitment of new players and their wage demands for playing in The Championship was enormous for a small club like Walsall. The search for quality players would take Paul Taylor, our player acquisition scout, across Europe and the world. The trials given to players were ongoing all season, as an endless search to build a team capable of at least staying in The Championship began.

We had our strong core of committed players that had achieved so much to get us promoted and the early signings were sound options. Tony Daley joined to prove his fitness and rebuild his career on the left wing. Carl Emberson joined from Colchester United, where he had been their first choice keeper, as competition for 'Wacka'. Tony Barras came from Reading to play centre-back and Mark Robbins, a former Manchester United star, joined our strike force for what we believed would be a great pairing with Andy Rammall. A whole host of foreign players began to appear for trials. The first one to be signed that season was Gabor Buckran, from Xerez in Spain, who would slot comfortably into our midfield and adjust well to The Championship.

The team went to France for a pre-season tour, unusual in our history, but a sign we were moving up in class and an attempt to blend the new players into our special team spirit that had achieved so much.

We started the season well with a draw at home against Swindon, 0-0, a win in the League Cup against Plymouth Argyle, 4-1, and a draw against Sheffield United in our first away match, 1-1. It was a surprise, when in our second home match against Crewe, after Mark Robbins put us in front, that we lost the game, 4-1.

We rallied immediately by battering Plymouth in the second match, 4-1 again. At that point, the Crewe game seemed just a blip.

Our next game would be the start of our Midland battles, which eventually would bring us the tag, 'Walsall Football Club, Pride of the Midlands.'

August 28th 1999 will long be remembered by the huge Walsall support that laid siege to The Molineux that day. Pete Waterman and I, along with our pal, Joe Savage, booked our seats with the Walsall fans that day, as usual. The Walsall fans knew that we always preferred to sit with them at away matches and we always enjoyed the banter and friendliness of the fans towards us. We had, however, misjudged the response that 'Pop Idol' was having during its first season.

The atmosphere was just brilliant as the Walsall fans began singing long before kick-off and erupted as our team came out onto the pitch. The long rivalry between Walsall and Wolverhampton Wanderers was particularly evident that day and the Walsall fans knew we had a brave team that might just be able to pull off an upset. Walsall responded to the noise of the fans and went after Wolves with complete disregard for their status as a 'big' team, attacking straight from the kick-off in a wave of determination and belief. We forced a corner after 3 minutes, taken by Darren Wrack, who found the head of Tony Barras and to the delight of the now screaming Walsall fans we were 1-0 to the good. Wolves' fans were already unhappy that day, they had not seen the acquisition of players they thought they needed for the campaign and were upset before the game started. The goal from Barras wound them up even more and the Walsall fans were not slow to remind them of their current plight. Their best player at the time was Andy Sinton and when Chris Marsh put in a strong but fair tackle that led to Sinton going off, their humour seemed to disappear completely. Wolves stuck to their task in front of the disgruntled fans and equalized after half an hour through Carl Robinson. This did not stop the wave of Walsall attacks or quiet our fans; Wolves were still in disarray and there for the taking. Just before halftime, Gabby Buckran delivered a cross from right midfield, Robins headed on and an incoming Andy Rammall bundled the ball into the Wolves net, 2-1, and the party started.

At halftime, Pete, Joe Savage and I went under the stand to visit the toilets. The Walsall fans, in a robust and joyous mood, spotted Pete, launched into a chant of 'Pop Idol, Pop Idol, Pop Idol,' and surged forward. Joe had no chance of protecting Pete with the on-rushing crowd, but we managed to bundle ourselves into the toilets, hoping for it all to quieten down. It didn't. The fans all charged into the toilets after us. We abandoned our proposed relief, went straight out of the other entrance and headed back to our seats, which was a task in itself. The fans meant no harm, they were 2-1 up against the old foe and celebrating, but for Pete, Joe and I, it was a scary situation; there was nowhere to go and the crush that was caused left us breathless. Fortunately, no one was hurt, in what was after all just fun and excitement, but we did realize after that situation that we may not be able to sit with the fans anymore, especially with potentially huge crowds. Away at Cheltenham on a cold Tuesday night was fine, but a warm summers day at the Molineux, 2-1 in front, was not possible anymore. 'Pop Idol' had landed.

Walsall win at Wolves 1999

We held on during the second half to record our first win of the season and what a place to do it. Did we love it? You bet we did. We left the ground with the joyous Walsall fans and saw the Wolves fans demonstrating to their Board of Directors outside the club's offices. Receiving a good 'spank' from the Saddlers was not on their list of good days out.

We drew our next game away at Norwich 2-2, but then the wheels came off, Andy Rammall got injured and we found it increasingly hard to score, putting more pressure on our defence. We lost 7 games on the bounce, 5 in the league and 2 league Cup games. That sequence dumped us at the bottom of the division.

Our next match was at home to Birmingham City on October 8th 1999; a Friday night and live on TV. I was planning on meeting Pete, Joe and my Sister Helen at the ground to watch the match, but unfortunately, I had been ill all week and my hopes of recovering in time to make the journey were sinking as the week went by. I left it until Friday morning, hoping I would miraculously feel better, unfortunately, that was not the case. Although I would have preferred to be at the ground, at least the game was live on TV and I could stay warm in the comfort of my living room and watch the super Saddlers take on the Blues.

With Rammall, Marsh and Waterman

Andy Rammall had got himself fit again and had played in the previous match, a defeat to Stockport County. Ray Graydon had worked the loan and transfer market and brought in Samassi Abou from West Ham on loan, to hopefully score some much needed goals, and Pedro Matias from Tranmere Rovers to play on our left wing as Tony Daley had failed to hold down a place in the side. Both would be in the team that night.

Pete, Joe and Helen were at the ground and I was at home, shouting at the TV in an attempt to urge the Saddlers on.

Birmingham City, obviously knowing we had given Wolverhampton Wanderers a rough ride, were not in the mood to be embarrassed. They came to Bescot a determined team and they probably had the better of exchanges during the first half. The second half began and Walsall, attacking their favoured Gilbert Alsop End, were making better inroads into the Blues defence. Bukran hit a long ball out to our right-flank, which 'Wracky' got to, gathered and put in a dangerous cross. Birmingham's goalkeeper got half a touch on it and Pedro Matias, who had been in Walsall for only a couple of days, put it back into the six-yard box, where that man, Andy Rammall, side-footed it home. Rammall went off on a run down the length of the Gilbert Alsop End, soon to be mobbed by the team and I was jumping around my lounge with all the energy I had left. 1-0 up against the Blues with twenty minutes to go. Blues had their moments, but none good enough to break down our defence. Midland Teams 0, Walsall 2. The 'Pride of the Midlands' were growing in stature.

Our next match was eight days later. It was my birthday and we were away at the Hawthorns to face West Bromwich Albion on October 16th. I had been invited up for a lunch and small celebration for my day. Glenda Devy, Dave Cox, from the old days at Walsall Football Club, along with Keith Bertschin, Mark Rees and Colin Brazier all turned up. We had a great lunch and some good stories and memories before watching the match. Walsall fielded the winning team that had beaten Birmingham City.

Again, we would be victorious. Again, Andy Rammall would get the only goal of the game. Again, we would win 1-0. It was all too much to believe. We had now defeated Wolverhampton Wanderers, Birmingham City and West Bromwich Albion all in the first two months of the season. We were now rightly crowned 'Pride of the Midlands.'

We were all on such a high after those victories. Pete and I travelled to Portsmouth to watch the next match three days later. 'Marshy' had phoned to say put a few quid on 'Wracky' scoring, he really fancies himself tonight. Jeff Peron, then at Portsmouth had got us the tickets. Unfortunately, they were in with the Portsmouth fans, albeit in the stand. Walsall came out and sure enough ten minutes in 'Wracky' scores and we are 1-0 up. The excitement of the goal and the bet, probably made us celebrate too keenly. Portsmouth fans are not that forgiving and so we started to take a little bit of stick from all around us. Having taken a bit too much stick, I did explain to someone from Portsmouth, that maybe they should be 'off.' Mistake number one of what was a long night. A heated discussion followed and we narrowly escaped a ruckus. Portsmouth then equalized and then went in front. There were a few referee decisions that night that were dubious and left a lot to be desired. Another Portsmouth goal went in, 'Wacka' kicked the ball away in disgust and got booked before Ray Graydon pulled him off the pitch. Tackles were now flying in and the home crowd were beginning to enjoy the moment. We were taking more stick from them in the stand. Portsmouth then scored goals four and five and we had been battered. The escape from the ground was quick as we expected trouble in the streets, fortunately, we escaped unscathed from what was a real come down from our recent victories. As we all know, that's football!

We had another poor run from then until Christmas and we were still at the bottom of the table as the New Year began. Adie Viveash rallied the troops and Ray Graydon went into the transfer and loan market as we made a valiant attempt to escape the looming relegation.

In came, winger, Kevin Harper; strikers, Jamie Forrester and Graham Fenton; midfielder, Tom Bennett and full-back, Ian Brightwell. Transferred out were Neil Pointon, Richard Green, John Keister, Siggi Eyjolsson, Wayne Thomas, Darko Mavrak and Jason Brissett.

There is no doubt, the Board and Ray Graydon were trying everything to stay in the division and we still believed we had a chance. We started the new year well, beating Bolton Wanderers 2-0, Sheffield United 2-1 and Crewe Alexandra 3-2. That brought Wolverhampton Wanderers to Bescot Stadium on January 29th. A good crowd of 9,422 packed our ground to see if we could achieve the double over our closest rivals. The Wolves fans had come for revenge as they had not enjoyed our 'Pride of the Midlands' taunts and our belief we were a better side than them. That Wolves team were on a good streak and wanted to give their fans something to cheer about, they came prepared and ready for battle and so were we. The game went end-to-end throughout the first half and most of the second and with only eight minutes left Wolves went 1-0 ahead through Neil Emblen. The Wolves fans were ecstatic and started celebrating their victory immediately, probably a little prematurely. Walsall at the time were a gutsy team and did not lie down no matter what the circumstances. Four minutes later, a corner came into the Wolves six-yard box and there was Tony Barras to poke the ball home. Oh dear, 1-1 and the Wolves celebrations became muted as the Walsall fans ignited and once again laid claim to the 'Pride of the Midlands' tag.

We stuttered and stammered through February and March, drawing, losing, with only a couple of wins. With 5 matches to go we were still alive and had a chance to escape relegation back to Division Two.

On April 15th we drew 2-2 with Crystal Palace at home. On April 22nd, West Bromwich Albion came to Bescot Stadium. They were also in trouble at the bottom of the table so we both needed a win. A crowd of 9,161 packed into Bescot with both sets of supporters vocal and nervous. WBA took the lead through Bob Taylor and although we pushed forward the halftime score remained 1-0 to West Brom. Two minutes into the second half Pedro Matias swung in a corner that was partially cleared and put back into WBA's six-yard box; again, it was Andy Rammall who scored. Then, with seven minutes to go, Matias again bent in a corner for Tom Bennett to head home and bring the points to Walsall in a 2-1 victory.

Two days later, our next match was at St Andrews against Birmingham City. For the only time that season, and probably at the most crucial time, we lost a match to our Midlands rivals, Birmingham winning 2-0 in front of 24,268 fans.

Two games to go and we still had a chance; we made some amends for a horrible night in Portsmouth by defeating them 1-0 in front of 8,151 fans, with Pedro Matias getting our goal.

It set up what was our final match away at Ipswich Town on May 7, 2000, another game featured live on TV. I'd been away in Los Angeles but knew the game would be on TV that day and knew only a win and 3 points would do. I rearranged my flight to fly through Saturday night and arrive back in the U.K. at 10:30am. By the time I'd cleared customs and got home it was almost 12:30pm. I set the alarm and slept for an hour and a half before settling in front of the TV to watch our fate unfold. I still believed we had a chance and I knew enough about football to know it's not over until it's over. I knew the team were going all out for it and believed they could do it having spoken to Chris Marsh from L.A.

As we all now know it was not to be, Ipswich would win the game 2-0 and make the playoffs, we would be relegated, but our team had never given up all season long. Our manager had tried everything with a small playing budget to bring in players that might help and, to be fair, a lot of them had played their part. Gino Padula had been spectacular since signing in November. Tom Bennett had played well. Paul Hall had settled in and done a good job. Our main problem had been scoring goals. Mark Robbins had just not hit a goal streak even though you could see he was very capable of doing so. He would go on to Rotherham and score a bucket load of goals, but it just didn't work at Walsall. The most unfortunate situation was with Andy Rammall. He was very important to our team, but he had a real in-and-out season with injury. Many fans believe, had 'Rambo' been fit all season, we would not have been involved in a relegation scrap.

Even though we were relegated, for me it was a great season. I was proud of the team and all they had achieved; we had the better of West Bromwich

Albion, beating them twice, we won 1 and drew 1 against Wolverhampton Wanderers and we won 1 and lost 1 against Birmingham City. You simply cannot do that without great heart and passion and Walsall were a great side.

Personally, when I look back over my own career, in many ways 1999 was a peak year. Jive Records sold more singles than any other record company did that year in the United Kingdom; an amazing achievement given we were so small compared to EMI, Warner Bros, Polygram, Sony and BMG. We achieved our own status by winning 'Label of the Year' for the first time; we would win it in each of the next three years, recording four 'Label of the Year' Awards consecutively. I was awarded 'Managing Director of the Year' in 1999, the year of our promotion and the first six months back in The Championship when we beat all our local rivals. It doesn't get any better than that. Our record label was the 'Pride of the Music Industry' and my team were 'Pride of the Midlands.'

With Mark Robbins and Pete Waterman

Chapter 23

The Greatest Day

Relegation in football is tough, it seems to hover over everything you do like a dark cloud; everything reminds you of your losing status, you have fallen or tripped and life does not feel the same.

The mood around Walsall Football Club and the town, somehow, was not of despair or depression this time it was of positivity, unusual after relegation. I believe the reason for this was Ray Graydon.

Ray was known as a tough disciplinarian and it is true the squad did not like the no mobiles, no baseball caps, wearing suits to training, all of this was much talked about. What Ray was good at was giving the players guidelines, definite boundaries that made them know exactly where they were on all issues. This gave them a security and concentration that enabled them to play their best, it also united the team spirit, they were all treated the same and became a unit. If you talk to players who signed for Walsall during Ray's managership, they all say that Ray Graydon was the main reason they signed for Walsall. They believed he would get the best out of them, no matter how he did it, that would happen. Hence, not answering your mobile at training or on a match day was a small price to pay to play at your best.

Leaving the club at the end of the previous season was Bjarni Larusson after 59 games and 3 goals. Bjarni joined Scunthorpe; he had been a good midfielder for Walsall and was much liked. Michalis Vlachos left the club after making 12 appearances and scoring 1 goal in our relegation struggle. Mark Robbins joined Rotherham and became a hero scoring nearly 50 goals for them; he played 40 times for Walsall and scored 6 goals. Mark was a great lad and I enjoyed many an after-match conversation with him, he has gone on to be a fine manager and I always wish him the best.

Adrian Viveash was the biggest loss. Adie was a big part of our team and would be missed. He joined Reading after making 202 appearances for the Saddlers and scoring 13 goals.

Ray Graydon began rebuilding the squad, selling, buying, loaning and giving endless footballers trials in the hope of uncovering gems for his side.

Andy Rammell had an injury-broken season in our relegation and after a disagreement with Ray was placed on the transfer list. Rambo would soon move to Wycombe Wanderers where he would become a hero to their fans. When Rambo left, there was great disappointment from the Walsall fans; he was a huge hero and a symbol of the 'never say die' attitude our team had played with. Rambo had played 69 league games and scored 23 goals.

Michael Ricketts got the transfer he desired to Bolton Wanderers and soon would become a Premier League player and play for England. We sold him for 500,000 pounds and he had made 76 appearances, scoring 14 goals in his first spell with the club.

Gino Padula, who had played amazingly well at left-back after arriving mid-way through the last season, was a talented player and we were very keen to keep him. Gino became elusive and Ray searched everywhere to talk him into signing for us, then one day he appeared and had signed for Wigan Atheltic. Padula played 25 great games for Walsall before moving on. One door closes and another one opens. The previous pre-season we had a left-back on trial, we had liked him but not offered him a contract. This time we did and he would become a hero at the Bescot. Signed from CD Longrones in Spain, in came Zigor Aranalde, he would form one of our best left-flank partnerships with Pedro Matias.

Paul Hall and Tom Bennett both signed for the club after playing last season for us on loan. They were both good additions to the squad and were already part of it all.

Graydon paid 10,000 pounds to Bristol Rovers for Andy Tillson, who at 34 years of age had played for the Pirates most of his career. He would captain our side and perform brilliantly during the season - a great man and player.

To replace Rambo and Mark Robins, Ray brought in three strikers. He had been after Brett Angell for over six months and he finally got his man. Brett was much travelled and had scored goals at every level and club he had been with. His career total would be 187 goals in 502 games; at Walsall he would make 61 appearances scoring 15 goals.

Darren Byfield left Aston Villa reserves to prove himself at league level with Walsall and would become an all-time hero.

The pre-season build-up had commenced with four days at Whittingham Army Barracks. The squad then moved on to a tour of Scotland and it was in the game against Raith Rovers we unearthed our gem and future huge Walsall hero. I spoke with Chris Marsh during the tour and he told me we had this striker on trial from Portugal, he came on hitting the full-backs, running the channels and scored a hat trick before halftime, then Ray took him off so no one would see him and steal him from us. I knew if Chris thought he was good he had to have talent. Ray Graydon would sign Jorge Leitao from CD Feirense in Portugal for 150,000 pounds. He would become the leader of our attack and a Bescot favourite.

The season started at Rotherham with Mark Robins making his debut for them and we paid an early price, Robbo scored from the spot in the first half and scored again just after halftime. 2-0 down and Robbo had started what would become a magnificent spell at Rotherham. Brett Angell dragged us back into the match with a debut goal and, on an incredibly hot day, we went after Rotherham. The pressure of attacking led to an equalizing own goal to bring the score to 2-2. Now with our tails up we went after the winner. Brett Angell scored his second goal on debut and the 3 points came home to Walsall. That opening match of the season set the tone for the team for the coming year. No matter what happened we always believed that we could come back, we were never beaten until the final whistle, our fitness and discipline were at a very high level. The players and Ray were committed to regaining our status back in Division One at the first attempt; our supporters who were at Rotherham believed it too and cheered the boys on wherever we played. In the league we won the first 5 games and shot to the top of the table; Rotherham away 3-2, Oldham at home 3-2, Swindon away 4-1, Oxford at home 3-2 and Wigan at home 2-0. The 5 straight wins at the beginning of the season was a club record and would deliver a 'Manager of the Month' award for Ray Graydon. The curse would strike from that award and we lost the next match at Bury 2-0.

October 2000 saw us win 3-0 against Stoke City, which would be the start of 8 consecutive wins at home. The TV cameras turned up to see our ninth home game and brought with them the curse, which stuck and broke the winning streak, a 1-1 draw against Rotherham was all we could manage. Rotherham and Walsall were both flying at this time and were first and second in the table, it would signal a poor patch for the Saddlers and Ray Graydon delved into the market to bring in some experience to see us through to the end of the season.

In came Barry Horne at thirty-eight years of age, from Kidderminster Harriers, to steady the midfield, along with Fitzroy Simpson from Hearts. Ronnie Eklund came and played a few games to help out and Don Goodman arrived from Motherwell to bring great enthusiasm and passion to our attack.

The main departure from the squad through January was the calling of time on the great Walsall career of Chris Marsh. 481 first team games and 'Lucky' was on his way to Wycombe Wanderers to link up with Rambo.

To be fair, we battled to the finish line, we were no longer in the running for automatic promotion, but wins over Bristol Rovers 2-1 and away at Port Vale 2-0 set up an end-of-season party at Northampton where Brett Angell scored a hat trick in a 3-0 win. Walsall had finished 4th in the table and now had the prospect of the playoffs. We had finished the season with those 3 straight wins, were confident and in form.

Jorge Leitao should take great credit for this season; he became our leading scorer with 20 goals, led our front line with power, commitment and passion and was voted our 'Player of the Year.' Known in Walsall as 'Gorgeous George' and 'The Portuguese Man of War,' a true hero and over the next few seasons, a Walsall legend.

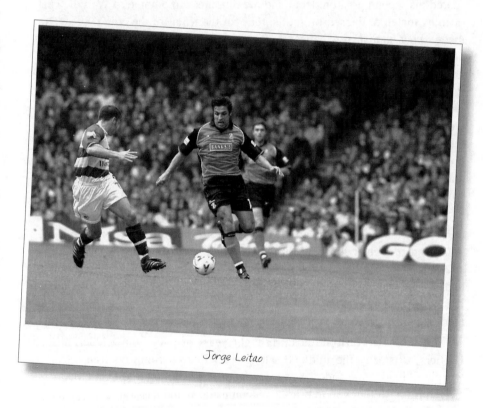

Jorge Leitao

Walsall had a couple of moments in the Cups that year that added to another fine season. In the League Cup Round One we beat Kidderminster Harriers, which brought West Ham United to Bescot Stadium. We just lost the first leg 1-0 after putting in a good performance. Pete and I were at Upton Park for the return. West Ham scored quickly but Jorge Leitao equalized after seven minutes. We then proceeded to take the game to West Ham and Mark Wright, making his debut, so nearly took the game to extra time.

In the F.A. Cup we dispatched Exeter City in Round One and Barnet in Round Two live on TV. Round Three drew us again against West Ham United at Bescot Stadium. The match was to be a pulsating affair and would be the lead game on 'Match of the Day' that evening. West Ham took an early lead, with Frank Lampard cutting through our defence after four minutes. This Walsall side was made of strong stuff and after slowly turning the match scored through Darren Wrack after thirty-two minutes. The second half began with West Ham showing renewed vigour and Kanute headed West Ham in front. 'Wacka' would take all the spoils that day for some outstanding saves during the match as West Ham grew in confidence. Kanute smashed in another to make it 3-1, still Walsall were not done. With two minutes to go, Brett Angell pulled one back and we went after the equalizer, but time was not on our side. In the after match interviews all of the West Ham players mentioned what a great goalkeeper Jimmy Walker was and what a good side Walsall were; we came out of it with honour and a great deal of credit.

The playoffs are always nervous affairs, the prize is so huge and the disappointment of losing is equally mammoth.

In finishing 4th we were drawn to play our first game away at Stoke City before having the possible advantage of playing the second match at home.

4,000 Walsall supporters made the journey to the Britannia Stadium to see the first game on May 13th 2001. Stoke believed that they would eventually be promoted and the total gate was 23,689. The first match ended 0-0, which was thought of as a satisfactory result by Walsall. In reality, we had been better than that and unlucky not to take a lead back to Bescot.

Pete, Joe, my Sister Helen and I were all in attendance, nervous, excited, hoping and praying that Walsall would make it to the Millennium Stadium for our first ever national final.

A vocal Walsall support of 8,957 assembled at Bescot on the evening of May 16th 2001. Stoke were a determined outfit and took the game to Walsall. After thirty-one minutes Graham Kavanagh struck an exceptional volley into the back of our net and then proceeded to celebrate in front of our fans, which upset them and our team, the celebration was excessive. That celebration galvanized our team and forward we went in search of an equalizer. On forty-two minutes we gained a corner, Tom Bennett sent in an in-swinging kick that somehow Stoke's keeper Gavin Ward fumbled and it ended up in the back of the net. That goal just before halftime changed the whole face of the match. Walsall went in on a high at halftime with the scores level and Stoke returned to the dressing room disappointed they had not held onto their lead.

During the first fifteen minutes of the second half the tie would be over, Walsall came out fully charged, attacking the vocal Gilbert Alsop End of the stadium. It took only two minutes for Pedro Matias to wriggle free and beat the offside trap to put us 2-1 up. We surged forward again at Stoke and they were forced into giving away a free kick just outside their box. Dean Keates dispatched the ball into the net to make it 3-1, just three minutes after Matias had scored. The Walsall fans went wild and the team went at Stoke to finish them off. Eleven minutes later a Stoke side, in disarray, tried to clear a ball across their own goal, Matias stuck out a leg and it cannoned into the net 4-1. We were on our way to the greatest day in our history. Stoke managed a consolation towards the end of the game but they were a well-beaten side at 4-2.

The town of Walsall was alive. The search for tickets was immense, as everyone wanted to be there at the Millennium Stadium to face Reading, who would feature two of our former players, Adrian Viveash and Martin Butler.

In the English football world, Reading were by far the favourites to progress to Division One. Their squad was valued at 6 million pounds and Walsall's at 180,000 pounds and that included 150,000 pounds for Jorge Leitao. Reading also had the goal scoring partnership of Jamie Curaton with 28 goals, and Martin Butler with 27 goals. The May 27th playoff final drew a crowd of 50,496. Walsall fans were outnumbered three to one; over 17,000 people had made the journey from Walsall down the M5.

Everyone from Walsall has his or her own personal story from that day which will always remain in the memory.

On Saturday 25th I drove from London to Cardiff to enjoy the whole weekend, staying in a hotel. I had dinner there that night and went over to see the Walsall staff, including Jeff Bonser and Roy Whalley who were dining in the same restaurant. We were all full of hope and excitement. On the day of the game I had a late breakfast and tried to stay calm as the atmosphere built.

Pete Waterman drove down on the day of the match and we met inside the stadium. My Sister Helen travelled down with Joe Savage and a group of Walsall die hards that always went to away matches in Joe's 'Venga Bus.' I knew my Sister would be safe with Joe.

The Walsall fans were there early, milking the atmosphere of what could be our greatest 'day out.' They were all dressed in red and white and, with great humour, were wearing Don Goodman wigs.

I walked around the Stadium saying hello to many of the travelling fans I knew before entering the Stadium. I will always remember the sight of those 17,000 fans and the noise they made before kick-off and during the match. It was a magnificent sight.

The Walsall fans out sang and made so much noise they drowned out the Reading fans and the reception they gave our team was enormous.

The match began and the Saddlers were soon on the back foot. Reading attacked us in waves and we were defending continuously, it took us fourteen minutes to have a speculative shot at the Reading goal. We seemed to have weathered the storm when on thirty-two minutes Jamie Curaton hit a shot from a throw-in. 'Wacka' seemed to have it covered but it slipped through his grasp and just rolled into the net, 1-0 to Reading. Murphy's law had struck, Jimmy had been having an outstanding season and it was unfortunate that he should make a slip in a match like that. The Walsall fans responded with a chant of 'Super, Super Jim, Super, Super Jim, Super Jimmy Walker' to rebuild Jim's confidence. Reading continued to throw everything at us and would soon hit the bar with Jimmy beaten. We all started praying for halftime so we could regroup, hopefully, being only 1-0 down. Finally, the halftime whistle came and we all breathed a sigh of relief that it was no worse than 1-0.

The Walsall side and fans regrouped in the break and again our side was welcomed back onto the pitch as heroes. Reading decided to come out slowly and take the sting out of our coming response, but to no avail. Walsall attacked straight from the kick-off. Dean Keates tested their keeper with a powerful free kick and three minutes into the second half Matias crossed for Andy Tillson to head back across goal, where Don Goodman hooked the ball into the net. 1-1, we were back in it. The Walsall fans went wild, including me, Pete, Joe and Helen.

The game was now end-to-end as both teams went hard at each other the 'ooohs' and 'aaarghs' rang out around the ground. Brightwell blocked and Jorge Leitao had a shot scrambled away as the half ticked away. A minute to go and Jorge ran sixty yards to shoot, but he had no power left and it was easily taken by the Reading keeper. Extra time was called as Ray Graydon went on the pitch to rally the Walsall side.

The first period of extra time began and disaster struck, a throw-in enabled Parkinson to cross into our box and Martin Butler rose to head it into the top corner. We were 2-1 down and all Walsall fans knew before the match that Martin would most probably score. It had happened at the worst time.

Seven minutes later Ray Graydon played his final hand, on came Darren Byfield for Jorge Leitao, Gabby Buckran for Tom Bennett and Matt Gadsby for Paul Hall.

As the teams turned around for the final fifteen minutes the score was still 2-1 to Reading. It would now take an enormous effort from a tiring Walsall side to overcome the odds beginning to stack up against us. After three minutes, Bukran played the ball into the Reading penalty area and both Darren Byfield and Dean Keates ran at the defenders. In a panic one Reading defender banged the ball at another and the result was a bizarre own goal from Tony Rougier, who really knew nothing about it as the ball cannoned off his head and into the net. The Walsall fans were now yelling, screaming, chanting and urging the team forward. I had no idea how the goal had arrived, it all happened so quickly, it seemed that Keatsie had somehow banged it in, it would take a few video re-runs to see how we had equalized. Reading were deflated, just twelve minutes from Division One. Walsall, however, were rampant; gathering the ball after the kick-off we went at them again, sixty seconds later, Ian Brightwell played a ball out to Darren Byfield who turned the defender and shot with his left foot, he had caught it sweetly and the ball shot inside the near post. We were in front at 3-2 with ten minutes remaining. That would become the longest ten minutes in Walsall's history. The drama still not over, Reading threw everything at Walsall and within a minute Tony Barras fractured a cheekbone in a collision with Adie Viveash. Barras was on the touchline pushing and shoving to get back on, the team doctor and Ray Graydon had to restrain Tony, who sat on the floor in despair as Walsall challenged for every ball in a desperate attempt to hold on with ten men.

Challenge after challenge went in on Reading as the time slowly ticked away. In what seemed like an age the referee finally blew for fulltime. Walsall had made it back to the First Division at the first time of asking.

Darren Byfield would remain a Walsall hero forever for his winning goal that day. 'Daz' had been disappointed not to make the starting line-up but the team had been saying all week that Darren would spring off the bench to claim the winning goal and so it came to pass. I think the team believed 100% that Darren would score when he came off the bench and that confidence saw us through. The team and Ray Graydon collected the trophy and the Walsall fans enjoyed every minute as they paraded in front of the fans.

Pete and I were invited to join in the celebrations with the team inside the Stadium after the match; we stayed there for a couple of hours enjoying the moment before making our way home.

That day was Ray Graydon's wife's birthday; Sue celebrated on that day of all days. The people of Walsall knighted Ray Graydon for that special day and achieving two promotions to Division One in three years with an un-fancied side. He is still referred to only as 'Sir Ray,' to this day, by the people of Walsall.

Ray Graydon and that team provided the people of Walsall with their 'Greatest Day.'

May 27th 2000-2001 Play-off final

With Don Goodman

Chapter 24

Chris 'Lucky' Marsh

Chris Marsh

I guess I first met Chris in 1986; he had been at Walsall Football Club and worked his way through the ranks. Over the next two years I would get to know him a little more, but gradually. 'Marshy' had played well in the youth team and reserves and was getting closer and closer to being a fulltime professional. As he is prone to do, he fell in with the wrong crowd, well, the wrong crowd being a crowd of one, the legendary 'Rico' Mark Rees. Its unfortunate that I was also known to frequent the wrong crowd as 'Rico' has always been one of my mates. Hence, I met 'Marshy.' I did go out on occasions with Reesy, Don Penn, Paul Waddington, Ian Paul and a young 'Marshy' used to tag along on occasions. 'Rico' got to know all of the young players at Walsall. Possibly because of his injury problems he spent more time with them than training with the first team. All of the youngsters also looked up to 'Rico,' the fans loved him and when fit, he was a frightening player.

Chris Marsh

I remember well the day 'Marshy' made his Walsall debut; there were 5,051 spectators in the crowd that day, January 2nd 1988. The visitors to Fellows Park were Rotherham United and we were in the process of spanking them 5-2, Nicky Cross getting three, David Kelly and Craig Shakespeare the others. We sent on two substitutes in the second half, first Trevor Christie and then

Chris Marsh

Chris Marsh. I was sitting with Reesy. Chris ran on, encouraged by Mark, 'Go on 'Marshy'.' He had only just got into position, right centre-midfield, when the ball dropped to him, he lashed it into the net and set off on a run. Reesy went mad. I was stunned and the crowd went up delighted, the disappointment as the referee blew for offside was immense. Trevor Christie had been late moving out with the defence and was caught offside. In today's world and new laws, would he have been interfering with play? I'm not sure he would. Had the goal have stood, timed at seven seconds, it would have been the fastest debut goal in the history of the game. The curse of 'Lucky' had struck.

Chris would be on the bench and get on a couple of times that season. In those days Chris was sporting the hairstyle of the day. In today's world the style leaves a lot to be desired, but back then it was all in the name of fashion. If you can remember Chris Waddle in his pomp with a hairstyle called 'The Mullet,' then you can picture 'Marshy.' Chris added some gorgeous blonde colouring to set off the look. I'm sure his Mom, who I know well, said 'You can't go out looking like that Chris' and he replied, 'You don't know what you're talking about Mom.' Looking back, I think she did. I must also add I have no room to talk as some of my early hairstyles could also be expressed as fashionable in their day.

In our promotion season Chris came on three times as we made our way into the now called Championship for the first time in twenty-five years. We had a fine side that season and to get anywhere near playing for the team shows the promise that Chris had as a player.

In our one season in The Championship, Chris played 5 times and made 3 sub appearances. He played mainly in midfield at the time, wide right, wide left and central, slotting in comfortably in all three positions. We were relegated the next season. During the next campaign, 1989/1990, Chris played in 11 games with two substitute appearances. He played mainly in central-midfield but also featured at left-back and on the right-flank.

In our first season in Division Four, Chris started on the left-flank, switched to central-midfield, filled in at right-back then went back to central-midfield, making 27 appearances. On February 2nd 1991, Doncaster Rovers were the visitors to the new Bescot Stadium, the result was a 1-0 victory to Walsall and marked the first goal scored for the club by Chris Marsh. His second would come at Halifax Town in a 5-2 defeat on March 2nd 1991.

In the 1991/1992 season Chris was established in the side, he would make 44 appearances scoring 3 goals. Position wise, the most appearances were in central-midfield, but he also played at left-back and on the right-flank.

It's fair to say that the Walsall Faithful took a while to become Chris Marsh fans. In his early days as a young player they gave him a rough ride, to be honest, I thought unjustly. If you know about football, it is not easy to constantly switch positions, most players will not do it; they become specialized in one area of the pitch and find it uncomfortable when changing position. 'Marshy' was being asked to play left-midfield one week, left-back the next, central-midfield, oh, tell you what, right-flank 'Marshy.' It is testament to his character and ability to be able to change position at the

Chris Marsh

drop of a hat and perform well with the crowd giving you stick; you have to be talented, strong and purposeful to withstand that.

The next season, 1992/1993, we would eventually make the play-offs but lose to Crewe Alexandra. Chris really established himself during this season and the fans began to turn around and realize what a player he was becoming. I believe this was due to the first time in his career he was allowed to play consistently in one position; he made 43 appearances and scored 3 goals.

It was during October 1992 that the buzz about Chris Marsh and a possible transfer started to rise. The scouts had been down to Bescot: Arsenal, Manchester United, Tottenham, Coventry and Liverpool were all taking a look. Liverpool had Graeme Souness in charge, brought in to rebuild an ageing Liverpool side. Young talented British players were the order of the day back then, long before the Premiership became international as it is today.

Chris Marsh

Liverpool confirmed their interest, which sparked the club and Kenny Hibbitt into action by making noises in the press that Kenny rated Chris highly and wouldn't want to sell, but 300,000 pounds would enable him to bring in new recruits. More scouts were arriving at Bescot; Everton, Norwich, Aston Villa, West Bromwich Albion, Derby County and Oldham were all taking stock of the situation. When Liverpool came to look twice more during the coming months, it seemed that 'Marshy' would follow a great deal of other Walsall footballers to move on to better things. Personally, although I would have missed 'Marshy,' I wanted him to get the move and have a chance at higher level, especially as it was Liverpool. I believe that he would have converted to right-back permanently at Liverpool, they would have enabled him to do that, whereas at Walsall we need players that can play well in different positions, mainly because the squad size is much smaller.

It would be soon after that that Chris injured his right ankle putting him out for most of the second half of the season. The interest cooled and never came back, Liverpool made their signings and Chris remained at Walsall. That's football and the curse of 'Lucky' struck again.

Chris, obviously massively disappointed, is not the type to dwell or whinge, he got his head down and had a magnificent next season playing either left-back or left-wing-back, chalking up 47 games and scoring 4 goals. He was never on the bench, was always first choice and only missed 3 games through injury.

In 1994/1995, even after playing a full season on the left side, Chris played almost the whole of the next season down the right of midfield. He seemed to enjoy the freedom of getting forward more often and would score 11 goals while making 49 appearances. We got promotion with a draw away at Bury, 0-0 in the final game. I was talking with Chris the day after as I had not been able to make the match, he told me in the second half, as Bury pressed, he was chasing a ball down our right-flank and was clear, the ball was heading out of play, but 'Marshy' knew he could get it. An over keen ball boy took a pace onto the pitch and picked it up. Chris going at full pelt was shouting 'drop it, drop it;' keyed up and into the game Chris thought the referee just might let him carry on. The kid dropped it, the referee blew the whistle and the young lad, with everything happening around him and the crowd shouting, just burst into tears. 'Marshy' in the heat of a promotion fight consoled the kid with a 'Don't worry, you're all right, it'll be okay' before heading back into position. That kid must be much older now but I bet he remembers that moment in his life. 'Marshy' at full pelt, screaming at you, can't be pleasant, let's be fair.

The following season, after promotion and eleven goals, Chris started on the right of midfield, quickly switched and spent half a season at left-back, then finished it on the right again.

In the summer of 1997, Martin Butler, a great mate of both 'Marshy' and me, was heading off to Cambridge United to be signed by Roy McFarland. It seemed that with the arrival of Jan Sorenson Chris may be available for transfer. Roy McFarland was showing interest in Chris and Walsall probably thought the deal might go through, depending on Cambridge paying the fee. Chris was then at Cambridge United training with them but not allowed to play in any games until the deal was completed. Walsall, in the meantime, were trying Darren Rogers, Dean Keates, Ian Roper and Stuart Ryder, all at left-back. I went to Cambridge a couple of times when Chris was there, watching the first team matches with him and Martin Butler play. It seemed a good club at the time and they were building a good side. I believe Chris thought maybe it was time for a change and was disappointed in not being included in Walsall's early plans that season. Whether it was Jan Sorenson or Jeff Bonser getting fed up with Cambridge or a combination of the two, Chris was on his way back to Walsall and the left-back position.

We thought at the time regarding the transfer to Cambridge that the 'Curse of Lucky' had struck again. However, 'Marshy' arrived in the dressing room, the boys happy to have him back and Hodgey had scrawled 'Welcome to our new left-back' all over the training board.

Chris played in 47 games that season at left-back, missing only 3 due to injury. He played at West Ham United in the Coca Cola Cup, Old Trafford against Manchester United in the F.A. Cup, and so nearly got to Wembley in the Auto Windscreen Shield.

It was obviously 'Marshy' that managed to get the only Walsall shirt to make it back to the dressing room that day at Manchester United, had it washed and then got all the boys to sign it for me. I was also pleased when I found out it was Platty's shirt, no one dared to take it off him I guess.

The 1998/1999 season will never be forgotten as the Ray Graydon group of no-hoper players and bookies bet for relegation, beat everyone in the Division and made it, after eleven years, back to The Championship. The last time Walsall played in that division 'Marshy' was just a first year professional all those years ago, he had come full circle.

Chris, for me, had his best ever season that year. His partnership with Wracky that season down the right side of our team was the best combination I've ever seen at Walsall Football Club, they were devastating. They knew each other's game so well and trusted each other positionally, the way they doubled up on full-backs and defended as a pair, you will rarely see better at any level of football. Chris played in 52 games and scored 1 goal.

Chris does not boast about anything he has achieved and is more likely to take the mickey out of himself, he rarely talks about the moments in his career. I know a few that he remembers with great fondness though and the goal that season is one of them. I think it was a magical moment to have played at Walsall all those years and been involved in an eleven year struggle to get back to The Championship. It was only right and proper that the player that had done the most for the club, during all those years, should be the one that scored that goal at that moment against Oldham. The moment we all knew we were back. The joy on the faces of the other players as they chased him down to the corner flag said it all, 'Marshy' is a legend and he's done it! I was with Chris after the game, the enormity of the achievement just sinking in, all he said to me was, 'Oh mate, that goal.' It was a truly great moment. I was in the stand with Pete Waterman, we both went wild when Chris scored and it was a moment neither of us will forget either. I would guess, if Chris were pressed on other moments of his career, I would say, the goal against Leeds United in the F.A. Cup and playing at Old Trafford against David Beckham were his highlights.

Our season back in The Championship, Chris played his part, although all of these years later Chris still pays for that season. His achilles was in bad shape. The trouble with achilles injuries is sometimes you can play on them, although I wouldn't advise it. Chris had an aggravated achilles injury all season; he should have stopped playing and rested it. Chris being Chris, had made it back to The Championship and was not going to miss playing in all those big stadiums and proving himself at a higher level.

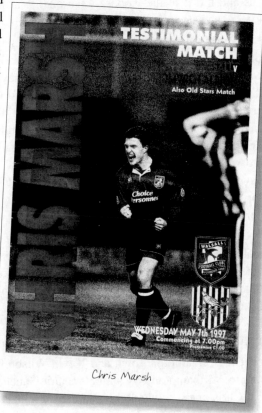

Chris Marsh

During the early part of 2001, the case of the missing coach appeared on Sky Sports News. I hadn't spoken to 'Marshy' before seeing the piece but I had a strong feeling I knew who might have took it. Tom Bradley, who had retired but could not get used to Saturdays without a match, returned to the club as kit man, he used to drive the bus with all the equipment and injured players to Lillishall. Tom unloaded the bus and was inside when Chris and Keatsie noticed he'd left the keys in. They took the bus and parked it in the woods, sneaking back into the dressing room without being missed. Ray Graydon and Tom sounded the realisation that the bus had been stolen. The boys were assembled and asked if they knew anything about it, all was quiet. They were then confined to the dressing room while Tom and Ray went in search of the missing coach. It could not be found. The boys were told they would stay in the dressing room until someone owned up. At that point 'Marshy' and Keatsie had to raise their hands, a hefty fine, all but Ray and Tom had a good laugh.

A couple of weeks later, Walsall were playing live on TV, as they warmed up during the 'kick in' the camera fell on 'Marshy,' the commentator, missing the over 450 games he had played for Walsall and the legendary status he had achieved, commented 'And there's Chris Marsh, the man who stole the team bus and hid it in the woods.' Live on TV in front of millions the 'Curse of Lucky' had struck again.

During January, a number of issues happened. Ray had signed Ian Brightwell, who had fitted straight into the team at right-back whilst 'Marshy' was struggling with his achilles problems. Ray liked Ian and 'Marshy' found it impossible to get back in his now favoured right-back position. There was also the pranks, the legendary status, the fans' favourite, sometimes all of that can work against you. Chris suggested it might be time to leave, wanting a first team spot on a weekly basis after all he had achieved. In March 2001, the move to Wycombe Wanderers came for a fee of 30,000 pounds. Wycombe were having a great Cup run and I went along with Chris to see Andy Rammall play for Wycombe in the F.A. Cup semi-final against Liverpool. They put up a great performance, eventually losing 2-1.

A few days later, Pete Waterman and I went to Wycombe to watch 'Marshy' make his debut at right-back. We turned up and went to the Directors' entrance where Chris had left tickets. The doorman looked at Pete and recognised him, giving us the tickets he said 'Who the hell is this Chris Marsh?' Pete took his ticket and when I got mine I told him 'Legend mate, that's Chris Marsh!'

I saw 'Marshy' play a couple more times for Wycombe, but at the start of the next season they started with a changed system and Chris was on the bench. Northampton Town and Kevin Wilson offered 10,000 pounds to take him to Northampton. Wycombe's Laurie Sanchez did not want Chris to leave, but Chris knew he would be guaranteed a place at Northampton and took the move. I think if you ask him now he probably believes he should have stayed at Wycombe, but in usual Marsh style, Chris just gets up and gets on with it.

Chris had two seasons at Northampton and I saw him play there a couple of times, he played right-back and centre-midfield, back to being the utility player. His stay was interrupted by the troublesome achilles and at the end of his contract Northampton were relegated and they did not renew. Chris had got it in his mind it was time to quit. I remember trying to talk him out of it. I had seen enough professional footballers retire when they could have had another season or two and how tough it is to re-adjust to 'normal life.' Roy McFarland, who had wanted to sign Chris to Cambridge, offered him a contract at Chesterfield, where he was then their manager, but I think Chris had already made his mind up. The achilles was still troublesome and I think he knew it would go completely if he carried on. So, a career that had seen over 500 professional appearances came to a close.

Chris was soon up and off again, straight into working and had some successes and a failure or two along the way. The driving company, Bostin' Baps the sandwich shop, the football coaching school, were all successes, the restaurant, probably not. The coaching in the U.S.A. and Australia were great excursions and the small comeback playing in Australia lasted only one game. Chris played midfield and came off with 'Man of the Match,' but I think he knew that the achilles would not stand up to it at all.

I guess I've known 'Marshy' over twenty-five years now and we have always been good friends, even when he has been in Australia or the U.S.A. we have kept in touch by email. When I've played football with him in Old Stars' games he has always looked after me on the pitch. He supported me through my record career and I supported him through his football career. He always came to my concerts and I watched him play.

Years and years ago I told him I'd trade all of my hits to run up the tunnel in a Walsall shirt on a cold January night in Hartlepool. He said he'd trade his appearances to experience all of those hit records. I guess we lived each other's dreams at close quarters.

We are still mates to this day. It's still hard to watch a match with Chris; he's not a great watcher. When he's at a game he still wants to play - true testament to a footballer with great courage, power, skill and a will to win.

Chris 'Lucky' Marsh, my mate.

With Rambo and Marshy

With Chris Marsh

Chapter 25

Punching Above Our Weight

Walsall were back in The Championship and we hoped that this time we could stay there. Yes, we wanted to do better than that, but the main objective was to stay in The Championship, come what may. Ray Graydon set about building the squad for the new season. Don Goodman signed on after being on loan last season. Similarly, after long negotiations, Fitzroy Simpson signed after his last term loan spell. In came Lee Harper from QPR as back up to Jimmy Walker in goal, Matt Carbon signed from West Bromwich Albion to play centre-back and we signed a tricky unpredictable right-winger from Brazil, Herivelto signed from Cruzeiro.

Soon into the season, Fredrick Biancalani signed from French side Nancy, primarily to play left-back, but Ziggy Aranalde was not going to lose his position without a fight.

Out of the club went Paul Hall after 51 appearances and 10 goals, joining league newcomers, Rushden and Diamonds. Also leaving was Gabor Buckran after 73 league games and 4 goals. Gabby joined Wigan Athletic and remains the only Hungarian to have played for Walsall.

The team that started the season was goalkeeper, Walker; back four, Brightwell, Tillson, Barras and Aranalde; midfield, Herivelto, Bennett, Keates and Matias and strikers, Leitao and Byfield.

The first match of the season would see us hold onto our 'Pride of the Midlands' crown. We were at home to West Bromwich Albion and it was a great way to start the campaign. 9,181 turned up with the noise level at full tilt as the teams began the match. In the first half both teams contested the match strongly before Herivelto wriggled his way down our right-flank and crossed for 'Gorgeous' Jorge Leitao to head us in front. The score remained the same until the second half when West Brom equalised through a thunderous shot into the corner of our net. The game could have gone either way after that. Late on in the game Keatsie sent in a free kick from our right-flank, which Barras headed towards goal, the keeper saved but fumbled and Barras followed up to poke it home. The Walsall Faithful erupted as we were back in the First Division, defeating our close rivals again and securing our first 3 points.

We drew our next match away at Preston, 1-1, but then went on a poor run of results. In our next 8 games we would only achieve 2 draws. We had a better October, winning 3 and losing 3. The run to Christmas brought 3 wins, 2 draws and 6 defeats. If we didn't know it before, we knew it now, we were in a fight for survival. During that first half of the season Chris Nichol had returned to the club as first team coach and we had used the loan system to bring in Tom Curtis, Thomas Thorgerson and Steve Chettle from Barnsley, all of who had several games in our first team.

January 2002 arrived and the month would bring incredible and surprising change. Carlos Andre came in on loan to bolster our midfield from Portugese side Vitoria Guimaraes and David Holdsworth joined on loan from Birmingham City to marshal our defence. On January 12th 2002, we lost 2-1 at Preston North End and then went to the Hawthorns to play West Bromwich Albion on January 20th. We lost the game 1-0, but it was more the way we lost it that caused the problem. The Walsall team was flat that day, unusual for a Walsall side in a local derby. The Walsall fans were disappointed but there were no chants or calls for the Manager's head, Sir Ray was too well respected for his achievements with our club. I think we all believed that somehow Sir Ray would pull the side together and make an attempt at fighting relegation. It was therefore a complete shock that on January 22nd Jeff Bonser fired Ray Graydon.

I believe the Board were worried that Walsall would again be relegated as they had been two seasons before. They probably also thought that if that happened it would be unlikely that Sir Ray could build another team to bounce straight back.

Jeff Bonser felt that Ray had lost the dressing room and could not motivate the team; he felt he needed to act quickly to give sufficient time to a new manager to escape relegation. It was a sad moment for Jeff as well. The conversation between Jeff and Sir Ray was short and quiet that day. Sir Ray Graydon left Walsall Football Club with great dignity, true to the man. He is still our most successful manager and will always be respected and loved in Walsall.

I only knew Sir Ray to say 'Hello' to during his days as Walsall's manager, but in the years that have followed I got to know him well through Footballer's Golf Tournaments and Testimonial golf days. I remember well his hole-in-one at The Footballers' Classic on the 12th hole on the South Course of La Manga; a shot over water, the ball ended up in the cup and was recorded by the TV cameras. Great shot, great man.

Personally, I could not believe Ray had gone, but football is a fast moving business and within a couple of days former Wolverhampton Wanderers Manager, Colin Lee, was appointed and Chris Nichol resigned his post.

Colin Lee set about changing the personnel straight away. Brett Angell, after 61 games and 15 goals, joined Rushden and Diamonds, as did Andy Tillson after 51 games and 2 goals. Darren Byfield was sold to Rotherham United for 50,000 pounds after 77 appearances and 13 goals.

Dave Merrington was appointed first team Coach and soon to arrive on loan would be centre-forward Marcelo and Walsall midfield hero, Martyn O'Conner, both from Birmingham City. Steve Corica joined from Japanese side Sanfreece Hiroshima; he had played at Wolves under Colin Lee and was an Australian International. Full-back, Gus Uhlenbeek, joined on loan from Sheffield United and the pace of change was breathtaking.

On January 26th our next match was in the F.A. Cup Fourth Round away at Charlton Athletic. It was described as a baptism of fire for our new manager.

Phil and Barbara Cokell, Phil being a lifetime Charlton fan, had invited me to the match. A great friend, he thought it would be good to enjoy a rare match between our teams. We had a great lunch and plenty of banter before the game began. Jorge Leitao had been dropped from the team a month before, but Colin Lee brought him straight back to lead our attack. On seeing the team sheet, I'd told Phil that Charlton were in trouble as 'Gorgeous' was back.

The game started and after only five minutes 'Gorgeous' robbed a Charlton player of the ball in our own half and set off down the left before cutting in and sending the most delightful curling chip shot over the Charlton keeper. Jorge would later say that it was the best goal of his career. Jimmy Walker was also having one of his days, whenever Charlton worked a position to score, 'Wacka' saved. The halftime score was 1-0 to Walsall and we set about the second half, not to defend, but to go forward again. After three good attempts at the Charlton goal, Pedro Matias sent Jorge through the middle and he coolly rounded the keeper before putting it into the empty net. 2-0 and an upset was on the cards.

After sixty-seven minutes Charlton were awarded a penalty. Their penalty taker was Graham Stuart. Charlton had played a game midweek and were awarded a penalty, which Stuart had taken and scored. The highlights had been shown on TV and I had sat at home watching. I knew Stuart would put the ball to Jimmy's right, I was screaming from the stand at Jim 'Dive right, dive right, 'Wacka,' dive right.' Jimmy would never have heard a word with a 20,000 crowd, Stuart hit the kick and Jimmy dived right and saved.

Jim told me afterwards he had been watching the same highlights in midweek and guessed Stuart would do the same thing as he had scored. A game turns on such moments and although Stuart would score later in the game we hung on to record a memorable 2-1 victory. It set up a home match in the Fifth Round against Fulham and although we put up a great fight we eventually went down 2-1.

Colin Lee had the most exceptional start to his career as Walsall manager. That Charlton match did a lot to recover confidence in the squad. The team that day was an attacking side. Wrack and Matias on the wings and Leitao and Byfield up front had pace and determination. Lee had returned to a 4.4.2. system. Sir Ray had been playing a more defencive 3.5.1 system, obviously to stop us leaking goals. The change and freedom of the system helped us win that match, along with a pent up Jorge Leitao, who had not started a game for over six weeks.

Colin Lee moved players in and out of the side searching for the right combination. We had not done well against our local rivals, won 1 and lost 1 against West Bromwich Albion, the defeat at the Hawthorns signalling great change at our club. We lost our home game 3-0 against Wolverhampton Wanderers and would lose the return at the Molineux on February 26th, also 3-0. Revenge for the 'Dingles' I guess.

Following the defeat at Wolves we had 10 games left in the season and there were six teams battling to avoid the final two places left for relegation. During the first 6 games of the 10 we won 2, drew 3 and lost 1. We were still in the bottom three with 4 games to go.

On April 1th away from home, Nottingham Forest were surprisingly beaten 3-2. No one saw that result coming and everyone had thought it was a home win for Notts Forest. This breathed life into our campaign and gave us hope that we might succeed, but it was still a long shot. Five days later, at home to Stockport County, in a nail-biting game we won 1-0, 'Gorgeous Jorge' coming off the bench to score the winner. These two victories lifted us out of the bottom three for the first time in two months. With 2 games left we headed for an away game at Sheffield United on April 13th, unlucky for some.

It had been twenty years since the 'great escape' at Sheffield United when Don Penn put us 1-0 in front with his penalty and Ron Green saved Sheffield's penalty in the last minute. Lightning striking twice, no, I don't think so, however, this is Walsall.

Sheffield United were safely in a mid-table position and were coming off a 3-0 victory in their last match. The game started and was full of tension; we believed we needed to win both our remaining games to stay in the division. Steve Corica was in great form and controlling the midfield, with Martin O'Connor protecting our back four. Two minutes before halftime Ziggy Aranalde got down our left-flank and centered, it went over Pedro Matais, but coming in at the back post were both Jorge Leitao and Darren Wrack. 'Gorgeous' made it just before 'Wracky' and slid the ball home; 1-0 to the Saddlers and halftime arrived. Sheffield United came out with renewed vigour in the second half and started to push us back. The longer the half went on the further we retreated. They were getting closer and closer to scoring, hitting our bar and the inside of the post. As time ticked on our play became even more desperate. The scoreboard flashed that our relegation rivals were losing and the Saddlers fans started going wild in anticipation of victory and safety. The referee awarded five minutes of injury time, which eventually became six, the team just kept throwing everything into tackles and clearances. Finally, the whistle came. The scenes of joy from our fans were immense. The team had given everything and had managed to survive relegation and remain a First Division club.

Our final home match was a carnival day out. Bradford City came to the Bescot and we would draw the match 2-2, with goals from Steve Corica. The joy that day was as if we had won promotion and in a sense we had, we would get to play again in The Championship. It was such a momentous occasion for a small Football Club, the last time we had achieved consecutive seasons in the First Division was forty years earlier.

The end of the season came with the news of the collapse of ITV digital. The renegotiation package valued at 315 million pounds was in trouble. This spelt a huge loss of revenue for Football League clubs and those in The Championship would be the worst hit. Players' wages had increased accordingly and smaller clubs could now not compete. Walsall being one of those clubs; the loss of revenue totalled 3 million pounds for the coming season. Our well-built off-field activities, however, gave us a better chance than most to survive the crash; it would still be restricting and it hurt. We also commenced redeveloping the Gilbert Alsop End of the ground into its current two-tier stand. We would start the coming season with only three parts of the stadium open.

The fans spent the summer basking in the glory of our 'great escape' and looking forward to the new season. Colin Lee set about building his own team and, what is now common in football, the revolving door of players coming in and going out started.

Transferred were: Ian Brightwell to Stoke after 84 games for Walsall, Tom Bennett to Boston United after 89 games and 8 goals, Carlos Andre, Dion Scott and Marcelo all moved on. The biggest loss was Dean Keates. 'Deano' is a Walsall boy and fans' favourite, so it was a disappointment that he could not agree a contract with his hometown club. He had made 159 league appearances and scored 9 goals and would join Hull City. Some believe that the great friendship between 'Wacka,' 'Wracky' and Deano had something to do with it, that Colin Lee did not like the firm bond between the three of them and that they were their own clique. Who knows if that is the real reason, but Dean's transfer came as a shock. Lee Harper also left the club as back-up keeper and joined Northampton Town. Don Goodman moved to Exeter City after 25 games and 3 goals and Fitzroy Simpson moved to Telford United after playing 63 times and scoring 4 goals for Walsall.

Matt Gadsby and Gary Birch were the best of our homegrown players in our first team squad apart from the much-loved Ian Roper, who had already established himself in the team. Gary Birch would remain with the club and Matt Gadsby, surprisingly, moved to Mansfield Town after 37 Walsall games; he would move again to Kiddiminster Harriers, before Forest Green and Hinkley United. All Walsall fans and players were devastated on September 9th 2006, when, during the game between Hinkley United and Harrogate Town, Matt collapsed and died; the muscle to the right ventricle of the heart had caused the heart to fail. Matt will always be remembered for his substitute appearance at The Millennium Stadium on our greatest day, when he put in tackle after tackle to protect our lead and gain the club promotion.

Our reserve team was still producing future football stars. Making an impression were Julien Bennett, a left-back or left centre-back, and striker Matty Fryatt, who had scored 43 reserve goals, 34 in the league games and 9 in 3 cup matches. They were not far away from first team games.

Colin Lee's signings began to arrive as the squad entered pre-season training and a tour of the West Country. Danny Sonner arrived from Birmingham City to play in midfield. Danny Hay, a central defender from Leeds United. Darren Bazeley arrived from Wolves to replace Ian Brightwell and David Zdrilic joined; an Australian centre-forward who had been playing in Germany for four years.

Gavin Ward joined as second goalkeeper to replace Lee Harper and we had trouble getting clearance for our Brazilian signing, striker, Junior.

The team that started the new campaign were goalkeeper, Walker; back four, Bazeley, Carbon, Roper and Aranalde; midfield, Wrack, Corica, Sonner and Matias and strikers, Leitao and Birch.

Martin O'Connor would be injured for the first month but would soon return to our midfield and David Hay would soon appear and hold down the centre-back position in partnership with Ian Roper.

We were a stronger side for our second campaign in the First Division. Although we were always in the lower half of the league we were more difficult to beat, forced draws instead of losing and so maintained a higher position for most of the season. Our strike force of Jorge Leitao and Junior was a real advantage; the two of them just hit it off together. It took a while for Junior to pick up the pace of the division, but when he did he looked dangerous. Opposing defenders had trouble with them both, if they decided to mark Junior out of the match that gave 'Gorgeous' more room and he could be devastating. The defence looked more solid and the midfield partnership of 'Skip' O'Connor and Steve Corica worked well.

Walsall had a good Cup run in The Worthington Cup, beating Shrewsbury Town in Round One, Nottingham Forest in Round Two, before losing to Blackburn Rovers on penalties after a 2-2 draw. In the F.A. Cup, we again showed a team spirit drawing at home 0-0 against Reading; we went to the Madjeski Stadium in the return. I remember having to attend a meeting at BMG Records that went on longer than it was supposed to, I got caught in a traffic jam in London for an hour and a half and by the time I got to the M4 I was seriously late. I bombed it all the way to Reading, just getting there as the teams walked out. We fought to a 1-1 draw, through extra time and won the tie on penalties 4-1. That brought Wimbledon to the Bescot and we got passed them 1-0. Round Five again came along and we had high hopes of making it to the quarterfinals drawing Sheffield United away. We went down 2-0. I suppose they decided it was time to stop our parties at their ground.

In the league there were some memorable moments. On October 29th, Pete and I brought to the Bescot a couple of mates from the Record Business that supported the visitors that night, Crystal Palace. We all came up in a Minivan and had dinner in the Bonser Suite. Steve Prebble and Steve Bradley were given some serious stick by Joe Savage and it all added to a great night.

That night we never looked like losing, a thrilling match. Junior scored twice and Corica, we were always in front, 1-0, 2-0, 2-1, 2-2, 3-2, 3-3, when in the last couple of minutes Palace broke away when we were going for the winner and scored 3-4. It had been a great game. Unfortunately, Pete and I had to travel back in the Mini-van with a pair of boisterous Palace fans. They had the best of us that season. In the return at Palace, where Pete, Joe and I were treated to lunch in what seemed like an underground bunker, they do not have Bescot's facilities, we went down 2-0. In fact, we haven't beaten Palace since the seventies when I was just a young man.

On November 23rd, when the visitors to Bescot were Gillingham and Pete Waterman opened the new two-tiered stand, we both enjoyed the moment and we enjoyed it even more when Junior scored in our 1-0 victory.

We were having problems with the Bescot pitch that season and it would come to haunt us. We had lost at the Molineux 3-1 at the beginning of the season and were very much looking forward to the return match at Bescot on January 11th. We played well that day and were holding a strong Wolves side at bay. I can still see the unfortunate moment when Danny Hay made a routine back-pass for Jimmy to clear. Just as the ball reached Jim and he took his swing, the ball hit a bump and bounced higher than his knee and started heading for the goal. 'Wacka' turned and made a run and a dive to prevent it crossing the line and scooped it out, the ball rolled to N'Dah who just pushed it home. We were gutted. Wolves won the match 1-0.

The second half of the season saw Rodriguez and Herivelto leave the club and a host of loan signings come in to help as we began to slide down the table. Neil Emblen from Norwich City, Carl Robinson from Wolves, Chris Suker from Manchester City, Jamie Lawrence from Bradford City and Vinny Samways from Las Palmas in Spain. They were all good players and added to our squad as we battled to stay ahead of the relegation places. Our plight was not as bad as the season before, it seemed we would just about escape any problems. Then, out of the blue, we were hammered at Preston North End 5-0 and 2-0 at Crystal Palace, we were right-back in trouble.

As April began we lost at home to Portsmouth, nervousness was beginning to set in. Then, all of a sudden, we won away at Gillingham 1-0, drew at home with Coventry 0-0, home to Norwich 0-0 and went to Grimsby on Easter Monday needing 3 points for safety; we duly got them with a goal from Junior in our 1-0 victory.

It was another feeling of promotion, never before had a Walsall side

Junior celebrates

played three consecutive seasons in The Championship. We were beginning to establish ourselves at that level. It had taken so much effort and passion to stay up and fight relegation for two seasons, I felt exhausted by the end of it all and I'd only been watching.

The relief brought a fine last home game against Derby County where Junior scored a hat trick in a 3-2 win. We lost our last match away at Sheffield Wednesday 2-1, but the season was over and we would have another chance in The Championship.

Junior would be our leading scorer that year with 15 goals, one of the best being the one against Preston North End at Bescot in a 3-3 draw. I was in the main stand as Junior cut in from our side, beat two players and curled it into the top corner - breathtaking. Ian Roper was 'Player of the Year' and we were all delighted that 'Ropes' had achieved that in The Championship when so many had doubted he could.

Almost as soon as the final ball was kicked players began leaving the club. Danny Sonner played 24 times scoring 4 goals and then joined Nottingham Forest. Tony Barras after 105 games and 9 goals joined Notts County. Fitzroy Simpson, who had gone and come back again, finally left. Sadly, the most high profile and Walsall legend, Martin O'Connor, left to join Shrewsbury Town. No one could believe we had let him go, he was our Captain and the strongest motivator in the team, it was believed to be a mistake.

As we always say 'That's football.' The new players started to arrive for our third crack at The Championship.

With Joe Savage and Jimmy Walker

Chapter 26
Magic Merse

As we prepared for the 2003/2004 season there was a good feeling around Bescot. We had survived in The Championship for two seasons and for the first time it felt as if we belonged there. Walsall Football Club had never played three consecutive seasons in that division, which in itself was a massive achievement. The team had got used to playing in front of massive crowds and Bescot Stadium was getting used to almost sellout crowds most of the time. Our suites were staging great lunches before the matches and entertainment in the evenings, the club was going places.

Players leaving the club in the summer were Gavin Ward our back up keeper to 'Wacka.' Gavin had always been first choice wherever he had played and had sat on the bench all of the previous season at Walsall, he understandably wanted first team football. 2003/2004 was also Jimmy Walker's testimonial year after ten years as Walsall's goalkeeper. Ward knew there would be no displacing Jimmy that season. The most disappointing departure was that of Junior. Walsall had worked hard to make a platform for Junior to use his undoubted skills; his partnership with Jorge Leitao was special and enabled him to play with freedom. Junior's hat trick in the final game at Bescot in the previous season against Derby County would come back to hurt us. After one season and 15 goals, Junior joined Derby County. He would never reach the same heights in the English game; his success had a lot to do with 'Gorgeous' Jorge Leitao. David Zdrilic joined Aberdeen after just 1 season at Walsall. He had been unfortunate, after getting into the side and scoring goals, he was injured and during that spell, Junior and Leitao formed their unbreakable partnership.

Colin Lee had masterminded two seasons without relegation and started to build a team to move us forward.

Neil Emblen and Simon Osborn, both former Wolves players, joined from Norwich City and Gillingham respectively. Stephan Oakes joined from Leicester City to add to the midfield.

Our reserve side was showing great promise and the next batch of footballers were making their mark. Strikers, Karl Hawley, Andy Bishop and Matty Fryatt; winger, Mark Wright and defender, Julien Bennett, were all nearing the first team.

Then came the biggest ever Walsall signing. There had been rumour that we might be signing Paul Merson; I had heard the rumour but just dismissed it. Merson had just had a fantastic season at Portsmouth and had one year left on his contract. He still lived in Sutton Coldfield after his years at Aston Villa. The travelling to and from Portsmouth was beginning to take its toll and with Walsall beginning to build a squad of experienced First Division footballers we became attractive to 'Merse.' Never before had a Walsall signing been shown live on Sky Sports. Never before had a crowd turned up at the stadium to witness a Walsall signing. Merson changed all of that.

Paul Merson in one fell swoop changed the whole perception of Walsall Football Club. Suddenly we were on the map and the confidence warmed the whole club and support like never before.

Everyone wanted the season to start and just couldn't wait.

The first match of the season was at Bescot Stadium and the opponents were West Bromwich Albion again. West Brom had built a great side and were favourites for promotion to the Premiership, which eventually they would attain.

August 9th 2003 was a boiling hot sunny day. A crowd of 11,030 turned up in good voice; the Walsall fans excited about the debut of Paul Merson in our colours.

The game started and WBA went at us with style and good football. For the first fifteen minutes, we were under the cosh, then, we broke down our right-flank, centered to the edge of WBA's penalty area and Paul Merson hit the most sublime volley straight into the top corner. It was a 'goal of the season' contender, given that it was a debut goal, it was Paul Merson and against West Brom. The Walsall Faithful celebrated like never before. Minutes later, Aranalde broke down our left-flank and centered, the ball was laid back to Merson again, on the edge of WBA's box, Merson just thumped it into the other top corner of the net. As Merse went on his run, the Walsall supporters celebrated, but after a moment of shocked delay. None of us had ever seen anything like it at Walsall Football Club, Merson was just magical. West Bromwich were now in a state of shock and disarray. Simon Osborn picked up the ball and just ran straight through the middle of their defence before hitting the post; the rebound fell to Jorge Leitao who gleefully rolled it home. We were 3-0 up against a good WBA side at halftime. West Brom came out in the second half determined to give their supporters something to cheer about, but slowly we ground them down and with fifteen minutes to go Steve Corica cut in from the right and put another one in the top corner, 4-0. Albion did pull a goal back late on, but nothing before or since has ever been seen like that at Bescot Stadium.

Merson said after the game, everything just went right today, it rarely happens but it did today. Gary Megson stated that Walsall probably scored three goals of the season today; there is nothing you can do about that.

Walsall went to the top of the First Division that day for our first and only time courtesy of our four-goal haul. Paul Merson would become known in Walsall as 'Magic Merse' or just plain 'Magic' for the best debut performance we had ever seen. Pete Waterman and I stood in the stand for a good ten minutes after the match trying to drink it all in, it was difficult to believe what we had just seen. Walsall had not only beaten West Brom, we had destroyed them and, what's more, the Baggies had not played badly. It was breathtaking and still is today when I think about it.

Three days later we were all back at the Bescot to watch our first game in the Coca-Cola Cup against Carlisle United. We all had 'Magic' fever. The game was 1-1 at halftime, Leitao having scored for us. In the second half, 'Magic' received the ball on the left wing and started to cut in towards goal. It seemed just the slightest movement of his body put the Carlisle defence on the wrong foot. As he approached the penalty area, he just rolled the ball into the bottom corner, the keeper having no chance from a twenty yard rolled shot - just amazing and spectacular. We won the game 2-1 and that goal deserved to win a game. The team that started that season was goalkeeper, Walker; back four, Bazeley, Hay, Roper and Aranalde; midfield, Osborn, Emblen, Samways and forwards, Corica, Leitao and Merson.

The first five months of the season were fantastic. We were playing well and we used the loan market to strengthen our side further. As we went along, Paul Ritchie came in from Manchester City, Deon Burton, Jamie Vincent and Gary O'Neil from Portsmouth and full-back Chris Baird from Southampton - all good footballers. On December 26th, we won away 1-0 at Cardiff and on December 28th a draw at Bescot 1-1 against Reading saw Walsall just outside the playoff places, 9th in the league. Just when you thought it was safe to go back into the water, the wheels came off. Danny Hay, knowing his previous injury was on its way back and that he could not cope with Championship Football, headed back to New Zealand.

In an F.A. Cup game at Millwall on January 3rd, Jorge Leitao and Jimmy Walker were both sent off in a tough and angry game, bringing suspensions.

Paul Merson left for Arizona for treatment and rehabilitation on his addictive problems.

Vinny Samways, whose family lived in Spain, was beginning to find the travelling and staying in a hotel tiresome. Our reserve goalkeeper got injured and we had to look around to get someone in quickly to cover Jimmy's suspension. Andy Petterson, known to Colin Lee, came in for his first match against Coventry City at Bescot. Also making his debut that day was Stefan Oakes in for Paul Merson. After thirty-five minutes Stefan Oakes was sent off for a tackle on his debut. We went 1-0 down before 'Wracky' equalized on halftime. The second half was a disaster, ten men and a nervous and unfamiliar keeper, Coventry just kept scoring; we lost 6-1 and were shattered.

We would begin a rapid slide down the table not winning for 10 games. Vinny Samways would leave for Spain, 'Magic Merse' would return, but not in the same frame of mind, and Colin Lee set about bolstering the team with loan signings to stave off another relegation scrap.

In came Craig Burley from Preston North End, Lee Bradbury from Portsmouth, Jamie McSporran from Wycombe Wanderers and Keith Andrews from Wolves. Young Walsall players Mark Wright, Kris Taylor and Matty Fryatt all made appearances as we tried to stop the rot.

The Easter holidays changed the path of Walsall Football Club. With 5 games to go we were 2 points above the drop zone, we lost at home 1-0 to Burnley and then had a disastrous 3-0 defeat at Gillingham, that signalled the end of the Colin Lee reign.

Colin Lee had decided to speak to Plymouth Argyle about their vacant Manager's position at a most crucial time in our season. Maybe he just didn't think we could get out of trouble this time or maybe it was a desire to return to his home area in the West Country. Whatever the reason, Jeff Bonser acted swiftly to try to save us from relegation. Paul Merson was named caretaker Player Manager, with Simon Osborn assisting. We had 4 games left when we went to Norwich in Merson's first game in charge and got battered 5-0. We all arrived at Bescot Stadium for the match on April 24th against Sheffield United, a team we had beaten in two of our 'great escapes.' As Pete and I arrived, Jeff Bonser called us over and asked Pete to go onto the pitch and speak to the crowd and get behind the team to help escape relegation. I went pitch side with Pete as he delivered an inspirational 'Churchillian' speech to the fans. Sadly, on this occasion, it didn't work and we went down 1-0 to a penalty.

Two games left, the first away at Crystal Palace where we never seem to get anything. With five minutes to go, after defending resolutely, the referee gave an unbelievable penalty kick. Jimmy saved the first attempt, but a Palace player followed up to score, again, we went down 1-0.

The final game of the season was at Bescot. 11,049 turned up to see another 'great escape.' We needed to win and Stoke City had to beat Gillingham for us to survive.

We went in front with a Simon Osborn goal, only for Osborn to later give away a penalty. 1-1, but worse was to come as Osborn was sent off for two bookable offences. Down to ten men and Walsall went ahead again through young Walsall winger, Mark Wright, 2-1. Two minutes to go and Rotherham were awarded another penalty, 2-2. Walsall threw everything at Rotherham in a last ditch attempt to win and a corner came in to Paul Ritchie who gleefully headed home. the Saddlers fans went barmy. Maybe, just maybe. The final whistle went, but moments later, we all knew the Stoke score, they had failed in their attempt to beat Gillingham.

After three great seasons in Division One we were relegated, not on points but on goal difference and that goal difference was ONE goal.

It seemed unfair that we should be relegated by one goal after all that effort over three seasons, however, they say the league table does not lie, after 46 games we were where we were, in the relegation zone and relegated.

The work that had been put in by Ray Graydon, Colin Lee and the Board of Directors had brought us six unbelievable seasons. Each one of those seasons provided promotion, relegation and 'great escapes' before we were finally back in what would now be termed League One.

Colin Lee had been a good manager for Walsall. He had been able to bring in players that would not have normally played for Walsall. Paul Merson remains our most high profile player and Vinny Samways was just tremendous in our midfield; in all of the football I've watched I've never seen a player retain the ball like Vinny. If today's stats had been around back then, I believe that Vinny Samways would have the highest total of completed passes; he just never gave it away.

Paul Merson was quickly named our new Player-Manager, with Simon Osborn as Player-Coach. There was a confidence around Bescot that just maybe, with Merson and a few good players, we could return straight away to The Championship.

It would be a tough job for Merson. There would be an exodus of players as we dropped a division. The role of player and manager is always difficult to combine, especially if you are the best player.

Matt Carbon, Jermaine McSporran, Aaron Kerr, Steve Corica and Paul Ritchie left the club immediately. Pedro Matias, a great favourite, who had spent five seasons on our left wing, racking up 141 league appearances and scoring 24 times, left for Blackpool. The biggest loss was Jimmy 'Wacka' Walker. Jim was offered a new contract but felt it was time to go and try to play at a bigger club and at a higher level. The supporters were disappointed but they understood. Jimmy had kept goal for Walsall for eleven years, making 475 appearances. He went with everyone's blessing and was sorely missed, joining West Ham United.

Neil Emblen, Darren Bazeley, Kris Taylor and Jorge Leitao signed new deals, along with Walsall Academy graduates, long-serving Ian Roper, Gary Birch, Mark Wright, Matty Fryatt, Julien Bennett and Daryl Taylor.

Our new season would soon commence with a brighter, focused Paul Merson in charge, ready to accept a new challenge as a League Manager. Youngsters Scott Dann and Leroy Williams were offered professional contracts during pre-season. Merson's first signing was Michael Standing from Aston Villa to fit into our midfield.

The opening game of the 2004/2005 season was at Bescot Stadium and the opposition Port Vale. Our team that day was goalkeeper, McKinny; back four, Bazeley, Emblen, Roper and Bennett; midfield, Standing, Kinsella, Merson and Wrack and forwards, Birch and Fryatt.

We all filed into Bescot that day to see Paul Merson's new side perform. Matty Fryatt, establishing himself in the side scored first from the penalty spot, with Port Vale equalizing later in the second half. It was a fiery game with plenty of yellow cards. With twenty minutes to go Merson threw on two of our teenage academy players, Daryl Taylor on the right-wing and Leroy Williams down the centre. The game changed as these two players ran at Port Vale with the freedom of youth. Williams picked up the ball went straight at the middle of Vale's defence and smashed in a goal to put us 2-1 up. Minutes later, an inspired Daryl Taylor scored the third and secured the points. Vale got a consolation with just seconds to go.

Walsall would have a goalkeeping problem for most of the season. Richard McKinney had signed from Colchester United and started the season, shortly to be followed by Mark Paston who came in from Bradford City. They had big shoes to fill. 'Wacka' gave the players and the supporters huge confidence and when the new 'keepers came in, their nervousness spread through the defence and into the stands. Eventually, Joe Murphy settled the situation when he came in on loan from West Bromwich Albion in mid-October. On his return to Albion, Dean Coleman made one appearance at Blackpool from our reserve side, unbelievably saving two penalties on his debut. Alan Oakes then signed from Derby County; not having a settled goalkeeper would not help our cause that season.

By September, after losing to Brentford at home, we were in the bottom four. Changes started to come with the signing of Mark Kinsella from West Bromwich Albion. Mark Wright had made the right-back position his own and that enabled Darren Bazeley to move to New Zealand.

We opened our F.A. Cup campaign away against Slough Town on November 13th. I'd arranged to meet Joe Savage at the ground and we sat in the stand with a small Walsall following. Slough took the lead. Merson tried to rally the troops playing in his first ever First Round F.A. Cup match. Eventually, Darren Wrack equalised just before halftime. Joe and I breathed a sigh of relief but we knew we were not playing well and Slough's goal had given them confidence. The second half was not pretty to watch, as we made no real impression on Slough. Then, with fifteen minutes to go, Slough Town scored what proved to be the winner; we were out of the Cup, humiliated by Slough. Joe and I trudged back to our cars and as soon as I got into mine to drive home, my phone started going with messages from football followers in the music business. I remained calm and took the abuse, but it was not what I needed that day.

Still hovering around the relegation places just prior to Christmas, we signed Marvin Robinson to lead our attack. Scoring after coming off the bench on his debut, a 1-1 draw with Bradford City, and then claiming two in his next game, a 3-2 win at home to Blackpool, we set off for Sheffield Wednesday on Boxing Day with renewed hope.

I had stayed overnight at my Sister Helen's and was due to pick up Pete from his home just outside Manchester before going across the Pennines to Sheffield. I hit an enormous traffic jam just outside of Stoke; an accident had closed all three lanes and I just sat there for three hours. Pete made his own way to the ground. I tried to cut across country in an attempt to get to the match, but I was still 45 miles away at 3:00pm. I turned the car and headed back down the M1, by the time I arrived home I had been in the car nine hours, missed the match and on top of that we lost 3-2. You've got to be tough to support Walsall!

January and February were tough in terms of results. We lost 5-0 at Colchester and Merson tended his resignation, which was not accepted. Four days later, we won against the odds at home versus Huddersfield Town, 4-3. After being 3-1 down, Matty Fryatt scored a hat trick to seal the points, Merson having opened the scoring himself.

As the transfer deadline approached, further new recruits came in. Andy Oakes in goal, Andrew Surman, a fine player from Southampton, Craig Pead from Coventry City, Anthony Gerrard from Everton's reserves, who would make his league debut straight away, David Perpetuini from Wycombe Wanderers and, finally, Julien Joachim from Leeds United.

Ziggy Aranalde left the club, relinquishing his left-back position after five seasons, 195 league appearances and 5 goals. Ziggy would play for Sheffield Wednesday before spending three seasons at Carlisle United.

During March, as we were assembling the new players, we had a 5-game losing streak, a draw at home to Torquay United stopped the rot and then the team finally clicked. We won all 5 of our remaining games: a 2-1 win away at Swindon, 2-0 away at Peterborough, 3-0 at home to Hull, where we secured our position in League One, 3-1 away at Hartlepool and, finally, 3-0 at home to Stockport County on the final day.

It had taken all season for us to blend a team together. Merson's assistants had been changed three times during the campaign, the goalkeeper five times. No one featured in all of the matches as we chopped and changed to find a good formula. Walsall were unpredictable, which still made them exciting to watch, losing 5-0 one match, winning 4-3 the next, winning 3-2 at Blackpool, losing 3-2 the next match at Sheffield Wednesday, you just never knew what would happen as you walked into the ground. Merson definitely kept the fans 'on their toes.'

Matty Fryatt was 'Player of the Year' in his first season, scoring 14 times in 24 starts. Paul Merson, with all his headaches of management, was still an unbelievable player, making it into the League One 'Team of the Year' at a canter.

It seemed that 'Merse' had gone through a tough first year management course, but had come out at the end with a winning team and a final position of 14th. Merson was handed a new contract and would enter his second season as Walsall Manager.

The early signs were good. Anthony Gerrard signed permanently from Everton, with him came Danny Fox, also from Everton, to play left-back. Steve Staunton signed from Coventry City, Chris Westwood from Hartlepool and Darren Wrack signed a new three-year deal that would include a testimonial in his final year.

Merson had chased Julian Joachim after his scoring spree in our last few matches, but an influx of cash into Boston United meant we could not match their offer.

The team that started the season was goalkeeper, Oakes; back four, Pead, Westwood, Bennett and Fox; midfield, Wrack, Standing, Osborn and Taylor K. and forwards, Leitao and Fryatt.

We started the campaign well, winning at Rotherham 2-1, at home against Nottingham Forest 3-2 and drawing at home against Southend United 2-2 in our third match. We stood top of the table.

The first five months of the season were satisfactory. Again, we had goalkeeping problems when Oakes was injured; Rene Gilmartin from our youth team played, John Ruddy came on loan from Everton and Joe Murphy again came in on loan, this time from Sunderland.

We tried again to find a winning formula and we chopped and changed the team; Merson only making a few appearances himself as he wrestled with finding a winning side. Walsall were not doing badly, but we were slipping down the league and we never looked convincing. We signed James Constable from Chippenham Town for 4,000 pounds; it would be the first transfer fee we had paid out in five years. Constable was a raw but strong centre-forward and looked a good capture. Ishmal Demontagne made his debut at Port Vale from our reserve side and scored, there was no doubt he was a very talented footballer.

On December 31th 2005, Bescot Stadium said goodbye to 'Gorgeous' Jorge Leitao. Jorge had been feeling ready to return to Portugal for some months and had received an offer from Beira-Mar to return home. The visitors were Blackpool and James Constable came off the bench to score both goals in a 2-0 win. The moment, however, was Jorge's, he wept as he ran on his lap of honour with the crowd singing his name. Jorge had been a great servant to the club, had always played with 100% commitment and was a hero and a legend in Walsall. After 230 appearances and 71 goals we said goodbye to 'Gorgeous.'

In January, we sold Matty Fryatt to Leicester City for a million pounds that included a sell-on clause for part of the fee in any future transfers. He left after 70 games and 27 goals. We also sold Julian Bennett to Nottingham Forest after 51 games and 3 goals.

We would only win 1 of our next 13 games. On February 4th we played away at Brentford. Pete, Susan and I went for lunch with a Brentford fan and Sony employee. Even though we were in a bad run, Dean Keates had just rejoined the club and we had hoped he might inspire the team.

Unfortunately, that was not to be that day, we were dreadful. Pete, unable to face it all, left as Brentford's second goal went in. Susan and I left as their third goal went in. As we were walking back to the car, the cheers told us that number four and number five had also been scored.

That match would be the end of Paul Merson's reign as Walsall Manager. We were now 1 point off the drop zone and falling fast.

Kevin Broadhurst was soon named our new Manager, with the brief of avoiding relegation. Susan and I went up to Bescot to see Keatsie's home debut, in which he scored, along with Andrew Barrowman in a 2-2 draw against Scunthorpe United. In Broadhurst's first 8 games we drew 5, won 1 and lost 2. It was a 'backs to the wall' fight with a side low on confidence. In the next 6 matches, at the crucial stage, we lost 5 and were relegated with 2 games to go. Kevin Broadhurst was relieved of his duties.

Richard Money was soon named as the new Manager for next season and he watched the last 2 matches, a win at Gillingham 1-0 and a 2-1 defeat at Bescot against Barnsley.

A season that had started so brightly, again, had turned into disaster. We were back in the basement division having used 47 players during the campaign.

Richard Money's job was not going to be easy. The team needed rebuilding and the desire was immediate promotion. League Two was not where Walsall Football Club saw its future.

Chapter 27
Champions Of Division Two

Life changes. It always will and always does. Walsall were playing in League Two and my life was changing too. During the early months of 2006, Walsall Council and Walsall Museum were planning a tribute to my life's work in the Music Industry that would be titled 'Kylie, Britney, Justin and Me.' The exhibition would display some of my 270 Platinum, Gold and Silver discs along with photographs and commentary on the hits and moments in my career. I was still under contract to Sony Records at the time as was my partner and friend Pete Waterman. We were both beginning to look at other projects rather than just making records, which we had been doing all our lives. The exhibition for me came around just at the right time and it felt like a return to Walsall after all that had happened. The people of Walsall would embrace my return and some 8,000 people would visit the exhibition, making it the most popular exhibition in the town's history. The press, radio and TV also embraced my return and for the term of nine months, in which the exhibition ran they were strong supporters. Walsall Football Club also supported me greatly. I wrote for the programme for two seasons and the club promoted me and I promoted it whenever I was on the radio or TV. Everyone knew I was a true Saddler and proud of it.

I will never forget the response of my hometown's people to the success in my career. I wanted them to feel part of it and they responded with a warmth and support I would never have imagined. It truly was a great period in my life; I was home and loved for it. My lasting memory is how proud my Mom and Dad would have been, if only they could have witnessed it all.

Pete was also moving into his great hobby and love of trains. He was developing his model train company, which took him all over the country at weekends to train gatherings and exhibitions. He would not be such a regular at Walsall F.C..

Since late 1996 until the coming season of 2006/2007, Pete and I had averaged between 30 and 35 games a season together. Watching Walsall Football Club all through those years, we had loved it all. We still talk about those times today and the Walsall days and nights out we had when we were part of it all with 'Marshy,' 'Wacka,' Keatsie and Wracky.

The coming season was exciting for me; all of the talk was that we were going for promotion at the first attempt. Dean Keates was back, Darren Wrack was nearing a return after a year out with injury and my old friend Martin Butler was about to return to lead the attack.

Richard Money had been appointed and as I'd been around the club in the summer I knew he would become a great manager for us with his meticulous preparation, fitness routines and confidence-building style - the right man at the right moment. All good Managers know, as Bill Shankley said all those years ago, a team needs a great spine within it, a great goalkeeper, a great centre-half and leader of the defence, a great midfield General and a great centre-forward. Get that right and you're on your way to building a winning team.

Richard came in and brought to the club, Clayton Ince from Coventry City to keep goal; he would prove to be the best keeper outside of The Championship division. We had Ian Roper and Anthony Gerrard as centre-backs, Dean Keates, an inspirational midfielder, and Martin Butler brought in from Rotherham to lead our attack. To build a team around those players suggested to me we had a chance of promotion from the off.

Clayton Ince at full stretch

I was at the club when Martin Butler returned for the first day of training. He greeted me with 'You're not still here are you?' You bet I was.

Richard also brought in Michael Dobson, who would play a major role in our midfield and Captain the side, Hector Sam, who formed a good partnership with Martin Butler, from Port Vale, during the first half of the season, Bertrand Bossu as back up keeper and Tommy Wright on loan. Mark Kinsella would hang up his boots and move to Charlton to join their coaching staff.

All was set and we started the season well, 3 straight wins and we were top of the table. We would not be out of the top two between then and Christmas as the first half of the season went to plan.

The team was goalkeeper, Ince; back four, Westwood, Gerrard, Roper and

Fox; midfield, M. Wright, Dobson, Keates and K. Taylor and forwards, Butler and Sam.

The team had a strong look about it and was settled after the previous two seasons when we had chopped and changed in search of a good combination. Our reserve side contributed under the guidance of Richard Money, with Scott Dann becoming a revelation in defence, Mark Bradley beginning to feature, as did Alex Nicholls, Ishmal Demontagnac, Troy Deeney and Manny Smith.

We held the top spot in the league until February when we had a blip of 3 defeats on the bounce. Richard Money acted instantly and brought in Kevin Harper and Kevin Cooper, who were both successful on our wings, and Trevor Benjamin to add strength to the forward line. Back came the Saddlers

Anthony Gerrard

again going 9 games unbeaten, including our win at Notts County.

3,000 Walsall fans made the trip to Notts County knowing a win would seal promotion. It would prove to be a tough match. Kevin Harper put us in front after seventeen minutes, but back came Notts County and it was no surprise when they equalized just before halftime. Notts County opened the better of the sides in the second half, but Walsall held on and with six minutes to go Dobson found Butler, who headed on to Benjamin and he buried it in the bottom corner. Walsall were up at the first attempt and back in Division One. The celebrations from the fans, players, management and directors were immense. The town had pulled together behind the Saddlers and we had bounced back.

Filled with confidence, everyone wanted to finish the season as Champions.

Walsall had only ever won one Championship in the club's history and that had been the old Division Four title in 1959/1960. We were in pole position; it was Hartlepool United or Walsall.

We had 3 matches left, 2 at home. Disaster struck when we lost the first 1-0 to Bury. 7,057 turned up to cheer us on against Wrexham, a game we won 1-0 with a goal from Demontagnac. Our last match of the season would be away at Swindon Town. Hartlepool United were at home to Bristol Rovers and top of the division, now favourites for the title. Bristol Rovers needed a point to confirm their playoff place. Swindon needed a point to confirm their third place position and playoff position. The permutations were endless, but it meant that all four teams would be fighting hard for their own futures. A sunny day in Swindon saw us all arrive in good voice and hoping for that unattainable Championship. 3,400 fans arrived from Walsall and I can still see them all packed in behind the goal.

Hartlepool took the lead in their match and all looked lost, our halftime score was 0-0. We went further away from the title when Swindon scored early in the second half. News filtered through two minutes later that Bristol Rovers had equalised from the penalty spot at Hartlepool. The tension began to build as we began to attack the Swindon goal in waves. Demontagnac was getting some rough treatment from the Swindon defenders and, in an attempt to make the officials do something about it, Richard Money over stepped the line and was dismissed to the stands.

Four minutes remained when news came through that Bristol Rovers had taken the lead. The Walsall fans' roar just filled the ground as they urged the team forward. If we could score, a 1-1 draw would bring the title to Walsall. We were on the edge of our seats as Walsall's renewed vigour forced them forward at a tiring Swindon side. With sixty seconds to go Dean Keates got the ball twenty-five yards out and hit it with everything he had got, it flew into the back of the net, 1-1. The title was coming home and the sight of the Walsall fans celebrating will live with me forever. The players celebrated with the fans as the final whistle blew; we had a Championship title for only the second time in our history.

Clayton Ince, Craig Pead, Chris Westwood, and Dean Keates were all named in the 'League Two Team of the Year.'

Dean Keates was top scorer with 13 goals from midfield and Walsall 'Player of the Year.'

Dean Keates with Walsall fans

Richard Money with the Trophy

Michael Dobson celebrates promotion

Walsall Council announced a civic reception and the team were to travel around the town on an open top bus before arriving at the Town Hall. I was honoured to be invited, along with Susan, to travel on the bus with the players waving to the supporters as we went and to also be invited to the civic reception at the Town Hall. We were with all the lads as they were presented with their medals and raised the trophy to the crowd outside the Town Hall; we then went inside for the reception and had a wonderful time. Susan and I had our photograph taken with Deano and the trophy. I was surprised when the photographer remarked it was the only photo Dean had smiled on all day.

After the reception, Susan and I were invited to have an Indian meal with Richard Money and Bill Jones. It was a great night and we discussed the season at length. We also talked about the coming season and I remarked that we must not lose Dean Keates, the talisman of the side, who was out of contract. I was alarmed that Richard would make no comment. It would be only two days later that both Dean Keates and Chris Westwood joined a buoyant Peterborough United. Deano phoned me and apologised for his glumness on the civic reception day, saying the contract talks were going on all day, while we were at the ceremony.

Keatsie is a Walsall boy and wanted to stay at Walsall. Peterborough United were offering an excellent deal for three years and Deano wanted a three year deal from Walsall to include a testimonial, but would take a lesser pay structure to stay, the club obviously refused. This would be a huge mistake. Keates was the heartbeat of the team at that time, top scorer, 'Player of the Year' and fans' favourite. To be fair, Walsall did try to get Peterborough to tear up Keatsie's contract when the Posh came in for Martin Butler. Walsall said they could have 'Butt' if they returned Keates. Neither club could agree and all we did really was upset Martin Butler who was also being offered a good contract. We should never have let Keatsie go, it was a huge mistake and would have repercussions throughout the coming season. I'm sure there is another side to the story that I don't know, but regardless of that, it was one of the club's biggest mistakes, just when we were on the up. Others leaving after our promotion were Craig Pead, Hector Sam, Mark Wright and Kris Taylor. The rebuilding would soon start and we looked forward again to our return to Division One.

For Walsall Football Club to win The Championship whilst my exhibition was running in the town was the most perfect ending to my return home. If I had written it down before it happened, no one would have believed it and I would have been called 'mad.' Nevertheless it happened and I will never forget it.

The summer rebuilding started with the signings of former players, Danny Sonner from Port Vale and Paul Hall from Chesterfield. These seemed strange signings to make and would ultimately be failures. The reasoning behind it was twofold: we had a very good group of young players and Richard Money felt he needed to add experience to the ranks, also, the atmosphere at our stadium was sometimes negative and he felt that Sonner and Hall knew the Stadium and would not be affected, hence, helping the young lads. More experience was brought in with Tommy Mooney from Wycombe Wanderers, Rhys Weston from Port Vale and Paul Boertein from Derby County. Edrissa Sonko arrived from Roda, already known as Mr Sunshine, to play on our right-wing.

The side took a while to settle and it would take 8 games for us to record our first victory, away at Millwall 2-1, with goals from Fox and Deeney. We were bottom of the table. The wins then started to come and we steadily began to rise up the table. During October, both Danny Sonner and Martin Butler left the club and Peter Sweeney would soon arrive on loan to play left-midfield. Michael Ricketts came in on a three month loan from Oldham, to return to the place it had all began for him and he settled in straight away, fired up to do well on his return home. Susan and I were at the Oldham game earlier in the season, when we lost 3-0, with Michael scoring their opener. Joe Savage and I had both told Susan that Ricketts would score that day and so he did. However, when he resigned it felt good to have him back in a Walsall shirt.

Danny Fox

The arrival of Michael Ricketts started the most unbelievable run of results. Ricketts played in 16 matches during his loan spell and we didn't lose one. It catapulted the side from the lower reaches of the division to 5th place in the league and in contention for the playoffs by mid-January 2008.

The team that had that run of results were goalkeeper, Ince; back four, Weston, Gerrard, Dann and Fox; midfield, Sonko, Bradley, Sweeney and Wrack and forwards, Mooney and Ricketts.

All was suddenly going well and all of the supporters thought we were in with a chance of a playoff place. The talk around town was that the last time we won a Championship in 1960, the following season, manager Bill Moore and his team, had gone right through the next division and been promoted as runners-up to Division Two, now called The Championship. The supporters knew that this team was good and that in Richard Money we had a manager that might just be able to pull off that feat. We know in Walsall that lightning can strike twice.

Mid-January arrived and it would be our most disappointing transfer window ever. Danny Fox was transferred to Coventry City; there should be no complaints from the Walsall Faithful on this issue as Danny would have been out of contract in the summer and would have left for nothing. Walsall had tried on several occasions to negotiate a new contract but none had been accepted, it was better to sell Danny at that point for a fee, which was believed to be around 600,000 pounds than to receive no income at all at the end of the season. The total shock was that within days Scott Dann also signed for Coventry for a fee believed to be around a million pounds. The Scott Dann issue would cause problems for Walsall Football Club and its supporters for the coming two or three years. Firstly, Scott came to the ground and requested a transfer, knowing of Coventry's interest most probably from teammate Danny Fox. Now, we know Scott was under contract, but if you keep a player who wants to leave you are most certainly asking for trouble. Walsall have a policy that attracts good young players to the club, they sign knowing that, if you are good enough, you're old enough to be in our team, that is the main reason good young players sign for Walsall rather than Wolves, West Brom, Birmingham or Aston Villa. If you then show you are not willing to sell them when their opportunity arises, again, you could stop the flow of good young players coming to our club. Walsall tried endlessly to sell Scott to Coventry but loan him back for the remainder of the season, but Scott did not want to do that, he wanted to play in The Championship alongside Danny Fox for Coventry, which would give him his best chance of settling in, you cannot blame him.

The Fox/Dann affair, which would cause so much trouble and loss of support, was something no one could do much about, that's football. Michael Ricketts' loan spell came to an end at the same time. Oldham suggested sign him or he returns. If we had signed Michael then we would have had to match or get close to a wage package that was too big for Walsall. We all know as well that Michael can be 'in and out' with his performances; although he had inspired the team during this loan spell there was no guarantee it would continue.

Supporters will now say that I'm backing mistakes made by Jeff Bonser, I don't think I am, I'm just relaying the facts as I know them. Was I disappointed that we lost three of our best players at that time in a matter of days? You bet I was. Those moves destroyed our chance of making the playoffs, but we have to deal with the disappointment, that is the big issue, blaming Jeff Bonser for something he could do little about is not the answer. In fact, Jeff Bonser, who is a fine businessman in realising the value of his young players, has continuously made more money in transfers for Walsall than he should have done. That still does not heal the disappointment of losing the chance that was before us at that time, but we should deal with the disappointment and not misdirect the blame.

Richard Money more or less had to build a new side contending for the playoffs. In came Lee Holmes, a fine loan signing for our left-flank. Kevin Betsy, from Bristol City, came in to play on the right-flank. Alassane N'Dour joined from F.C. Troyes to play midfield and Aaron Brown came in from Reading to try and fill the gap left by the Scott Dann transfer.

Scott Dann

Ultimately, it would be to no avail, we began losing crucial matches at crucial times, the balance of the team had changed and by Easter we were out of the running for a playoff place. As soon as that was realised Richard Money resigned. Was it lack of support? Was it that our ambition did not match his? Was it just the sheer disappointment that we all felt? Whatever the reason, we lost a great Manager who had changed our club around in two years when we were in the doldrums and facing League Two. Well done and thanks, Richard Money.

Some have said that even I became a 'stay away' during this spell at Walsall Football Club. Not true. I had, for the first time in my life, a new freedom in not being under contract to any record company. Susan and I had decided to spend time in California, visiting Santa Barbara, Las Vegas and Palm Springs. The trip was almost two months and we enjoyed every minute.

Jimmy Mullen was promoted to Manager of Walsall Football Club and immediately after the game against Hartlepool, a 2-2 draw that Susan and I attended, players started to leave: Stefan Moore, Tommy Mooney, Edrissa

Sonko, Bertrand Bossu, Paul Hall and, with great sadness, Ian Roper, after nearly 400 games and 7 goals. Many supporters, including me, didn't want 'Ropes' to go. He had never given less than 100% in any game; he had played and held our defence together for all those years. I watched with delight on TV when he scored that goal for Kettering Town against Leeds United in the F.A. Cup - just brilliant.

Darren Wrack also left the club after 380 appearances and 52 goals. I spoke to him on that day of the Hartlepool match when he was told he was not required. He was disappointed and so was I; Wracky had become a mate over all of those years. I went to Kettering, along with Susan, 'Marshy' and Craig Lang, to show support for him when he signed for them. Wracky was a great Walsall player and a hero to our fans.

Under Richard Money we had two great seasons, The Championship and a good run at the playoffs. The new season again would be not long in coming. It would be the first since 1972 that I didn't have a close friend in the side.

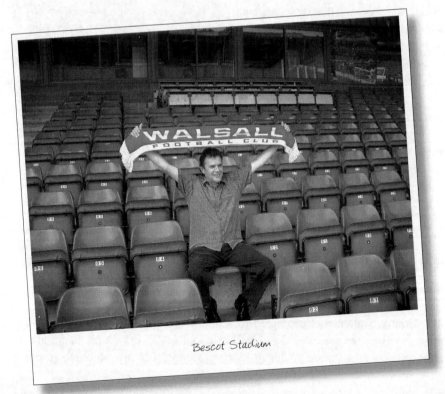

Bescot Stadium

Chapter 28
Long Distance Supporter

During the summer, I had decided to write a book about my life and career in the Music Industry, from my early years in Walsall, through all the hits to my return to Walsall for the exhibition. During the nine months of the exhibition, press, radio, TV, the people of Walsall, had constantly asked when I would write the book, something I never had any intention of doing. Susan had been with me through all of the promotion of the exhibition and had constantly been suggesting that I should do it. Having concluded a lot of business arrangements and having some free time, it had to be now or never, and so I began the long task of writing the book. This meant that as long as I had a computer I could work anywhere in the world. Susan and I had also really enjoyed our time in California, so the idea came that maybe I should write in a warmer climate and we should miss England's winter weather.

We made arrangements for two long trips, one to Florida for November, December and January, returning to England for a couple of weeks before heading for Marbella in Spain for six weeks. This meant I would miss most of the season at The Banks's Stadium. For the first time in my life I began to learn how to be a long distance supporter. My friend Joe Savage would text me after every match with the result, the scorers and a few words describing how we played. The Internet became my Walsall source of information; reading match reports, the manager's view, the new signings, in fact, everything I could learn about what was happening back home. I could read the *Express & Star* Walsall page daily, the Saddlers website, Up the Saddlers site and Walsall Mad. Then, a few days later, I could see the goals in a short piece of footage on Virgin or the BBC website. That all became part of my day, along with writing and my passion for playing golf, now that the legs have gone and there is no more football.

At the beginning of Jimmy Mullen's reign, I was impressed by the signings, all of which looked solid: Stephen Roberts from Doncaster Rovers, Jabo Ibehre from Leyton Orient, Dwayne Mattis from Barnsley, Sofiene Zaaboub from Swindon Town, Michael Ricketts from Oldham, Stephen Hughes from Coventry City, Chris Palmer and Marco Reich. These players and the squad we already had, along with our young players, Deeney, Smith, Taundry, Bradley, Sansara and Nicholls, looked as though we should be able to compete in the

Division for 2008/2009.

Susan and I made a couple of trips to the Banks's Stadium before we left for Florida and I was impressed by Jabo, Stephen Hughes, the early performances of Reich and Mattis, Roberts and Gerrard looked solid in front of Clayton Ince and the full-backs had experience.

By the time we left for Florida we were doing okay, but the cracks were beginning to appear. At that time, I thought it might just be a bad patch as we lost the 3 games in October. However, as we now know, November and December got worse, the supporters were on the back of Jimmy Mullen and soon he was relieved of duty.

Chris Hutchings and Martin O'Connor were appointed in January 2009 and the side began to look more solid and began to get some results. I was delighted that Martin O'Connor had returned to the club and was hoping that his enthusiasm and passion for our side would rub off on the players and we could build a winning side with 'Skip' as part of the management team. Now that one of my friends was involved again I felt attached to the team. We had a good run, but we petered out towards the end of the season finishing 13th in the Division. I only attended three matches that season as we spent so much time out of the country. I missed most of Jimmy Mullen's matches in charge but was ready to be at the ground more in the coming season.

As we returned to the U.K., Michael Ricketts, Stephen Hughes and Paul Boertein were released.

During the summer, another of those life-changing moments came along. I was expecting to see more of the Saddlers during the coming campaign, but soon realized that life might just not be the same for a while.

My daughter, Josephina, in short, picked up a golf club at the age of 14 and had the most amazing natural talent. Within three and a half months Josie was in the Middlesex squad and within a year would be a 10-handicap player and selected for Middlesex first team. This changed weekends for both Susan and I. Saturdays and Sundays were now focused on golf as I became, driver, coach, caddy, secretary and practice companion. I am not complaining; to see exceptional talent is amazing, to see it in your daughter is unbelievable.

Hence, Saturday's had to be rearranged and for Susan and I to get to Walsall and back, for the most part, was impossible. Again, the Internet and Joe Savage were my saviours as I kept up to speed with all things Saddlers.

In what seemed like another teambuilding summer, Palmer and Zaaboub left the club, Jabo Ibehre joined MK Dons, Stephen Roberts, after a fight with injury, had to retire and Anthony Gerrard finally got his move to Cardiff City for 250,000 pounds.

In came Mark Hughes from Northampton, Steve Jones from Burnley, Josh O'Keefe from Blackburn, Sam Parkin from Luton, Peter Till from Grimsby, Matt Richards from Ipswich, Jamie Vincent from Swindon, Darren Byfield returned on a six-month deal and Clayton McDonald was soon to arrive on loan.

The stability of the Richard Money era was well and truly over. Although a lot of the players signed were good footballers, it seemed we had returned to the days of trying to find the formula rather than knowing what the formula was and signing players to fit into it.

When games were close to London it was much easier for me to get Josie dropped off and be able to pick her up after her match wherever she was playing, hence, I was at Wycombe Wanderers for the game on October 31st. What a match to pick. We were 2-0 down at halftime and looked like a shambles, it could have been more. I was with Joe Savage and we were talking to some of the Saddlers fans while we had a cup of tea at halftime. They said to me that the side could be 2-0 up and lose 3-2 or the other way round, evidently, it had been the same for a couple of months. Walsall could only play for half a game, but when they did they were great. I took it all with a pinch of salt thinking it was just supporters talk and just could not believe what I saw during the second half, Walsall were a different side. We quickly got one back through Steve Jones, 2-1. We then really went after Wycombe and you could see they were wobbling. Jones scored again, 2-2. Then, as the game drew to a close, Alex Nicholls nipped in with the winner, unbelievable. I left the ground that day with Walsall fans laughing and saying, 'Told you so.' I managed to have a few words with 'Skip' O'Connor who told me he thought we were three or four quality players short of a good side. 'Skip' was motivating the side as always with everything he had, but the side had not got enough.

During November, Susan and I managed to get to the 2 games at Brentford on the 21st and 28th, one in the league and one in the Cup. We had a hard fought draw in the league, 1-1, with a goal from Steve Jones who was in good form and looked our best player. A week later we were knocked out of the Cup 1-0 when Brentford rearranged their team and outplayed us.

We managed to get to the Banks's on December 5th for the visit of Southampton. My Sister Helen always comes to the games whenever we can get to Walsall and did so that day. Southampton played us off the park but I was delighted to see Darren Byfield get a goal in our colours.

By mid-February we were still in with a chance of the playoffs with wins at Leeds United and at home to Brentford, however, we slipped back into the pack after failing to win in the next 4 matches, one of which was March 13th away game at Orient, another one I could get to easily and still do my fatherly golfing duties. We lost 2-0 that day and were just dreadful. Fans will remember Troy Deeney's outburst after the match and Deeney did look the only good Walsall player on the park and the only one really competing. I saw 'Skip' after the game in the underground car park at Orient. I said, 'Alright Skip' he replied 'You must be joking after that!'

We did finish the season well, only losing 1 game in our last 8 matches. It lifted us to a finish of 10th in the league, our strongest finishing position for five seasons. I believe that Chris Hutchings and Martin O'Connor had milked everything they could out of our team that season and the end of season finish looked promising for the next campaign.

I did manage another trip to Wycombe Wanderers on February 6 for a game against Yeovil Town. Wycombe were deep in trouble and facing relegation. They had signed on a short-term contract, Dean Keates, after his two promotions with Peterborough United. I spoke to Keatsie and he got tickets for Susan and I to support him on his debut at Wycombe. Keatsie was just the same, buzzing all over the midfield and he put in a great ball for Wycombe to score. We had a drink after the game and Deano told me he had got close to returning to Walsall, but they had not committed to a deal and with a young family Deano took the deal with Wycombe. In the end, Wycombe would just be relegated and Dean would sign a two-year deal with Wrexham close to where his wife's family lived. It's a shame he did not make it back to Walsall for one last hurrah, I believe he would have done another good job for us in midfield.

Immediately the season was over players began to leave the club: Sansara, Mattis, Till, O'Keefe, Bradley, Parkin, Weston and Ince, after 152 league games in goal for Walsall, retired and returned to Trinidad and Tobago. As we got close to pre-season training Mark Hughes left for Australia and Rene Gilmartin, who had finally established himself in the first team, was transferred to Watford. The biggest move was Troy Deeney's transfer to Watford. They had been after him for quite sometime and would get their man with an offer of 500,000 pounds. I believe the Saddlers fans thought overall it was good business and we wished Troy the best in his new career.

The vast amount of players leaving meant again we were in for a massive recruitment surge. Just prior to the season, in came goalkeepers Jonny Brain from Macclesfield and David Bevan from Aston Villa. Aaron Lescott from Bristol Rovers, Oliver Lancashire from Southampton, Paul Marshall from Manchester City, Ryan McGiven on a season-long loan from Manchester City and Jon Macken from Barnsley. The squad looked thin on the ground as the campaign started and a whole rash of loan players began to appear: David Davis from Wolves, Martin Devaney from Barnsley, Reuben Reid from West Bromwich Albion, Liam Dickinson also from Barnsley and Andy Butler to plug our leaking defence. The run-up to Christmas was an absolute disaster. The Walsall fans were calling for the head of Chris Hutchings for months as the team struggled to find any rhythm or confidence.

We were at the opening game of the season against MK Dons and watched our 2-1 defeat. I was then at Orient on September 28th for the 0-0 draw, when our defenders did not want to pass the ball back to Jonny Brain, who was obviously shot confidence wise. It was a terrible match and Orient were no better, but we battled hard for the point.

Susan, Helen, Joe and I were all together again on October 23rd for the game against Tranmere Rovers when we were smashed 4-1 at home. We hit the bottom of the league and looked completely gone, devoid of confidence and organization. I read all the abuse on the Internet that was falling upon Chris Hutchings and the criticism of a Walsall side playing 'lump ball.'

Just when all seemed lost we pulled a 1-0 victory at Charlton, the only match we played during December as the weather obliterated the football programme. I guess we all hoped that somehow, during the break, the team would regroup and come out for the second half of the season fighting. Unfortunately, when we did return to playing we lost 2 games heavily, 3-0 and 4-1 and that signalled the end of Chris Hutchings and Martin O'Connor.

I don't personally know Chris Hutchings, but I know a lot of people in football who do, they all say what a nice guy he his and so I believe that to be true. Somehow, he could not find a team to respond to what he wanted. I was disappointed for Martin and spoke to him briefly the day after he left. Martin just said 'That's football,' but I know his love for Walsall Football Club and it hurt him badly.

Dean Smith, another former player who I've known since the days he first broke into our team, was appointed initially for 2 games and then until the end of the season. The brief was to save us from relegation, this would not be a 'great escape,' it was more of a 'Mission Impossible.' We were 8 points adrift of the safety line with no games in hand and a team devoid of confidence. Dean had done a great job with our youth side and at least knew all the players, their faults and capabilities. I read how some supporters said that Dean was the cheap option, but I believed it was astute to give him the job if he wanted it. Everyone who worked at the club believed the job that Dean had done after Mick Halsall had resigned was exceptional. Dean had folders of training schedules that he had collected over the years and changed everything in terms of training from day one. The promotion of Jon Whitney was smart; we all know that Jon has always been Mr. Positive. The second brilliant move was to bring in Chris Nichol. We needed Chris to give the defence confidence. Lancashire, Butler, McDonald and Smith all have ability and to coach them in the proper way was necessary. We all know that Chris made an outstanding player out of Ian Roper, the lynch pin of our defence for seasons. I was also impressed that Dean did not go out and sign a rash of loan players; he pushed confidence into the existing players and gave them all a chance. The 3-3 draw at Tranmere and the 2-2 draw at Bristol Rovers showed a marked improvement, which was almost overnight. I know we then lost a couple of games, but we were unlucky to do so, the 1-1 draw against Oldham, when we were unlucky not to win, and then the 6-1 thrashing of Bristol Rovers could not have been thought of only four weeks before.

The signings on loan of Mathew Gill and Jason Price were good in that they were battling players that wanted to do well, not just in town for a run out. The Carlisle away win was exceptional, the Bournemouth defeat unlucky, even Bournemouth thought they were lucky to take all 3 points.

We bounced straight back with a 1-0 win against relegation rivals Dagenham. When it looked as though we would never score, no matter how many chances we created, Will Grigg came off the bench to win the 3 points. A 2-0 reverse at Colchester set up 2 home games, against Rochdale on February 26th and Southampton on March 1st. Susan, Helen, Joe and I had lunch in the Bonser suite, meeting up with Chris Nichol in the car park. He said today's game against Rochdale would be tough. So it proved, although we penned them in their own half for the first period, they were a strong, organized, commando-type team. Rochdale played better in the second half, the score remaining 0-0, but I saw it as a point gained rather than two lost. I was at the computer all night watching the score as we faced Southampton; a good shout went up in North London when Jon Macken put us in front in the second half. Our defence held firm under the onslaught and we secured three valuable points, which lifted us out of the relegation places for the first time in five months. Walsall were now 5th in the recent form guide in the division, a testament to the effort they were putting in.

Jimmy 'Wacka' Walker was back in our goal and the Southampton match was his 17th since his return to Walsall. 'Wacka' was on his way to achieving the milestone of 500 games for Walsall if he could remain fit and healthy.

The following Saturday, March 5th, Susan and I were invited to Swindon Town by match sponsors, Cat Communications, to see the game against Walsall. Craig Lang is the owner of the company and although now living in Swindon, is a Saddler through and through. Joe Savage, Craig's wife Penny, the staff of Cat Communications, Stefan Gamble and some of the boys who work in the Bonser suite on match day, were all invited.

Fitzroy Simpson also came along to see the game; he also lives in Swindon now. We had a good chat, as it had been some years since I'd seen him, we commented that, given our position in the league, a point from today's game would be great.

That match was my first chance to see the new signings, Emmanuel Ledesma, the striker from Argentina and Marc Antoine Gbarssin, the French defencive midfielder. Swindon opened well for their new Manager Paul Hart, who had replaced Danny Wilson only two days previously. Dean Smith changed our midfield to cope with their system and the game was a hard fought midfield battle with few chances at either end. Gbarssin, after taking ten minutes to settle down, had a good game and got better and better as the game went on. Strong in the tackle, he looked a good loan signing for the rest of the season. Emmanuel Ledesma looked a dangerous player who could be full of surprises, however, he had to do a job at Swindon that curbed some of his natural flair. Tom Williams slotted in well at left-back and the team seemed to be taking shape. We eventually managed a 0-0 draw and came away with a point. Jimmy Walker's fingertips, in the last minute, deflected a Swindon shot that looked in all the way, onto the underside of the bar and out. We had now achieved a clean sheet in 4 of our last 15 matches; 'the Chris Nichol effect' was beginning to work.

We were at home the following Tuesday versus Leyton Orient, who were in a fine run of form; we would eventually lose the match 2-0, putting us back into the relegation zone with 10 matches left to play.

The game away at Yeovil was a big match. Yeovil were two points and two places above us, a win there and the task would seem a little easier if only for a week. I was playing golf that day; finishing the game I turned on the radio as soon as I got in the car. Fifteen minutes later I heard with great joy, that Jon Macken had tapped in to give us the lead. I would learn later it was against the run of play and Yeovil were battering our defence. Just minutes before halftime Yeovil equalized, and during the second half they probably should have gone in front, we held out and nearly snatched it at the end when Ledensa hit the underside of the bar only for it to bounce clear. Nevertheless we gained a point that might still prove valuable; we remained in the bottom four on goal difference.

The following Saturday, March 19th, Hartlepool United were the visitors to Banks's Stadium. We started poorly and were 1-0 down at halftime. Soon after the break we went 2-0 down and all was looking lost. Dean Smith put on Emmanuel Ledesma and in one of the biggest turnarounds ever, we clawed our way back into the match. First, Will Grigg spun on a ball on the edge of the box and fired it into the net. Ledesma crossed for Darren Byfield to equalize minutes later. The crowd and the team were set alight by the breathtaking display of Ledesma. Julien Gray followed up a shot to make it 3-2. Manny Smith headed home the fourth and Ledesma finished off the afternoon in the ninetieth minute with a direct free kick for his first Walsall goal. Ledesma was named 'Man of the Match' for the thirty-eight minutes he played, probably saving our slim chance of escape from relegation, as all the teams around us won. It was one of those special afternoons when against all odds we returned a 5-2 victory, we remained in the bottom four, but still in touch with the teams ahead of us.

I spoke to Jeff Bonser later that week. He had not been to a match since the opening day of the season, feeling his presence at matches was a negative and his popularity with the supporters at its lowest ebb. He told me he listened to the games on the Internet in the comfort of his own lounge and then watched the videos of matches later. That day he was considering opening a bottle of wine to drown his sorrows as we went 2-0 down, the comeback started and Jeff was alone, jumping around his lounge as the goals began to go in. No matter what anyone thinks, I know Bonser is a true Saddler and will always be one; the team and the results matter to him.

Our next game, with 8 matches to go, was an away game on Friday 25th at MK Dons. Susan and I had been invited to the game by an old music pal of mine John Aston. I also knew Pete Winkleman, Chairman of MK Dons, well from his days in the record business. We had a great evening, made even more special by the gaining of a point in a 1-1 draw. We managed to catch up with

Chris Nichol before the game and spoke with Mick Kearns, Dean Smith and 'Wacka' after the game. It had been quite some time since I'd seen Wack and some things never change. Wack was in great form. The team had an enforced layoff due to the fixture schedule and I didn't think we needed that at the time. We had a good confident head of steam going against relegation and needed to keep it going by playing. During the enforced layoff Dean Smith was awarded a two-year deal to be Walsall Manager. I thought it was deserved and the performances of the team since he had taken charge were a vast improvement on what had gone before. Dean Smith had given, not only the team, but also the whole town, a belief that we may just escape relegation even though it looked like 'Mission Impossible.'

Our next game was against relegation favourites Plymouth Argyle at Home Park. Their loss of 10 points through entering administration had hurt them badly in terms of league position. On the day, only 'Wacka' turned up putting in a great display, the rest of the team struggled to find their form and we found ourselves in 22nd position after the 2-0 defeat, but still in touch and still in with a chance. Our next 3 games were all at home and would define our season and finishing spot in the table. First up, were Brentford on Tuesday April 12th, it was to be Jimmy Walker's 500th game for the club, a massive achievement. I decided to make the trip from London to pay my respects to a Walsall legend and lend my support to the challenge of getting those 3 points. The feeling was if we lost that match we would probably be doomed. We didn't start well and for the first forty minutes looked out of touch and lacking in confidence, going behind to a goal from a corner. On forty minutes, 'Wacka' punted one up and Jon Macken volleyed in from thirty yards. 1-1 at halftime and as the second period began we looked a different team with much more confidence. Jordan Cook, on loan from Sunderland, spun in the box and put us 2-1 in front. Brentford came back soon after just as we looked like winning easily, capitalizing on a misjudgment by Richard Taundry they levelled us at 2-2. Within two minutes Jon Macken bustled one over the line and we regained our lead at 3-2, that was how it stayed and the 3 points were ours. Those points moved us out of the relegation zone on goal difference and put us back in with a chance. Brighton secured promotion that night by doing us a favour and beating Dagenham. Brighton would be our visitors on Saturday and we left the Stadium hoping they would go on a two-day celebratory bender, rendering them under par for Saturday. Hope is found in the strangest of places.

Unfortunately, Brighton would be made of sterner stuff and claimed the Division One title at the Banks's with a 3-1 victory. We got caught twice at the start of each half and although we put up a good fight Brighton probably deserved their win. Our 'run in' problems were compounded with an injury to Clayton McDonald that would end his season and Ledesma's unfortunate sending off during the match meant a three game ban that would put him out of the team until the last match of the season at Southampton.

Our next match looked like a 'must win' game at home to Sheffield Wednesday. I was playing golf that day in a St George's Day competition and wouldn't be attending the match. I remember turning up for the golf game and thinking about the afternoon's game against Sheffield more than my own preparation. We took an early lead through Jon Macken, only for Wednesday to equalize and the game then became a midfield affair with few chances. A 1-1 draw was not what we needed, but now the league table suggested it would be two teams from three for relegation. Swindon Town and Plymouth Argyle looked gone, Dagenham and Redbridge, Walsall and Bristol Rovers were all locked on 44 points with 3 games to go.

Our next match on Easter Monday now looked critical, it was an away game at Oldham Athletic. London to Oldham is just too far and being Easter Monday I was involved with family duties, but I kept nipping out to the car to hear how the lads were doing. All seemed to be going well, with a goal from Tom Williams putting us in front. A lead we held until the eighty-eighth minute when a twenty-five yarder flew into our net. Another 1-1 draw brought huge disappointment as we nearly had the 3 points, the results again went for us and we moved out of the relegation zone by a single point with 2 games to go.

Everything now rested on our last 2 games at home to Charlton and away at Southampton a week later. We needed to beat Charlton to stand any chance of survival.

The Charlton match grew in importance during the week. One of the most important games at the Banks's stadium in recent years and I was not going to miss it. The call across the Internet and the local papers for a good Walsall support in our hour of need was evident. All that had gone before was history and all that mattered was a win on Saturday.

My daughter Josephina and I made the drive from London to Walsall, met up with my Sister, Joe Savage and Craig Lang for lunch at the club in the Bonser suite before settling down to the tension of the game. It would be a good performance from the team, a couple of early scares, but we soon got a grip of the game and scored on thirty minutes through Will Grigg. The second half started and Charlton had a go to level the match, but we stood strong and began to attack their goal. Julian Gray added to our total and we saw out the match, a 2-0 victory.

The Saddler Girls

My Sister Helen

My Daughter Johanna

My Daughter Josephina

My Wife Susan

Back inside the Bonser suite everyone was looking for the other scores, which had not been kind. We remained 1 point above the relegation zone with 1 game to go.

I met with 'Wacka' after the game who told me he thought we would win at Southampton and stay in the division, as did many of our supporters, buoyed by the euphoria of the win against Charlton.

As the coming week progressed the reality of going to Southampton in front of 32,000 fans celebrating their promotion seemed more and more daunting. The other game with the most importance was what looked like an easier fixture, Peterborough at home to Dagenham and Redbridge, if Peterborough won we would stay up regardless of our result and Dagenham would be relegated.

1,700 Walsall fans attended the match at Southampton and sang their way through the game. We were under the cosh from the start and, although we rallied, Southampton struck twice in two minutes before Julian Gray pulled one back just before halftime. Peterborough were beating Dagenham 1-0, but Daggers had hit the bar and the post, they were far from out of it. Walsall started well in the second half and were unlucky not to equalize, then, everything started to change. Supporters were watching and listening to the Peterborough game on the radio. In a blaze of scoring Peterborough went two up, Southampton made it 3-1 and then Daggers collapsed, 3-0, 4-0 and, finally, 5-0, meant Walsall would achieve 'Mission Impossible' and the 'great escape,' remaining in Division One against all odds. The whole stadium celebrated, Southampton's promotion and Walsall's escape, it had become one of those memorable moments that are talked about for years to come. It was probably one of the toughest 'great escapes' in our history. 8 points adrift on January 3rd, bottom of the table, we had survived against all odds.

Dean Smith, in his first ever management position, had, in five months, engineered the greatest turnaround in fortune and in Walsall he was rightly 'Lord of the Manor.'

The Final Whistle

Chapter 29

Banks's Stadium And The Land

The Banks's Stadium and the land on which it sits had been put up for sale in March 2011. The selling agent appointed being DTZ. It seemed that after twenty-three years of service that Chairman, Jeff Bonser, at the age of sixty-eight, had decided that his time was coming to an end.

The Stadium and the land had been separated from the club many years before during 1989 and so two separated companies controlled Walsall Football Club.

Although, throughout many years, Jeff Bonser and Chief Executive Roy Whalley had said many times that the club was for sale, no serious attempts had been made to buy the club and/or its land.

I would guess, in an attempt to lessen Jeff's responsibilities and to work towards selling the Football Club, the Stadium and the land was put up for sale.

The Football Club had for many years paid rent to operate at the Stadium, a rent that was now 477,000 pounds per year. The Stadium and seventeen and a half acres were rumoured to be valued at somewhere between 5 and 7 million pounds, although no fixed price had been set and offers were invited.

Slowly, between March and April, all supporters had become aware that when the Stadium and the land were sold, most probably it would be sold to property developers. Within the contract it was reported that the Football team had the balance of a first term of 17 years, followed by a further 30-year option to play at the Stadium. How solid that covenant was no one really knew.

Some took the view that all would be fine and we'd fight it later if necessary, others began to worry that if the Football Club hit bad times and went into receivership that would open the door to demolishing the Stadium and building warehouses and apartments on the land, thereby making a fortune from the initial investment and Walsall losing their football team.

As time went on it became clear and worrying that big companies across the country saw this as a good deal, guaranteed rental income and the possibility that if the Football Club began to collapse, real money could be made.

The team at this time looked like it would be playing its football in Division Two and its Chairman was preparing to leave in the near future after 23 years of solidarity. All did not look good.

I suppose being well known in the town for my hit records and music career many people began to talk to me about the situation at the games and thought that I should do something about it. The supporters groups, the Saddlers club, Walsall Trust and Unity, all had differing opinions, but they generally believed that the Stadium and the land should be returned to the Football Club.

Personally, and after twenty-odd years apart, I could not see that happening. The Stadium and the land had too much value to just be returned and no one in the previous 10 years had made an offer sizeable enough to allow that to happen.

The dilemma began to occupy my mind. The love of my local team had stayed with me throughout my life and the thought that just maybe the club would no longer exist and league football would not be played in Walsall was just too much to consider.

I was talking to Joe Savage on the phone about our chances of beating the drop one day and Joe mentioned the problem of the Stadium and the land. We spoke again a couple of days later and again we spoke about the Stadium deal. Joe said, 'You might just have to do something about that you know, if you don't no one else will.'

That one sentence struck a chord in my mind and I began to think, he's right, if no one does anything then this land will find its way into the hands of companies outside of Walsall, who have no interest in the town and probably even less in the Football Club. It seemed to me, I either ignore it or do something about it, even if I fail, at least I would have had a go. Better to have tried and failed than to have not tried at all.

I explained everything to Susan and suggested I should try. Susan said that the club had always been my passion and that if I wanted to try that she would support me in the task and let's just see where it goes. I also spoke to my Sister Helen, who suggested that if I didn't try I might always regret it and that I should give it a go. Then, speaking with Joe, I decided I would make a plan and try to do something. Put a plan into action and just see if there was support and try to make a difference.

I knew that in the past Walsall Council had either shown some interest in the Stadium and the land or had been spoken to by the club. Nothing had ever happened, but it had been reported in the local press that enquiries had been made or at the very least talked about. My belief was that if we could convince the Council to buy the Stadium and the land, it would guarantee that the facility would always be there for the supporters and people of Walsall. The council would benefit from the rental income and would protect the Football team, the town's flagship.

I began to read about other town's councils buying the land that their Football Clubs resided on and either purchasing their Stadium or having part ownership of it. The situation was clear; the Council should do this for the town and its people. The advertising, investment and income that the Football team brings to our town have nothing but a positive effect. A league football team is written about in all of the local papers and then in the national papers. The results every time they play are nationally printed, the results and goals broadcast almost daily on Sky Sports. A town without a League Football Club becomes lost on the map of England. All football supporters know where League clubs are, where their towns are, without them you become lost.

It seemed to me that the first place to start was with the supporters clubs: Walsall Supporters club, Walsall Trust and Unity. If I could enlist their support I could at least begin a campaign.

I began to set about getting names and addresses of the most influential people at these organizations. It was a hit and miss affair, names came easily, but addresses were slower to arrive. I used some of my old contacts in Walsall, some music promotion people I knew, people from the Council and got a couple from the Football Club. Having got what I thought were the right people I wrote to them all and asked if they were prepared to come along to a meeting.

After the initial letter, I was then able to communicate with them all via email. The date was set for Wednesday May 4th at The Queen's Head in Wednesbury, 6:30pm. Joe had come to the rescue in sorting out the venue.

Susan and I drove from London to Walsall that day, had a bite to eat at my Sister Helen's and then Helen joined us and Joe at The Queen's Head to confront the supporters and talk about my plan of action.

Slowly, everyone began to arrive as we had set a 7:00pm start time; we were probably underway at 7:15pm. Susan, Helen and Joe sat behind me as I addressed the group. I spoke about my plan to try and get the Council to buy the Stadium and land, the supporters made it clear that their first plan would be that the Stadium was returned to the club, but I explained why I thought that would never happen, slowly, they believed that my option was a good second.

We spoke for nearly ninety minutes before I felt I needed a break and called for a fifteen minute recess. In short, I'd taken a good battering. The supporters knew everything about our little Football Club, in far more detail than I knew. They all still lived in the town and the team was their complete passion, I was wilting under the strain, but still had heard no better idea and so was sticking to my guns. The break allowed me a few minutes to think and regain my composure. I believed I'd won over more than half of the lads but was still under fire from the rest.

I began to speak again and started with, 'You know what lads, if you really don't wish to go forward on this issue it's really okay, I can easily get in my car and drive back to London and play golf. I'm here because I wanted to try and do something to protect the Football Club, if it's not to be, it's not to be.' Those few words changed the landscape, they were honest words and the supporters' groups responded to them.

I had written an 'open letter,' which I intended to send to the *Express & Star*, hoping that they would print it and the campaign would commence. We all agreed, with relegation staring our team in the face, their final game at Southampton being the coming Saturday, we would delay any movement until the following Monday. This would also give me time to approach the evening paper. The meeting finally broke up around 10pm. Susan and I headed back to London supported by the Saddlers club, Walsall Trust and Unity and we had a start.

The *Express & Star* is the country's largest evening newspaper, covering the whole of the West Midlands. In these days of free newspapers you still have to buy the *Express & Star*.

Chris Marsh, former Walsall player, with nearly 500 appearances for the club, had been a mate of mine for over twenty years. I remembered he had told me about Nick Mashiter at the *Express & Star* and he felt that after many interviews he was someone who could be trusted to do the right thing and respect confidences.

On Thursday May 5th 2011, I called Nick Mashiter. Fortunately, he was aware of my career, which made life easier and we began to talk about the current state of Walsall Football Club, the Stadium, the land and what might happen in the future should the land be sold to property developers. I sent him the copy of my 'open letter' and agreed nothing would happen until after the Southampton match. Over several conversations during a two-day period I knew that the letter would be printed on Monday May 9th.

That Monday, after Walsall had somehow completed the 'great escape,' the supporters and the town were alight, the newspapers would be full of this incredible achievement and we were about to launch our campaign to hopefully unite the town's Football Club with the town's council, protect our Stadium and land and move into a secure future that would deliver the next hundred years of football in the town.

During Monday, the phone was hot between Nick and I, the news team at the *Express & Star* had seen Nick's piece and wanted to take it over. I told Nick to tell them I would only talk to him and in doing so, try to offer him some protection within the paper. I did not want Nick to lose the story.

Eventually, it was worked out, the story would be front page and a credit of Nick Mashiter would be printed. I had never thought that this story would be a front page item. I had only thought of it as 'Sport,' back page or inside the back page amongst the reports of the 'great escape.' The campaign had started and started with unbelievable exposure. My story, letter and face blasted across the front page.

The letter immediately hit home and ignited already buoyant Saddlers supporters after the 'great escape.' The Internet, such a major tool these days, was buzzing with comments from the fans and people of Walsall.

The previous Thursday, May 5th, the local elections had occurred in Walsall. This would become crucial as the campaign developed. The Conservatives, led by Councillor Mike Bird, had been in power for some time, but it was felt around the town that there might be a change coming.

On May 5th a change did occur and Walsall was left with a hung Council, Conservatives losing seats and ending up with a count of 28, Labour gaining to 26 and the Liberal Democrats holding the balance with 5, plus one other, making up the 60 councillors.

Councillor Bird had made it clear over the past few years that he had no interest in the Banks's Stadium or Walsall Football Club and would never entertain the Council getting involved. Had the Conservatives won the election the campaign would never have gotten off the ground. Now, with a hung Council, if the parties did not form a coalition then every major issue would have to be voted on by the 60 councillors, a score of 31 yes votes would pass anything on the agenda.

On Tuesday, May 10th, under the title of 'Walsall Fans Back Jenkins' Idea' the *Express & Star* printed the story of the backing from 'The Saddlers' club, the Walsall Trust and Unity. With it came more and more Internet chatter and support from the fans and the town.

NOW LET'S BU[Y] THE STADIU[M]

By Nick Mashiter

SADDLERS fans today celebrated the greatest escape in the club's history – as a millionaire fan urged the council to buy the stadium and secure the side's future.

Despite losing 3-1 to Southampton, Walsall beat the relegation drop by a point after Dagenham collapsed 5-0 at Peterborough on the final day of the season.

Now, music producer and lifelong Saddlers fan Steve Jenkins – who has worked with Britney Spears, Justin Timberlake and The Stone Roses – is urging Walsall Council to buy the up-for-sale Banks's Stadium and safeguard the club's future.

Jenkins, a former MD of Jive Records, has written an exclusive open letter to the Express & Star calling on the council to act on the club.

Belief

He said: "Having had time to think about the situation, it is my firm belief that the best way forward for Walsall Football Club for the land to come under the ownership

Staying up – Saddlers fans fly the flag as news comes in of their rival's collapse   Millionaire fan Steve

Jenkins renewing his call to council

MILLIONAIRE Walsall fan Steve borough's councillors to follow the by buying the Banks's Stadium. In [...] producer insisted he is [...]

Fans back Jenkins call

FANS today backed Steve Jenkins' Banks's Stadium vision and urged the council to consider his proposal.

The music producer and lifelong fan yesterday called for the council to buy the ground and end the uncertainty surrounding its future.

It has been on the market for two months with an asking price believed to be around £5m.

Supporters' groups want the council to seriously think about the plan.

"They would be investing in the people of Walsall," said

Council urged to back Saddlers

by Nick Mashiter
n.mashiter@expressandstar.co.uk

WALSALL COUNCIL were today facing mounting pressure to help the Saddlers safeguard their future after Labour called on them to meet the club.

The party want the council, which is under a minority Conservative rule, to hold "urgent talks" with the club and fans about the sale of the Banks's Stadium.

In a statement they stopped short of saying the council should make a bid for the ground but insisted the local authority should take a more proactive role in the sale process.

It follows a campaign, led by music producer and lifelong fan Steve Jenkins, to convince the council to buy the freehold.

Council leader Mike Bird has dismissed the idea, insisting they cannot afford to invest, despite the extra £250,000 in rent a year the council would receive from the Saddlers.

Labour leader Tim Oliver said: "This out of hand rejection of a role for the council in the club's future is

short sighted, to say the least. The club has a fantastic reputation within football as a well run, family friendly team which projects a positive image for the borough nationally. It would be wrong of Walsall council to refuse to help secure the Saddlers' future so we are calling for all p[...] urge Mr B how hom [...]

at Bescot. We understand that around 20 other local councils around the country have come to such arrangements for the benefit of their communities.

The ground has been on the market for two months and the *Express & Star* understands it has a price tag of £5m. Jenkins fears for the club's future if a private investor buys the land and added: "I'm delighted we're moving forward and the council are starting to recognise this could be a [...]

Jenkins will seek talks on ground sale

MILLIONAIRE Walsall fan Steve Jenkins today called for a swift end to the Banks's Stadium saga and revealed he will seek talks with the council.

The music producer and lifelong Saddler insisted the local authority buying the ground represents the best option for them and the club – despite the council's reluctance.

Leader Mike Bird dismissed the proposal on Wednesday claiming they didn't have the cash and had to slice £70m off their budget.

Mr Jenkins wrote an open letter to the Express & Star

by Nick Mashiter
n.mashiter@expressandstar.co.uk

on Monday revealing he fears for the club's future should the stadium, which has been on the market since March, end up with [...]

Millionaire fan calls council to buy ground

A millionaire Saddlers fan urged the council to buy the stadium and secure the side's future as fans are celebrating the greatest escape in the club's

COUNCIL BOSS RULES OUT BUYING STADIUM

Authority does not have money to purchase Saddlers' home

By Elizabeth Joyce

Walsall Council today ruled itself out of ever buying Banks's Stadium – following pressure from a millionaire superfan.

The cash-strapped local authority said it wished the club well but would not be buying the stadium and surrounding 17 acres of land at a time when it has to save £70 million.

[...]elong Walsall fan Steve [...]ed with Britney Spears, [...] Stone Roses – is urging [...] he up-for-sale Banks's [...] club's future.

[...]ive Records, has written [...] the press calling on the

[...]e to think about this sit[...]at the best way forward [...] is for the land to come [...] council.

[...]eguard the club's future [...]n remains at the Banks's [...]ld gain possession of an [...]unity asset.

Councillor Bird, sensing the wave of support from the town's people, did his best to stop the momentum by issuing a statement, which was printed on Wednesday May 11th. Bird stated that the Council would not be buying the Stadium or land under any circumstances and flatly dismissed the idea.

On reading this statement, I thought the response was too quick. How could Councillor Bird have spoken to all of the councillors in such a short period of time? How could he have gained so much support to just end the discussion on whether this was a good or bad opportunity for the town of Walsall? I soon decided that this outburst was a personal view, backed up with no support from the other parties or councillors. It felt like someone who before the election had complete control somehow had not adjusted to the now hung Council.

I decided after a night of thinking about the whole campaign, I didn't believe Mr. Bird's outburst at all, it was just him trying to dampen the now building campaign and I decided to attack again.

On Friday, May 13th, under the heading 'Steve Jenkins seeks talks over the future of the Saddlers, again I spelt out the message, reserving special attention and respect for Mr. Bird, but stating that I believed his view to be a personal one and that we now knew that we had 1 vote against and 59 still to go. Without saying Mr. Bird didn't have the power to just stop this discussion, I had suggested it. That piece set the course of the campaign over the coming weeks. Mr. Bird's poorly thought out dismissal just poured petrol onto the fire. Now the town's people, before just looking on, did not like the way I had been treated and dismissed out of hand. The campaign doubled overnight.

Over the weekend, I felt the campaign was back on track and building pace. I had the supporters and some of the people of Walsall but needed to keep on building the support in the press and adding to it.

Chris Marsh, my great friend and Walsall legend, did an interview with Nick Mashiter that would be printed on Monday May 16th, titled 'Walsall legend backs Steve Jenkins.'

Chris's story added more momentum to the campaign and suggested that now I had the support of the players; when you have player support normally the wave of supporters follow and that happened again, the support grew overnight. Every time a newspaper story hit, 'Up the Saddlers' website carried the story and the Internet chatter increased. More and more of the town's people were talking about the Saddlers and the Stadium.

Steve Jenkins

The following night, Tuesday May 17th, Walsall Football Club's Stefan Gamble issued a statement from the club. Stefan is the Chief Executive of the club and stated that Walsall F.C. welcomed Steve Jenkins' idea, especially as the supporters backed it.

For me that was all well and good, but I needed the Chairman and owner Jeff Bonser to verbally back the campaign. As much as Jeff was not popular with the supporters, without him, they tend not to believe that the club would support anything. I made a phone call to Jeff Bonser and we talked for over an hour on the issue of Banks's Stadium, the conclusion was he would back the idea wholeheartedly and make a press statement that would go to press.

I also asked for all of the brochures from DTZ, the selling agents, and further information about how Walsall Football Club was a mainstay in the town for Walsall people. I wanted to write a letter to all of the sixty councillors with all of the information so that not one Councillor could say 'I know nothing about it.'

I also spoke with The Saddlers club, Walsall Trust and Unity to write a letter that could be downloaded, signed and sent to the public's local Councillor backing the campaign. I worked for two complete days on setting up a Friday 13th attack that would cause huge repercussions and leave no way out for councillors to ignore this campaign. We all now worked hard to time an attack for 2:30pm on Friday, May 13th 2011.

The time was chosen as that is when the *Express & Star* evening edition hits the streets. That night the *Star* carried the two reports of the 'Fans Letter Campaign' and a photograph of Jeff Bonser above the heading 'Jenkins vision has Bonser backing.'

At 2:30pm the fans letter was posted on all of the websites to be downloaded, signed and sent off.

At 2:30pm the detailed DTZ brochures and information sheets hit the Council House and were put into every councillors post box, no one was missed.

All I could do then was wait.

The first few days of the coming week were ignited again by Internet chatter. Councillor Bird had contacted the *Express & Star*, Sports division, with a story of a 'Mystery Buyer' he had spoken to who had reportedly offered a 4.5 million bid, was a Walsall man and not a property developer. The Sports

296

division declined to print the story without naming the Walsall man, Bird declined to issue the name, no story. By Thursday May 26th, an incensed Bird called the news department and insisted the story was printed and it became a front page item. Bird obviously thought this would deflect the pressure from the Council and send the fans and people of Walsall off in another direction.

Initially, I thought the idea of deflection was a good one and gave full credit to Bird for his actions. I thought long and hard over a sleepless night that evening. By the morning I had thought about there being several interested parties in buying the Stadium and to me and the people of Walsall they were all 'Mystery Buyers,' again, we decided to attack.

On Monday, May 30th, under the title 'Walsall Council Told To Put Banks's Stadium on an Agenda.' I reaffirmed that Mr. Bird's view was personal and the story remained the same, 1 against, 59 undecided. I also spoke about the other 'Mystery Buyers' and that whoever the Walsall 'Mystery Buyer' was he would be better advised to talk to DTZ or Walsall Football Club than a Councillor who had no interest in the Football Club.

Again, the outburst from a determined Mr. Bird had backfired, the Internet chatter was huge about Council deflection and the campaign was one that just would not go away. Our breakthrough came the following day. On Tuesday, May 31st, Tim Oliver of the Labour Party issued a statement, which was reported in the *Express & Star* under the heading 'Talks on Walsall's Banks's Stadium urgent says Chief.'

The following day, June 1st, 'New Twist in battle for Banks's Stadium.'

The report featured Ian Shires of the Liberal Democrats calling for talks with the three major parties over the Banks's Stadium after the wave of public pressure.

We had finally forced the Council to commence proper talks about the Stadium and land; The Banks's Stadium was now a political hot potato.

It seemed now that there was little more to do. Two of the three leaders of the political groups had come out in favour of, at the very least, some form of discussion on the Banks's Stadium affair. The other, Councillor Bird, was still against any such discussion and continued with that stance.

I was no longer in control of events; we just had to await the outcome of internal meetings within the Council.

On June 6th, The Supporters clubs got in touch and asked if I would write a letter to the fans purely for use on their websites. This just happened to coincide with a report from Rotherham Council that they had lent Rotherham United Football Club 5 million pounds towards building a new stadium. I wrote a summery piece of how far we had come over the past six weeks and that we must now exert patience as the Council were preparing for a meeting. I also incorporated the news about Rotherham United. The *Express & Star* picked up on the piece and published a story on June 7 titled 'Steve Jenkins Makes New Point.' I had not envisaged that happening, but it sparked plenty of discussion on the Internet and probably more than had gone before. I can only surmise that the increase in 'chat' was caused by the realization that we were getting closer and closer to a meeting between Walsall Football Club, DTZ and the Council.

The online chat was more intense than ever, mostly for, but, as always, some against. The ones that were against still had no alternative for the security of the Stadium and land, only proposing that the Stadium be returned to the Football Club. That was never going to happen, having been separated for nearly eighteen years, valued at around 5 to 7 million pounds. Who would agree to that proposal? It was just not reality.

I did read all of the 'against' pieces, the conspiracy questions, the demands, the questions about my life and character, my relationship with Jeff Bonser. None of which had any effect on the stance I had taken. The only one that got to me a little was when someone questioned my being a supporter of Walsall Football Club. That one stuck in my throat for a day or so. After all of the years of travelling 250 miles for a home game, to have my dedication to the Football Team questioned was a step too far. I reasoned with myself that it was just an uninformed view.

The conspiracy theory that I was somehow in league with Jeff Bonser over the whole affair was based on a visit Jeff had made to my exhibition in the town some four years earlier. The report was still available on my website and the fans that had generated a hate for Jeff Bonser within themselves, could not cope with the fact I had given credit to Jeff Bonser for securing our Football Club for over twenty years.

On that issue, when you look around the Football League clubs and see how many have gone into liquidation, how many are struggling under huge debts, how many have fallen into the Conference from The Championship or League One, you see my point. The Stadium, the conference facilities, the entertainments programmes all contribute to 40 percent of the income to operate our football team. That takes years of hard work. I still believe it's only right and proper to give credit for those achievements.

As for being in league with Jeff Bonser, I hadn't spoken to him in over two years before I started on the campaign. During the campaign I spoke with him twice, the first time to obtain his support and six weeks later to wish him well when the meeting with the Council came around.

Some fans will always dislike Jeff Bonser no matter what he does. I thought it unbelievable that even in Dean Smith's 'great escape' only weeks before, no credit was given to the financial safety of Walsall F.C.. No one seemed to acknowledge that, had Plymouth Argyle not gone into administration and been deducted 10 points, no matter what our team had done, if that had not happened, we would have been a goner and in Division Two. I guess that's football. I was used to half the public saying a record of mine was great and the other half saying it was useless. Their views had little effect on what I believed in. I never got too 'high' when a record got to number one and never got too 'low' when a record I thought was a hit, stiffed badly. I think I always had the same attitude, play the game, win, lose or draw, shake hands afterwards, accept the result and move on. In keeping those emotions in check, I didn't waste any time and moved on swiftly to the next challenge. I do accept that I had a few good nights out when we hit the number one spot on occasions, but not every time.

'Steve Jenkins Makes New Point.' This put the Council under more intense pressure. Councillor Bird responded by pushing forward the bid made by local businessman, Geoff Dance, for the Stadium and land, to deflect from the announcement that the Council were meeting with Walsall Football Club and DTZ at 6:30pm on June 21st.

The announcement made by Tim Oliver, leader of the Labour Group, that the meeting had been called, should have been front page news after a six-week campaign. Bird saw it coming and named Mr. Dance, which took the headlines. Tim Oliver's announcement was buried within the piece.

'Boss Behind Bid To Buy Banks's Stadium Named.'

This was a great disappointment for me after all of the hard work the supporters and I had put into the attempt at getting the meeting. However, the meeting was on.

The whole Mr. Dance affair was a deflection, but the timing and then further plagiarism of our campaign did irritate me. I thought long and hard about responding, but decided not to lower myself to their level. The truth would eventually out.

I would learn a few days later that a so-called Walsall supporter who had attended my initial meeting with the supporters groups and worked for the Council, had introduced Mr. Dance to Councillor Bird in an attempt to obviously further his career, have some influence over the future of Walsall Football Club and generally become the 'Big I Am.' This again was a disappointment, to be attacked from within. He did not want to be named as he called the supporters groups together to push the bid by Mr. Dance. I wonder why? For me, he would always be a 'Dingle in Disguise.'

Tuesday, June 21st, the longest day of the year, Summer Solstice arrived. Jeff Bonser, Roy Whalley, Stefan Gamble, Adam Davey and Nick Allen from DTZ all presented to 22 councillors, including 8 members of the Conservatives and, surprisingly, Ian Shires of the Liberal Democrats.

The *Express & Star* had written about the coming meeting that day under the heading 'Walsall Talk to Labour councillors,' the local BBC News had also carried the story that night.

The early reports were that the meeting had gone well, with an exceptional performance from Roy Whalley. Jeff Bonser had stated his position clearly and the councillors realized the community part of the Football Club clearly for the first time.

The following morning I woke with the feeling we still had a chance. It was disappointing only 22 councillors had turned up, but the disappointment was tempered with 8 Conservative councillors attending under the complete dismissal of the proposal from their leader. Also, Ian Shires attending opened up another door. All we could do was wait and see if Tim Oliver felt he had enough support to take the proposal to a full Council meeting. I believed, after all we had done, we still had a fifty-fifty chance.

At 4:45pm on Wednesday 22nd a press release was issued from the Council saying that the meeting had been a positive one and that the financial officers of the Council should be instructed to look further into the financial implications of buying Banks's Stadium and land, both the benefits and risks, which would lead to further meetings on this issue.

Although this seemed painstakingly slow, it is the way it works at Council level. I believed it was slow but sure progress. I also believed the more the proposal was looked at and investigated the more it made sense.

On Tuesday 28th, Councillor Tim Oliver, appeared on BBC West Midlands talking about the Council moving forward with the Banks's proposal. I wrote a ten point letter explaining all that the people of Walsall and Saddlers supporters should know. This appeared on the front page of Up the Saddlers website and caused enormous debate.

I had originally wanted to issue the ten point letter via the *Express & Star*, however, the editor of the paper had decided not to carry further stories on the issue until a conclusion had been reached regarding a meeting within the Council. Some thought that Councillor Bird had requested that no more publicity on the proposal should be issued as the pressure was building and building on the Council.

On Wednesday 29th, Councillor Bird was interviewed on West Midlands radio, again stating that the Council would not become involved in the buying of Banks's Stadium. Geoff Dance was also interviewed as one of the bidders in the same interview. This was to backfire immediately. Councillor Bird was less than complimentary about my involvement and came out with outrageous statements about Jeff Bonser's pension and the Conservative Group's administration roll within Walsall. I listened to the interview later and felt there was now an air of desperation within his answers. Later in the day, I began to receive emails from Walsall supporters that they now had lost any faith they may have had with the Geoff Dance bid and the only way forward was to put even more pressure on the Council to put the Banks's Stadium on a Council agenda.

'10 Points Walsall People Should Know.'

Walsall Football Club's Stefan Gamble issued a statement from the club via the *Walsall Advertiser* on Thursday 30th. His letter to the *Advertiser* was very detailed, however, the *Advertiser* used only a few points and reported more in general terms, which didn't have the real impact it should have done.

The following three weeks were slow. The *Express & Star* had chosen not to revisit the subject until there was something positive to report; understandable. The *Advertiser* had also reached a point where something had to happen. Radio and TV had also made their reports and had the programmes of debate. There was a feeling that something just had to give before the campaign would move forward or end.

I read many times on the Internet that some supporters and Walsall people were wondering where I had gone. Had I lost interest? Didn't I care anymore? Was I frustrated by the Council and just walked away? None of that was true.

I could not continue just saying the same thing. We all knew if the land and Stadium could not be reunited with the Football Club, then the safest and best place for it was with Walsall Council. Everyone knew that to be true and the rental income was advantageous to both Walsall and the Council.

The next critical point was Monday July 11th, the Council meeting. Would we make the agenda and be voted on? Councillor Bird was doing his best to keep it off the agenda and Councillor Oliver was doing his best to get it on. There now seemed a growing feeling the Stadium was becoming more and more of a political battle. The longer it went on the more unreasonable Councillor Bird appeared.

I believed the Stadium would feature in the Monday 11th meeting. I don't know why, I just believed that if it didn't the outcry would be huge and the Council, for or against, knew it and they would not take that risk.

Eventually, on Friday 8th, news leaked that the Council would put on the agenda the proposal that the financial review of the Stadium and land should be passed and voted on. We all thought that this had been done. Councillor Oliver had asked for it to be done, but Councillor Bird had vetoed the request, all without having majority control of the Council. The feeling was that the more Councillor Bird said 'no' the more councillors thought it was unreasonable and started to support that it should be done at the very least. My immediate reaction was that of disappointment. The financial review had not even been done. However, I soon returned to the positive, if the review was passed then the Football Club, supporters and town people would benefit on all fronts.

The campaign was still alive, at least until Monday. I also thought that it was still a foolish decision not to at least look at the proposal knowing all the financial facts, given the publicity, support and desire of the Walsall people.

Monday, July 11th, 2011, will remain a crucial date in the history of Walsall Football Club. The Council met that evening and decided not to pursue the financial review of the Stadium and land.

Councillor Mike Bird had done an impressive job, a late addition to the agenda was a discussion that all Council staff would have to take a 20 to 30 percent reduction in their wages to help with the under pressure financial situation the Council found themselves in. This was followed by a passionate speech by Bird about the proposal of the Stadium and land, which resulted in a collapse of support by the floating councillors and the motion to investigate was lost. The Council issued a press release the following day stating that they would not pursue the proposal and added that 50,000 pounds was too much of a cost considering the financial situation. Obviously, that also was misleading; they could have reviewed the idea at no cost and would only incur cost if they then operated due diligence in proceeding.

Bird had misled the public throughout the previous two months, had stood alone in his personal determination to have nothing to do with the Football Club, but had politically won the game. For that alone I have a good deal of respect for him as a political operator. I also believe I have always been the same, in that when I won during my career I tried to underplay it, in defeat I tried to shake hands and suffer with dignity.

Many supporters and fans wanted and expected me to make comment in the press and slaughter Bird. I was never going to lower myself to that.

The fact of the matter was that Councillor Bird was wrong not to even review the proposal. To not do that was egotistical and showed him in some people's view a dictator, even though he did not have a majority in the Council building. Equally, it also showed a lack of character from some of the other councillors that did not stand their ground.

Why should I slaughter Councillor Bird for his beliefs? He was a formidable opponent and in my book, even though I didn't enjoy defeat, he deserved respect for his stance. In the past, Councillor Bird has supported ideas for our Football Club. He was instrumental in supporting The Sunday Market at the stadium; he also supported the building of our billboards that bring in so much income to the club. He may not like football and obviously does not want Council involvement in the Stadium or land, but as a Councillor he has put in many years of work on behalf of the town of Walsall. I will always respect these deeds.

We lost the Council vote 28 to 24, with 8 abstaining.

The campaign/adventure was over. There was no resurrecting the situation. The only way the Council would buy the Stadium in the future was if the Labour Party were voted into power that would mean waiting a year and relying on the fate of an election.

I believed I had to wait to see what would happen next. Would the offers on the table from other parties now be reviewed? Would the Stadium be sold very quickly? Just what would happen no one knew and so I decided to let the dust settle before making a move, if any.

I still felt that I would do all I could to make Walsall Football Club as safe as possible for the future generations of Walsall people, but how, I had no idea at this point.

Steve Jenkins

Finally, as this chapter concludes, I would like to thank the Saddlers Club, Walsall Trust, Unity, Nick Mashiter of the *Express & Star* and the people of Walsall for their support of me during those three months.

There is no doubt that the Council owning the Stadium was the safest place for the Football Club and as 25 of the 92 league clubs are in partnership with their local councils, it was and is a safe way forward. That Walsall's Council chose not to embrace the flagship of the town seemed to suggest that Walsall as a town was going backwards at an alarming rate. We had already lost the Walsall Illuminations that brought thousands of visitors to the town and the Football Club has even more visitors per year than that glorious light show around the Arboretum. I felt a great sense of loss all round for the town of my birth, a town I have always loved, and its Football Team.

A few months later, the Stadium and land was withdrawn from the market. What happens next? Who knows? But I still believe change will eventually come.

Chapter 30
Jeff Bonser... Guilty

The story of Jeff Bonser and Walsall Football Club is an incredible one when you look at it over twenty years. It's not only Jeff though, you have to put into the mix Barrie Blower and Roy Whalley. The first thing to say about the three of them is they are all Walsall people and love Walsall Football Club.

I have known the three of them a long time, without Barrie, and make no bones about this, there would be no Walsall Football Club today; his passion and love of the club, saving its existence in the 1980's, he was 'King' of the Walsall fans and gave his time and energy to save us when all looked lost.

During his Chairmanship after Terry Ramsden, he, Jeff and Roy masterminded the move from Fellows Park to Bescot Stadium. In the face of two relegations and against all odds they built our stadium. That in itself should warrant a long standing respect. It cost three million pounds to build and at the time they had little assistance or help. Imagine taking on a project like that and pulling it off - incredible.

With Jeff Bonsor

The subject of Fellows Park is a touchy one, for me and for many others. It was the ground where my Grandfather and Father supported Walsall Football Club, whenever I visited after their passing it connected me to them. I worked there and broadcasted for many seasons. The games against Manchester United, Liverpool and Newcastle United, our playoff victory against Bristol City and Ned Kelly's hat trick all happened at that stadium and long will it remain in our memory. So much so, for me, I have never visited Morrisons and never will.

However, Fellows Park was not for the 1990's, 2000's and onwards, in truth, the place was falling down, we had to go, if we had not, there probably would be no Walsall Football Club today and if there was, we would probably be in the Conference or worse. Blower, Bonser and Whalley put us on the right track and there is no argument about that.

Barrie Blower is still going to all of the Walsall matches to this day. He still lives all our promotions, relegations, management changes, rebuilding of teams and has been a great ambassador in opposing boardrooms for twenty years. League clubs across the country welcome Barrie to their boardrooms, I know because I've been there and seen it. Barrie, quieter these days, still is prone to the occasional roar of encouragement to the team from the Directors' box; he is and always will be a Walsall boy and a Saddler.

Jeff Bonser has supported Walsall from boyhood. I asked him who was his favourite player years ago and he told me that Tony Richards had given him the most pleasure in a Walsall shirt. Jeff is from the terraces, something that has been forgotten over the years; he built a successful business in Walsall and with the money he made from that he invested in his passion and gave his spare time to Walsall Football Club. Bonser is a Walsall boy and another Saddler, first and foremost.

Roy Whalley joined Walsall Football Club in 1986 and so has dedicated twenty-five years of his life to the club. I have seen Roy at almost every away match I've ever been to; he has travelled the country from top to bottom for twenty-five seasons. I have never known anyone with so much outward energy in support of the Saddlers. Roy is a little more vocal than Barrie at games from the Directors' box and fidgets constantly in his seat as he tries to force the ball into the goal on behalf of Walsall F.C.. If you care to have a conversation about a Walsall match from twenty years ago, Roy would have been there and can most probably name the team and recall some of the action. There is no doubt he is a true Saddler. Roy's wife Jane is a long-suffering Saddlers supporter; she has had no choice and accompanied Roy through all those motorway miles.

I mention the background to these men as at times I have been accused of supporting them when the fans have been upset about a transferred player or lack of investment in the team. Well, as you can see, I know they are as passionate about Walsall Football Club as I am, if not more so. They have put their lives into it and for that I afford them my respect.

The main person singled out for abuse from a section of our fans is Jeff Bonser. He knows, as I do, if you're the Boss it comes with the territory. When things go well you normally don't receive praise, but you don't get any abuse.

When things go badly, it's all your fault and you receive all of the abuse. I believe he would say fair enough to that reasoning. The problem has been over the past six or seven years Jeff has had to take an unbelievable amount of 'stick,' which in a lot of ways has been uncalled for.

Supporting a small Football Club, I believe, has its advantages. The highs of promotion or cup 'giant killing' cannot be felt to the degree we feel it from better-supported or bigger clubs. Relegation is relegation, even Manchester United have felt what that feels like and they like it as much as we do.

Walsall's problem is its location, being in the middle of Birmingham City, Aston Villa, West Bromwich Albion and Wolverhampton Wanderers, means we will always be the 'Cinderella' club. I would suggest if you are unhappy with waiting for our moments of going to the 'Ball,' which will always be few and far between, become a 'Baggie' a 'Blue' a 'Villain' or a 'Dingle.' I must admit I will never ever become one with you, but we all have a choice.

Recently, I was at Swindon for a Walsall game, both sides facing relegation, but Swindon's gate was 10,000 plus. Are they better than us? The league says not, yet because of their geographical position, with no league clubs close by, they can get big crowds even when facing Division Two. The season before they had made the playoff final and lost, they had sold their centre-half and two strikers that had scored 47 goals between them. They had made 5 million pounds from those players.

One of their directors is in the top 10 richest men in the U.K.. Given that, an income of 5 million pounds from transfers and gates of 10,000 when you're losing and Danny Wilson still could not buy new players to help fight relegation. Now that makes you think doesn't it? Therefore, I believe, it is not just Walsall Football Club that sells its players to raise money to pay wages for the current and next campaign, it's across the board of lower league Football Clubs. You have to know where you are and what you're doing to move forward. We all have to do that in our own lives and operating a football team is no different.

So, are Jeff Bonser, Roy Whalley and Barrie Blower guilty of operating our Football Club properly for over twenty years and keeping it afloat? I'd say yes! Guilty as charged.

The building of Bescot Stadium, now known as The Banks's Stadium, which I struggle to get used to, has been impressive. I don't think any of us doubt that issue. I remember my first visit and it was an impressive sight when I saw it driving into the car park. For Walsall Football Club and the town to have a stadium like that warms the heart. I felt it was a cold stadium to start with watching football matches, but as it built its history and magical moments it became home. I know my Grandfather and Father would have gone there if they could and so I feel their presence there, after all, it is the team not the stadium.

It was 1990 when Bescot Stadium opened. Two years later, the club built the all-weather sports pitch behind the Gilbert Alsop stand, opened The Sunday Market, which attracts up to 20,000 people and is the biggest market in the Midlands, and erected two large advertising hoardings facing the M6.

The all-weather pitch helped our team in their training and brought income into the club as it was used for all sorts of football games throughout the year. It brought life to the Stadium site in the evenings.

The Sunday Market was sheer brilliance. To attract that many people to the Stadium site on a Sunday, coupled with that income coming into the club, was an exceptional business move. The whole town had advantages from that idea.

During 1993, Daewoo agreed the biggest ever sponsorship deal in Walsall's history to have their name on the hoardings facing the M6, so, within three years, the Football Club had a vast income that was not related to the gate money.

In 1994, that off-field income had risen to over 1 million pounds.

In 1995, to increase the off-field income, Walsall F.C. erected another illuminated board facing the M6. You have to say that Jeff Bonser learns quickly and goes for the opportunity twice as fast.

Three years later, in 1998, we opened a function room for 300 guests to stage events and conferences. The Bonser suite would bring enormous income over the years into the club. During 1998, another advertising site, a monopole, was erected on the Bescot car park for more off-field income.

In 2002, to add seating to the stadium and increase gate returns the Gilbert Alsop stand became a two-tier affair and opened. The name changes over the years for all of our stands for sponsorship money has also increased the revenue coming into the club.

In 2003, a new gymnasium and media room were built inside the Stadium and we became an all-seater to fall in line with F.A. rules. A year later, the Stadium suite was opened under the Gilbert Alsop stand and increased our conference and event facilities capacity up to 700 people.

In 2006, a 120-room hotel opened on the Bescot site. This enabled companies to stay onsite and use the Stadium facilities for conferences and it also enabled us to put up players whilst they looked for more permanent accommodation after signing to the club.

A year later another new advertising sign was built, the largest free standing advertising site in Europe, taking advantage of the busiest stretch of motorway in the country. The new club shop also opened.

In 2008, our new Football Club training ground opened at Essington, featuring a gymnasium, medical room, changing rooms, kit and boot room, video analysis room, offices, dining room and kitchen.

2009 brought an overhaul of the Stadium offices, the dugouts and the press and radio facilities. The work on our stadium has never stopped since the day it opened twenty years earlier.

All of this has been done regardless of our fortunes on the pitch. It has also been done without our club going bankrupt, into administration, out of business and all those other phrases that we have grown used to with other Division One and Division Two Football Clubs. On top of that, we have never fallen through the trap door into the Conference, which a whole host of clubs have done.

In a lot of ways, Walsall Football Club has progressed when most others have failed and has become a role model for Football Clubs across the country. I'm sure if you asked the other 45 teams that play in Divisions One and Two if they want to swap? The response would be enormous.

Hence, for protecting and maintaining the club I love, is Jeff Bonser guilty?

Yes, Sir, guilty as charged!

When I drive into the car park at The Banks's Stadium I'm proud of what has been achieved. I'm proud of the Stadium, the town and our Football Club. The facilities and the environment are sometimes much better than the performance of the players and team. Not always though and that keeps me driving the M1 and M6 as I have done for over thirty years.

The supporters, as all supporters do, want a winning team, I want one too. And because of the incredible achievements at the Stadium site they believe that all of the money has gone into development rather than into the team, which brings the most criticism and abuse.

The truth of the matter is a football team loses money every year it exists. The rise in players' wages at all levels far outweighs the income from attendances, that's not at Walsall alone, that's all over the leagues. Even Manchester United and Chelsea try to breakeven by selling players. United did it with Ronaldo and do you think United wanted to sell a player like that? It so nearly happened with

Rooney. Chelsea apply their team balance sheet slightly differently because of Abramovitch. That's because he's one of the richest men in the world. If only he had chosen to come and live in the cultural backwaters of Walsall we could have been in the Premiership, it would only have taken a couple of seasons. I don't know what was wrong with the man? It would have been much more rewarding for his soul and Jeff would have sold it to him, I'm sure.

You have to decide how you are going to operate your team. Walsall set a budget for the season for wages, it is then up to the Manager how he manipulates his budget, but I can tell you, it is mostly topped up, re-constructed half way through the season and normally means Jeff Bonser and the Board put more money in. Football has changed; it is no longer about transfer fees, it's about wages and length of contracts, that's what brings players to the club. That, and the facilities at our new training ground, helps us bring new players to the club because the training ground is really the players' home not the stadium. If they can see themselves in good surroundings day after day, it helps them make up their mind to join Walsall rather than go somewhere else.

Jeff Bonser, guilty of trying to bring players into the club and provide great facilities? Guilty as charged. Our youth system has been one of my greatest joys over the years. I love that we develop young footballers well, give them an opportunity in our first team, where hopefully they do great things for the club, and I'm happy when they get the opportunity to play at a higher level and a better club. No matter who is in charge of our youth development, Bill Jones, as Youth Development Officer, has been a constant. To have watched so many football matches with him has been an honour and a pleasure; he is another true Saddler, a great and funny man. Sometimes I wish our young players would stay at Walsall a little longer, but opportunity is opportunity and you have to take it when it comes. You would and so would I, so we have to deal with the disappointment and move on. Jeff Bonser can do as little about when opportunity knocks as you or I. One thing I would say is this, if another club comes in for one of our young players, Jeff Bonser is the best man to make the deal for Walsall Football Club. He has learned the business by concluding transfers over many years and has made very few mistakes. In fact, we all rejoice when an amount of money comes into the club from Jeff's 'sell-on' clauses inserted into contracts.

Jeff Bonser, guilty of making as much money as possible from transfers of Walsall players? Guilty as charged!

The business of 'The Pension Fund' that owns our Stadium and land is something that brings so much abuse to our Chairman and Board. Now, I do not know all of the ins and outs of that arrangement and my view is that it is none of my business. However, I do know one thing about pension funds in the business arena, which all supporters should understand. Football Clubs are not seen as good business ventures by banks. I think everyone would agree with that. Therefore, if you are going to invest in facilities at a Football Club, where are you going to get the money? Where do you finance stadium improvements and entertainment facilities that all clubs are trying to do to increase people coming to a stadium that otherwise is only used once every two weeks? The banks will not give you money, the Council, certainly for the moment and during the past twenty years, will not give you money, except on one occasion for Walsall many years ago, so, how are you going to improve and protect the club? Well, if it were me faced with those problems, I would take the most valuable and only asset, form a company with a solid income basis and, in times of need, borrow money to finance improvements against that asset. It's business, plain and simple. It's not about creaming the money off the top it's about building something that no one will invest in. Then, some twenty years later, when you have worked six days a week each of those twenty years to build it, a group of people say 'Yes, very good, now give it away, give it back, just walk away.' I ask, if that were you, what would you say? I bet it starts with 'F.'

Hence, I am not offended by the so-called 'Pension Fund,' it is not the problem. The problem is we cannot find a new Abramovitch that will buy the Football Club, the Stadium and the land, if we could do that it would end all of the unrest, abuse of the Directors and provide more income to finance the team. With that knowledge is our Board of Directors, including Jeff Bonser, clever and forward thinking businessmen? I believe, guilty as charged.

I don't know all of the Walsall Directors, some I only know well enough to say 'hello.' They know me as a supporter and someone who had a few hit records over the years, but they all treat me well when I see them. Over the years I've got to know better Jeff, Barrie, Roy and Nigel Bond, who has been a great and dedicated Director since he joined the Board.

The 'new' boys, Stefan Gamble, Chief Executive and Dan Mole, Club Secretary, have both been at the club for years and have worked their way up the ladder; these two bring a lot of enthusiasm to the club and have my complete support. Their forward thinking ideas and prompting of the other board members is an advantage to Walsall Football Club. They are Saddlers without doubt and I hope their new initiatives with season tickets, under-12,

16 and 18-year-old proposals works well. We need the young people of the town to support our team or else everything we've been through over the years will come to nothing. Walsall Football Club's history must continue and be retained. Walsall without a football team would be much less of a place.

During 2011, in our 'Mission Impossible' escape from relegation, I believe even the 'Bonser Boo Boys' were alerted to the job Jeff has done. With us languishing in the bottom four, Plymouth Argyle went into administration, moving us up the table after their 10 point deduction and leaving us 1 point from the safety mark overnight. I believe this registered with the supporters that blamed the Board and Jeff for everything. I even read 'Let's hope Bonser doesn't want his money back!' I don't wish administration on any Football Club, I love football too much, but I believe that more and more clubs will go into administration in the current climate. It would be a strange affair, if, by clubs going into administration, Walsall climbed the league and the divisions mainly because of their well-run philosophy.

Walsall Football Club has been for sale for years. Anyone could have come in and bought the club and the land it sits on, it's obvious that it is not an attractive package. It's not about buying and selling players and the ego of promotion, you have to be prepared to spend most of your time raising money to keep the club in operation, selling advertising, getting sponsors, operating the conferences and entertainments and events, without all of that you have no football team. If you do take all of that on, yes, you may feature in the newspapers, on radio and TV, but lose a few matches and you are the reason it all went wrong. On top of that you have to spend six days a week working and only possibly get ninety minutes of enjoyment on a Saturday. That enjoyment may turn to pain, as we all know.

'Steve Jenkins and Pete Waterman to buy Walsall Football Club.' I've seen that headline many times and each and every time it has been untrue. Pete loved his time supporting the Saddlers, but I can honestly say, our conversations about buying Walsall Football Club were only when the rumours started and it was never a serious option. The reason, in short we do not have enough money. It is not only the buying of the club, if you want to make a difference, you have to be able to put in millions to buy a team that can fulfill your dreams and you have to understand that you could probably lose it all. Football is not a good investment, it is a passion and a hobby. Jeff Bonser would have been a much richer man had he curbed his passion for his local football team and remained a supporter. Pete and I chased our dream making records and fortunately had hits. We no longer have the passion, drive, commitment and youth to start another business and try to make it work.

I am a supporter of Walsall Football Club and I will be for as long as I'm breathing. Owning and operating the club is not my passion, supporting the club is. I'm a Saddler and proud of it. I believe everyone in Walsall knows I will do all I can to help the club, it is a constant in my life and I love it, however, I have no wish to be in charge of the constant strain of raising money to keep it afloat. I don't want to operate the Stadium and Bonser suites or all that goes with it. I know what it takes and it's a fulltime job.

During the summer push for the Council to buy the Stadium and the land, I considered becoming directly involved in the club, however, the more you learn about operating a Football Club in today's market, the more you know it is a thankless task and could be very expensive when the marketplace goes against you. In the current troubled times anything can happen. Today, I'm happy doing the things I like to do and believe I've earned the right to do so after forty years of giving my all to music. I will give my time and effort to promote Walsall and Walsall Football Club for as long as I can, just as I always have done.

Hence, I give my support to Jeff Bonser and the Board of Directors at Walsall Football Club, they have taken the chance and stuck in there when the going has become tough. If someone comes along and buys the club then we should also support them. Maybe they will be better or invest more money into the team, who knows? For now, our club is still safe and I believe it will remain so for as long as Jeff Bonser and the current Directors are there.

I also support The Saddlers club, Walsall Trust and Unity. All of the people in those organizations are passionate about Walsall Football Club and I'm all for people who are passionate about the team, there are quite simply not enough of us.

Chapter 31
The Ginger Mourinho 2011/2012

The summer break had been all about the sale of the Stadium and the land. Every week Walsall Football Club was in the newspapers or on the Internet sites as the campaign to get the Council involved continued.

The press, TV and radio kept Walsall F.C. constantly on the minds of the people of Walsall where normally the off-season brings with it few reports from local Football Clubs.

Dean Smith's 'Mission Impossible' escape from relegation had breathed new life into Walsall Football Club. The press surrounding the sale of the Stadium had added even more enthusiasm for the coming campaign.

We had released nine players: Matt Richards, Julian Gray and Emmanuel Ledesma had been offered new contracts with a deadline, which they all missed, allowing Dean Smith to move forward with new signings. As the return of pre-season training commenced new players started to arrive: Matt Sadler, a left-back from Shrewsbury; Kevin Hurst a left-winger from Carlisle; Ryan Jarvis a striker from Leyton Orient; Claude Gnakpa, a right-winger from Luton Town and Adam Chambers, a midfield player from Leyton Orient. They all left with the current Walsall players for a pre-season tour of Scotland, playing a couple of games before returning home to face both Wolverhampton Wanderers and Aston Villa in pre-season friendlies. Along the way, three trialists signed one-year deals: goalkeeper David Grof, defender Lee Beavers and midfielder Anton Peterlin.

The season opened with a home game against Leyton Orient. We played well with our new team and won 1-0. A thirty yard screamer from Adam Chambers on debut, against his former club, sealed the points. I missed the game as I was playing golf in Rick Wakeman's Charity day for Sparks, playing alongside former snooker star Willie Thorne. We managed a 7th place finish in what was a hugely successful day for Sparks.

Once again we were out of the League Cup at the first attempt, just three days later at home to Middlesborough losing 3-0. It was the fifth consecutive season that we had fallen at the first hurdle. Adam Chambers' sending off after twelve minutes meant taking on a Championship side with ten men. The team performed heroically, but it was too big a hurdle to overcome.

The second match of the season away at Hartlepool resulted in a 1-1 draw. We achieved a penalty after three minutes dispatched by Jon Macken, our first penalty awarded since September 2009. We led for only two minutes before a huge kick from Hartlepool's keeper and an unfortunate bounce deceived super Jimmy Walker and a bundled equalizer ended the scoring. Unfortunately, a double sending off just before halftime meant the game would be played throughout the second half with ten men versus ten men. Andy Butler, our captain, received a harsh red card, which would be appealed against days later.

Butler's red card would be successfully appealed against and that enabled him to play away at Sheffield United. We took a two-goal lead through Hurst and Grigg before a disastrous fifteen-minute second half spell where Sheffield scored three goals and won the match. It was, however, our best performance of the season so far for an hour of the game.

The following home match against Yeovil was disappointing, a 1-1 draw. Jon Macken fired us into the lead, but it was short-lived as Yeovil equalized and the two teams just cancelled each other out.

The August Bank Holiday fixture was away at Bournemouth and the Faithful headed for the south coast. Susan and I drove to Bournemouth on the Friday, dining in Poole that evening and spending some time in Bournemouth.

Jon Macken, who had started the season well, had turned his ankle in training and would not be fit. Jimmy Walker would be called back to London with a personal problem and so David Grof would make his debut in goal. Ryan Jarvis would lead the attack and Manny Smith returned to the side in place of Oliver Lancashire.

Bournemouth started with great pace and cut through us on three occasions. We had been lucky to survive, but we did not panic under the pressure, slowly, we regained our composure and pushed forward. Sadler broke free and sent in a cross that was handled and a penalty was given. Ryan Jarvis sent the keeper the wrong way and what seemed against the run of play we were 1-0 up. From then on we played with great confidence and although Bournemouth had a couple of opportunities we went in one to the good at halftime. Ten minutes into the second half a Hurst corner found the head of Jarvis and we were two up and then never looked like losing. It had been a great weekend.

It seemed that Dean Smith had moulded a good group of players together. They were not the finished article yet, but they were playing for each other and could all handle the ball. We were playing neatly and positively; the 3 points from Bournemouth put us up to 10th in the league, a sound first month of action.

Soon after the game, Susan and I left for Spain; Josie our daughter was attending the TSA golf academy in Alhaurin, set in the mountains inland from Marbella. We decided we should be around in Spain, not near the Academy, but close enough should Josie have any problems settling in a different country.

It would be 16 games before I saw the Saddlers play again. In those 16 games we would only win 2, against Preston North End in the league and Exeter in the F.A. Cup. Our fall down the division would put us back in the relegation places and the win against Exeter was in the Second Round of the F.A. Cup.

It seemed that after our bright start we were in trouble again. I had read, almost daily, the reports from the *Express & Star*, the Official site and Up the Saddlers for the fans' views and then watched the goals on those two-minute match reports on the BBC Internet site.

I believed that although the team hadn't 'clicked' it was not too far away. Maybe I'm such a 'red-eyed' supporter I can't see the wood for the trees, however, my belief was that this team had something about it. 'Wacka,' Grof, Westlake, Lancashire, Smith, Butler and Sadler are good players. Taundry, Chambers, Hurst, Peterlin and Gnapka, along with loan players, Martin and Wilson, seem solid without being overly creative, but those players are hard to find. Nicholls, Macken, Patterson, Grigg and the emerging Bowerman all have something, but our lack of goals is where our problems had been.

Fortunately, Dean Smith has not come in for the usual 'stick' handed out after losing streaks; this had been good to see. I believe it takes time to build a good team, allowing the younger players to gain enough experience and confidence to perform consistently. For me, in due course, Westlake, Lancashire, Smith, Taundry, Nicholls, Patterson, Grigg and Bowerman can all become solid members of our team and have the potential to win games for us. That they have come through the ranks at Walsall is testament to our set up. I'm aware that Olly Lancashire did not come through the youth team, but his development as a young player over the past eighteen months has been at Walsall.

What seemed like my first match in months was the away game at Stevenage, Walsall's first ever visit to their ground. I was pumped up for the match and really looking forward to seeing the boys. Stevenage was also only thirty minutes drive from our home, so that was a real pleasure in terms of my normal travelling time to see the Saddlers. Susan and I saw all of the Walsall Directors, as ever, passionate about the team and looking for points on the board. We spent time with Chris Nichol and Nick Mashiter, spoke with Dean Smith, while a hot and sweaty 'Wacka' jumped on me after his warm-up.

I managed to speak with some of the Walsall supporters prior to the game as well. It felt like I was back home with my people and I was desperate for any kind of result.

All of us know that Stevenage have a system, which had seen them win two promotions in two years. Whether you like the system or not, they know how to play it and are fully committed to it. Any lack of commitment in your own team and they will put you away. As they came out, it seemed to me that part of the system was that you also had to be six feet two and over to get in the side, it was going to be a tough afternoon.

I thought our team gave everything in the onslaught that came at us. Our full-backs stayed tight to our centre halves. Lancashire and Smith were solid and defiant. Taundry, Chambers and Wilson, who I thought looked a class player, fought hard all afternoon. Nicholls, Macken and Grigg attacked and defended from their forward position in a committed team effort. Sitting close to the dugouts, after about sixty to sixty-five minutes, you could see the Stevenage bench becoming tetchy as we stuck to our task. We had our moments of fortune and we could have nicked it through Jon Macken late on. It was good to see George Bowerman come on for fifteen minutes and he was not troubled or nervous of the pair of giants that were marking him, he tried hard to move them around and cause problems. The 0-0 score line was probably a fair result. Susan and I enjoyed every minute of it. I believe we had to work incredibly hard to achieve that result and it showed that the team had a real spirit.

Finally, I enjoyed Richard O'Kelly's return to the club, it may only be for a short time to help out Deano, but I'm sure Richard will bring something to the team in the coming weeks. He was always good to have in the team, the dressing room and training pitch in his previous days at Walsall.

Two weeks later, I was back at the Banks's Stadium for the visit of top of the table Charlton Athletic, this time as a guest of Cat Communications. Craig and Penny Lang, with their company, have always been great supporters of Walsall F.C. and I join them most times they are at the Stadium. Charlton were on a run of 8 consecutive wins and we were staring straight down the barrel. The press boys were taking bets on 4-0 to Charlton, 3-1 to Charlton and so on. No one gave us much hope. As usual, as with a lot of Walsall sides over the years, we rose to the occasion. The match was a great one, open and end-to-end. We scored first through Jon Macken and then dropped deeper looking to defend until halftime. The equalizer came on the stroke of halftime and we went in a little disappointed not to hold onto our lead. Walsall came out in the second half and pushed Charlton back, we were unlucky not to go in front again. Sadly, Matt Sadler made a tackle on the half way line to stop a Charlton breakaway and was ordered off for a second bookable offence. With ten men we hung on for the final few minutes to gain a credible draw. Three days later, I was listening to the radio, as we took on Dagenham and Redbridge in a replay in the Second Round of the F.A. Cup, following our 1-1 draw at Dagenham the previous Saturday. We already knew our prize for winning would be a Third Round draw at home against Millwall, not a glamour tie, but a chance to win against a Championship side on our own patch. Unfortunately, it was not to be, a poor performance against a poor side and following 0-0 at fulltime and 0-0 after extra time we went out 3-2 on penalties. We also lost Manny Smith to a fierce kick in the head and Ollie Lancashire to a torn hamstring. It was a terrible night and one I was fortunate to miss. The problem with nights like that are plentiful; losing to a poor side we should have beaten, injuries to our two centre-halves that had been playing well and keeping our Captain, Andy Butler, out of the side and the sudden loss of form just three days after holding a flying Charlton. Financially, it was also a disaster. The loss of 25,000 pounds for getting to the Third Round, plus the income from a bigger game against Millwall and the possibility of winning and progressing to the Fourth Round, we may just have lost 60 to 70,000 pounds in one night. That money is critical to a small club like Walsall.

We returned to action the following Saturday in the league playing Chesterfield, who were bottom of the table in a terrible run of form, and Walsall were looking to win and forget about the F.A. Cup. We again took the lead through Alex Nicholls and held on until ninety minutes and forty-five seconds before disaster struck and Chesterfield equalized, sixteen seconds remained in the game. Sometimes football is the cruelest of games.

Boxing Day 2011 was the first time we had played on that day for three years. The previous years' games had been postponed due to poor weather. The attendance was due to be exceptional. Sheffield Wednesday would bring almost 4,000 fans and fill two sides of our stadium. Walsall supporters would come out for the traditional Boxing Day game in larger numbers and the gate would be our biggest for over two years; 8,600 were there to witness the game. Sheffield Wednesday were on a great run, undefeated in 8 games, winning 7 and drawing 1. Their supporters were buoyant and vocal, the odds were stacked against us and we were clear favourites to lose the match.

The atmosphere was great as the game started, noise seldom heard in recent times at the Banks's. Our players were inspired and went toe-to-toe with Wednesday, giving as good as we got. 0-0 at halftime breathed confidence into our players. Wednesday upped their game at the start of the second half, Walsall responded and were just on top when, shortly after Paterson hit the bar with a great drive, Wednesday broke free and scored. It felt unjust, the team did not drop their heads and went in search of an equalizer and the Walsall supporters began to make a noise as the players attacked our favourite end. We had a few half chances but time was ticking away. Dean Smith sent on George Bowerman and Claude Gnapka in a final throw of the dice in search of the equalizer. The board went up and displayed five minutes of injury time. Within seconds, Gnapka cut inside, beat one player and hit a shot at goal; a deflection saw it fly into the Wednesday net, Walsall supporters rose in jubilation. With four minutes left they screamed the team forward. Two minutes later, Sadler centered for the Saddlers and Manny Smith delicately lobbed the ball into the Wednesday net, 2-1. The Christmas and Boxing Day Party started as Wednesday supporters immediately headed for the exits. The unbelievable had happened, the press had already written of our loss, rewritten our draw and finally rewritten again our victory. As I walked from my seat to the Bonser suite, hoarse from encouraging the team, the joy written on the faces of Walsall fans I knew and didn't was immense. A huge relief and burden was lifted, we had taken on one of the best teams in Division One and won. The result lifted us out of the relegation zone and up to 18th in the league. We all hoped that we had turned a corner, possibly, just possibly, our young team may have finally clicked and the second half of the season would see us rise to safety from relegation in our Division. Boxing Day 2011 could just be a turning point.

The next three matches were not as we had hoped, a bruising 0-0 draw at home to Rochdale, a 2-1 loss away at Bury, and then, after playing Bournemouth off the park at home and being 2-0 up, we conceded an equalizer just thirty seconds before the end of the match to register a 2-2 draw.

On January 14th 2012 we were just outside the relegation zone and playing away at Brentford. It had been 'Wacka Week' in the buildup to the match; James Walker was to beat Colin Harrison's appearance record for the club with his 530th appearance. Susan and I had a short journey to Brentford in honour of Jim's feat.

Walsall were in a determined mood, no one wanted to lose on such a day for Jimmy. Brentford, just outside the playoffs, were thinking of victory and 3 points. Every one of the Walsall players put in a great shift, we looked a decent side and probably created more chances, even though there were only a few during the game. The best chance fell to Brentford when they burst through and had a one-on-one with Jimmy Walker. As usual, Jim stood up until the last moment and pulled off a textbook save. We broke away twice in the closing minutes and so nearly gained a win but had to settle for a 0-0 draw. That point kept us out of the relegation zone again, but this time only on goal difference. It seemed we had found our best team and we were difficult to beat, however, we were not creating enough chances and wins were elusive. The following week's 1-1 draw away at Carlisle was a good point, but we had not played well. Alex Nicholls equalized with ten minutes to go from the penalty spot on his 200th appearance for the Saddlers.

The transfer window closed on January 31st. Claude Gnapka after 26 appearances and 2 goals moved on to Inverness Caledonian-Thistle. In came Florent Cuvelier from Stoke City on an initial one month loan. That day I was in Walsall on other business but had made appointments in mind that the Saddlers were at home to Notts County that evening with a 7:45pm kick-off. We needed a win, Walsall were out of the drop zone by goal difference, but only 1 goal, Scunthorpe, just below us, had one game in hand and it was beginning to look ominous. Jimmy Walker returned to the Banks's Stadium after breaking the appearance record. On hand was Colin Harrison, the previous record holder with 529 appearances, to give 'Wacka' his award. Also there that night were Nick Atthey, with 502 appearances, and my old friend Kenny Mower, with 496 appearances. I had a good chat with Kenny, as I had not seen him in three or four years and a quick chat with Colin Harrison who I had not seen for five years. To say I was desperate for a win was an understatement. The relegation places looming and with Martin Allen managing Notts County; it's fair to say I'm not a fan. Allen coaches his teams into a ruthless approach to the game, that coupled with the nonstop verbal from the bench always makes games against his teams tough, uncompromising and raises the level of aggression from both players and fans. It is not pleasant to watch. Notts County flew out of the traps, pinned us back and scored after three minutes through Lee Hughes, another player not favoured by the Saddlers fans, however, his goal was a class turn and shot, leaving Jimmy Walker no chance. On a freezing night we lost both Walker and Macken to hamstring injuries by halftime and were barely in the game. After halftime we made a better fist of the match, had what looked like a good goal disallowed for a push on the keeper when it looked like he just dropped it and would never break down the County defence again. Florent Cuvelier came on for twenty minutes and looked a good player, livening up our attacks from midfield, but we would go down 1-0 on the night.

I spent some time with Kenny Mower after the match and saw Jimmy Walker pick up another award from the Supporters Trust, but it was a long drive back to London.

On Valentines Day, Pete Waterman and Helen Dann joined Susan and I for dinner at our home. We kept checking the score at Oldham and from being 2-0 down we made a valiant attempt with a goal from Flo Cuvelier on his full debut and so nearly snatched a point but for Alex Nicholls' penalty miss in the last minute.

Susan and I left for Las Vegas on February 16th. Our marriage had been arranged for February 22nd and we were both looking forward to the day and ten days in Vegas. On February 18th a loud roar went up in the Palazzo Hotel on the Las Vegas strip, Walsall had recorded a 2-0 home victory against Wycombe Wanderers. An even louder roar went up on the following Tuesday as we recorded our first back-to-back wins of the season, away at Scunthorpe United, a 1-0 victory courtesy of a Flo Cuvelier goal. Flo had changed the style of play from our midfield and seemed a player with a great future. Walsall confidence on the Las Vegas strip was at a high level the following day as Susan and I married. The following Saturday I was nervous in looking for our result, just hoping we had not lost; great joy was felt as we had drawn 0-0 away at Preston and from the reports were unlucky not to record a third win on the bounce.

Susan and I left Vegas on Monday February 27th for a day's travelling, Vegas to Miami and then Miami to Barbados, where an old Music Industry friend, Steve Prebble, had lent us his villa on the island as a honeymoon present. The villa was delightful and we settled in for a sixteen-day stay of sunshine, swimming and local food. We were also completing the final corrections on my first book about my life in the record business *The Future is in the History*.

The first Saturday of our stay saw Walsall draw 1-1 away at Leyton Orient with an injury time equalizer from Olly Lancashire. We had survived again, kept the unbeaten run going and were climbing the table. On Tuesday March 6th we signed Sam Mantom on loan from West Bromwich Albion, again, to strengthen our midfield. Mantom started the match against Sheffield United that night and scored his first professional goal to open the scoring. Twice we went in front to be pegged back before Alex Nicholls got the winner with nine minutes to go. A 3-2 win and we were finally out of the relegation places. Saturday March 10th was something of a disappointment, we bossed the home game against Hartlepool but we could not find the net and recorded a 0-0 score line. We were now six games unbeaten had a new central-midfield and David Grof was keeping the legendry Jimmy Walker on the bench holding on to the goalkeeping position.

Susan and I returned from Barbados on March 15th before flying to Innsbruck on March 17th to see our other daughter Hanna perform in the musical Hair.

That day our undefeated run ended at Yeovil Town, we went down 2-1, with two deflected goals, which I saw on the Internet, Sam Mantom having opened the scoring for Walsall. The game also featured the return of Emmanuel Ledesma from Argentina, once again joining Walsall for our last 11 games of the season. His unpredictability and skill could again earn us valuable points as he had done last season.

Monday March 19th, Susan and I returned to England again, completing nearly five weeks away from home but with memories of a trip of a lifetime. All our flights, hotels, villa, shows in Vegas and marriage had worked incredibly smoothly. We were now looking forward to the launch of my first book and hopefully an escape from relegation for my favourite team for the second year running.

On Tuesday, I was close to the radio again as we played away against Sheffield Wednesday in what would be a disappointing few days. We drew 2-2, on the face of it, looking a great point, but the curse had struck again, a ninety-six minute equalizer robbed us of three valuable points and dumped us back in the bottom four. We now had 9 games to go and with 2 home games in succession coming up. We needed a couple of wins to put breathing space between the drop zone and us.

Stevenage arrived at Banks's Stadium and provided their own brand of 'up and at 'em' football; always a bruising encounter and a hard fought 0-0 draw added a point to our total. The Tuesday night home game against Colchester came quickly. 1-0 down after eleven minutes we fought back with goals from Ledesma, Sadler and Bowerman to record a 3-1 victory and secure three valuable points, lifting us out of the relegation zone by two points. The following Saturday we were away at Rochdale, below us in the league and fighting for survival. All was going well in the first half, a 2-0 lead put us in a great position, Ledesma scoring his second goal since returning to the club. The second half completely turned around, Rochdale eventually coming back to 2-2 and then scoring to make it 3-2 four minutes into injury time. Straight from the kick-off we punted a ball forward and our Captain Andy Butler equalized with seconds to go. It was draw 19 of the season. There was a lot of debate about whether it was 2 points lost or 1 point won. Whichever was the view we had added another point to our total and stood just above the relegation line, 5th from bottom on 43 points and 2 points ahead of Wycombe.

Traditionally, a First Division Football Club needs 50 points to survive relegation; we needed at least 7 points from 6 remaining games. Next up was Chesterfield at home, below us in the table and fighting for their lives.

I couldn't make it to Walsall for the match as my daughter Josie was playing golf for Middlesex first team and duty called. I decided to settle for the Internet live blog and Sky Sports Saturday. I think we all knew a win against Chesterfield would ease our troubles and put us in a good place for the remaining games, but a loss would damage our position and chances. The closer it came to kick-off the more I knew I could not just sit and watch the blog or TV. I headed for the driving range to practice my golf and pass the time. On returning home we were winning 3-2 with ten minutes to go, Ledesma scoring twice and Mantom firing us in front again. We had, in fact, fallen 1-0 down, pulled back to 2-1, 2-2 and then gone ahead again. A determined Chesterfield were fighting for their lives. The final whistle came and I breathed a sigh of relief, 3 more points to our total.

On Easter Monday, Susan and I decided to catch the tube and cross London to see the game against Charlton Athletic. A short bus ride and we were inside the ground just prior to kick-off. Charlton Athletic were top of the league and close to promotion. We joined about 300 Saddlers fans behind the goal and they were in good voice. Walsall played well; Ledesma was a cut above anything on the park, always involved in corners, free kicks and constantly demanding the ball, and by far the best game I'd seen him play. Walsall fell behind in the first half but put in a fantastic performance. During the second half Charlton hardly made an attempt at our goal as we pressed for the equalizer. There is no doubt Walsall were the better team, looked more threatening and had better players with more of the play. We lost 1-0 but Saddlers fans left the ground with great pride; the probable Champions had been bashed in their own backyard. The relief from Charlton fans at the final whistle was immense. The silver lining of the day was that both Wycombe and Leyton Orient had lost. Orient were level on points with us and Wycombe four points adrift. There had been no real change but we had inched a little closer to safety. 4 games to play and possibly 4 points needed.

Disappointment would come again at home the following week against

Tranmere Rovers, a reasonable performance but unable to convert our chances, which led to undue pressure on our defence and we finally cracked to go down 1-0. Results had been kind and we still stood 3 points above the drop zone as we looked to the next away match at Exeter. It was going to be difficult. If Exeter lost they were relegated for sure and they were going to give everything they had.

We started well and seemed in control of the match. 2-1 up with twenty minutes to go, then, Manny Smith got sent off for a second bookable offence, which looked harsh and Exeter went in for the kill, scoring three times and recording a 4-2 victory. We had now lost 3 games on the spin and had 2 games to play. Fortunately, we were still 3 points ahead of Wycombe who occupied the final relegation place with 2 games left to play. It was going to be a nail-biting finish and go right to the end of the season for the second year running. My wife Susan, on hearing the result against Exeter, said 'I don't think I have the stomach for all of this again.' As I've always said, you've got to be tough to be a Saddler.

Saturday April 28th arrived and I was launching my autobiography *The Future is in the History* at the New Art Gallery in Walsall. The launch had been arranged for 12:00pm as I was hoping to attend the match against Huddersfield at 3:00pm. The launch was a great success and I was personally delighted that Chris Nichol, Chris Marsh and Martyn O'Connor all turned up to support me. We were all finished by 2:00pm and a gang of us headed for the Banks's Stadium. The Bonser suite was packed having served one hundred and fifty lunches. Walsall people had turned out to support the team in the hope we could win the match and escape relegation for the second year running.

Jimmy Walker had been recalled for the match even though David Grof had done well in goal over recent matches. 'Wacka's' experience to calm the defence was a good call, I felt, by Dean Smith. Unfortunately, Huddersfield scored after two minutes and took the wind out of our sails. We all felt that Ledesma was fouled in the box after nine minutes, but the referee declined our calls, wrongly, we believed. Huddersfield were the better team over the forty-five minutes and we had a worrying halftime, however, right from the start of the second half we seemed to have found new belief and after four minutes Cuvelier scored to level the match at 1-1. It was pretty much one-way traffic after that, we battered Huddersfield with more and more pressure but could not find the winner. Deep into injury time a huge roar went up from behind the home goal, quickly it spread around the ground that Notts County had scored with seconds to go against Wycombe and were winning 4-3, this meant

Walsall were safe from relegation. The relief from our bench and the players was noticeable. The final whistle blew and the joyous Saddlers fans invaded the pitch. Personally, I was still not sure and quickly went to the Bonser suite to watch the TV. Wycombe had been winning 3-2 with one minute to go, Notts County had scored two goals in two minutes and turned the match around. Seven minutes of injury time had been added, but it was true, Walsall were safe from relegation. The Bonser suite was filled with smiling faces, it meant a lot to the faithful fans; everyone was congratulating each other, a great moment after months of uncertainty.

I could not have hoped for better that day, it was my wife Susan's birthday, my book launch was a success and Walsall had retained their League One status, a fine hat trick.

The following Saturday our last game of the season was away at MK Dons. The Dons were safely in the playoff positions and had won 4 games on the bounce and looked in great form. the Saddlers supporters, as usual, fancy dressed for the final day and there was a huge following assembled behind the goal to sing their way to the close of the season. Susan and I drove up from London, a much shorter drive then the usual Walsall trips, and joined them behind the goal with Big Joe Savage meeting us inside the stadium. The Walsall fans are always kind to me and they came up in twos and threes to say hello, it was a great atmosphere.

Walsall were in good shape; freed from the worries of relegation they set about the task of winning the final game. MK Dons, surprisingly, looked tired and lacklustre as we controlled the game from the off. Nineteen minutes in and Will Grigg got free down our left wing, cut inside and hit a beauty into the far top corner, 0-1 and the party started in earnest. MK Dons never threatened throughout the game and only in the final minute of injury time did Jimmy Walker need to make any save of note. It had been a brilliant day after almost a full season of worry.

The day after, Susan and I were in Walsall and with my Sister Helen we went to the 'Player of the Season' dinner. Andy Butler won 'Player of the Season' for the second year running, Mat Sadler, the 'Players' Player of the Season,' Jamie Paterson 'Young Player of the Season' and Malvind Benning 'Apprentice of the Year.' The final award, 'The Lifetime Achievement Award' went to James Walker in the season that he broke the club appearance record, which had stood for thirty years. It was a great night and everyone enjoyed the evening immensely.

The following morning I was on BBC WM with Adrian Goldberg for an hour playing records from my career and relaying the stories behind the hits. All in all, it had been a great bank holiday weekend and we returned to London in high spirits, another season was over.

Football is football and it never rests, next on everyone's mind was the retained list of players and those that would be departing. On Wednesday May 9th, the lists were published. Leaving the club were Jon Macken, Olly Lancashire, Kevan Hurst and Anton Peterlin, whilst contract offers were made to Manny Smith, Mat Sadler, Emmanuel Ledesma, Alex Nichols, David Grof, Richard Taundry, Daryl Westlake, Lee Beavers and Jake Jones. The remaining players were already contracted for the following season and within seven days James Walker would decide on his future in talks with Dean Smith. I believe we all hoped that 'Wacka' would play on.

Walsall Football Club had provided another season of drama. In recent seasons it seemed as though we were relegated, promoted, playing for a playoff position or in the past two seasons escaping relegation with the last throw of the dice. We were not a club that had seasons of mid-table complacency. Personally, I believe that is what keeps you on the edge of your seat; desperation, pure joy and deep depression, the emotions of being a Saddler. Another season would come soon enough. The next one for me would be a special one.

Chapter 32

50 Years A Saddler

The summer had been one of the wettest in history; a few days of sunshine but mainly overcast, with storms that seemed relentless. The Queen's Jubilee, the European Football Championships and the London Olympics had filled our TV screens and brought a feel good factor to a nation in recession.

Walsall Football Club had tried to keep the basis of the side together, but one by one the players who were offered contracts saw their futures elsewhere. First to go was Alex Nicholls to Northampton Town on a two-year deal. Although I was sad to see Alex leave, I thought it was a good deal for him and he probably needed a change having been a Saddler his entire career. Mat Sadler joined Crawley Town, a club well financed and an offer too good to refuse. Emmanuel Ledesma joined Middlesborough on a three-year deal; again another good contract and move that Walsall could not compete with. Lee Beavers joined Mansfield on a two-year deal, Daryl Westlake moved to Sheffield United, again, on a two-year deal and Manny Smith, another player who had spent his whole career at Walsall, left for Notts County. As supporters, we all felt that Ledesma was worthy of a Championship side and were not surprised, the most disappointing was Manny Smith, who had developed into a fine centre-half and would surely be missed.

David Grof signed his contract and soon after the legendary James Walker signed as player/goalkeeping coach for the new season. Richard Taundry, after looking around, returned to sign on again. Jake Jones signed an initial six-month deal.

As the players returned for pre-season training we had a threadbare squad, our attempts to retain players had largely failed. The news that the loss of TV revenue had cut the playing budget by twenty-five percent brought with it some doom and gloom from the supporters.

We were in the process of building a completely new side. The positive in that was that Dean Smith would be able to mould a side together exactly as he wished within the constraints of the budget.

Good news began to come in. Richard O'Kelly returned as first team coach after his spell at Hereford United. I felt, with Dean, Richard, the positive Jon Witney and the passion of James Walker, our coaching staff were the best we had assembled since the Richard Money days. They were all Saddlers and knew our club, team and supporters jointly over many years.

Ashley Hemmings was first to sign on from Wolverhampton Wanderers, a winger with pace and trickery. Having spent part of last season on loan at Plymouth Argyle, he had gained some league experience and was looking to push on and prove himself in our team.

Flo Cuvelier rejoined from Stoke City on an initial six-month loan deal. There was no doubt our fortunes had turned around during the previous campaign on his arrival, he had given us both energy and composure in our midfield and this was a hugely positive move.

Next in, Dean Holden, ex-Shrewsbury and Rochdale right back or centre-half; having played over 400 league games he would bring some experience to our defence.

Fabian Brandy, a Manchester United youth and reserve player, had lost his way in the two years since leaving Old Trafford with average spells at Hereford, Gillingham and Notts County, but we hoped his talent would come through after being given a chance in our side.

Connor Taylor, a striker from Aston Villa's reserve side who had shown great pace and ability during a trial, signed on and being eighteen years old could develop and have opportunity at Walsall.

Paul Downing, twenty years old, signed from West Bromwich Albion, a central defender who had gained league experience whilst being on loan from WBA at Rotherham United, Shrewsbury Town and Barnet.

We signed James Baxendale, a nineteen-year-old winger who had come through Leeds United's youth set-up and had spent a season at Doncaster Rovers.

Ben Purkiss, a right-back or central defender, signed after spells with York City, Oxford United and Hereford. Nicky Featherstone, a midfielder, signed after playing for Hull City, Grimsby Town and Hereford.

Further good news came during this spell of new signings as we added to our team budget via a sell-on clause in the contract of Anthony Gerrard as he moved from Cardiff City to Huddersfield. Sheffield United paid compensation for our former youth player Daryl Westlake and we would return to TV on October 14th, the live game away at Shrewsbury Town, which would bring in further money.

The season would start at home in the Capitol One League Cup match against Brentford, with the league fixtures commencing the following Saturday, August 17th, at home to Doncaster.

It was rumoured that more signings would arrive at the club in between the Brentford and Doncaster games, but we were almost ready to go. We had a young squad with a point to prove, but all came with a history of being comfortable on the ball. As we had not signed a big centre-forward to hold up play it seemed we had set up a squad that would retain the ball and play a passing game, traditionally, this style of football is favoured by the Faithful and was encouraging. Nearly all of the new signings had been on trial at the club during the pre-season training and so had played and trained together for a month before the first match.

Hope springs eternal.

Personally, this would be my fiftieth season as a Saddlers supporter. Our home game against Preston North End on September 22nd 2012 would be exactly fifty years since I walked through the gates of Fellows Park with my Grandfather Harry Jenkins to watch the 1-0 victory over Rotherham United with a goal from George Meek.

star.com   DY   Saturday, September 22, 201

Mogul marks 50 years of watching team

The man who discovered Britney Spears celebrates his 50 years of supporting the Saddlers today – and to mark the occasion he has written about his memories in the club's programme.

Bloxwich-born Steve Jenkins, a close friend of former Pop Idol judge Peter Waterman, was just eight when he attended his first game at Walsall Football Club's former Fellows Park stadium on September 22, 1962.

He attended with his father Alan and grandfather Harry Jenkins, and the game saw the Saddlers notch up a 1-0 victory over Rotherham United, the only goal coming from George Meek.

"The my biggest memory was seeing the pitch for the first time," he says. "It was September, so the pitch was in the best shape possible before a

Report by Mark Andrews
mark.andrews@expressandstar.co.uk

full season of football, and it was breathtaking."

Steve, now 58, went to Joseph Leckie School in Walsall, and began his music career as a DJ on the club scene around the West Midlands.

As well as producing Britney Spears' hit Baby One More Time after being blown away by her audition, he has also worked with international stars such as Kylie Minogue, David Bowie and Billy Ocean.

He says the match against Rotherham was the start of between 1,500 and 2,000 games he has attended over the last half century, watching the Saddlers home and away. He has even arranged

business meetings in the US around flights back to home, to ensure he does not miss any games.

His weekly trips to see the Saddlers aroused the curiosity of music mogul Pete Waterman, who soon joined him in becoming a fan of the club.

"These days I live in London, so it is 120 miles there, and 120 miles back, and the journey's back always seem a lot longer when we have not done very well," he says.

But he writes in today's programme: "I do not regret one minute of the travelling, the joy and the disappointment of all those years. "Our football club has kept me connected to Walsall, to my family and the memory of my dad, mum and grandparents, and I believe they would have been proud of my loyalty to the club."

Producer – Steve Jenkins

A Lifetime with the Saddlers

The season got underway with the visit of Brentford in the Capital One Cup. Ashley Hemmings scored after eight minutes, Brentford had a player sent off and we progressed to the Second Round for the first time in years. Out of the hat came an away game at Premier League Queens Park Rangers. This was good news on two counts for me: one, we would get the chance to play Premier League opposition and two, Queens Park Rangers is a short distance to travel from my home.

The league campaign started seven days later with a home match against Doncaster Rovers, recently relegated from The Championship. James Chambers had signed the day before on a non-contract basis to play left-back following an injury to Richard Taundry. For the first time in years I would not be at our opening home league fixture. My daughter Josephina had been awarded a golf scholarship in America and was off to Oklahoma that weekend to play in the National American Golf Leagues whilst attending Seminole College. Susan and I were very proud of her and we were there to see her off at Heathrow in the next stage of her life.

Doncaster Rovers played well and won the match 3-0, but the reports suggested that Walsall had retained position of the ball well and were developing as a new unit. Two exceptional goals had undone us that day.

The games come thick and fast at the start of the season. The following Tuesday we drew 1-1 away at Oldham, an equalizing goal from George Bowerman brought home the point and we had registered on the board. The following Saturday, the away game at Notts County was a tough one, County had won their opening two fixtures and traditionally it's a difficult place to get a result. Walsall came through the test scoring with eight minutes to go and registering our first league victory of the season, 1-0, with a goal from Andy Butler.

Whilst the Saddlers were in Nottingham, I was watching Charlton versus Hull City; the first time ever I had seen other teams play before attending a Walsall game.

During the summer, Susan and I had been invited to Chris Marsh's wedding to Sabina. It had been a great day and evening, many of my old friends had been invited and it was fantastic to chat and find out how they were all doing. In attendance were Mark Rees, Adrian Viveash, Phil Hawker, Keith Bertschin, Wayne Evans, Darren Wrack, Clive Platt and many more friends from over the years. Keith Bertschin had just moved from Sunderland to Hull City that day to join up again with Steve Bruce's coaching staff. I had said to Keith whenever they were in London to let me know and Susan and I would come along to see the team. I also wanted to see how Matty Fryatt had developed in his years since leaving Walsall. Keith phoned on the Friday and said Hull were at Charlton and would we like to come along. Hence, we watched a 0-0 draw that Hull City were unlucky not to win after battering Charlton in the last twenty minutes. Unfortunately, Fryatt was suffering from an achilles injury and was unavailable that day. We met up with Keith after the match and spent half an hour chatting about the match and old times. I was in a great mood having seen Walsall's victory on my phone, it felt like the season was well and truly under way; as we left Charlton I was already looking forward to Tuesday night at QPR.

Tuesday soon came around and we were off to QPR. I felt the excitement of seeing the new Walsall side as we approached the Loftus Road Stadium. Walsall had signed left-back Andy Taylor during the day and he would make a good debut that night. Over 300 Saddlers fans had made the trip to London and were in fine voice before and during the match, which we would eventually lose 3-0. No surprise in the result given the many world-class signings QPR had made during the summer, but they were made to work hard that night as Walsall showed true grit and determination. I was most impressed with the team: a defence that had experience, coupled with a midfield and forward line that was filled with young exciting players. No one in our team had a bad game; they all believed in what they were doing. Dean Smith and Richard O'Kelly were seemingly on their way to building a good side growing in confidence. Our young players stood up to the Premiership side and showed the 'no fear' attitude that youth brings. Cuvelier, Featherstone, Hemmings, Paterson, Grigg, Baxingdale, Bowerman and Jones all gave a good account of themselves and were comfortable with the ball. The Capital League Cup was over for the season for Walsall but it had provided a great night out at QPR.

September started with a home match against Brentford. After scoring twice through Paterson and Bowerman within a minute of each other midway through the first half, we led 2-0 at halftime. Brentford applied the pressure in the second half but we held out until four minutes from time when Brentford scored and then equalized in the final minute. To miss out on 2 further points was a disappointment, however 1 point gained was positive. The following Saturday we were at home again, this time the visitors were MK Dons. We scored after seventeen minutes through Dean Holden and this time saw out the match to win 1-0. A confident Saddlers side went to Portsmouth and recorded a 2-1 victory with goals from Baxingdale and Cuvelier, both glorious strikes lifting us up the table to 5th position.

The week commencing September 17th was a big one for me. I would be seeing Walsall play twice, first up was an away game at Stevenage, always a tough fixture and this season would go some way to show how far our young side had developed. My wife Susan, our friend singer/songwriter Phil Ryan and I headed off for the short journey from home to Stevenage. Before the match started I bumped into James Walker; suffering from a calf strain 'Wacka' was just watching and sat with us for the game. I had a great time with 'Wacka' reminiscing about days and matches from the past and discussing the new team that had been assembled in the summer. Walsall started the game well but it was a tough encounter; Stevenage had done their homework well, tight marking our most creative players Patterson and Cuvelier who struggled to find freedom. Stevenage took the lead and held it until halftime. Walsall started well in the second half, stuck to our game plan and were rewarded with a George Bowerman headed equalizer. It looked as though we may go on to win the match, but Stevenage scored with a thirty yard attempt that was a fine goal. Again, we went after the equalizer but got caught on the break and Stevenage scored again to close the match. Although we had lost 3-1 there were many positives to come out of the match: we continued to play football, did not let our heads drop and were still competing to the very end.

September 22nd the visitors to the Banks's Stadium were Preston North End. Just coming off a 5-0 victory they were in a strong and confident mood, it would be another tough test.

The journey up from London was difficult; an accident on the M1 meant we had to cut across country to join the M40, a journey that would take three hours with us arriving at the stadium at 2:15pm. I had written programme notes remembering my first visit to see Walsall play fifty years before, taken by my Grandfather Harry Jenkins, a Saddlers supporter all his life along with my Father Alan Jenkins. Being a Saddler was a family affair. My Sister Helen joined us on the car park and Joe Savage was waiting inside; we were all looking forward to the game on this anniversary day.

Walsall started well, pinning back Preston, creating half chances and pressurizing, so much so, we were caught on the break and found ourselves 1-0 down. It seemed to make no difference as Walsall continued to press, scoring through James Baxingdale with a great chipped lob; we went in at halftime scores even. We expected an onslaught from Preston in the second half but our young team completely outplayed them in what was one of the finest performances from a Walsall side I had seen in over five years. George Bowerman was fouled in the box and converted the penalty and two minutes later stroked the ball home from twenty yards to make it 3-1. Walsall were unstoppable, kept the ball and Preston's keeper did well to keep the score at 3-1.

With minutes to go, Baxingdale, then Paterson and then Grigg were substituted to standing ovations. I had not seen that in the stadium in years. The supporters stood and applauded for minutes afterwards as our players waved to the fans from the pitch. It had been a magical day, one I would not forget and for it to happen on my 50th anniversary was a moving moment.

The journey home was another long one. Choosing to go back on the M40 was okay until we approached junction four at Wycombe, another accident had closed the motorway. Again, we had to cut across country, another three-hour journey in the car. It had not dampened the spirits though; Walsall's performance was worth it.

A fine September would be completed with a 2-1 victory at Bournemouth, putting the team just outside the playoff positions. George Bowerman would be awarded 'Young Player of the Month' in Division One for September, Dean Smith nominated for 'Manager of the Month' and Flo Cuvelier nominated for Division One 'Player of the Month;' awards and nominations for a team that were considered relegation favorites at the beginning of the season.

A lot of press had been generated and much was made of the team being very young yet extremely good footballers, also, that the Board of Directors had set in motion with Dean Smith a directive that the team would play attractive attacking football, played primarily on the floor with an emphasis on passing, ball retention and control. They saw the future generating players primarily from our youth team in the hope that the fans would connect with the players once more and unify the supporters in a true local fashion. As a directive, by the end of September, we had gone a long way towards that goal and I believed that come what may it was the only way forward for smaller clubs to operate, given the tough economic climate and the guidelines enforced by the F.A.. I believed our management and directors had made a sensible but tough decision that had ignited the supporters and word was spreading through the media.

We now faced 3 consecutive home games; 2 in the league and 1 in the Johnson's Paint Trophy. Confidence from September suggested we just might push on. Unfortunately, that was not to be, losing 2-1 to Leyton Orient, a wonder goal securing the points for Orient. Then, a 2-1 loss to Carlisle, scoring their winner in the ninety-second minute, and, finally, a loss to local rivals Port Vale in the Cup, 2-2 at fulltime and losing on penalties.

Sunday October 14th was a special day for me. Walsall were live on Sky TV away at Shrewsbury Town and it had been four years since we had been featured live on TV. The absolute joy of not having to travel to watch a match and being able to see the boys play in the comfort of my own lounge was something not to be missed. 1,400 of our supporters made the short journey from Walsall to Shrewsbury and packed into one end of the ground. The team started like an express train; how we were not 4-0 to the good after twenty minutes was only due to a fantastic performance from Shrewsbury's goalkeeper who would win the 'Man of the Match' award. Against the run of play, from a corner Shrewsbury took the lead and held on to gain the points. Shrewsbury were better in the second half but Walsall still created four or five chances. How we didn't win that game was a Shrewsbury miracle. The commentators, watching public and press all made comments about the footballing ability of our side, we were just coming to terms with losing again. The final 3 games of the month saw us draw at home 2-2 with Crewe, equalizing in the ninety-first minute, losing 1-0 at Sheffield United, Dean Holden being sent off after seventeen minutes and playing the rest of the match with ten men, then, finally, a 1-1 draw away at Bury.

In our 7 games during October we had lost 5 and drawn 2, yet all of the talk was still about how exciting our team was. Yes, we were inexperienced and probably didn't know how to close a game out when in a winning position, however, this was much better than watching ageing footballers seeing out their career in the lower leagues, these were young footballers giving everything for the group. There were no cries for the Manager's head, everyone still believed we had something special here and if we kept on playing the way we were then results would come. November was going to be interesting.

The month started with our Manager, Dean Smith, signing a new two and a half year contract. I believed this was great news. Continuity and stability would now be enforced at the club; Dean would now be able to feel secure in his drive to play attractive attacking football.

The F.A. Cup Round One was on the horizon. Our first game of the month would be away at Lincoln City in that competition. We believed our superior ability would see us through this game, but the F.A. Cup is the greatest leveller, as we all know, and it's the reason why the competition is loved among football followers. We were lucky to escape with a late equalizer from George Bowerman in a 1-1 result; the replay would be at the Banks's Stadium in ten days. We returned to football league action and put in one of our worst displays of the season at home to Scunthorpe losing 4-1. The following Saturday we made the drive to Walsall to see the home game against Swindon Town, this time we had an easy run with no hold ups and had lunch in the Bonser suite before the match. Sam Mantom had returned to the club on loan from West Bromwich Albion to bolster our midfield after the injury loss of Flo Cuvelier. We would lose the game 2-0 after falling behind after ninety seconds, not the start we needed. We pressed on and got a good hold of the match and were the better team either side of halftime. Just when we looked like the team that would score the next goal, we got caught out and conceded a second goal, which finished us off. There was no doubt about the effort the team had put into the match and I thought we were unlucky not to get the equalizer from where we might have pushed on to win. The highlight of the day was the full debut of Malvind Benning at left-back; he played magnificently and looked like a great player for the future, winning the 'Man of the Match' award.

Our third home game in a row was the return F.A. Cup fixture against Lincoln City. We started well, but Lincoln were no pushover, after taking the lead we found ourselves 2-1 down, equalizing again with minutes to go and taking us into extra time. I think we believed we would now go on to win but Lincoln would not lie down and scored the winner dumping us out of the F.A. Cup and recording our third straight loss at home.

We had now gone 11 games without a win; the supporters were becoming very vocal about our predicament and making what I felt were rash statements about the set up of the team and our management. Personally, I believed we still had a good team and good squad, many of whom were just finding themselves at Division One level. The loss of Flo Cuvelier was an important factor; he was the mainstay of the team and probably the best player at the club. Our goalkeeper David Grof looked devoid of confidence and I think this spread to the defence, causing extra care at blocking shots and not playing with total freedom and confidence in the keeper behind you. If Flo could get fit, along with the return of Sam Mantom in midfield and a change of goalkeeper, the team would look stronger and turn the corner. I could not believe that our experienced goalkeeper Jimmy Walker was not in the team.

Dean Smith acted quickly, bringing in Aaron McCarey, Wolverhampton Wanderers reserve goalkeeper, on loan initially for a month. McCarey is highly thought of at Wolves and may just breathe confidence into the defence.

Our next 2 matches were tough, away at Crawley Town, having a good season and 4th in the table, then, three days later, away at league leaders Tranmere.

Cuvelier would not be fit for either match but was recovering. Confidence was low with the fans but we went to Crawley and should have won the match, ending with a 2-2 draw, but playing well and being the better side. Fabian Brandy played ninety minutes for the first time this season after injury and more importantly scored our first goal, his first in nearly three years. We all hoped that this might spur Brandy on to realize a potential that is there for all to see.

Buoyed by this result we went to Tranmere and got another point in a 0-0 draw, again creating the better chances and looking the better side. Now 13 games since our last win, the coming home match against Hartlepool, adrift at the bottom of the table, was one we were looking to win. Unfortunately, we went 1-0 down after twenty-five minutes. Equalizing after halftime, we proceeded to batter the Hartlepool goal in a one-sided second half, but again could not manage a winner. October and November had been winless, stretching 14 games; we were hoping December might be kinder. We were only 3 points above the relegation places and were desperate not to fall into another relegation fight.

Susan and I left England on November 29th, we were spending a couple of months in Venice, Florida, to escape some of the winter weather and also see our daughter Josephina, who was at college in Oklahoma but would be coming to Venice for almost four weeks during her Christmas break. The Internet would be my source of Saddlers information over the next couple of months.

The Saddlers next game was December 8th. After a two-week lay off, no cup action for the side, was an away match at Coventry; it meant a good travelling support and high hopes. We took the lead and then conceded five goals, a disastrous day. A week later we conceded a goal in the final minute to draw 2-2 with Yeovil. We were on the edge of the relegation zone without a win in 16 games and it was not looking good.

Finally, on December 22nd, we beat Colchester 1-0; our seventeenth attempt to record a win. Buoyed with relief the Boxing Day game was a glorious 4-2 victory away at MK Dons. Our final game of 2012 was away at Leyton Orient and we lost 2-1 having dominated the game.

A New Year and new hopes; we were moving away from the relegation zone and playing with more confidence and belief, we would win the next 4 games and charge up the division.

On January 4th we played Portsmouth live on Sky TV. I knew the game would be broadcast around the world and set about finding a bar to watch. For two days I visited bar after bar, driving all around Venice and towards Sarasota. I drove both Susan and Josephina to distraction with an intense determined search to watch the match. Unfortunately, no one was showing the game. Susan believed she could find it on the Internet and eventually she did. We joined a Mexican film website and were able to watch the game. Pure joy. I saw Fabian Brandy and Will Grigg score the goals in our 2-0 victory in our villa on Plantation Golf and Country club, Venice, Florida. Walsall won 4 out of 5 games in January, losing to Colchester at the end of the month before bouncing back with 2 more wins at the start of February.

As Susan and I returned to England on February 5th Walsall were now just 4 points from a playoff position. We had 47 points and we were the best team in England in all four divisions over the last 10 games. The supporters, only two months ago thinking of another relegation fight, were now dreaming of a playoff position. Along with the wins, our Manager, Dean Smith, was awarded 'Manager of the Month' for January; after the last few seasons, it is indeed a funny old game.

The team had made great strides. The January transfer window had closed and although there had been interest in our young players we had managed to hold on to them all. Sam Mantom and Craig Westcarr both signed permanent deals and James Baxingdale, Mal Benning, Paul Denning and Andy Taylor signed extensions to their contracts. It looked for the first time in years that there would not be a mass exodus at the end of the season and a complete rebuild in the summer for the next season. We did lose Richard O'Kelly, our Assistant Manager, to Bristol City, which was a disappointment. He had done a fine job. His replacement, David Kelly, was applauded in but left nine days later to join Nottingham Forest, both had offers they could not refuse. The career of the legendary James 'Wacka' Walker came to a close as he retired from playing at the start of February and left the club. Our record appearance holder will be missed, but we all wished Jimmy, Richard and David all the best for the future.

As I settled back into life in England Walsall had 14 matches left to play in the season. The first of which was a home game with Notts County; a 1-1 draw was thought of as a fair result. Will Grigg scored our goal from the penalty spot and County equalized in the second half.

Our next game was away at Brentford, a match I rarely miss. Brentford is the closest game to my home and provides the joy of returning home in twenty minutes after the match. Fortunately, Susan and I were invited by the Walsall Directors to spend the afternoon with them. I met with Stefan Gamble, Leigh Pomlett, Richard Tisdale and Roy Whalley. It was the first time I'd seen Roy since the announcement of his retirement at the end of the season. Although remaining on the Board, Roy had called time as Commercial Director. Roy Whalley had given over twenty-five years of service to Walsall Football Club and for many years had run the show on so many fronts; he had been Chief Executive, Club Secretary and Commercial Manager all rolled into one, an immense workload. Next season Walsall would be a different place without Roy being at every game working away. He will now enjoy just supporting the team on match days instead of all those duties.

I also spent some time talking with Stefan Gamble, now in his third season as Chief Executive; the first two seasons had been a baptism of fire involving two consecutive relegation fights. Stefan was enjoying life much more knowing we needed only 2 points to guarantee safety and we were still in February.

Dan Mole, the Club Secretary, had organized the tickets and passes for me. Dan too had taken on one of Roy's roles and has grown into the job and is now established at the Football Club. Nina Best has been assisting Roy in the Commercial Department as Commercial Executive and, I believe, come next season will take on more of the workload as Roy departs. The club is moving forward on all fronts.

The Brentford game would end 0-0, but it was a great game with two fully committed sides. Brentford probably had the better chances but we were organized and they could not break us down, every one of our players put in a great shift and knew what was expected of them. After not seeing the team for some time, I thought we looked a good side, difficult to beat and lots of creativity going forward. Ben George also made his debut at right-back from our Academy and looked good in his first match; solid throughout and made a good clearance off our line when we were under pressure.

Three days later, we were away at Carlisle recording a 3-0 victory, a Will Grigg hat trick, and our team were applauded off by the Carlisle fans for a fine performance. Shrewsbury Town were dispatched 3-1 at home in our next match and a point gained at, promotion chasing, Swindon Town followed with a 2-2 draw. The team had hit a fine run of form. Our next match was at home to Tranmere who had topped the table for most of the season. We made our way up to Walsall for the evening match. Tranmere started well and pinned us back in our own half for the first twenty minutes. Slowly, we got a grip of the match and started to make inroads into the Tranmere defence. 0-0 at halftime, we came out and proceeded to grind down Tranmere. Fabian Brandy ran straight at the Tranmere penalty area, wriggled his way in and was up-ended. Will Grigg dispatched the spot kick, 1-0. Soon after, Craig Westcarr hit a thirty yard scorcher, 2-0 and the game was almost over. The most impressive part of the whole match was how our young team wore down a good Tranmere side that eventually just ran out of ideas.

The following Saturday Crawley Town came to the Bescot Stadium for their first ever league visit. Crawley were a potent side and looking to get back into the race for a playoff position. We found ourselves 2-0 down, although most thought undeservedly so, it was minute eighty-nine when Paterson fired in our first goal to make it 2-1, with four minutes of injury time to go. Inspired by the goal, Walsall went all out to equalize, Taylor put in a great cross and Grigg slotted it home 2-2. A most unlikely comeback showed the belief and never-say-die attitude of this team. In the circumstances it felt like a win rather than a draw. Hartlepool away were next. We were in the depths of a terrible weather front: snow, ice and a biting wind. Somehow, Hartlepool got the match on when most were postponed, but the weather was the real victor, a 0-0 draw resulted with few attempts on goal. Another point added to our total; we were 3 points off a playoff position with 6 games to go. Our team had gone 10 games undefeated and Will Grigg had scored 8 times in 5 games. That goal scoring run had put Will in a group of Walsall strikers that had achieved a cluster of goals in a few matches, legendary names: Gilbert Alsop, Tony Richards, Allan Clarke, Harry Middleton, Alan Buckley, Don Penn, David Kelly and Kyle Lightbourne.

We were in a viciously cold March, possibly the coldest on record and the weather forecast suggested it could be a white Easter. Snow had fallen and then frozen with no sight of the temperatures improving, a strong northern wind meant it felt like minus three, four or five degrees.

Traditionally, the Easter games in the league programme go some way to deciding the relegation, playoff and promotion places. A cluster of games and 9 points to play for would mean a constant shifting of league position. Walsall would play away at Yeovil on Good Friday. Yeovil were in the playoff positions 3 points ahead of Walsall. Easter Monday would see Coventry City arrive at Bescot Stadium, 1 point and 2 positions below us but likely to go into administration, be deducted 10 points and end their season. The following Saturday would see Sheffield United at Bescot, games in hand, 4th in the league and going for automatic promotion. All big games and big crowds, it would be an exciting Easter, one way or another, for the Saddlers.

Walsall fans made their way down the M5 to Yeovil, a traffic jam would mean a few would miss the start of the match. Yeovil felt a win would end the Saddlers dreams of a playoff position and they were probably correct, a win for the Saddlers would close the gap and put them right in the mix. The game would end 0-0 with both sides trading punches for ninety minutes; a game of few opportunities and a result that helped neither side greatly. The Walsall local press felt that the 0-0 result was beginning to suggest the end of our rise up the table and possibility of a playoff position. Personally, I believed a point was a good return from a Yeovil team that had performed well all season and had total belief they would make the playoffs themselves. The key to it all would be our two forthcoming home games, if we could win them someone would slip up and we would be much closer to the dream, lose and we would be out of it.

Football is football and all that matters is the next match. The old saying of one game at a time is true, if we could beat Coventry City it would give us confidence that we could beat Sheffield United, a draw or loss would see our hopes begin to diminish.

Coventry City had been having a good season on the pitch but had gone into administration and consequently deducted 10 points only days before. I'm sure, with 3 games over Easter, they felt they could get 9 points back and probably still have a chance of the playoffs. On Good Friday they had beaten league leaders Doncaster Rovers 1-0 at the Ricoh Arena and arrived at Walsall full of confidence having beaten us in the previous November 5-1. They believed this game would provide another 3 points to their total.

We left London early on Easter Monday arriving at my Sister Helen's at 11:30am for bacon sandwiches and then going on to Bescot Stadium. We were displaying some of my gold discs that day at the game and selling copies of my autobiography before and after the match.

Being a local derby, the crowd had swelled to 8,000; the City fans were confident and in good voice, drowning out our local support early on. Coventry were a good side and after the early exchanges this looked a tough match, both good footballing sides, playing with confidence and determination. The Walsall fans began to find their voice as we started to find our rhythm and attack the Coventry defence. After thirty-three minutes Jamie Paterson wriggled into the box and found the net 1-0. At halftime the general feeling was we were looking in good form. Coventry were good but not hurting our defence and not really forcing our on-loan goalkeeper Sam Johnstone into making saves, we had a chance.

Nine minutes into the second half James Baxendale, in our side due to the injury of Will Grigg, drove into the Coventry penalty area and was scythed down, the referee pointed to the spot. I felt the tension, our regular penalty taker Grigg was injured, if we could score we would be on our way to 3 points. Craig Westcarr grabbed the ball, a confident sign, ran up and sent the keeper the wrong way, 2-0. Walsall, now very confident, attacked to finish off the game. Fabian Brandy, turning this way and that, was fouled three times within a couple of minutes and off went Coventry's Jordan Stewart for a second yellow card offence. Now down to ten men Coventry tried hard to get back into the match but were caught on the break. After Paterson's free kick, Westcarr headed home and with three minutes to go Westcarr set up Paterson, 4-0.

Personally, I was stunned, our team had played fantastic passing football; Coventry City were a very good side and yet they had been well beaten, the 3 points were ours. As we went back inside to see the other results, Yeovil had won again, hence, we were still 3 points from the playoff position, but the table had tightened up. More teams had a chance, pressure would build and all that mattered was our next match on Saturday at home to Sheffield United.

That day would mark the one hundred and twenty-fifth anniversary of the formation of Walsall Football Club to the very day, April 6th 1888, and it would hopefully be a day to remember.

Again, Susan and I hit the M1 from London. Fortunately, although it was busy, we made good time, arriving at Bescot just after 2:00pm. I spoke with a lot of the supporters as I walked around the ground, I just couldn't sit still. We had a famous Balti pie to settle the nerves.

The first half was all Walsall; we battered Sheffield United, making them look old and slow. Chances came and went, finally, Westcarr scoring just before halftime. Sheffield stunned and embarrassed by their first half performance were a better side in the second half, equalizing after sixty minutes and it became a tough game, Sheffield taking no prisoners with their tackling. The game ended 1-1. We were the better side but just could not force home the advantage. I thought our team played well and could not have done more, it was just one of those days when the ball just didn't quite drop in the right place. The league point had come at a cost, Andy Taylor had left the field early, Andy Butler took a brutal challenge and looked in trouble and Fabian Brandy was struggling to walk and those injuries would take a few days to assess. As we returned to the Bonser suite, the results showed that Yeovil had won again, but others had lost; Tranmere just couldn't get a win and Swindon were faltering but had a game in hand.

On the Sunday I did what most Walsall supporters did I guess, look at the table and every team's fixtures to see if we still had a chance. My conclusion was that we had to beat Scunthorpe on the coming Saturday and hope someone slipped up. Only a win would do and after that we would have to win our final 2 games; hope was still in the air. Saturday 13th came and all was going well with two minutes to go in the match. The results had gone our way and we were 1-0 to the good at Scunthorpe, unfortunately, that was when they equalized and the game played out to a draw. As the analysis began, we were 1 point closer to the playoffs in 7th position, but Swindon, just above us and the only team we could catch, had a game in hand and were a point better off. We still had a chance, but slimmer I felt. The good news of the day was that Will Grigg had returned to the team after injury and scored our goal. It was his twentieth goal of the season, the mark that strikers are judged by. Grigg was Walsall's first striker to achieve that feat since Jorge Leitao in 2001.

Swindon played their game in hand and returned to form, winning 3-0, leaving us now 4 points adrift. If Swindon won on Saturday there was nothing we could do. Swindon duly won their second home fixture of the week, again 3-0. Walsall were winning 1-0 at home to Bury, but again conceded in the final minute to play out a 1-1 draw. By that time we already knew that Swindon had won and our chance of the playoffs had gone. It had, nevertheless, been a fantastic season. Our team were now 15 games unbeaten in their bid for a playoff position and they had narrowly missed out. One game remained away at Crewe. The final game of the season has traditionally a carnival atmosphere; our team, for all of their effort, deserved a grand send off.

We would lose our final game at Crewe 2-0, conceding two goals in the last twelve minutes, the first of which was a poor penalty decision by the official. However, it had been a tremendous season and our final finishing position of 9th was testament to our improvement over the season.

Surrounding our club was a feel good factor; our season ticket sales were up twenty-five percent, there was a strong belief in our Manager and the young exciting players in our team.

My fiftieth season had been a great one. The special memory for me was the game against Preston North End on September 22nd, fifty years to the day that I had first watched the Saddlers play with my Grandfather. We were outstanding that day, sweeping aside Preston 3-1; the ovation the players received on leaving the pitch will remain with me for years to come.

Chapter 33
Walsall F.C. The Premiership

At the time of my exhibition at The Walsall Museum during 2006 and 2007, featuring some of the platinum and gold records from my career, I was constantly asked 'What is your favourite Walsall F.C. eleven?'

I had a lot of agonizing over that question and once or twice in interviews tried to fumble my way through an answer. Each time I made an attempt, I looked at the team afterwards and had missed someone who just had to be in the team. In writing this book, I knew at some point I would have to have another attempt at a Walsall side. Since knowing that, I've made several attempts and I'm afraid after fifty years of supporting the side and watching the team play I could not narrow it down to eleven players.

As a compromise for my own mind, I decided that if I wanted a squad to take Walsall Football Club to the Premiership what would that look like?

Hence, I decided that would be the approach I would make at selecting a group of Walsall players from over all of those years, with the aim of making it to the Premiership.

They would all have to be in the peak of their powers, there would be no transfer issues as they would all remain in the squad for the duration of the attempt. They would all be happy contractually and it would be just about winning matches and promotion.

On that basis, I will now reveal my squad:

Goalkeepers.

I've allowed myself three goalkeepers, to cover for form and injury and to change as we entered other competitions such as The League Cup, The F.A. Cup and The Auto Windscreen Shield.

James 'Wacka' Walker.

Mick Kearns.

Ron Green.

Some supporters may think I should have chosen Phil Parkes for his fantastic career and for what he went on to achieve after playing for Walsall, however, I'm happy with my picks.

'Wacka' holds the appearance record for a Walsall player. Mick Kearns has been around Walsall Football Club for years and is part of the place. Ron Green grew into being a great goalkeeper and played for us during two separate spells, as did 'Wacka' and Mick. They are my favourite Walsall goalkeepers.

Right-Backs.

I've allowed myself two right-backs for the squad, both of which would never let you down in terms of passion and commitment.

Brian Caswell.

Chris Marsh.

Left-Backs.

Again, two players for this position.

Kenny Mower.

Colin Harrison.

Kenny holds the appearance record for a Walsall left-back and Colin Harrison has held the all-time appearance record for a Walsall player. I found it impossible to have a Walsall squad without Colin; he deserves his place in any squad and played some great games in the full-back position, although he played all positions for the club. I would also mention, Mick Evans, Derek Statham, Neil Pointon and Gino Padula, who had a magnificent half a season in our colours, but two was the limit.

Centre-Backs.

As with most squads it's best to have four centre-backs, to cover for form and injury, therefore, I have allowed myself four picks.

Stan Bennett.

Adrian Viveash.

Peter Hart.

Scott Dann.

Stan is my all-time favourite Walsall centre-half. His commitment and passion for the club was always at the highest level and I missed him greatly when he retired. Adie was a class centre-back. 'Harty' was always solid and I never saw anyone get the better of him in that position. You may feel that Scott does not deserve his position in this team; my reasoning is that I believe Scott Dann is one of our greatest finds. Once he established himself in our defence he was the lynchpin, when he moved to Coventry City he was their captain in a matter of months. His next move to Birmingham City saw him move into the Premiership and handle the higher level with ease, fantastic player and in my squad. All of these centre-backs were also good with the ball at their feet; they could play the ball out of defence.

Right-Flank.

Mark 'Rico' Rees.

Darren Wrack.

'Rico' was just frightening for opposition defenders, his pace and determination above normal. In those days defenders regularly used to hit wingers in an attempt to see if they had any flaw in their passion for the job and to let them know it might be a tough afternoon. If they did that to 'Rico' all it did was wind him up, make him angry and more determined.

'Wracky' was part of what I believe to be the best right-flank partnership with 'Marshy' a Walsall side has ever had. During the first season under Ray

Graydon, which resulted in promotion, those two were just outstanding, both defencively and as an attacking unit.

Centre-Midfield.

I've allowed myself five picks for this area of the team, mainly because this is the most competitive part of the pitch and the engine room of the team. All of these players had great engines, now called 'box-to-box' players. All had good control and were great passers of the ball. As important, when they didn't have the ball they 'buzzed' around the opposition trying to get it back and protect our defence.

David 'Mini' Preece.

Martin 'Skip' O'Connor.

Nick Atthey.

Craig Shakespeare.

Dean Keates.

Left-Flank.

Two picks, again, for the left-flank.

Colin 'Cannonball' Taylor.

Jeff Peron.

'Cannonball' was just a remarkable player. 189 goals from the left wing is one of the best scoring records for a left-winger in the history of the game. I've still never seen anyone hit the ball that hard. 'Jeff' had only one season in our team but we all remember it. He made so many goals that season and became a Walsall favourite. He was a completely different style of player to 'Cannonball' but very effective.

Strikers.

Allan 'Sniffer' Clarke.

Alan Buckley.

David 'Ned' Kelly.

Kyle 'Killer' Lightbourne.

Paul Merson.

Strikers, I guess, are always the most contentious issue. My reasoning is this: 'Sniffer' was my favourite boyhood hero - he's in. Alan Buckley's name will always be linked with Walsall; our all-time leading scorer has to have his place in the squad. 'Ned' was another of our great finds, his goals for us and his style of play make him a must; his hat trick in the playoff final said it all. 'Killer' is one of our latter day heroes; quiet, skillful, with pace, a deadly combination.

Paul Merson is probably the best player ever to wear a Walsall shirt.

I must also mention George Kirby, Jorge Leitao and Andy Rammall, all of which stood a chance of being in the squad as proper centre-forwards; all were outstanding in leading the Walsall line.

So, there it is, my 25 Walsall players that I would put together in an attempt to go for the Premiership after watching Walsall sides for the past fifty years. I'm sure you might disagree with some of my picks, but that's football, a game of opinion. One thing I know is if I could get those players back in their 'pomp,' our stadium would be full to watch them play.

On a personal note, I'd like to thank all of those players mentioned for the pure joy they brought me whilst supporting Walsall Football Club.

The other question I'm always asked is 'What are my favourite Walsall F.C. moments?' I guess a lot of my favourites might be yours too:

1. I think the stand out moment for all Walsall supporters that were there would be our playoffs final win against a good Reading side at The Millennium Stadium Cardiff in 2001 and Darren Byfield's winner.

2. Only slightly ahead of my number 3 choice, and purely because it was twenty-five years in the making, is our playoff final win against Bristol City at Fellows Park in 1988, the day of 'Ned' Kelly's hat trick.

3. 1999's promotion to Division Two (The Championship) at Bescot Stadium versus Oldham Athletic, particularly the moment of Chris Marsh's goal.

4. The Milk Cup run of 1983/1984; the great Walsall victorious nights out at Arsenal, Rotherham and Liverpool, with Mark 'Rico' Rees creating havoc in the opposing defences.

5. The F.A. Cup run of 1974/1975, especially the victories against both Manchester United and Newcastle United at Fellows Park.

6. Richard Money's Championship season, especially the 1-1 draw at Swindon Town when Dean Keates secured The Championship with a minute to go.

7. Chris Nichol's promotion season of 1994/1995.

8. May 2nd, 1981, the 'great escape' at Sheffield United; Don Penn's penalty and Ron Green's penalty save.

9. August 9th 2003, Walsall 4, West Bromwich Albion 1; Paul Merson's debut and his two first half goals.

10. 2002 at The Molineux, our 2-1 victory, when Andy Rammall let Wolverhampton Wanderers know they were not the Champions of the Black Country.

'Who is your favourite Walsall Manager?'

I believe a lot of Walsall fans would say Alan Buckley, probably for his goal scoring feats as well as his years as our Manager. I agree that 'Buck' is a Walsall legend and became a good Manager for us. I also believe that Sir Ray Graydon would probably be everyone's number one choice and rightly so, we have only been led into The Championship on four occasions, once by Bill Moore, once by Tommy Coakley and twice by Sir Ray Graydon. What makes the feat even more incredible is that Sir Ray did it twice in three seasons - remarkable.

However, the question is 'Who is *your* favourite Walsall Manager?' For me that is Chris Nichol. I believe in his style and method and the way he coaches the younger players, turning them into proper professionals. I know his achievements for our club are not as great as Sir Ray's, however, it's Chris Nichol for me.

Our greatest Managers, I believe, are the ones that built promotion-winning sides that won over a nine-month period, and so, I believe, there are five that should be ranked:

1. Sir Ray Graydon for two promotions to The Championship.

2. Bill Moore for two consecutive promotions, including the Fourth Division Championship.

3. Richard Money for his Championship winning side.

4. Tommy Coakley for his promotion to The Championship.

5. Chris Nichol for his promotion winning team.

Chapter 34

The 125th Anniversary Dinner

On April 28th 2013, the day after our final game of the season, Susan and I drove up from London and, along with my Sister Helen, went to the Bescot Stadium to attend the 125th Anniversary Dinner of the formation of Walsall Football Club, incorporating the 'Player of the Season' Awards.

The event was a sellout and full capacity of the Stadium suite with over four hundred people attending. The Chairman, Directors, Manager, staff, players from past Walsall teams and the current squad were all in attendance in what turned out to be a fabulous evening.

The main awards were Will Grigg voted 'Player of the Season,' Jamie Paterson 'Young Player of the Season' and the retiring Roy Whalley 'The Lifetime Achievement Award' for twenty-seven years of service to the club.

With Roy Whalley

Some of our greatest players returned for the evening to present various awards: Nick Atthey, Alan Buckley, Mick Evans, Colin Harrison, Peter Hart, Ken Hodgkisson, Stan Jones, Mick Kearns, Kyle Lightbourne, Albert

McPherson, Chris Nichol, Richard O'Kelly, Andy Rammall, Ian Roper and Allan Clarke.

With Allan Clarke

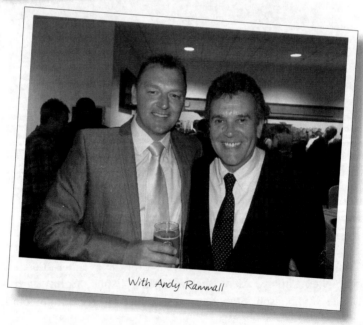

With Andy Rammall

For me it was fantastic to catch up with some of the players that were friends of mine through the years. The big moment was to spend a good ten minutes talking with my all-time hero Allan Clarke. 'Sniffer' told me that after all of the teams he played for and managed there were two results he looked for on a Saturday, those of Leeds United and his first club Walsall. When he played for Walsall I boyhood worshipped him from the terraces, never having the opportunity to talk to him, so that moment and conversation is a huge memory for me personally; it seemed to complete the circle of fifty years of supporting the Saddlers.

I started writing this book in January 2011. We were 9 points adrift from the safety line and staring relegation to Division Two full in the face. No one gave us a chance of escaping and few teams have achieved an escape from such a position. We escaped relegation, escaped again in 2012 and now, in 2013, we're looking upwards. We had turned the corner. Apart from the hard work of the Chairman, Directors and staff, the forward thinking, passion and playing philosophy introduced by our Manager Dean Smith has turned the club around. It was great to see happy, supportive fans believing that the coming season would be another good one.

There is some sadness as I conclude this book. The reality is the bulk of my supporting days of Walsall Football Club are behind me and I will probably never write another book about the club. It is doubtful that I will witness the 150th Anniversary Dinner. The generation gap between me and the current squad means that I will not form long friendships with the players as has happened in the past, yet I look forward to watching them play and the homegrown players develop into the professionals of the future. My joy is the development of our youth team, to watch the players get their chance and over a couple of seasons become the mainstay of our team. Should they then go on to play at higher levels with other clubs I'm immensely proud of them and without doubt they all remember the little West Midlands club that gave them their chance.

I believe there is an abundance of young talent that is coming through at Walsall. Like the record business, in some ways, it's a game of chance, you never really can tell who will go on to have long or short professional careers, but watching and hoping gives me immense joy.

Our 'Young Player of the Season' probably leads current graduates that have established themselves and given me great enjoyment for the past two seasons, Jamie Paterson. Will Grigg's development into a leader of the line, a fine striker and 'Player of the Season' has been immense. I'm a fan of George Bowerman, he has that striker's instinct. Malvind Benning, to me, looks a Premiership footballer of the future. I'm interested and hopeful in watching the development of Kieran Morris and Ben George and I hear good things about first year professionals Matt Preston and Reece Flanagan, although I've yet to see them play. Hopefully, some of these players will go on to achieve the consistency of Paterson and Grigg, becoming Saddlers heroes of tomorrow. One thing is for sure; they will be encouraged from the stands by this Walsall Boy that had a few hit records.

The best part of Walsall Football Club for me at present is the development of Dean Smith as Manager. I've known Dean since he was sixteen or seventeen years old and playing for our youth and reserve teams. I watched his development at Walsall, saw him play for Hereford, Leyton Orient and Sheffield Wednesday, captaining all of those sides, and I was pleased for him when he went into youth management at Orient and then assistant manager, before returning to Walsall, firstly as youth coach.

With Dean Smith

I like that Dean is a thinker and quieter than most Mangers on the touchline. I'm no fan of some of the League One Managers that come to Bescot with their sides and a couple of assistants that scream and shout all match long. In my mind I always think, what have they been doing all week long, did they not train and prepare to play Walsall? Did they not work out their marking from free kicks and corners? Did they not work on their system and pattern of play? The incessant screaming and shouting suggests they didn't. I do believe in changes and reaction to opportunities that can be seen during a match, but constant yelling at players is not the way forward.

Dean also knows Walsall and knows that even though we are a small club with a tight playing budget, as supporters we like the game played on the floor, the ball passed and retained. Whenever Walsall has had a manager that prefers to play the ball long and hard, even if they achieve results they are never embraced. We may be small, but as supporters we have knowledge about how the game should be played and what is pleasing on the eye.

Dean reminds me on occasions that, in his mind, even though my music career is now over, I'm still a legend to him. That comment is based on when I worked with The Stone Roses and they were in their first flush of success and they played what is now seen as a historical gig at Spike Island. Dean was a young professional at the time and up to speed with the music of the day. He asked for and got tickets from me to the gig and still remembers it well. I understand he still plays The Stone Roses records to the current squad on the coach and in the dressing room. I'm sure the players are not as enthusiastic about records made twenty-odd years ago.

My hope is that Dean Smith remains at Walsall Football Club for a very long time. I believe in him and his philosophies. It will not always go to plan, football never does, but stability with a Manager of a Football Club is proven as the way to go.

I've now lived and worked in London for thirty years, if I could have stayed in Walsall and still pursued my career I would have done so, but that's life. It has meant that a home game is a 250-mile round trip. The funny thing about all the M1 and M6 driving over the years is that on the way up to Walsall I'm full of dreams. In those dreams it's always a great afternoon, we always win four or five nil and have a great time. Reality and life, unfortunately, is not that way. When we have played poorly or lost the drive back is tough. I get in my car on the Bescot car park and I know it's two hours to get home if I'm lucky, if there is traffic or an accident then it's three hours or more. Most times it's 8:00pm to 8:30pm when I get back. I cannot believe I've been doing that run for thirty years and I still believe it's worth it.

Many of my friends in the music business are Arsenal, Chelsea, Tottenham, West Ham and Fulham supporters and they find it difficult to believe I still drive all that way to watch Walsall. Many times they have said Arsenal are playing Manchester United come and watch a real game. The only time I have been is if Walsall are away at Carlisle or Rochdale, which is just too far from London. When I do go I don't get that 'buzz' that a Walsall game gives me. Whether we are fighting relegation, going for the playoffs or promotion, no matter what is happening it is all important to me. Victory and 3 points warm my Walsall heart like no other football match. I love football so I do watch teams on Sky, all the England games and sometimes 'Match of the Day,' but only the Saddlers give me that 'buzz.'

My book about my music career *The Future is in the History* has done well, received great reviews and sales, but, most of all, ended a professional chapter in my life. I loved music and still do, it was good to me and I feel lucky that I have spent my life making records and fortunately had hits.

This book, I guess, is my life in Football and although this could well be my only book on Walsall Football Club, I feel it does not close a chapter in my life. As the terrace song goes 'I'm Walsall 'til I die' and I will forever be a Saddler.

See you at the match. 'Come on you Saddlers!'